SPLM/SPLA

INSIDE AN AFRICAN REVOLUTION

Dr. Lam Akol

Copyright © Lam Akol
This edition by Africa World Books, 2018.
ISBN 978-0-9876141-6-2

Cover design, typesetting and layout: All in One Book Design, Western Australia

First edition 2001, Second Edition 2009, Third Edition 2011.
National Library Cataloging – Sudan
962. 4043
    L.S.
    SPLM/SPLA – Inside an African Revolution./Lam Akol._3rd ed._Khartoum Printing Press, 2011
        Serial No.106/2001
        432p; 24cm
        ISBN: 978-99942-990-6-5
        1. Sudan – History – Civil wars, 1983-2006
        2. Civil Wars, Sudan
        3. SPLM – Sudan
    A. Title

Dedication

This book is dedicated to the memory of my parents; my brother, Dr. Justin Papiti Akol; my cousin, Awang Akot Ajawin; and my brother and comrade-in-arms, 1st Lt. Daniel Dak Akol.

About the Author

Dr Lam Akol Ajawin was born in 1950 in Athidhwoi village north of Kodok town. His father was a Medical Assistant (MA).

He obtained a BSc (Eng) degree in Chemical Engineering from the University of Khartoum (1975), M.Eng degree in Petroleum Engineering from Heriot-Watt University, Edinburgh (1977) and PhD degree in Chemical Engineering, Imperial College of Science and Technology, University of London (1980). He was awarded Honorary Doctorate in Political Science by the University of Juba in 1999.

He worked as a Teaching Assistant (1975-1976), as a Lecturer (1980-1986) in the Department of Chemical Engineering, University of Khartoum, part-time Lecturer in the University of Gezira (1982-1984) and Chairman of the Board of Directors of Port Sudan Refinery (1985-1986).

He has been active in politics since 1965, becoming President of the Students Union for Southern Sudan (SUSS), Khartoum Government Secondary School branch for two consecutive terms (1968-1970). In the University of Khartoum, he was a member of the Political Bureau and Executive Committee of the African Nationalists Front (ANF) for two terms (1973-1975).

As a member of the Council of the Khartoum University Teachers Union (KUTU) (1984-1986), he was active in the organization and execution of the March/April Uprising which brought down the May regime of Nimeiri in 1985. Afterwards, Dr Lam and other compatriots founded the Sudan African Congress (SAC) which won two seats in the Constituent Assembly elections in 1986.

He joined the SPLM/SPLA in 1983. In 1986, he went to the field of combat and was appointed alternate member of the Political-Military High Command the same year. He served as Zonal Commander of Northern Upper Nile (1987-1988) and Southern Blue Nile (1990-1991), and held several political and diplomatic positions in the Movement.

He was one of the three leaders of the Nasir Declaration on 28 August 1991.

He was Chairman and Commander-in-Chief of the SPLM-United (1994-2003).

He was Minister of Transport (1998-2002), Administrative Supervisor of Western Bahr El Ghazal State (2005) and Minister of Foreign Affairs (2005-2007).

He founded with other colleagues the SPLM-DC in June 2009 and was elected its Chairman. In January 2016, the name was changed to the Democratic Change Party.

Currently, he is the Chairman of the National Democratic Movement.

He published two other books: *SPLM/SPLA: The Nasir Declaration* and *Southern Sudan: Colonialism, Resistance and Autonomy.*

Contents

Preface to the First Edition

The SPLA (Sudan People's Liberation Army) hit the headlines of the news media for the first time in the closing months of 1983 and it remained on the news ever since. Few, however, knew anything about the inner workings of the SPLA or its political arm, the SPLM (Sudan People's Liberation Movement).

This book is an attempt to shed light on the origins and organization of the SPLM/SPLA and the conduct of the war by the guerrilla movement. It is not a history of the SPLM/SPLA but a contribution to it from my perspective. The events covered are those in which I was directly involved in my capacity as an active member of the SPLM/SPLA and part of its leadership. The period covered ends with the overthrow of the Mengistu regime in Ethiopia in May 1991.

It is my sincere hope that this work will provoke debate on the issues connected with this movement that has shaped Sudan's politics since 1983 in no small way.

My thanks go to the many friends who encouraged me to put pen to paper in order to produce this book. Special thanks are reserved for my wife, Rebecca Joshua Okwaci, and my son, Ganjwok, without whose support and understanding it would have been impossible to embark on writing at all.

Lam Akol
Nairobi
August 1995.

Preface to the Second Edition

Since it was first published in 2001, the book has been in high demand. But rather than reprint, two factors made it necessary to issue a new edition of the book: the quality of printing of the first edition left a lot to be desired, and it was necessary to correct some of the typographical errors that appeared in the book. The editing was also an opportunity to elucidate on some points. However, the bulk of the material remained unchanged.

Despite strenuous efforts to get the work done much earlier, many official assignments made it difficult for me to find time to do the editing. This is the reason for this rather long time it took to complete work on the second edition.

The only new addition is a chapter on the Comprehensive Peace Agreement signed in Nairobi on 9 January 2005. Although the nature of the book and the sequence of events do not favour the new addition, many friends have been pressing me to include it since this edition is coming out after this historic agreement, and none of the negotiators has written about it. As the whole struggle was for the attainment of peace, I got persuaded to do so. This appears as Chapter 10.

I am thankful to all those who read the first edition and made important comments.

Dr Lam Akol
Khartoum
August 2008.

Preface to the Third Edition

It was exactly two years ago when the second edition of this book hit the shelves of book stalls. Before the end of 2011 the copies produced had run out. It was, therefore, necessary to reprint. However, this was an opportunity to correct the minor typographical errors that appeared in the second edition.

This edition went to the printers immediately after the Southern Sudanese have voted in the referendum for self-determination as stipulated in the Comprehensive Peace Agreement (See Chapter 10). Final results confirmed an overwhelming vote for secession. Therefore, the Sudan will never be the same again. Nevertheless, it is our sincere hope that peace will continue to prevail between the North and South Sudan.

I am thankful to all those who took time to read the book and made useful suggestions for improvement.

Dr Lam Akol,
Khartoum,
January 2011.

Preface to the Fourth Edition

This is the fourth edition of this book. The previous editions were in 2001, 2009 and 2011. The book has been in high demand in Sudan(s) and East Africa but its exposure to readers beyond this geographical area was limited due to the scope of publication.

This edition is prompted by two considerations. First, there is a pressing need to get it to more readers across the globe. Second, the current state of turmoil in the new state, South Sudan, has left many pundits wondering as to what went wrong in a country that was full of hope and promise when it was declared independent in July 2011. This book does not claim to provide all the answers but it has clearly shown that the state of political disorganization of the SPLM/A, the ruling party, since its inception was a disaster in the waiting. Perhaps the readers may want to refresh their memories by going through the arguments put forward in that direction more than 16 years ago.

As always, I am grateful to all who advised me to republish the book and also to those who helped me in any way to prepare it for publication.

Dr Lam Akol,
Addis Ababa
August, 2017.

CHAPTER I

Events in the South

Flurry of Political Activity

T HE YEAR 1980 started rather harshly for Southern Sudan. February saw the coming into force of the "High Executive Council and Regional Assembly Act 1980" issued by Nimeiri and on the basis of which he dismissed the Regional Assembly of the Southern Sudan and dissolved the High Executive Council then under the presidency of General Joseph Lagu. This Act practically replaced the "Self-Government for the Southern Provinces Act 1972", most commonly known as the Addis Ababa Agreement, without following the stipulated amendment procedure. The newly elected regional government presided over by Mr Abel Alier was just a few months in office when the North provoked another controversy.

The People's National Assembly was discussing the "Regional Government Act 1980" for the division of Northern Sudan into six regions. A map attached to the bill to show the borders of the new regions also showed some parts of Southern Sudan adjacent to the North added to the latter. This triggered off an angry reaction all over the South and demonstrations of protest were staged. The issue was only resolved after Nimeiri intervened and formed a Committee that recommended the withdrawal of the map and that the borders of the South and the North would remain as stipulated in the Addis Ababa Agreement. Nevertheless, the incident helped fuel suspicion between the two parts of the country.

Hot on the heels of the border issue followed, in 1981, the controversy over the location of Sudan's second refinery to refine the oil discovered in Bentiu in Southern Sudan. The Southerners had assumed that the refinery would be built in Bentiu where the oil was discovered but the central government wanted it located in Kosti in the

North. The Southern public and Government in Juba were opposed to this. The Regional Government made representations on the issue to Nimeiri but Nimeiri insisted on his position. Finally, the Regional Government caved in and decided to persuade the Southern public to do the same but the public unflinchingly poured scorn on both the regional and central governments.

These two incidents will help shed light on the degree of mistrust that had developed in the South since the regional government was set up in 1972. The feeling was not without foundation. The provisions of the agreement were not strictly adhered to. Nimeiri felt at liberty to overlook some articles of the Self-Government Act 1972 at the acquiescence, if not the connivance, of those in charge of the regional government in Juba. A few examples will suffice. In December 1973, in the first elections to the Regional Assembly, Mr Abel Alier accepted to be nominated by Nimeiri, before all the elections results were announced, as the sole candidate of the SSU to the presidency of the HEC. This was contrary to the provisions of the Act which stipulate that nominations and elections to the post be made in the Assembly. Members of the Assembly did not insist on challenging Nimeiri's action, thus, setting a precedence which the central government had always exploited in all subsequent elections of the President of the High Executive Council. In 1974, the sudden announcement of advanced plans on the digging of the Jonglei Canal provoked popular protests. However, the public were soon to discover that their President of the HEC, Mr Abel Alier, was as committed to the digging as Nimeiri and was in full picture of the plans just made public. The Regional Assembly was kept in the dark. In March 1975, hurried moves towards the integration of the Anya-nya into the army, again contrary to the provisions of the Addis Agreement, resulted in an armed rebellion in Akobo by some of the absorbed Anya-nya fighters. A number of them withdrew into the bush. It turned out that the plan, originating from Khartoum, had the blessing of Juba. In 1976, there was a similar incident of armed rebellion in Wau and in February 1977 came the more serious Juba Airport mutiny. Adding to these a host of failures by the Regional Government in administering the South, it would hardly surprise anyone that the disillusionment in the South with the implementation of the Addis Ababa Agreement before its fifth anniversary was widespread. Nimeiri was condemned for reneging on the agreement while the Southern politicians in Juba were despised for having allowed themselves for self-interest to be used by Nimeiri in his destructive machinations against the South. Nimeiri's confrontational attitude with the South became more pronounced following the "National Reconciliation" agreement with the Northern opposition in July 1977.

This atmosphere of popular dissatisfaction was ripe for political mobilization and agitation on what action to take to remedy the situation or even to bring about a revolution. A number of underground organizations were born at different times all claiming to proffer solutions to the agony of Southern Sudan. In spite of the difference in organizational structures, tactics and stridency of the language in expressing the objective pursued, all these organizations were calling for a separate and sovereign state in Southern Sudan to be realized through an armed struggle (they differ on the timing). They argued that the Arabs were determined to oppress the South and impose their Arab-Islamic culture to supplant the African culture of the Southerners; that the only way to survive this onslaught was to resist in the only language the North understands, armed struggle; that compromise solutions such as the Addis Ababa agreement have sufficiently proved the futility of any peaceful settlement with the Arabs which falls short of total independence of the South and that the Southerners must rise to continue with the noble struggle interrupted by the Addis Ababa Agreement of 1972. Some of these underground movements in the late seventies were: NAM, JAPO, SSLM and MTLSS.

The National Action Movement (NAM) started distributing propaganda leaflets in the second half of the seventies and was believed to be run by politicians identified with the former SANU who were by then out of the regional government in Juba and were preparing to win the Regional Assembly elections scheduled for early 1978. Some elements sympathetic to the Sudanese Communist Party (SCP) were also identified with NAM. Not much of its objectives were known until a document on NAM written by, purportedly, its Chairman, Mr Matthew Obur, was published in the early eighties.

JAPO was an acronym of an acronym, so to speak. It stands for JUWAMA African People's Organization, and JUWAMA itself is coined by picking up the first two letters of each name of the three main towns in the South: Juba, Wau and Malakal, and joining them up in that order. It was formed by some of the Southern students who were studying in Egypt in the late seventies. Some of them had graduated by 1980.

It was with JAPO that I had the most extensive and closest contacts. I had separate discussions in Khartoum with a number of JAPO leading figures on the future of Southern Sudan. One of them was James Wani Igga who was introduced to me in 1980 by a mutual friend, Othom Rago Ajak. James Wani had just graduated from the Faculty of Commerce in Zagazig University in Egypt. Later that year he got employed in an insurance company and got transferred to its branch office in Juba, his home town. In the period he spent in Khartoum we held serious discussions on the struggle and how to bring together the disparate Southern Organizations that claim to be fighting for the same objective. With him was Abraham Wani Ywane who was then studying in the School of Telecommunications in Khartoum. We agreed to work together. We continued to meet whenever James Wani came to Khartoum on duty.

The SSLM was the political wing of the Anya-nya that negotiated the Addis Ababa Agreement. It is known that the name has been used by more than one underground movement thereafter. The one meant here was a leftist organization that was active among the students in Malakal in the late seventies. Three of its leaders; Lokurnyang Lado, Pagan Amum and Nyachugak Nyachiluk, slipped into the bush in 1982. Their organization hit the news when they launched the daring attack on Boma Mountain in July 1983 and seized some foreign tourists hostage. The story of how the group ended up in the SPLA in 1984 remains a mystery shrouded with sad memories. The other two had conspired against their leader, Lokurnyang Lado, arrested him and handed him over to the SPLA. He was later executed without trial by a fire squad in Bonga to mark the graduation of Koryom division in 1984. Pagan Amum himself was a member of the fire squad that shot Lokurnyang dead!

The Movement for Total Liberation of Southern Sudan (MTLSS) was short-lived. After issuing their first leaflet some of its leaders were arrested in Juba. It was reported that they managed to escape from prison later on but nothing has been heard of the TMLSS again.

These were some of the political movements that were mobilizing the people and preparing them for action. One was also aware of the activities of some of the absorbed former Anya-nya officers but their efforts were directed towards frustrating the government plans to transfer units of the absorbed Anya-nya to Northern Sudan. It is extremely doubtful that they attempted to organize into a political organization capable on its own of wresting power in Juba or somewhere else by the force of arms.

Most pathetic was the stand of the Southern politicians on the repeated encroachments of the regime into the constitutional powers of the South. They did not seem to feel the threat. They continued bickering with acrid acrimony that knew no bounds. For example, when the "High Executive Council and Regional Assembly Act 1980" was introduced and used by Nimeiri in February that year to dismiss Lagu's government, the group of Abel Alier welcomed and celebrated the move. None bothered to question the constitutionality of the Act itself; the end justifies the means! The group of Joseph Lagu were later to turn to the same Nimeiri to use extra-constitutional means to effect the division of the South. As a matter of fact, Nimeiri found it more easy and expedient to get his schemes through by manipulating the two groups one against the other.

This was the situation I found in the country when I came back from Britain in July 1980. As we shall see, neither the South-North nor the South-South relations showed any sign of improvement. The controversies over the border issue in 1980 and the location of the oil refinery in 1981 have already been discussed. Other events will be dealt with in turn. The events that led to the division of the South will be discussed in more detail as this was a turning point in Southern politics.

Division of Southern Sudan

The scheme to divide the Southern region into three was first brought into the open in February 1981 in a conference of the Sudanese Socialist Union (SSU) in Khartoum. The issue came up as part of Nimeiri's speech to the conference. While discussing the speech some members of the conference from the South took exception to the proposal arguing that this matter was not discussed by the SSU organs in the South and, according to the SSU rules, could not be raised in that meeting. It was then that Nimeiri dropped his bombshell; that the idea was not his but a demand from some prominent Southern politicians in a petition to him on the matter. In the conference itself, very few Southerners, notably Mr Philip Yona (from the Moru tribe in Equatoria), supported the idea of dividing the Southern region. The overwhelming majority opposed it and put their signatures on a memorandum to Nimeiri requesting that the proposal for the division of the South be withdrawn from the conference agenda until it is first discussed by the SSU organs in the South.

A few weeks later Mr Joseph Lagu published a booklet calling for the division of the South citing "Dinka domination" as the justification for that. In this booklet, Lagu listed the regional ministers and senior SSU functionaries in the South according to whether they were Dinka or non-Dinka by tribe, and concluded that the Dinka tribe has got more than its fair share of the cake. The booklet of glossy printing, was distributed and widely so, free of charge. Many of Lagu's opponents believed that the booklet was financed by Nimeiri's government if not by him personally.

Shortly after the publication of Lagu's booklet, Ambassador Philip Obang, Secretary-General of the "Friendship, Solidarity and Peace Council" of the SSU and a former Commissioner of Upper Nile Province (1976-78), lent his support to Lagu's call for division. He put his views across in a series of mimeographic tracts circulated in Khartoum.

The Southern Sudanese opposed to division did not take the writings in support of division seriously. For the first few months, save for two exceptions, no response was forthcoming. The two exceptions were: a tract I wrote and issued in April 1981 titled "South Sudan: Whither?" and an anonymous booklet written by a shadowy group calling itself "Solidarity Brothers". The booklet was printed by the Government printing press in Juba, much to the annoyance of Nimeiri. He accused Abel Alier of being behind the project.

A number of Southern intellectuals were very much concerned from the very beginning and wanted a healthy debate on the issue. At their prompting, the African Nationalists Front (ANF), the organization of Southern Sudanese students in the University of Khartoum, organized in March 1981 a rally in the University Campus. A wide cross section of Southerners were invited to participate. The list of speakers included the two publicly known proponents of division of the South; Mr Joseph Lagu and Ambassador Philip Obang. From the National Assembly in Omdurman came Mr Elia Duang Arop, whereas Mr Peter Gatkuoth Gual, the Vice President of the HEC, and Mr Angelo Beda, the Speaker of the Regional Assembly, represented the Regional Government in the South. Finally, the University teaching staff and students were, respectively, represented by me and the President of the ANF.

The rally was well attended and all those invited to speak, except Philip Obang, turned up and presented their points of view. Mr Lagu's position did not find any noticeable backing from the audience. The other speakers, while acknowledging that grave problems existed in the running of the affairs of the South, did not think that the solution was to be found in the division of the South into smaller and weaker entities. Unhappily, that was the last public rally of its kind combining as it did all shades of opinion on this serious matter. Events on the political front moved faster than everyone thought. The divisionists abandoned dialogue and resorted to writing secret memoranda to Nimeiri urging him to effect division by a decree.

In October 1981, Nimeiri dissolved the Regional Assembly, dismissed the HEC and appointed an army general, Major-General Gismalla Abdalla Rasas, as interim President of a new HEC which the order of appointment proclaimed was to be a transitional government that will supervise the setting into motion the constitutional measures leading to a plebiscite in the Southern Sudan on the issue of division. The new HEC was to accomplish its task within six months. Curiously, Nimeiri dissolved the regional setup not on the basis of the Regional Self-Government Act 1972, which contains no provision for dissolution, but on the strength of the so-called "The High Executive Council and Regional Assembly Act, 1980". This last act was first issued as a provisional order in February 1980 to dismiss Mr Lagu's HEC. It had remained on the statute books ever since. When the Act was first applied Abel's group was jubilant and not only did they not question its constitutionality, it was also suggested that some lawyers of the group took part in drafting it. Little did they countenance that they can be paid back in the same coin. It was the turn of Lagu's group this time round to rejoice. But the big loser in this unscrupulous infighting was the people of South Sudan.

The three most senior posts in the new HEC went to army officers (all from Bahr el-Ghazal province) and the rest of the regional ministers were civilians, all of them from the "Change Group". Abel's group was not represented. The Major-General and the two Brigadiers (Andrew Makur Thou and Joseph Kuol Amum) were promised that they will go back to the army at the end of their tenure in the HEC. This was not to be. When their HEC was replaced by an elected government in 1982 the three officers were retired at the ranks they held.

After assuming office and taking charge in Juba, Major-General Gismalla Abdalla Rasas, was not as enthusiastic to division as his boss wanted him to be. On the contrary, he was on record stating in a public gathering that the Regional Government in the South was hard won coming as it did after 17 years of war and hardships and that the Southerners should remain united. This and similar sentiments filtered through his speeches from time to time. No doubt they must have reached the ears of Nimeiri.

As mentioned earlier, the Government of Gismalla Abdalla Rasas was to prepare the citizens of the Southern Region for a regional referendum to decide on the division of the South in fulfilment of the provisions of Article 2 of the Addis Ababa agreement 1972 which stipulates that any amendment of the agreement must be approved by a three-quarters majority of the People's National Assembly and confirmed by two-thirds majority in a referendum carried out among the citizens of the Southern Region. Elections to the National Assembly (dissolved together with the Regional Assembly in October 1981) were carried out in December 1981. The newly elected National Assembly was to take a stand on the division issue. It held its first session in February 1982 in which Nimeiri delivered a policy statement charting the legislative programme of the assembly.

In his policy statement, President Nimeiri surprised observers when he decided not to bring up the issue of division before the National Assembly. He, instead, called for fresh elections in the South with the objective of:

> … maintaining the unity of the region, whilst at the same time allowing enough consideration to the other point of view by seeking more administrative decentralization by the proper application of the People's Local Government Act, 1981, and other administrative reforms.

This statement made many Southerners to conclude that the division issue was over. Their trust was misplaced. Nimeiri was buying time and his backing down on proceeding with the referendum can only be explained in terms of the realization that, in a free and fair referendum, all the indications were that the Southern people would have overwhelmingly rejected division and this would frustrate his designs.

The newly elected Regional Assembly met in Juba in June 1982. The policy statement of the HEC, delivered to the Assembly in July, committed the regional government to the very reforms Nimeiri articulated in his speech to the National Assembly earlier in February. Despite the commitment, Nimeiri was not prepared to give the Southern Region a chance and in less than a year he decided to act.

On the 5th of June, 1983, Nimeiri issued a decree dividing the Southern Region into three regions of Bahr el-Ghazal, Equatoria and Upper Nile. This action was in gross violation of Article 8 of the Constitution 1973 and Article 2 of the Addis Ababa Agreement. The decree was issued as a Republication Order No. (1), 1983.

9

The Debate on Division of the South

The debate on division of the South in 1981-1983 was highly charged with emotions, acerbity and hard feelings. In a sense it was a dialogue of the deafs with neither side willing or ready to listen to the arguments of the other. Accusations and counter-accusations were traded between the proponents and opponents of division thus polluting the atmosphere for any healthy dialogue on so important an issue.

Opponents of division averred that the whole issue was yet another ploy from Khartoum to weaken the South and drew attention to the relish and alacrity with which Nimeiri undertook the project. History was adduced to lend support to this argument. Southern Sudanese still remember how the Round Table Conference held in Khartoum in 1965 foundered on two main issues the South was not ready to compromise on: Northern insistence that in any regional setup in Sudan, the South must be broken down into its three constituent provinces and that Khartoum must choose the head of any Regional Government in the South. Furthermore, the opponents of division argued that unity is strength and whatever differences existed among Southerners, the only guarantee for their survival is in sticking together. Finally, they contended that the matter should ultimately be settled in accordance with the provisions of the Addis Ababa Agreement 1972 (Article 2).

The proponents of division on the other hand were harping on the record of the regional governments since 1972. They reasoned that unity is not just being within a common geographical border but rather an association of the people for a common purpose; a practice of togetherness in action and a feeling of mutual support without discrimination against each other. They made it plain that those who were at the helm of affairs in the South, while paying lip-service to the unity of the South, have been pursuing divisive policies. To support this point, a catalogue of grievances was produced. As to sticking to the provisions of the Addis Ababa Agreement, they were blunt. What they wanted was a divided Southern Sudan and it did not matter to them how it came about. The end justifies the means!

The protagonists on the issue of division of the South or maintaining it united contrasted sharply in their methods and means to have the final outcome in favour of each's side. The divisionists put together a well-orchestrated campaign of mobilization and appealed to the masses in Equatoria and elsewhere in the South to support them in their struggle to rid themselves of 'Dinka domination'. Their campaign caught the imagination of the people in Equatoria and Western Bahr el-Ghazal where they received an overwhelming support. Many people joined the bandwagon and "Kokora", a Bari word for divide equally, became a household word in the South. So, when the results of the 1982 elections to the Regional Assembly were announced, it was hardly surprising that the divisionists swept the board in Equatoria winning almost all the Assembly seats allocated to it.

In contrast, those calling for the unity of the South were led by the politicians who were entrusted with the administration of the South since 1972. They presented a lack-lustre campaign. They could not defend their record in government, the achievements were minuscule and the failures monumental. In government they paid little heed to the Southern opinion and when they later lectured to the people about unity they sounded drab and hence unconvincing. In reality they looked like a besieged group crying out to save their jobs! They lost the argument from day one for they were not with the people and hardly identified themselves with their interests (for example, the borders issue of 1980 and the refinery issue of 1981). Hence, most of them sought legalistic arguments as to how a miracle would be needed to overcome the constitutional hurdle.

More damaging to the case of those who opposed division is that those who led them could not break ranks with and take on Nimeiri by exposing his lack of impartiality on the matter. Some deluded themselves into believing that they can lead anti-division campaign while still ensconced in the Political Bureau of Nimeiri's SSU. This was the case with Mr Peter Gatkuoth Gual, Mr Bona Malwal and Mr Abel Alier himself. When the Council for the Unity of South Sudan (CUSS) was formed in December 1981 to lead the campaign against division they shied away from being identified with it although they were known to be supporting its objectives and methods.

This ambivalent stand of the big shots in the anti-division camp did not escape the notice of the divisionists and were quick to exploit it. For instance, in the rally organized in March 1981 by the ANF which was referred to earlier, Joseph Lagu shocked the packed audience when he said:

> All arguments so far against the division of the South are based on the fear that if the South was to be divided, we shall become weak. Why do we [Southerners] need to be strong? Whom are we fighting against?

In posing such a strange question, Lagu, no doubt must have been hoping to elicit a direct answer that will put the interlocutor on a direct collision course with Nimeiri. Significantly, one speaker after another avoided making any comment on Lagu's remark. But at question time, Mr Ambrose Ring Thiik, by then a member of the Regional Assembly and Chairman of the SSU Assembly Body (equivalent to the chief whip in a parliamentary system) took up the gauntlet. Without mincing words, he told the gathering that if Lagu had forgotten he should be reminded that the struggle of the South against the Arabs of the North was not yet over. His fellow ministers in the Regional Government, who were seated in the front row, sank in their chairs in extreme embarrassment. Since his University days as a student, Ambrose Ring Thiik has made a name for bluntness, or what others will call a loose tongue. The regime did not forgive him for this and he got arrested in 1982 together with a number of other politicians opposed to division.

Elections of the Regional Assembly, 1982

The 1982 elections to the Regional Assembly were of special significance, coming hard on the heels of the acrimonious debate on the division of the South. For sure, division was not the issue of the elections campaign; for the Regional Assembly has no constitutional say on the matter and, as referred to earlier, President Nimeiri had suspended the issue from discussion in his speech before the National Assembly in February 1982. However, the polarization engendered by the division debate influenced in no small way the outcome of the elections and the subsequent formation of the High Executive Council.

Since the signing of the Addis Ababa Agreement in 1972 up to its abrogation in 1983, politics in the South were dominated by underground competition between the two main parties in Southern Sudan before Nimeiri made his coup d' etat in 1969, namely, the Southern Front and SANU. In theory these parties, like other parties in the country, had been banned to be replaced by the SSU as the sole political organization to which all active politicians must belong. Most of the SSLM politicians identified themselves with SANU. This was the broad pattern but the division was by no means neat. There was a few exceptions. For example, Clement Mboro who was the leader of the Southern Front up to the advent of the May regime, kept changing sides between the two groups. So did others like Andrew Wieu who was a prominent leader in SANU during the parliamentary era. The two groups assumed different names at different elections to the Regional Assembly. The Southern Front group, led by Abel Alier, has been variously known as Abel's group (most of the times), Group of Dinka Unity (1980 - 1981) and Unity group (1981 - 1983). The SANU group which had no one particular leader assumed a number of names as well: Aru's group, Lagu's group, Group of Change (1978 - 1980) or Group of Change 2 (1982 - 1983).

Broadly speaking, the competition to elected positions in the South was between the two groups under whatever label each assumed at different times. The new element in 1982 elections was that a new group calling itself the Redivision Group led by Lagu emerged in Equatoria but most of its active members were from the Group of Change. This new group contested the elections in Equatoria on the ticket of calling for the division of the South and were elected on that basis. In the other provinces of Bahr el-Ghazal and Upper Nile, the division of the South was not a contentious issue and, with a few minor aberrations, elections went ahead as previously in 1973, 1978 and 1980.

An event of great significance and which would have broken the pattern of politics in Southern Sudan took place in December 1981 when the Council for Unity of South Sudan (CUSS) was born. CUSS brought together prominent Southern politicians regardless of their groupings, who were opposed to the agitation of Lagu for division of the South and stood in support of the unity of the Southern Region as stipulated in the Addis Ababa Agreement. Led by Clement Mboro, CUSS membership included such prominent figures as Joseph Oduho, Matthew Obur, Andrew Wieu and others. They wrote a letter to President Nimeiri outlining the objective of the formation of CUSS and requested him to allow them to operate freely as the divisionists are allowed by the central government. Nimeiri's reaction was to arrest the leaders of CUSS but they were later released in time before the 1982 elections to the Regional Assembly. CUSS enjoyed wide support among all sections of the Southern Sudan political scene: politicians, intellectuals, youth and students.

Most observers assumed that CUSS would lead the anti-division camp into the Regional Assembly elections through to the formation of the High Executive Council. They were disappointed. After its leaders were released from detention CUSS was not heard of again and the old shadowy groupings reemerged and the politicians melted into them. Therefore, there was no united body that fought the elections to preserve the unity of the Southern Region in the way the divisionists held on to their slogans of dividing the South as their electioneering platform. The demise of the CUSS was a clear example of the short-sightedness of those politicians who were opposed to the division of the South. It is hard to believe that they took the word of Nimeiri at face value when he declared in February that there shall be no division of the South. This is simply because the divisionists' agitation did not stop because of that promise. If anything it intensified and taken through to the Regional Assembly elections as mentioned earlier. Moreover, there were allegations from the anti-division camp that Khartoum was giving financial support to the divisionists. What for if the division issue was dead and buried?

The explanation has to be found in the power struggle for the presidency of the upcoming HEC. Abel Alier and his closest associates (Bona Malwal, Peter Gatkuoth, Hilary Paul Logali) were not in the executive of CUSS. When CUSS was formed, they supported its objectives and everything it stood for but the four of them chose to continue as members of Nimeiri's Political Bureau of the SSU. At the time of the elections the four of them showed interest in becoming the next President of the HEC. So did others within CUSS who belonged to the Group of Change. Later events proved this point. The leader of CUSS, Clement Mboro, who many observers assumed would be the sole unity candidate for the presidency of the HEC, was shunned by Abel's group (now calling itself the "Unity group"). Abel Alier allowed his own name to go forward. When it later became clear that the tide was running against him he withdrew, but some of his close associates such as Bona Malwal thereupon nominated themselves. The wheeling and dealing continued for some time during which Bona Malwal and his supporters had harsh words against Clement Mboro. Subsequently, all the aspirants in Abel's camp stepped down to endorse Clement Mboro but this was after a lot of damage has been inflicted by them on the credibility of their own candidate. It was too late and they all knew Clement Mboro had lost the race before the votes were cast.

After a lot of behind-the-scene horse-trading, the Regional Assembly finally sat to elect the two most important positions in the regional government: the Speaker of the Assembly and the President of the H.E.C. The first went to Matthew Obur Ayang beating Martin Majier Gai of the Abel's group. As to the election of the President of the H.E.C., Joseph James Tumbura won by 62 votes against 49 votes for Clement Mboro.

The events that took place afterwards are well documented and need not be recounted here. In February 1983, Joseph James Tumbura wrote a secret petition to Nimeiri demanding immediate division of South Sudan. In March 1983, Matthew Obur Ayang, the Speaker of the Regional Assembly and Dhol Acuil Aleu, the Vice-President of the H.E.C., whose support of Tumbura swept him to power, were humiliatingly arrested in Khartoum and thrown into Kober prison. The two remained in jail for over a year. On their release both went to Addis Ababa to join the SPLA but this was not without its problems as we shall see.

CHAPTER 2

The Underground Days

The Attack on Bor, Pibor and Pochalla

ON THE 16TH OF MAY 1983, the garrison in Bor, which was manned by a unit composed of the absorbed former Anya-nya officers and men, was attacked by a force from the Army Southern Command HQ in Juba. The attacking force was commanded by Col. Dominic Cassiano, himself a former Anya-nya officer. His mission was to quell, by force, the mutiny of Bor garrison. The force in Bor, commanded by Major Kerubino Kwanyin Bol, put up stiff resistance before it was dislodged and withdrew into the bush. Major Kerubino himself was wounded during the battle but managed to withdraw together with his force to the country side. Similarly, the force in Pibor, commanded by Captain Riek Macuoc which belonged to the same battalion as the force in Bor, was attacked on the 18th by the same force that attacked Bor garrison. It also withdrew into the bush and linked up with the force withdrawing from Bor and the force that was in Pochalla.

There have been several versions advanced as to what were the causes of the mutiny in Bor, who were the actors in it and what their roles were. This is an area we shall return to later. What is not subject to dispute, however, was the gist of the build-up to the showdown which was as follows. It has already been mentioned that, contrary to the provisions of the Addis Ababa Agreement, Khartoum had decided to transfer some units of the absorbed Anya-nya from the South to the North. Battalion 105 in Bor was one of them and received the order of transfer sometime in 1982. In line with the rest of their former Anya-nya colleagues all over the South, the battalion in Bor was opposed to the transfer and was dragging its feet in executing the order. The matter was complicated by a discovery of financial irregularities in the accounts of the battalion. Major-General Siddiq al-Banna, the Commanding officer of the Southern Command, ordered that the discrepancy be accounted for and that unless this was done no salaries would be paid to the battalion. No explanation was forthcoming from Bor garrison. As tension grew between the military in Bor and Juba the politicians stepped in. Several high-level delegations from the People's Regional Assembly and from the High Executive Council in Juba with the consent of the army commander, shuttled between Bor and Juba trying to find a solution to the problem. It appears by the end of 1982 the politicians had given up on their mediation, probably preoccupied with the rapid political developments taking place then on the issue of whether or not the South be divided into three regions. After that it was clear, from a strictly military point of view, that the force in Bor was in mutiny and its command in Juba was bound to take action. An attack on the mutineers in Bor was planned in Juba and executed resulting in the clash of May 16, 1983.

On the 6th of June, Major William Nyuon Bany, a former Anya-nya officer and a close friend of Major Kerubino Kwanyin Bol, took action. Word had reached him that a force was being sent from Malakal to arrest him. He rounded up the Northern officers and men under his command in Ayod and killed them before he withdrew with the rest of his force, entirely from the former Anya-nya, and the police into the bush. The day before, some hundreds of miles away, Nimeiri had declared the division of the Southern Region into three regions. It looked certain the confrontation was unavoidable.

The incidents of Bor, Pibor, Pochalla and Ayod could not be said to have been triggered off by the popular discontent then prevalent in Southern Sudan but nonetheless, they provided the spark needed to transform the mass anger into mass action. The news of the armed confrontation spread like wild fire. Students, workers and government officials trekked to the Ethiopian borders, where the soldiers had withdrawn to regroup and reorganize, to join the revolt. These groups linked up with some elements of the Anya-nya-2 in Itang, Ethiopia, in order to form an organization that will wage an armed struggle against

Khartoum. The SPLA captured the headlines in the closing months of 1983 as that kind of organization but little was known about the bitter infighting that led to its birth and left in its wake internecine inter-fighting among Southerners that was to continue for years to come.

Joined the SPLA

The SPLA declared itself a socialist movement fighting not for the separation of the South, as the Southerners expected, but for a united Socialist Sudan. It was to wage a protracted armed struggle starting from the South but which would engulf the whole country in a socialist transformation. It defined the problem as that of underde-velopment which was not limited only to the South but to other parts of the country as well. According to the SPLA, power in Khartoum has been a monopoly of pseudo-Arabs (the term was later modified to the phrase "minority clique") that defined everything in Sudan from its Islamic and Arab perspective. All these have to be brought to an end by the restructuring of power in the country. This information on the SPLA was contained in a letter signed by Col. John Garang which he sent to some of his friends in Khartoum. I came across the letter in October 1983 from Mr Philip Chol Biowei, a friend of mine and coeval in the University of Khartoum. He was in the Faculty of Arts and specialized in History. We stood on the same side most of the times in the students' politics and did some research together in our opposition to the Jonglei Canal in 1974. We shared other political activities during and after the University days. However, ideologically, we were poles apart; Philip Chol is the kind of person the neo-Marxists would describe as a "reactionary" and others to the right thought he was opinionated. Nevertheless, I liked him for his forthrightness; he would hardly be neutral on any issue. We remained friends ever since.

Philip came to me in my office in the Faculty of Engineering one afternoon rather more serious than usual. We sat down and ordered for tea. We chatted as usual but I could see something was bothering him. After the tea he requested me to bolt the door which I did and came back to sit. Then without introduction he brought out from the pocket of his shirt folded pieces of paper which he passed to me across the table and asked. "Have you seen this?" I first looked straight into his face and our eyes met, then I picked up the paper. It must have passed through a number of hands before for its outer parts looked a little worn out. I opened it and started reading. It was a serious stuff. I read it over again and then raised my head and answered Philip's question in the negative and gave the paper back to him. He went right ahead to give his opinion. He supported wholeheartedly, he said, the rise of the Southerners to fight for their rights long denied by Khartoum and betrayed by the Regional Governments since 1972. But he asked and his eyes twinkled, what is this diversion of the cause? Who wants socialism or the unity of Sudan? As I expected, he went on to disparage socialism and dismissed the call for a united Sudan as nothing but tactical. I had a long discussion with Philip Chol on the matter at the end of it I told him that my advice to him as a friend would be not to oppose this movement and in fact if he could make it he should join. The reasons I gave to Philip in support of the SPLA, though it was my first time to get its message, will be explained below. Weeks after our discussion, I heard that Mr Philip Chol Biowei had joined the SPLA. Whether our meeting had anything to do with his decision I cannot tell because we never had time to sit again. He was thrown into jail in 1987 and remained there without charge or investigation.

I went home that evening and thought deeply over the matter. Here I was, already involved in underground organization to mobilize the Southerners for action, and for good or for worse, action has already started in a serious way. The conditions of a revolution were ripe. Any hesitation or insistence on parallel organization could only lead to more confusion among the intellectuals and division in the ranks of the masses. The South could not afford any further division after the bitter experiences of a few months ago of the "Kokora". Yes, the issue of the ideology or the political line of the new movement must be reviewed. But this could better be done when in it rather than from outside. I concluded that if I were to be consistent I must join the SPLA. Two days later I found a friend who could deliver a letter to

Col. John Garang in Addis Ababa. I wrote to him informing him that I had somehow come to read about the SPLA and its objectives, have decided to join it and wanted to proceed to Addis Ababa and from there to the field. Col. John Garang wrote back in about a week in the last week of October but there was no reference in his letter to the letter I wrote to him. I even noticed that my last name was misspelt. In this letter he said I should remain in Khartoum to mobilize and organize the people to support and join the SPLA. He pointedly added that I was appointed a member of the Central Committee of the movement for organization with immediate effect. He closed by saying that he had just finished watching a TV film in which a torrent was washing away big logs of wood and likened the SPLA to that current and its enemies to the logs of wood.

Before I could elaborate on why I decided to join the SPLA, a little digression is necessary to answer the question on whether or not I had met Col. John Garang before then. This question is important because acquaintance with each other could have a strong influence on one's decision one way or the other. Indeed, I did meet Col. John Garang in Khartoum a couple of times. But all these were casual meetings and in the presence of other persons; we never had a serious discussion so that each of us may know where the other stood on issues. The first time was in my office in the University when he came in the company of his colleague in the army and my cousin, Col. Yoannes Yor Okuc. The latter had requested to be given a lift by Garang to my office so that he can discuss a personal matter with me. It was in the afternoon and Col. John Garang had gone to collect his son, who was with them when we met, from the school. We greeted each other and got introduced. Col. Yoannes Yor told me they were in a hurry and we had a few minutes alone outside the office discussing what he came for after which we went back into the office to join Col. John Garang and his son. Soon after, all of them left. The second time was in March 1983 in Garang's office in the Military Research Department I had gone with Mr Philip Chol Biowei to see him so that he can help us get a permit from the State Security Organ in order to visit Matthew Obur Ayang and Dhol Acuil Aleu who were arrested earlier and were held incommunicado in a security house. He seated us and served us tea. He did get the permit and took us past the guards in that house where we went and met the detainees. The last encounter was in Khartoum airport in March 1983. I had given a lift to somebody who was staying in my residence and was flying to Malakal early that morning. Col. John Garang said he was seeing off his colleague, Lt. Col. Francis Ngor, and others who were also leaving for Malakal on the same plane. A few weeks after, Col. John Garang took leave and went to Bor. The clashes of May 16, 1983 took place while he was there. He never went back to Khartoum again.

As alluded to already, what made me join the SPLA was not much the socialism it espoused or the unity of Sudan it set itself to preserve but basically the idea of the Southerners getting organized politically to wage a revolutionary armed struggle. Organization is the *sine qua non* for any social transformation. This is what has been lacking in the South, whatever objective Southerners have been struggling for. The people's war is waged and won by the masses. It is therefore, imperative that those leading the struggle undertake prior political work in mobilizing and organizing the people. In this, the SPLA had a good start or so it seemed. As to socialism, it cannot exist without a social base unless it is utopian socialism which does not concern us here. Furthermore, the essence of socialism as any person who has undertaken a serious study of the subject would recognize, is democracy. There can be no socialism without democracy. I consider myself a socialist and here stems my opposition to single party politics as practised by the SSU in Sudan and other parties elsewhere. Without exception, single-partyism leads to authoritarianism which is the antithesis of democracy. For me, however, what was needed at this stage and given the state of affairs in the South was not a socialist but a broad-based national democratic programme that would unite all the active forces of the society and marshall their energies single-mindedly towards waging the people's war. There are many experiences from the so-called "third world" countries especially Africa to learn from.

The call of the SPLA for a united Sudan surprised many Southerners most of whom had thought it was continuing the war staged by the

Anya-nya. Such an assumption, however, ignores important developments that took place since especially in connection with the South-
South relations after 1972. The monolithic South of the sixties could
hardly be advanced in 1983 when the Southerners were chasing
themselves away from each other's region while the Northerners in
all those regions were undisturbed! Those who thought this was an
ephemeral situation were absolutely in the wrong. This is not to
suggest that it was Southern disunity that drove the SPLA leaders
to take refuge in the unity of the country. Far from it. Unity by its
very nature, whether among Southerners or between Southerners and
Northerners, must be for a purpose and is always conditional upon its
acceptance by the parties involved. Unity will not be achieved simply
because somebody is calling for it or bent on imposing it on the others.

The central issue, it must be stressed, was the emergence of a
political organization that will ensure the participation of the masses
in the struggle. It is true the struggle must be waged on clear and
well defined objectives but these objectives can always be reviewed
periodically by the organization in the light of the prevailing realities
and circumstances of the struggle, otherwise they become idols to be
blindly worshipped. Revolutions have no room for blind faith.

The task the SPLA leader had entrusted me to undertake was
exacting and risky. It demanded vigilance and watertight precautions
to guard against Nimeiri's notoriously ruthless State Security Organ
(SSO). At the same time it necessitated reaching out to the people in
order to recruit them into the movement. I settled for the well tested
cell-system of clandestine work. For the membership of the primary
cell Edward A. Lino was an obvious choice. Apart from other considerations, I was convinced he knew more about the SPLA than he was
willing to admit. When I opened the subject to him he readily agreed
to serve. Then together we studied other suitable candidates. We finally
agreed on two other names. One was Dr Peter Nyot Kok of the Faculty
of Law, University of Khartoum and the other a senior official in the
Government who shall remain anonymous for the time being (call him
Mr X). Mr X was not much involved in politics but had very useful
connections. The four of us eventually sat, agreed on what had to be

done and mapped out how to do it. We used to meet ordinarily once a week and more frequently when the situation demanded.

The nature of the task demanded us to move slowly but surely. Nevertheless, in one year we managed to establish secondary cells in Khartoum and some key towns in the South. The primary cell had even expanded to eight including representatives from the army and the police. Most of those recruited proceeded straight to join the SPLA in the field, as the vast majority have done, or in Addis Ababa. It must, however, be stated that a good number of them did not need much persuasion to join; their concerns were more on how to get there physically. In the other direction, it must be admitted that the political atmosphere created by the controversy over the division of the South and the split within the fighters themselves had a considerable adverse effect on our recruitment efforts. Although the numbers were big, more than 90% of the recruits hailed from the Dinka tribe, the Nuba mountains taking up most of the remaining percentage. The imbalance was politically disturbing and I do not remember a single meeting we held without discussing ways and means of involving the other sections of the Southern community in the SPLA. The cell also carried out periodic analyses of the political situation in the country and related aspects and made reports on them which it shared with the SPLA HQ in Addis Ababa.

Mobilization and Recruitment

In November 1983, the SPLA launched its first major military operations in Nasir and Malwal Gahoth which shook the regime in a no small way. Immediately after, the regime published in the government-controlled press what it claimed was the SPLA Manifesto and Penal Law as proof of its being a communist movement. Attention was focused on the definition in the Penal Code of the SPLM as the "Marxist -Leninist Movement" and other terminologies in the Manifesto judged to be communistic. Many critics of the regime dismissed the regime's propaganda as its usual communist scare tactics and that the documents were a forgery to suit this purpose. Well, it turned out the documents were authentic. They were sent to Col. Pio Yukwan Deng, the army commander in Nasir and a former Anya-nya officer, who Col. John Garang wanted to win over to the SPLA. He passed the documents over to the Government instead! That was the first time for me and my colleagues in the cell to read the Manifesto of the SPLM.

The Nasir incident and the visit of an SPLM delegation led by Mr Joseph Oduho to Europe early 1984 had the effect of precipitating an immediate revision of the Manifesto and the Penal Law with a view of "toning down" the doctrinaire language. The result was a Manifesto with a pink cover that had remained unchanged up to today. We were sent copies of this newly published Manifesto in Khartoum, some autographed by Col. John Garang and addressed to specific personalities that we had to contact and try to persuade to join the SPLA. One of them was Mr Daniel Kodi Angelo, member of the People's National Assembly in Omdurman.

Daniel Kodi comes from Heiban district in the Nuba Mountains. He was a practising Catholic and a political activist. I did not know him well before and so I left the initial contacts with him to Edward Lino who knew him well. In the first two or so meetings, Edward passed to him an SPLA mimeographed tract titled "An Appeal to the people of the Nuba Mountains". There were similar separate appeals to the people of the South, the Fur, etc. Daniel Kodi's reaction was enthusiastically supportive. They arranged with Edward to meet me. In the meeting we reviewed the situation generally until we came to the SPLA and his stand. I then gave him the autographed copy of the Manifesto and the compliments of Col. John Garang. He told me what I had already been briefed about by Edward and finally declared that he had decided to join the SPLA and will be making arrangements to leave as soon as possible. Indeed, he left Khartoum for the SPLA HQ within a week.

Before his departure, Daniel Kodi gave us invaluable brief on the approach to the political work in the Nuba Mountains. We could have hardly made any headway without that advice. But our work in the Nuba Mountains got an unexpected boost from an unexpected source; Nimeiri himself! In 1984 the regime announced that a "racist plot" -

the stereotype expression - to overthrow the regime led by Fr. Philip Abbas Ghabbush was uncovered and arrests were effected among army officers, NCOs and men from the Nuba Mountains and the South, but the vast majority were from the Nuba Mountains for alleged involvement in the coup. Fr. Philip Abbas himself and some of his closest aides were arrested. Edward Lino of our cell was also arrested. These developments took place after Nimeiri had declared in April 1984 the state of emergency to apply the strict punishments provided by the Islamic laws which he had introduced in September 1983. As a result justice or injustice rather was being dispensed through kangaroo courts; the so-called "Prompt Justice Courts". After the announcements and the arrests, the usual vituperation and trial through the media followed and continued for a few weeks. The minds of the public were prepared for the worst; to raise arms against an Islamic state which Sudan was declared to be, was punishable by death. Suddenly came the surprise. Nimeiri announced that he had pardoned all those involved in the coup in response to a plea from Fr. Philip Abbas for the President to grant him and those with him pardon. The proceedings were performed in one of the kangaroo courts and covered by the TV and other government media. All the accused were there, the plea for pardon by Fr. Philip Abbas and the President's proclamation acceding to the plea were read before them by the "judge". The court declared that they were set free and each of them should resume his normal duties in his previous employment. All the civilians resumed their duties but the army High Command cashiered all the accused military personnel. Among them were two Southern officers: Major Niknora Magar Aciek and 1st Lt. Pagan Atien.

In the period between the arrest and the dramatic pardon an important figure in the Nuba politics, Yousif Kowa Makki approached me that he wanted to join the SPLA. Yousif Kowa was by then a member of the Regional Assembly of Kordofan region in El Obied. I first met him in the house of Fr. Philip Abbas Ghabbush together with a friend of his, Abdel Aziz Adam El-Hilou, also from the Nuba Mountains (with roots in the Masalit tribe in Darfur) and an official in the National Corporation for Electricity in Khartoum. Both of them graduated from the Faculty of Economics and Social Studies, University of Khartoum in 1979 but Yousif was much older. He had worked as a teacher for years before taking up University studies. I knew both of them were involved in an underground organization known as "*Jubhat Nahdhat Jibal El-Nuba*", which may be translated as the Nuba Mountains Development Front (NMDF). I also learnt from Yousif about the difficult relationship bordering on animosity between him and the Governor of Kordofan region, Major-General (Rtd) El Fatih Bushara, a close confidant of Nimeiri. I could not forget our meeting in Fr. Philip's house that day for an occurrence that I witnessed and still remember quite vividly.

Abdel Aziz, Yousif and Fr. Philip were in the study of the latter when I arrived in the house. I got seated in the sitting room where a number of other people were seated waiting to see Fr. Philip. Philip's son was informed of my presence and he went in straight to his father. Without delay he came back and ushered me in into the room. We greeted each other warmly and Fr. Philip introduced me to the other two as a close ally he trusted enormously. He also introduced them to me as comrades in the struggle for the freedom of the oppressed. Both of them said they had heard a lot about me before. We sat down and, as usual, got into discussing politics and the situation in the country. Then Fr. Philip asked the other two that the three of them continue with what they were doing and not to mind about my presence because he had confidence in me and considered me as one of them. He also asked me not to mind waiting while they went ahead with what they were doing. I told him that what suited him was all right for me. So they went ahead. Fr. Philip then started to conduct an oath-taking ceremony.

The ceremony entailed the following. A small quantity of salt was added to a tea glass about one-third full with water and stirred so that the salt dissolves. Then the tip of the thumb of the person taking oath is pricked with a needle and a drop or two of the blood coming out is made to fall into the salted water in the glass. The water is stirred again for the blood to diffuse into the water. After this the person recruited drinks most of the solution leaving a small quantity to be drunk by the person conducting the oath. This exercise is preceded by a pledge of loyalty to the organization made by the person taking oath. Fr. Philip conducted this ceremony first for Yousif Kowa and then again for Abdel Aziz Adam El-Hilou. When it was all over, we resumed our discussion for a while after which I asked permission to leave.

Some weeks later when the regime announced the foiling of the "racist plot" and effecting arrests among the military and civilians as referred to earlier, the above oath-taking procedure was described with graphic details in the government press as part of the confessions made by some of the soldiers arrested. On reading all this in the press, I immediately began to be seriously worried about the fate of my three friends. Hence, when I was approached by Yousif Kowa that day expressing his desire to join the SPLA in the field I was fully aware of the dangerous consequences any delay could cause. The day he was leaving, I arranged for Yousif Kowa to meet Dr Peter Nyot and after that we all went together to see Dr Hunud Abia Kuduf, in his office in the afternoon. Dr Hunud was a Lecturer in the Faculty of Law and he hailed from the Nuba Mountains. He represented a conservative view, a sort of let-the-others-do-it attitude. We deliberately wanted Yousif to get his views first-hand so that he also appreciates the complexity of the issues at hand. I drove Yousif to the airport in my car that evening and bade him farewell. We met again two years later.

Abdel Aziz Adam El-Hilou did not enjoy the high profile Fr. Philip and Yousif Kowa enjoyed and that was probably why the security did not seem to hunt for him. Of course, he took the necessary precautions in the first few days but ultimately it was business as usual. After the departure of Yousif, Abdel Aziz became the head of the SPLA cell among the Nubas. A quiet unassuming personality, Abdel Aziz was an excellent organizer and he proved to be an invaluable asset in our work. With him we managed to recruit a good number of people from the Nuba Mountains into the SPLA and sent them to the field. A number of the officials, Telefon Kuku, Yousif Kara, Awad El-Karim Kuku left together one day and were to make their impact in the SPLA later. Eventually, Abdel Aziz himself found it untenable to continue and had to join the others in the field of combat. He measured up to the expectations.

If Fr. Philip Abbas Ghabbush was planning a coup d'etat, the state

security must have been following his actions closely. The early intervention of the regime by making the arrest too soon before the plan
had developed also meant that it did not allow enough time for a body
of evidence against the plotters to build up. This could be a possible
explanation to the dramatic Presidential pardon as a way of getting
the regime off the hook. But the most important lesson those arrested
and released that day came out with was that a coup in Khartoum by
the Nubas has no chance of success. This was an important turning
point because a number of Nuba politicians, counting on the large
percentage of the Nubas in the non-officers ranks of the army, had
entertained such an idea. Some of them used to wonder as to why
they should join the SPLA when power can be taken in Khartoum.
Unrealistic as it is, it had the effect of confusing the masses.

From Southern Blue Nile area, I had met, in 1984, at the Staff
Club in the University of Khartoum a gentleman by the name Malik
Agar. He was a school teacher attending a training course at the School
of Extramural Studies at the University of Khartoum. He was politically conscious. We exchanged views on the situation in the country,
first in general terms and later on in relation to the SPLM/SPLA. We
found ourselves in agreement on all the issues we discussed. Finally, he
expressed interest to join the SPLM/SPLA and described to me how
he could reach there through Kurmuk and Dul. Arrangements were
made for him and he eventually left, joined the Movement, underwent
military training and was commissioned a First Lieutenant in 1985.

Our cell was also active in anonymous leafleting, so to speak,
on some important occasions such as the Conference on African
Liberation Movements held in Khartoum in 1983, the visit of the
U.S. Vice-President George Bush to Sudan in 1984 and the visit of
the U.S. roving ambassador, General Vernon Walters also in 1984. On
the first occasion, the regime produced a booklet entitled "Perspectives
on the South" that praised the division of the South into three regions
as being a response to the wishes of the people and as a means of
bringing the government nearer to the masses and so on. This booklet
was distributed to all the delegates that attended. They came from
all over Africa. We thought a refutation of the claims made in that

booklet was necessary, otherwise the delegates would leave with a wrong impression about the situation in Sudan. The paper entitled "The Unmaking of the Addis Ababa Agreement" was produced in mimeographic copies and discreetly distributed among the trusted delegates. It was decided to sign it as by a "Study group for the liberation of the Sudanese People."

The U.S. Vice-President visited Sudan in February 1984 ostensibly to assess the hunger situation in the west of the country. However, that was the period when the U.S.A. was supplying the Government in Khartoum with considerable military and economic assistance. Nimeiri had effectively succeeded to put his communist-scare card into fruitful use. This of course, in addition to the regime's support for the Camp David Accords between Egypt and Israel of 1979 persuaded the U.S. Government to support it, its repression and oppression not withstanding. It was necessary to seize this opportunity to let the U.S. Government at the highest level get the other point of view. A letter was written to him-in the name of the same group above - analysing the situation in the country and calling for the U.S. Government to discontinue its assistance to the dictatorial regime. The letter was delivered together with a letter to the U.S Vice-President signed by a number of Lecturers from the University of Khartoum giving a similar advice.

The Reagan Administration sent its roving ambassador, General Vernon Walters, to Khartoum in 1984 in a visit the regime described as in consolidation of the ever growing friendship between the Sudan and the U.S.A. Apart from meeting officials of the regime, General Walters spared some time to listen to the other points of view. The cell put its ideas in a letter written and passed to him on this visit.

These few examples will do. The problem with anonymous letters is that the importance that may be attached to the contents is far reduced than if it were signed. But all the same, they get read anyway, especially when the presentation is responsible and devoid of invective language and material that could easily be dismissed as nothing but mere propaganda.

On receiving copies of the Manifesto, the cell discussed it and made its observations about it. I also shared it with some trusted Northern friends. In general they were so much elated by the SPLA's call for a united Sudan to the extent that in my view, blunted their ability to evaluate in a critical way the other points of the Manifesto. One notable exception was Mrs. Sua'd Ibrahim Ahmed, a lecturer in the School of Extramural Studies, University of Khartoum and a senior member of the SCP. She made her critique in form of notes which she discussed with me. She was incisive and to the point, dealing first with the general tenor of the document and then turning to the specifics. In brief, she thought the leaders of the Southern movement ought to be commended for their foresight in calling for a united Sudan but criticized the historical analysis in the Manifesto and the claim of the SPLA to be a national, rather than a Southern ,movement as unrealistic and ignored objective realities of the Sudanese society. It was on the ideological orientation of the movement that she had most reservations. For her, words such as "bourgeoisified bureaucratic elites" and "minority clique" – used in the Manifesto - were unscientific and lacked any class content . Of course, she questioned the SPLM's claim to be the vanguard of the socialist revolution. She advised the SPLA not to think of overjumping social stages of development. I found her comments useful and shared her ideas with my colleagues and later on with Col. John Garang.

After joining the SPLA, my dialogue with James Wani Igga and his group continued. In fact, the discussion acquired special significance for two reasons. First, there was the exigency of the change of the strategy and tactics since we last met. Second, a real tough and uphill political work was called for in Equatoria. The overwhelming majority of Equatorians supported the division of Southern Sudan into three regions and their dreams of an Equatoria region had just been realized before SPLA operations became news inside the country. It was, therefore, perceived by many Equatorians that the SPLA was formed by the Dinkas to reverse their hard-won achievement. Consequently, the attitude of the Equatorians towards the SPLA was decidedly hostile. It was imperative to change this attitude if the movement was to succeed.

The most controversial issue in our discussions was the SPLA's call for the unity of Sudan. James Wani and his friends thought this was incompatible with the aspirations of the Southerners for a separate independent state. I argued otherwise stressing that any unity, even on the social level between a man and his wife, is always conditional and would only stick if the conditions attached to it last. A call for something, I went on, did not necessarily guarantee its attainment; the Anya-nya called for separation and ended up in a united Sudan. I also quoted the situation in Chad by then where the "green line" divided the country into two. The most necessary condition for success, I always contended, was the existence of a strong and united political organization that would organize the masses of our people and involve them in the armed struggle. This condition could not be achieved if the Southerners continue to be divided. Ultimately, James Wani Igga and his group agreed to join the SPLA. He formed a cell in Juba that did considerable work given the very difficult conditions under which it operated. In 1984, James Wani and a member of his cell, Scopas Loboro Kenyi, were tipped off that the SSO agents were after them. They escaped arrest by a whisker and found their way to the SPLA HQ.

The Death of Benjamin Bol Akok

The work of the cell was not without jolty moments. One such moment related to an incident that took place in September 1984 which shook all of us. We received news from the SPLA HQ in Addis Ababa that Benjamin Bol Akok, the SPLA representative in London had died of liver failure. Benjamin was a well known politician in the South having served as a regional minister, deputy speaker and as member of the People's Regional Assembly several times. There was no record in his medical history of liver problems. Soon rumours began to spread in London and Khartoum that he was killed by the Ethiopian Security with the personal connivance of Col. John Garang. The cell found the story of the SPLA HQ difficult to believe. We held a long difficult meeting on the subject after which it was decided that I go to Addis Ababa to find out the truth for myself and report back.

I did go to Addis Ababa in October. The news we received from London was that Benjamin Bol Akok was asked to disembark by an Ethiopian Security agent from an Ethiopian Airline flight bound for London via

Frankfurt. On the same plane was Costello Garang Ring, the SPLM representative in Germany. Costello continued his journey. Apparently, the wife of Bol was informed in advance that her husband and Costello were on board that plane. When her husband did not arrive London on the plane, she began a series of telephone contacts with Addis Ababa and with Costello in Berlin enquiring about her husband. These contacts and other investigations, according to the version from London, revealed that right from the airport, Bol was taken to a security cell where he was subjected to severe torture. When he fell unconscious, he was transferred into another cold underground cell where the torturing continued, this time with the participation of two SPLA personnel. It was reported that Bol died that night, his body put into a coffin by the Ethiopian authorities which was closed and handed over to the SPLA for burial in Addis Ababa. The report went on that Joseph Oduho and Martin Majier Gai, the only two senior members of the movement who attended the burial, had demanded from the security agents who accompanied the coffin that it be opened for them to have a last view of their dead comrade. The Ethiopian security refused the request emphatically. Faced with this flat refusal, the two gentlemen had no choice but to bury the coffin they were told contained the body of Benjamin Bol Akok. It is further reported that Dr John Garang and Dhol Acuil Aleu did not attend the burial on the grounds that they were busy attending the meetings of the founding congress of the Workers Party of Ethiopia taking place in Addis Ababa by then.

The key people I wanted to talk to in Addis Ababa were: Dr John Garang, Joseph Oduho and Martin Majier. In the event, I was only able to meet Dr John Garang accompanied by Salva Kiir, Dr Riek Machar and Gier Chwang Aluong. The last came with Dr John Garang in the car when he came that afternoon to meet me in the hotel I was accommodated in. The other two had come from Bonga training centre a few days earlier and were accommodated in the room next to mine in Meskel Flower Hotel in Addis Ababa. I did not know of their presence in the hotel until I met them in the presence of Dr John Garang.

We held a formal meeting in which I raised the serious concern shown by the Southerners inside the country and abroad about the death of Benjamin Bol Akok and that I was sent by the cell to take back the true story. Dr John Garang was the only person to speak and he insisted on the original version that Bol died of liver failure. When I requested to be given permission to meet Joseph Oduho and Martin Majier, Dr John Garang replied that they were very far away and it was not possible for me to see them during my visit. After that, I briefed them about the general political situation in the country. When Dr John Garang was about to leave the hotel, he called me out where we had some time alone before he and Lt. Gier Chuang drove away. During that short meeting he spoke disapprovingly of Joseph Oduho, Martin Majier and the politicians in general. I spent two days in Addis Ababa but still could not be allowed to meet the other two key figures in the case. When I arrived back to Khartoum, I reported to the cell in detail what I found in Addis Ababa.

Dr Barnaba Marial Benjamin, who was Bol's colleague in the London SPLM office and a medical doctor by profession, gave an interview to the BBC Focus on Africa programme in which he courageously affirmed that Benjamin Bol did not have a record of liver problem and, therefore, could not have died of a liver failure.

When I later joined the ranks of the liberation army, the SPLA, I continued my uncompleted investigation by talking to persons who were in the know. The evidence was conclusive. Bol died under torture and not because of liver failure.

The Case of Matthew Obur Ayang

After his release from detention, Mr Matthew Obur Ayang left Khartoum with his family for Addis Ababa to join the SPLA in July 1984. On arrival he was accommodated at Harambee Hotel in Addis Ababa. Matthew Obur spent many days without meeting Dr John Garang who was by then in town. This behaviour angered Obur who took it as a snub. Also, over the same period, Obur had opportunity to meet a number of SPLA and former SPLA personnel in Addis Ababa who gave him a negative picture about the movement and the way it was being run. Somehow, he also managed to communicate with

Joseph Oduho and others on the situation in the SPLA which was not at all complimentary. Apparently, as a result of the information he had gathered in Addis Ababa and his own experience there, Matthew Obur must have taken a decision not to join the SPLA after all. On coming to know about this, the SPLA's reaction was to accuse him to the Ethiopian authorities of being an agent of the Libyans planted to divide the SPLA! By that time, the relations between Libya and Ethiopia were strained although this did not come out to the open. Since then the attitude of the SPLA towards Obur became less than friendly. The death of Benjamin Bol Akok, a close friend of Obur, pushed matters to a breaking point from the side of Matthew Obur.

When I visited Addis Ababa in October 1984, the Ethiopian security official who received me at the airport and took me in his car to Meskel Flower Hotel, told me in the car that "Obur is giving us much trouble". He did not elaborate and I did not want to show interest. In fact, the remark worried me greatly - could Obur have been killed and nobody knows about it? I controlled my worries and pretended to be normal. When I met Garang that afternoon, I raised the matter with him and asked if I could help in straightening things out with Obur. He gave me Obur's telephone number at the hotel and advised that, for security reasons, it was better for me to phone him when I was in Nairobi which was the next leg of my journey.

Indeed, I phoned Obur from Nairobi and we had a long conversation. He related to me his misgivings and what he had found out about the movement in Addis Ababa. Among other things, he made it plain that Dr John Garang was under the control of the Ethiopians and that the movement cannot succeed without being free to chart its own course. He also told me that some combatants who had just come from the field had assured him that Samuel Gai Tut, his chum and political ally, was still alive and that he had sent a message to Gai. I tried to talk him out of this impression stressing to him that Samuel Gai Tut was positively identified dead and that no useful purpose would be served by pretending that he was still alive. I noticed that he did not quite agree with this point of view. It is to be recalled that the Anya-nya 2 continued to deny Gai's death for a very long time after the event. Some statements bearing a forged signature of Gai originating from Addis Ababa were circulating in Khartoum long after his death. Matthew Obur must have met some of the authors of these documents in Addis Ababa.

After my conversation with Obur, I wrote a report to Dr John Garang on the gist of our discussion and recommended that dialogue with him should continue as it was clear there were a lot of misconceptions which could only be straightened through face-to-face discussions.

Later on, through the good offices of the Kenyan authorities, Matthew Obur Ayang moved to Nairobi where he stayed with his family. However, in late 1985, he was deported to Khartoum at a 24-hour notice in a move many believe to have been at the instigation of the SPLA.

Nimeiri's Peace Games

So much for the underground.Overground, before the year 1983 was out, SPLA's military operations begun on a high gear, kept on the pressure on the government troops in the South and did not show any sign of slackening. In December, Nimeiri visited Nairobi and had discussion with President Daniel arap Moi. No doubt their talks must have touched on the situation in Southern Sudan. But Nimeiri's big catch in that visit was in the person of Clement Mboro, a veteran Southern politician who went into exile there after the division of the South and was jailed by Nimeiri in December 1981 for this reason together with 23 other members of the CUSS executive committee of which he was chairman. Nimeiri assumed Clement Mboro supported the SPLA and he was delighted when the latter accepted his offer to go to Khartoum with him to involve him in some role that would help bring the war to an end.

The arrival of Clement Mboro in Khartoum in December 1983 was received in Southern circles with incredulity and astonishment. How he could listen to Nimeiri, a man he knows and everybody else knows as capricious, so soon after the division of the South and the imposition of the Islamic laws was mind-boggling. But there he was. In the comfort of the Grand Hotel in Khartoum and with the slogan of "Love, Peace and Unity" – which he copied from Moi's Nyayo – always on his lips, Clement Mboro started in earnest to work on a programme for peace that Nimeiri had asked him to produce. Dr Peter Nyot and I met him in his hotel not long after his arrival and several times thereafter. We were more concerned to find out from him what guarantees Nimeiri had given him that the endeavour was a serious one. No satisfactory answer was given. Many other Southerners who had discussions with him reached the conclusion that nothing serious was on offer. After a few weeks Nimeiri could not even reply Clement's requests for an appointment to see him, then he began to complain of "being cut off" to anybody ready to listen to him and finally he was blaming Joseph Lagu for his misfortune with the President! Lagu had become the second Vice-President since 1982 replacing Abel Alier. The crafty Nimeiri was biding his time. Then in 1984, Nimeiri decided to make a humiliating gambit, he offered to Clement Mboro the position of a Minister of State in charge of the smooth implementation of the division of the Southern region into three regions. The desperate Clement swallowed his pride and accepted to serve in a position that guaranteed the implementation of a policy he had detested all along. His peace initiative died before it had begun.

By mid 1984 the government troops in the South had been pushed to the defensive in specific fortified garrisons while the SPLA combatants were freely roaming the countryside. Yet, the regime continued making exaggerated war claims in an attempt to mislead public opinion. In the top echelon of the regime, however, the situation was different. The gravity of the war was dawning on them. In 1984, the People's National Assembly held a number of closed sessions to discuss the situation in the South and how to bring the war to an end. In addition to the members, top SSU leadership, senior army officers, and supporters of the regime judged to be knowledgeable on the South were invited to attend and contribute to the discussions. Joseph Lagu, and the Governors of the three Southern regions were also in full attendance. The meeting went on for days and it was subsequently announced that a summary of the proceedings was prepared and submitted to the President. Days wore on into weeks and months and the President was tight-lipped on the issue.

On March 3, 1985 - the regime marks 3rd of March every year as "Unity Day"- Nimeiri suddenly announced the formation of a "National Committee for Peace" that was to look into the war situation and talk peace with the SPLA in order to resolve the conflict. The Committee was under the chairmanship of Sirr El-Khatim El-Khalifa, the former Prime Minister in the October 1964 Government, who had served the May regime as a Minister and in a number of other senior positions. The Rapporteur was Andrew Wieu Riak, a former Minister in the Southern region. The membership included Northerners and Southerners. The real surprise, however, was the inclusion of Dr Peter Nyot's name and mine in the list of those appointed to the membership of the Committee.

Dr Peter Nyot and I were appointed to the "Peace Committee" without prior consultation and were at a loss trying to figure out who might have proposed our names. Personally, I did not know Nimeiri and I do not remember having met him at all. In any case, both of us were resolved not to sit on the committee but decided that our rejection should be expressed in a way that will deny Nimeiri the propaganda value he wanted to gain from this bogus committee. Our plan was to bring together most of the leading Southern politicians in Khartoum and write a joint letter to Nimeiri analysing the situation and suggesting that it was him alone who can provide a solution to the problem he had created. With the exception of the Governors and a few others, we approached all who matter and it was agreed that a meeting be held in the house of Abel Alier who together with Isaiah Kulang, were also appointed to the committee.

The meeting took place and it was agreed that the letter be written and an outline of its contents was worked out including the decision to reject serving on the committee. The meeting also resolved that the letter was to be drafted by Abel Alier to be ready for signing by all two days after. We left the house happy that this was yet another opportunity to show Nimeiri that the South was still united in its rejection of his machinations. At the appointed time, we converged in the house of Abel Alier. He told the meeting that the letter was ready but added, much to the astonishment of everyone, that he alone will sign it. He did not give any reason for his unilateral decision. Needless to say, the suggestion could not be accepted as it defeated the very purpose of the collective action. All the same, nothing could be done and we singly dispersed to our homes in disappointment. Days later, in the evening of March 27, 1985, we viewed Abel Alier and Isaiah Kulang on the national television attending the opening session of the "Peace Committee" which Nimeiri had addressed that morning before he took off for Washington. The two gentlemen did not see any inconsistency between refusing to serve on the committee and attending its opening session!

Nimeiri did not return from that trip to the American capital, Washington; there was a change of guards in the Republican Palace in Khartoum on the 6th of April.

CHAPTER 3

The Uprising Days and After

The Brewing Storm

SUDAN'S ECONOMY, in the closing years of the seventies, was showing signs of enormous strain and by 1980 the Sudanese pound had been devalued several times beyond recognition. As a consequence, there was rise in inflation and unemployment in addition to the other difficulties caused by the austerity programme imposed by the IMF which the government resorted to as a succour. Naturally, the professional and trade unions struggled to protect the standards of living of their members being eroded by the inflation. Top on the agenda of these unions towards the end of the seventies and in the early eighties was their demands for the Government to raise salaries and wages so as to counterbalance the effects of the rocketing inflation. The progress of negotiations with the Government on salaries and wages and the improvement of working conditions was slow.

As the war broke out again in the south in May 1983 even the most optimistic about any improvement in the economy had to give up hope. Then followed a series of strikes notable among them was the Judges strike which was followed in September by Nimeiri's imposition of the Islamic laws. This last move was a bombshell that heightened the tension and shifted the confrontation with the government to the political gear.

The reaction of the professional and trade unions to the imposition of Islamic laws was predictably furious, and the confrontation with the regime took a sharp turn to the worst. In December, Nimeiri dissolved all the professional and trade unions, only the Khartoum University Teachers Union (KUTU) escaped the onslaught. Late in December,

Ustaz (Mr) Mahmoud Mohammed Taha, leader of the Republican Brothers, was tried for apostasy by a tribunal under the Islamic laws and was sentenced to death by hanging. Despite protests and pleas for commutation from many quarters from within and without the country, Nimeiri went ahead and Ustaz Mahmoud Mohammed Taha was hanged on Friday morning on the 18th of January 1984. Inspired by the example of El-Ghurashi in the October 1964 Uprising, the professional and trade unions were looking for a martyr and Nimeiri, unwittingly, gave them one in the person of the septuagenarian Islamic thinker. The murder of Ustaz Mahamoud Mohammed Taha became the focus of political agitation and the symbol for unity against a repressive regime.

The professional and trade unions defied the dissolution order and carried on to operate clandestinely. They continued to meet and this time the objective was to overthrow the government through a general strike. For this to be realized it was necessary to mobilize the membership of the unions and the public in general. The tasks were defined. An example of such mobilization effort was a political rally held on the University campus on the 18th of January 1985 in commemoration of Ustaz Mahmoud Mohammed Taha. It was organized by KUTU and representatives of many professional and trade unions took part. The Trade Unions Alliance was born just after that date.

The Intifadha

On the 26th of March 1985, Nimeiri was addressing an SSU meeting in which he announced new increases in the prices of essential commodities when students demonstrations broke out that evening in Omdruman. Significantly, they set the building of Wad Nimeiri Transport Company and the cars found there on fire. This is a company owned and run by Nimeiri's brother, Mustafa. For the next three days the demonstrations spread into the other parts of Omdurman and went on late into the night. These also extended to Khartoum and Khartoum North. Nimeiri dismissed the demonstrations as acts of "hooligans instigated by remnants of the Baathists and Communists" and proceeded on a prearranged visit to Washington for a medical check-up. The professional and trade unions organizations, under the banner of Trade Unions Alliance, which were in constant consultations all this time, decided to declare a general strike all over the country on Wednesday the third of April and to come out on demonstration that day. The procession was to move from opposite the Faculty of Medicine and follow the Palace Road to converge with the other demonstrations opposite the Republican Palace to deliver the petition demanding the resignation of the Government. I was in the procession and although the Police exercised restraint some agents of Nimeiri's Security Organ were out for trouble. They threw in tear gas cannisters and rubber bulltes. My colleague, Dr Taisier Mohammed Ali of the Department of Political Science, who was not far away from where I was got slightly wounded in the neck by a fragment.

In view of the near unanimity of the popular discontent, the army, which High Command was still supporting Nimeiri, was threatened with a dangerous split. The middle ranking officers established contact with the Trade Unions Alliance and held a series of meetings with the top brass of the army to persuade them to "side with the people". These negotiations were not easy and went on for days. The Commander-in-Chief, General Abdel Rahman Mohammed Hassan Siwar ed-Dahab, who was Nimeiri's Minister of Defence, a religious man of Khatimiya sect background invoked Islam to argue that he had given his *"Baiyaa"* – oath of allegiance – to Nimeiri which cannot be abjured. Later on, an Islamic way was found to untie the Gordian knot!

The greatest difficulty, however, was in getting the main parties, the Umma and the DUP, to sign a joint political charter with the Trade Unions Alliance (TUA). Central in this was how to phrase the cancellation of Nimeiri's Islamic laws for inclusion in the Charter. Although these two sectarian parties have been opposed all along to these laws, they feared to be outbidden by the Muslim Brothers who supported the laws and whose effective propaganda machine equated opposition to these laws with opposition to Islam. Negotiations went on to the small hours of the morning of the 6th of April some hours

41

after the army High Command had been persuaded to take action. The compromise phrase was "the repeal of the September Laws". The avoidance by the two parties of any explicit mention of Islamic or Sharia laws, though secured the signing of the Charter and the birth of the National Alliance for National Salvation, remained a time-bomb that eventually blew off the democratic set-up four years later. On the morning of April the 6th, General Siwar ed-Dahab, in a terse speech announced that the army had decided to side with the people. Amid jubilations the crowds applauded the decision of the army, thronged into Kober prison and set the political detainees free. The popular Uprising has triumphed, or so it seemed!

The National Alliance for National Salvation (NANS) had agreed with the army leadership to meet at the army GHQ on the morning of the 6th of April to discuss the arrangements to govern the country in the transitional period leading to the General elections all over the country. When they arrived the meeting hall, they were not alone. Some prominent leaders of the Muslim Brothers were there together with a number of persons they claimed to be representing trade unions outside the Trade Unions Alliance (TUA). The NANS objected to the presence of the Muslim Brothers, the pillars of the just overthrown regime, in such a crucial meeting. The generals insisted that they were to listen to the views of all sections of the Sudanese political spectrum! Although the generals endorsed the Charter of the NANS, it soon emerged that they had no intention of adhering to its provisions. They ignored the transitional structures suggested in the charter in which power at the top (the supreme council and the council of ministers) was to be shared between the constituent parts of what was then termed "the three sides of the triangle": the political parties, the professional and trade unions, and the army. The army usurped the supreme authority and formed not a supreme council of five but of fifteen, all army generals! This body was termed the Transitional Military Council (TMC).

The TUA retired to the University of Khartoum Staff Club, which had become the HQ of the NANS, to review the attitude of the army High Command and decided that the strike, which had not then been lifted, was to continue until the army reaffirms its commitment to the letter and spirit of the Charter. On its part, the army issued an ultimatum that it will be left with no alternative but to take firm and decisive action against what it called some elements bent on continuing with the strike for narrow political interests. The TUA consulted with the political parties in the NANS and it was clear that the Umma party and the DUP were not only opposed to the continuation of the strike but blessed the step that the Supreme Council be formed entirely from the army. To avert the inevitable split that would have occurred within the NANS had the TUA decided to take on the generals, the strike was lifted. Since then, the NANS lost the initiative as the leading body of the Uprising. In the official terminology, the generals, the Umma party and the DUP, changed from using the expression: "March/April Uprising" to "*Intifadhat Rajab*" – *Rajab* Uprising-in conformity with the Islamic revival!

The concurrence of the Umma party and the DUP with the generals was not by accident prompted by the spur of the moment; it has deeper roots. The top brass of the Sudanese army has always been a conservative force with strong links, family or otherwise, with the two major religious sects - the Ansar and the Khatimiya - whose followers, respectively, form the bedrock supporters of each party. In fact, the two parties were uncomfortable in an alliance, the NANS, in which, in their views, everybody else, parties and unions alike, was leftist in ideas. Their eyes were fixed on winning the upcoming general election and cared less about the drastic reforms the NANS called for. Consistent with this line, the DUP later pulled out of the NANS but the Umma party, more adept than its sectarian rival in cajoling the left, stayed on board to ensure the stultification of the leading body of the popular revolution.

The Reaction of the SPLA

Meanwhile, the reaction of the SPLA to the overthrow of Nimeiri was being eagerly awaited. From the first day the regime of Nimeiri fell, leaders of the NANS have been making appeals to the SPLA to lay down its arms and join the Uprising. Radio SPLA, which is well listened to in Sudan, made it known that the leader of the movement, Col. John Garang, was going to deliver an important speech on April the 9th stating the position of the movement on the developments in the country. On the appointed date, microphones were installed in all corners of the University Staff Club connected to a powerful radio so that everybody can hear the speech directly. At 3.00 p.m. (Sudan Local Time) Radio SPLA started transmission and the leader of the SPLA began to speak. There was complete silence in the club, except for the voice of Col. John Garang, all were attentive listening to every word being said. The speech went on for almost one hour, the full transmission time of the radio station. In his analysis, Col. John Garang distinguished between two aspects of the change that had taken place in Khartoum: a genuine popular uprising against the regime which he identified with and supported, and a military coup staged by Nimeiri's Chiefs of the General Staff which he condemned for, in his view, it robbed the masses of their hard won victory and was bent on continuing with Nimeiri's regime without Nimeiri. He gave the generals seven days to resign and hand the power back to the people. At the end of the broadcast, I could see a general disappointment in the faces of the listeners. Somehow, the leaders of the NANS had assumed that the leader of the SPLA was going to go to Khartoum once Nimeiri has been ousted for they saw in him an ally against Nimeiri. Both the NANS and the SPLA leader made mistaken assumptions and correspondingly erroneous conclusions regarding the forces that led to Nimeiri's overthrow and the relative strength of each. This aspect of the Uprising will be dealt with elsewhere in this book.

Reaction of the Southern Politicians

It is necessary at this point to go back to April the 6th to consider the reaction of the Southern politicians to the change. It will be remembered that when the May regime on assuming power decreed the dissolution of the political parties then in existence, the Southern Front and SANU complied and all their leaders joined the regime. Also, when the Addis Ababa Agreement was concluded on February 28, 1972, the leaders of the SSLM on their own dissolved the movement and melted into the SSU, the regime's infantile political party. Therefore, when the underground struggle against the May regime was being waged, there was no Southern party involved for there was none in existence. The Southern presence in the anti-Nimeiri struggle in Khartoum was almost non-existent except for the one or two of us holding offices in the professional unions. This is the background to the events to follow.

In the evening of April the 6th, a number of Southern politicians held a meeting in the office of the "White Stork Company" in Khartoum-2, owned by some of them, to review the situation. The meeting was on the advice of Lt.Col. Mathiang Malwal. Those present included Ezekiel Macuei Kodi, William Ajal, and others. I happened to be there and was invited to attend. Lt.Col. Mathiang Malwal opened the meeting by stating that he had just been to the office of General Siwar ed-Dahab and that the latter, who had served previously in the Southern command in Juba, was willing to hear the views of the Southerners on the situation and the way forward. He suggested that these views be put in writing in a letter to Siwar ed-Dahab as Head of the Transitional set-up which he can take to him. The idea was discussed and approved. The letter was written and signed by all of us and by others who did not attend the meeting but agreed to the contents. Among other things, it called for the cancellation of the Republican Order No. 1 dated 5/6/83 that divided the South into three regions. The letter, however, neither claimed to be speaking for anybody other than those who signed it nor did it commit the signatories to continue working together.

The attitude of the leadership of the army of being selective on which parts of the Charter to respect and which to disregard created a new fluid situation altogether. As Southerners, we were concerned about a number of issues: what will be the attitude of the new order toward the war in the South, will it be a "jaw-jaw" or a "war-war"? What about the administration in the South, will the one regional Government be set up or will the South continue as three regions? What about Southern participation in the transitional institutions;

will it be substantive or will it continue to be in peripheral capacities? etc. In addition, of course, to the other issues of national nature, such as the Islamic laws, human rights, how long should the transitional period be, etc. Some of these issues were addressed in the Charter and the new situation meant that fresh negotiations were to be sought with the generals to know the exact position. But, who will negotiate on behalf of the South or at least put across a Southern Viewpoint?

Some of us, mostly University lecturers discussed these matters in the Staff Club. Among those involved were Dr Akolda Man Tier, Dr Peter Nyot Kok, Dr Paul Wani, Dr Banaia Yongo-Bure and I from the University. We agreed to form a political body that will articulate our concerns and present them to the TMC. The body would also apply to join the NANS. We finally resolved that a general meeting with Southerners in Khartoum be called to discuss the proposal.

The Southern Sudanese in Khartoum (SSK)

A few days after our discussions at the Staff Club, a meeting was convened in one of the University lecture rooms. The meeting was briefed about the situation since April the 6th, the need to have the voice of the South heard, and the discussions that have been taking place in the staff club. The proposal was then presented to the floor. After a frank and healthy debate the meeting agreed to proceed as suggested. The points to be included were discussed and agreed upon.

Finally, it was decided that, for the time being and to keep the doors open for many more Southerners to join, the organization was given the tentative name: "The Southern Sudanese in Khartoum (SSK)." The same group that called for the meeting were given the task of formulating the points agreed upon as a programme of action and present it for approval in another meeting. This task was duly accomplished. The meeting was convened and the programme endorsed on April 11, 1985.

We presented the programme of the SSK to Brigadier General Osman Abdalla Mohammed, member of the TMC in charge of political affairs, in a meeting we held in Nimeiri's Military Academy near the Ministry of Health on the Nile Avenue. He discussed with us the points contained in the programme and was visibly impressed by our approach to the issues. We agreed to meet again. Later in the afternoon he gave a statement broadcast over Radio Omdurman in which he commended the approach of the SSK towards the solution of the Southern conflict from a national perspective.

There was no difficulty encountered when I presented the application of SSK to join the NANS. What was needed was to endorse the charter which we did. Thus, the SSK became a full member of NANS, the first to do so after the signatories to the charter.

Consultations on the transitional setup

After the near collision between the NANS and the TMC on the latter's decision to monopolize the supreme power to the exclusion of the TUA and the parties, the two sides settled for dialogue. High in the agenda were the issues of the structure of the Transitional Council of Ministers and the length of the transitional period. After lengthy discussions, it was agreed that the Council of Ministers will be composed of civilians all nominated by the NANS save for the Minister of Defence, who will be nominated by the army, and the Minister of the Interior, to be nominated by the police force. Of the civilian Ministers, three seats will be reserved specifically for the Southern Sudanese. Agreement was also reached on an interim period of twelve months as from the moment the Council of Ministers takes the oath of office. The NANS argued for a shorter period than was in the charter in order to rid itself as soon as possible of the military. After this followed a protracted discussion within the NANS on the formation of the Transitional Council of Ministers.

The political parties in the NANS, especially the Umma party and the DUP, wanted to be represented in the Cabinet. The TUA argued otherwise, maintaining that what was needed to prepare for a healthy democratic era was a Cabinet of technocrats that enjoyed the confidence of all the parties to the alliance that brought Nimeiri down. After many days of discussion, the Umma party and the DUP conceded to the TUA that the Cabinet be formed from non-partisan technocrats but insisted that all the nominees must be vetted by the NANS as a whole to ensure their independence from partisan allegiance. A number of conditions which must be met by a candidate to the cabinet were set. One such condition was that the candidate should not have served in any political capacity under the May regime. Another phase of long discussions followed on the vetting of the candidates to the Transitional Cabinet. It was not a pleasant exercise to get all the members of the NANS to agree on somebody. A lot of details about a candidate, some of them quite personal, were unearthed and discussed.

Despite this finicky exercise, none of the parties was interested in discussing the nature of and nominations for the three cabinet seats reserved for the South. It was understood that this was the work of NANS which was entrusted to submit its nominations of the civilian members of the cabinet to the TMC for approval. Edward Lino and I represented the SSK in these meetings held in the Medical Doctors Club and no satisfactory answer was forthcoming from the TUA, the North's usual way of taking the South for granted.

The NANS managed, at long last after many days of tedious debate, to put together a list of the Northerners nominated to be Ministers in the Transitional Cabinet. Oddly enough, there were two nominees to the office of the Prime Minister for the TMC to choose one from! If the NANS could willingly relinquish to the military what was clearly within its power to do, can it justifiably blame the military for encroachment? Possibly, the NANS did not consider the implications of having the TMC, which they have already come to be suspicious of, to choose a Prime Minister for them. The list of all candidates considered for the office of Prime Minister was finally shortened to two: Dr El-Jizouli Daffallah, President of the Medical Doctors' Union and Mr Mirghani El-Nasri, Chairman of the Bar Association; both organizations are founding members of the TUA and played a great role in the uprising. The TUA should have given itself time to come out with one nominee even if it meant more delay in the formation of the Cabinet. In the process the TUA chose the easy way out and the TMC was quick to exploit this window for its political advantage.

A few days after the NANS meeting in the Doctors Club, the meeting of the SSK with Brigadier-General Osman Abdalla Mohammed that was agreed upon earlier took place in Nimeiri's Military Academy. With him was Brigadier-General Taj - El-Sir El-Badawi, the Director of the Academy. The SSK was represented by Dr Peter Nyot and myself. The TMC member raised the issue of the formation of the Transitional Cabinet and southern participation in it and wanted to know the SSK's view on the matter. We stressed to him that there was a gulf of lost confidence between the South and the North and hence the first step was to embark on building confidence between the two parts of the country more by deeds than by words.

On the Southern participation in the Cabinet, we told him that the form it will take will contribute either positively or negatively to the confidence-building all desire to achieve. We told him that we felt the Southerners would feel there was a real change to the better if Southern participation in the Cabinet was not, as previously, confined to insignificant portfolios. We gave him a copy of a press release issued by the SSK on the subject. In the paper, the Cabinet portfolios were listed under three categories: supremacy, economy and service ministries. It was suggested that the three portfolios for the South should be selected as one from each of the above three categories. We assured him that the SSK would consider participation in the Cabinet if the above requirement was met. He was replying when Lt.Col. Mathiang Malwal entered the room, greeted us and proceeded to where the Brigadier was sitting and whispered some words into his ear. After that the Lt.Col. left the room.

When we were alone again, Osman Abdalla told us that Lt.Col. Mathiang Malwal had told him that there were a number of Southern politicians outside who wanted to see him and that if we did not mind, he wanted to meet all of us together. We told him it was all right. Then entered Mr Samuel Aru Bol, Oliver Batali Albino, William Ajal and others. Lt.Col. Mathiang Malwal said he was going to fetch some

Southern Military officers whose views will benefit the discussion and Osman Abdalla told him to go ahead. Dr Peter and I wondered whether all this was by accident or something was up but thought we should allow the events to take their course.

Samuel Aru did not have much time to waste, he went straight to the point. He had come to Osman Abdalla mandated by the Southern politicians to agree with him on the three Southern nominees to the cabinet. He went ahead and gave to the TMC member the three names put forward by them: Samuel Aru Bol, Peter Gatkuoth Gual and Oliver Batali Albino. Significantly, Samuel Aru stated that they were ready to serve in any portfolio but added that if there was something like a "Deputy Prime Minister" he would be so glad to add it to his portfolio!

Brigadier-General Albino Akol Akol, speaking on behalf of the Southern officers in the army, added his bit to the unfolding drama. He gave a boring speech on why it was necessary at that stage to have the commissioners in the Southern provinces (there were eight of them) appointed from the military. Col. James Yol who was sitting next to him was nodding in approval as Akol Akol spoke. Whether by chance or by design, Osman Abdalla did not ask if any of us representing the SSK wanted to speak. We did not insist and so the meeting was over. That was the last time we saw Osman Abdalla in private discussion.

When the Cabinet was later announced, the list of Samuel Aru had gone through. He was made Deputy Prime Minister and Minister of Irrigation, Peter Gatkuoth Gual, Minister of Transport and Communications and Oliver Batali Albino, Minister of Labour. All of them were prominent figures of the May regime! A few months later, Oliver Batali Albino was dismissed from the Cabinet for alleged involvement in a drug scandal that happened at Jeddah airport in Saudi Arabia. Of course, Brigadier-General Albino Akol Akol was appointed one of three military governors in the South and Col. James Yol and a number of other army officers from the South were appointed commissioners to the eight Southern provinces.

It was earlier mentioned that the TUA played into the hands of the TMC by presenting to it not one nominee but two for the important office of the Prime Minister. Right from day one the TMC had sufficiently shown its lethargy towards implementing the drastic reform programme advocated by the NANS and especially the TUA within it. Therefore, common sense would suggest that under the circumstances, the only course of action left for the TUA was to ensure the control of the Council of Ministers if the programme of the uprising were to have any chance of implementation. This is so because during the transition there was no constitution to guide the division of powers between the TMC and the cabinet. The Prime Minister, no doubt, is the hub of the Cabinet. The two gentlemen proposed for the office contrasted widely in their political convictions. Although at some stage of his life he was associated with the Islamic Socialist Party, Mirghani El-Nasri was viewed by the sectarian parties as a socialist. That for them, was enough reason not to support his candidature. In contrast, Dr El-Jizouli Daffallah was a devout Muslim and some Leftist would go as far as to suggest that he was a fundamentalist. As expected, the conservative TMC influenced by the two sectarian parties and the Muslim Brothers picked the latter. Thus, El-Jizouli Daffallah became the Prime Minister of the Transitional Cabinet of the uprising. The NANS was in for an uphill struggle.

The portfolios reserved for the army and police were duly filled. The Ministry of the Interior went to the Chief of Police, Lt.General Abbas Medani but the Ministry of Defence went, rather incongruously, to Brigadier-General Osman Abdalla Mohammed. There were at least two reasons why the appointment of Osman Abdalla as Minister of Defence could be considered out of norm. First, he was a member of the TMC which wielded supreme power and which appointed the Prime Minister and his council of Ministers and to which the Cabinet was answerable. Protocolwise, he could not be answerable to the Prime Minister. Second, the TMC had retained the command of the army. The Chairman of the TMC was the C-in-C of the army, his deputy, the Deputy C-in-C and the 3rd in the hierarchy of the TMC, Lt. General Mohammed Tawfig Khalil, was the Chief of Staff. Osman Abdalla was very low down in the hierarchy of the TMC, he was the 13th in line. Where does he fit in such a situation as Minister of Defence?

The long and short of it was that Brigadier-General Osman Abdalla was no Minister of Defence for the Cabinet had no say on anything related to the army, this power rested firmly in the hands of the TMC or, to be more exact, the three top members of it. His presence in the Council of Ministers accorded the TMC the opportunity to follow, first hand, the deliberations of the "civilian" cabinet.

With all the parts in place the Cabinet was finally completed and announced. Dr El-Jizouli Daffallah and members of his Cabinet finally took the oath of office before the Chairman of the TMC on the 25th of April. After weeks of suspense there was a sigh of relief that the Council of Ministers was at long last formed.

The Structuring of NANS

Since the 6th of April 1985, the NANS had little time to structure itself. The alliance has by now considerably expanded in membership as newly formed political parties and some trade unions joined. With the hectic weeks of haggling out of the way the NANS could embark on internal reorganization. As indicated earlier, the NANS comprises two components: the TUA as one component and the political parties as the other. This was the case on the night of the 5th of April and continued to be so, the fad about the 'triangle' not withstanding. The only new development weeks later was that the number of the political parties had increased. The TUA had its own Secretariat under the Chairmanship of the Doctors Union with the Engineers Union as the Secretary-General and other offices allocated to the other professional and Trade Unions. The difficulty was with the political parties none of which would accept to be subordinated to the other. It took several days of discussion for the NANS to agree on a Secretariat for the alliance. The Chairmanship of the NANS would be by rotation on a monthly basis between the TUA, the Umma party and the DUP. In addition to these three members of the Secretariat, two other members were the Sudanese Communist Party and the SSK. The Secretariat had no power to take policy decisions, its main function was to follow up the implementation of such decisions and to represent the NANS on occasions where it would not be possible to have the whole membership present. The NANS also agreed on the Engineers Club in El-Aamarat as the meeting place of the Secretariat, as frequently as necessary, and the whole body of NANS which had ordinary meetings once a week; every Tuesday. I was the leader of the SSK's three representatives to the NANS. The other two were: Dr Peter Nyot Kok and Mr Edward A. Lino.

Four main issues occupied the attention of the NANS and featured in its discussions: the Islamic laws, peaceful resolution of the war, the transitional constitution of the Sudan and the electoral law.

From the moment of the imposition of the Islamic laws by Nimeiri beginning with the penal code in September 1983 followed by a series of other laws thereafter, the issue has been a thorny one. Some political analysts believe Nimeiri took the move to pull the rug from underneath the feet of the Islamic-based sectarian parties, the Umma and the DUP. Even the Muslim Brothers who were by the time in power with Nimeiri were as much surprised by the decision as everybody else. In fact, the laws were being issued not from the office of the Attorney General but from the Palace! The reaction of the Umma Party and the DUP was halfhearted opposition. Their position was that, whereas they were for Islamic laws and an Islamic constitution for the Sudan, they opposed Nimeiri's laws because they were not truly Islamic! The Muslim Brothers, on the other hand, were smarter. They gave their full unreserved support to Nimeiri for having at last, applied *"Sharaa Allah"* - God's laws. They organized mass demonstrations of support for the Islamic laws and their leadership, from Dr Hassan Abdalla El-Turabi downwards, had sworn an oath of allegiance to Nimeiri as the Imam of the Muslims in Sudan! This was the state of affairs among the Islamic-based parties when the uprising was brewing. The other political parties and professional and trade unions in the NANS were all for the repeal of the Islamic laws to be replaced by the 1974 secular laws, amended to purge them of any provision restrictive of basic freedoms.

The debate within the NANS, because of this wide divergence of views, could not go beyond the phrase already contained in the

Charter which skirted not only calling the laws by what they really were, Islamic laws, but also the vital point of the laws replacing them once repealed. The position of the two parties, the Umma and the DUP, on the issue continued to harden as the Muslim Brothers, through an effective press, stepped up their accusations that these two parties had allied themselves with the communists to repeal the Islamic laws. Eventually, the DUP withdrew from the NANS on the issue. The TMC and the Prime Minister seized on this difference and declared that the Transitional setup was not qualified to decide on the Islamic laws and, therefore, they will remain on the statute books until the elected government decides on what to do with them.

On the war raging in the South, the NANS was at one that the only option was a peaceful resolution of the conflict through negotiations with the SPLA and called for a cease fire between the warring parties to create an atmosphere conducive for the talks to take place. In spite of the unanimity on the policy, this was the area where the NANS received its greatest setback, for no aspect of the policy was effected. Cease fires were declared always unilaterally, and never implemented. The parties that controlled the war machine were out of the control or influence of the NANS. At the end, the NANS ended up on the defensive against the unfair barrage of accusations leveled against it of being a fifth column to the SPLA!

War or Peace?

A number of events led to the difficulties faced by the NANS in its attempts to bring about a political settlement to the war. The deadline Col. John Garang set in his April the 9th speech for the TMC to resign passed, not unexpectedly, without event. This was followed in May (the 26th and 27th) by another speech over Radio SPLA in which Col. John Garang vowed not to talk to the TMC while expressing readiness to talk to the civilian cabinet. The reaction of the TMC was predictably hostile. It concluded that the SPLA was not ready for peace and stepped up its preparations for war, both militarily and politically. In its political mobilization for the war effort, the TMC found a most faithful ally in the Muslim Brothers, now under a new rubric, the National Islamic Front (NIF). The NIF press, comprising two daily newspapers and two weeklies, were full of diatribes against the SPLA portraying its leader as a "traitor" and an "agent of communism" and that the nation must mobilize all its resources to fight the threat. The NANS was not also spared of the venom of the NIF press. Its conciliatory tone was adduced by this press as evidence of collusion with the SPLA since both organizations were communists inspired and controlled! The NIF did not stop at that, it backed its words by deeds. It called for countrywide contributions, in cash and in kind, to support the army in its war in the South and organized demonstrations of support that marched to the army General Headquarters in Khartoum pledging their unreserved support for the army in its war against the SPLA. One such demonstration, on the 5th of September 1985, dubbed "Sudan Security March", handed over to the army leadership the contributions collected by the NIF and was addressed by TMC members expressing deep appreciation for the national efforts exerted and sacrifices made by those concerned in supporting their national army.

Militarily, the TMC which controlled every aspect of the army, continued with the war plans already set in place before the departure of Nimeiri to Washington. In addition to this, the TMC was able to blow out of proportion small incidents of armed attacks on villages by some SPLA deserters as proof of the SPLA's lack of commitment to any ceasefire. A lot of hullabaloo was made in the NIF press on an alleged SPLA attack on "El-Gardud" village in Southern Kordofan and another village South of Kosti town in the White Nile province. The Umma party which believed the areas concerned fell within its sphere of influence did not want to be outsmarted by the NIF and condemned the SPLA in the strongest possible terms. It rhetorically asked: what does the SPLA want?

On the other hand, some actions of the SPLA helped strengthen the hands of the war mongers adding to the isolation of the NANS or those elements within it still committed to the political settlement of the conflict. The SPLA's incursion into the areas around Kurmuk in September 1985 with a force under the command of the SPLA's Deputy leader at a time when the NANS were busy making preparations to receive in Khartoum a delegation of the SPLA led by the same man, could not be explained in anyway other than as lack of seriousness. Also the ill-advised action by the SPLA in the same month to hand over a letter to the Prime Minister under the escort of the SPLA force in the government garrison in Nasir, rather than in Addis Ababa where the letter being replied was handed over, played into the hands of the war mongers in Khartoum. The TMC and the NIF were quick to seize on these incidents and others and made a lot of capital out of them. In fact, Osman Abdalla, the Minister of Defence addressed a meeting of the NANS in which he explained what happened in Nasir as a stratagem by the SPLA to capture Nasir and that if it were not "God's care" and the "alertness of our gallant armed forces" the worst could have happened in Nasir. He went on and added that the capture of Nasir was to lead to an attack by the same force on Bor! Such was the extent of disinformation. When I asked the Minister of Defence, in the same meeting, to elaborate more on how the rebels walking on foot at that time of the year when the ground was muddy could exploit a success in Nasir to attack Bor some 300 km away, he was caught off balance. He was counting on an audience that did not care to know how far apart Nasir and Bor were. Dr Ali Abu Sinn of the NUP followed and cautioned the Minister of Defence against army attempts to manipulate the politicians. In any case, the NIF press had a field day over the Nasir incident calling the letter a "booby-trapped parcel". For one reason or the other the letter could not arrive from Nasir and a copy had to come from Addis Ababa adding to the state of confusion on the whole affair.

True to its policy, the NANS exerted commendable efforts in order to bring about a political settlement to the war. As soon as the position of the SPLA on the transitional setup became known, the NANS sent a special envoy, Dr Farouq Ibrahim, to Addis Ababa to meet with the leaders of the SPLA and explain to them the situation from the NANS perspective. In Addis, the envoy met a delegation of the SPLA led by Major Riek Machar Teny, the office manager of Col. John Garang, and included comrade Dhol Acuil Aleu and others. In a series of meetings the two sides briefed each other on their respective positions and exchanged views on the situation of war and peace in the country. Dr Farouq Ibrahim went back to Khartoum and rendered a comprehensive report to the NANS on his meetings with the SPLA delegation in Addis Ababa. On the basis of this report the NANS decided that it was necessary to involve the Council of Ministers: first, by issuing a general declaration committing itself to a peaceful settlement of the conflict and, second, by getting the Prime Minister to write a letter to Col. John Garang, the leader of the SPLA, on the Government's readiness to enter into negotiations with the SPLA. The Council of Ministers agreed to the proposal and made a draft of the declaration for the NANS to approve. The draft was discussed and, after some minor amendments, approved by the NANS. The letter of the Prime Minister was ready in June 1985 and both the Declaration and the letter were taken to Addis Ababa the same month by Dr Taisier Mohammed Ali to hand over to the SPLA. This is the letter which Col. John Garang did not reply until three months later. He had his reasons for the delay as we shall see later!

After that Dr Taisier went on a number of official missions to Addis Ababa to continue dialogue with the SPLA on peace. In one such mission he was entrusted to find out the view of the SPLA on the possibility of it sending a delegation to Khartoum to conduct meetings with all concerned and to see for itself the situation inside the Capital. According to Dr Taisier's report to the NANS, the SPLA officers he met, Captain Deng Alor Kuol and Captain Mark Maciec, assured him that the SPLA was willing to send a delegation to Khartoum if their security could be guaranteed. The NANS welcomed this as a very positive development and a sign of good will. It immediately embarked on seeking the security guarantees from the TMC and the Council of Ministers which were readily offered. On obtaining these guarantees a programme of the visit was put together and Dr Taisier was sent back to Addis Ababa to show it to the SPLA for possible addition or subtraction. This time it was none other than Col. John

Garang that he met. Dr Taisier, somewhat in high spirits in what seemed like a breakthrough, reported to the Colonel on what had transpired in Khartoum, that everybody was looking forward to meeting an SPLA delegation in Khartoum as this will be a practical way of dispelling the fears and illusions about the movement and concluded by the assurances given to the NANS by the TMC and the Prime Minister on the security of the delegation and that the NANS had drafted a programme for the visit that it wanted to share with the SPLA. After the niceties, Col. John Garang told a startled Dr Taisier that the SPLA had never ever committed itself to going to Khartoum under the security guarantees of anybody other than the SPLA, and that the SPLA was indeed willing to go to Khartoum if its delegation was allowed to march there escorted by a force of two battalions for its security! Dr Taisier related to him his previous discussion with the Colonel's new office manager, Capt. Deng Alor Kuol and his assistant, Capt. Mark Maciec, and stressed that there was no way a suggestion of a force marching to Khartoum can ever be considered by the authorities in the Capital. The meeting ended not on quite a friendly note. When he reported to the NANS days later Dr Taisier Mohammed Ali could not hide his disappointment with the encounter. That was the end to any attempt to invite an SPLA delegation to Khartoum. A few weeks after, Radio SPLA announced that Lt.Col. Kerubino Kwanyin Bol, the Deputy leader of the SPLA was in the Kurmuk area on his way to lead a high-level SPLA delegation to Khartoum when he was intercepted by the forces of the TMC!

The Koka Dam Conference

The NANS did not despair in its effort despite obvious obstructions from the warring parties and continued contacts with the SPLA. It was finally agreed that the NANS would meet the SPLA in Addis Ababa to discuss the peaceful resolution of the problem. This meeting took place in the Koka Dam resort, 100 km South of Addis Ababa, in the last week of March 1986 when the political parties were busy with the general elections scheduled to take place in the first week of May. This took some steam out of the event. The NANS delegation, on which I was a member, had to wait for two days for the arrival of the SPLA delegation. Finally, the SPLA delegation arrived Koka Dam led by Col. John Garang, his second-in-Command, Lt.Col. Kerubino Kwanyin Bol and Major Arok Thon Arok. The lists of the two delegations were exchanged over dinner. Eyebrows were raised on the side of the NANS for the inclusion in the SPLA's delegation of the name of Dr Mansour Khalid, an outstanding figure in the May regime but had resigned some two years earlier.

The opening session of the Koka Dam Conference was open to the press and started at about 10.00 a.m. on 22nd March 1986. It was opened by Mr Yelma Tadesse from the Ministry of Foreign Affairs representing the Ethiopian government. Mr Tadesse was a former Ethiopian ambassador in Sudan, in fact the last one, and knew the country well. He expressed the wish of the Ethiopian government and people to see that the bloodletting in the sisterly neighbour, Sudan, is brought to an end by peaceful means and wished the delegates well in their deliberations. He was followed by Dr Khalid Yaji, the Chairman of the NANS. In his speech Dr Yaji thanked the Ethiopian Government and people for hosting the conference and went on to state that the aim of the meeting was to prepare a conducive atmosphere for the holding of the constitutional conference that will discuss the major problems facing the Sudan. Dr Yaji then moved on to point out the failure of the transitional government to implement the objectives of the uprising but stressed that "... the democratic dialogue and solving our problems through democratic means is the only option adopted by all the forces of the Uprising, and willingly accepted by the Sudanese people as a result of their long experience". He added that: "we are aware of the challenges that are faced by this option and the dangers that surround it". Dr Yaji also devoted part of his speech to underline the necessity and urgency of bringing the fratricide to an end and that the human and economic resources consumed by the war could have been directed towards a comprehensive economic development of the country.

Col. Dr John Garang then took the rostrum and addressed the meeting for about three hours. He started by thanking the Ethiopian Government for hosting the meeting and apologized for the delay of his delegation saying that he was busy directing military operations in order to repulse a concentrated attack launched by the government troops against the SPLA. He spoke at length about his vision of what a "United New Sudan" should look like in terms of justice, balanced regional development, identity, etc. that should be agreed upon and embodied in the constitution. Col. Garang told the meeting that he will not discuss with them military issues for two reasons: these issues are of a technical nature, and that the delegation of the NANS did not represent the Government which is directing the war against the SPLA. On the upcoming elections, the leader of the SPLA rejected the exercise totally arguing that the elections will only be conducted in the North without the South. He advised that the elections should have been preceded by the holding of the constitutional conference in which the SPLA will take part. Col. Garang concluded by saying that: "dialogue is good as it leads to more dialogue which may lead to peace."

Both Mr Yelma Tadesse and Col. John Garang, whose delegation was led by Lt. Col. Kerubino Kwanyin Bol, left the meeting after the opening speeches.

When the conference was about to get to business, Dr Nasir El-Sid, leader of the Islamic Socialist Party and member of the NANS delegation, took the microphone and informed the press corps that he had a statement to make. He stated that it was a principled position of his party not to deal in anyway with the pillars of the May regime and, therefore, he cannot be party to talks with the SPLA if Dr Mansour Khalid was a member of the SPLA's delegation. He declared that because of the fact he was walking out of the talks and left the room. He was supported by the representative of the Libyan-supported "Popular Committees" of Mr Abdalla Zackaria who walked out with him. Major Arok Thon Arok, who introduced himself as the spokesman of the SPLA's delegation, got up to reply. He said Dr Mansour Khalid had left the regime before it fell unlike others who waited until the last minute and picked up spoils, that Dr Mansour Khalid had written a book that exposed the ugliness of the May regime and concluded, rather firmly, that none has the right to choose the other's delegation. The NANS delegation retired for consultation on the issue and it was resolved that we continue with the talks regardless.

We held an afternoon session that day which was the first and last plenary session. After that the two delegations formed smaller committees to continue with the discussions. The NANS side was led by Mr Awad El-Karim Mohammed, the Secretary General of the NANS, while the SPLA side was led by Major Arok Thon Arok. The discussions went on for three days. On the issues discussed, it was only the Umma party which had a different outlook and eventually it was the Umma party that needed to be persuaded to a common position. On every point discussed, the representatives of the Umma party, Mr Idris al-Banna and Dr Bashir Omer, would contact sayed El-Sadiq al-Mahdi in Omdurman by telephone to get his consent. We did not know if the other side had noticed this but it was quite embarrassing for us. Finally, agreement on a general framework for the political settlement of the conflict was reached and signed on behalf of the SPLA by Lt. Col. Kerubino Kwanyin Bol and on behalf of the NANS by Mr Awad El-Karim Mohammed. It became known as the Koka Dam Declaration.

The NANS delegation went back to Khartoum satisfied with the achievement. However, developments in the country towards electing a democratic government overtook some provisions of the Koka Dam Declaration. The two sides in the Koka Dam Conference agreed on the necessity of creating "a New Sudan that would be free from racism, tribalism, sectarianism and all causes of discrimination and disparity", and that "the process leading to the formation of a New Sudan should begin by the convening of a National Constitutional Conference." Point 2 of the Koka Dam Declaration stipulated that the two sides agreed that the essential prerequisites which would foster an atmosphere conducive to the holding of the proposed National Constitutional Conference are:

1 The matter under discussion be defined as not the "Southern Problem" but the national problem.
2 The lifting of the state of emergency.
3 Repeal of the "September 1983 Laws" and all other laws that are restrictive of freedoms.
4 Adoption of the 1956 constitution as amended in 1964.
5 The abrogation of the military pacts concluded between Sudan and other countries and which impinge on Sudan's national sovereignty.
6 A continuous endeavour by the two sides to take the necessary steps and measures to effect a cease fire.

The Koka Dam Declaration spelt out the agenda of the Constitutional Conference and that it shall be held in Khartoum during the third week of June 1986, provided the prerequisites above have been met. The two sides also agreed to set up a liaison committee comprising five members from each side to follow up the implementation of the provisions of the declaration.

The Transitional Constitution

We now turn to the debate on the Transitional Constitution. The issue was as sensitive as the debate on the Islamic laws for it is the nature of the Constitution that governs the kind of laws derived from it. The debate started with the laws and we have already seen how it was settled in favour of the Islamic laws. The Alliance had thought it would write the draft transitional constitution and then present the draft for discussion with the TMC and the Council of Ministers. This continued to be the belief until suddenly in October the NANS discovered to its dismay, that the TMC had formed a committee to draft the transitional constitution and that the committee had completed its work and reported back to the TMC! Worse still the NANS discovered that Mr Mirghani El-Nasri, the Chairman of the Bar Association and member of both TUA and NANS, and one or two lawyers representing the Umma Party were on the Committee of the TMC! The committee was headed by Brigadier-General Mahmoud Ahmed Hassan, the legal adviser of the TMC. The Committee had succeeded to maintain complete secrecy on its deliberations. The most controversial part of the transitional constitution was the article on the sources of legislation which reaffirmed Islam and custom to be such sources. It was a similar article in the 1973 constitution that was used by Nimeiri to impose the Islamic laws ten years later. The NANS wanted the Constitution to be silent on the sources of legislation as the Transitional Constitution of 1956 was. The NANS demands to open the matter to discussion were ignored. Its case was further weakened by the participation of some of its members in the TMC's committee. In the end, in what has by now become a trend, it had to settle for the *fait accompli.*

The Electoral Law

The Law governing the election to the Constituent Assembly was a very controversial issue. The Sudanese have learnt very early in their experience with elections how the electoral law influences the final outcome of the balance of forces in Parliament. In 1953, the victory of the NUP over the Umma Party was ascribed as much to the popularity of the former as to the exclusion from the voters registers of the migrants from Western Africa who were believed to be Umma supporters. These migrants were registered in 1958 elections which the Umma Party won thus lending support to the premise. The issue at stake this time was in relation to the role of the so-called "modern forces". Simply put, the modern forces meant the professional and trade unions. It has been recognized that this group has been the most effective in overthrowing the two military dictatorships which had ruled Sudan (in 1964 and 1985) yet when the elections were held only the "traditional forces" get elected. Discussions were held in the NANS with a view of finding a formula which can guarantee the representation of the modern forces in the upcoming Constituent Assembly. All members of the NANS, except the DUP, agreed that the elections law must provide for reserved seats to be filled by the modern forces. In opposition, the DUP argued that the elections are governed by the principle of one-person-one-vote and as such allocating special seats for special groups will contradict this basic principle of democracy. When the DUP withdrew from the NANS there was unanimity on the matter. However, as was the case on many issues, the Umma Party was not sincere in its acceptance of the principle. In their manoeuvres with the TMC, the three parties (Umma, DUP and NIF) made sure nothing was heard again of the modern forces. This was replaced by reserved seats for the "Graduates", defined as any holder of a post secondary school diploma or degree which duration of study extended over at least two years. When the Graduates seats were allocated later, it was arbitrarily decided that each region of the nine regions of Sudan would form an electoral college and that each of these colleges would send a number of graduates to the Constituent Assembly equal to one-tenth of the geographical constituencies in the region. As if this was not enough rigmarole already, the TMC added another absurdity: whereas the graduates in the country are only allowed to vote in the regions they reside in, those abroad were free to choose any of the nine regions where to vote for the Graduates Seats!

The NANS argued, to no avail, that even if the principle of the Graduates Seats were to be accepted it will only make sense if the elections to the reserved seats were conducted nationally with the whole country as one electoral college. This was also the only way to justify the voting of the graduates abroad as Sudan's electoral laws do not cater for voters outside the borders of the country. The Graduates seats of 1965 elections was a case in point when all the graduates in the country voted to elect fifteen members of the Constituent Assembly to fill the seats reserved for the graduates. However, it was precisely this experience that the traditional parties did not want to be repeated, for in those elections the Sudan Communist Party won twelve out of the fifteen seats. Hence, the complication on the issue cannot be attributed just to amateurism. In the end, the TMC had its way and the electoral law came out without consideration to the views of the NANS.

The "Racist Plot"

In late September 1985 the government in Khartoum announced that it had uncovered a racist plot to overthrow the government. It elaborated further that the plot involved a military coup d'etat master-minded by Fr. Philip Abbas Ghabbush, the leader of the Sudan National Party (SNP), to be executed by his fellow Nubas and some Southern Sudanese in the army and that once the coup had succeeded the SPLA would be invited in to take charge of the country's affairs. The statement went on to claim that some politicians in Khartoum from the SNP and from the South were behind the plot, and concluded that the soldiers entrusted to execute the coup were arrested just before their Zero hour and that the arrests of those involved was still going on. Dr El-Jizouli Daffallah delivered a speech on radio and television on the alleged plot. His racist language went beyond what was usually heard from the establishment on similar "racist coups" and that speech went unpublished up to today.

That evening, Lt. General (Police) Abbas Medani the Minister of the Interior and Mr Omar Abdel Aatti, the Attorney-General, went to the Engineers Club to brief the NANS on the matter. I was not there when they did the briefing. That evening I went to the University Staff Club as usual and the discussion there centred on the Prime Minister's irresponsible and emotional speech. Two days later I came to know that the police were looking for me in connection with the plot. I was very much surprised by the news. On the 2nd of October, I drove my car to the police HQ after my morning lectures were over. I went straight to the office of the Minister of the Interior but did not find him in. There I met Lt. Col. (Police) Salih El-Jak Salih, who I know very well from Malakal. He seated me and we chatted for some time. Then he told me that there was a warrant of arrest from the Attorney General's office to put me under detention in Kober prison. I told him it must be a case of mistaken identity but assured him I was at his disposal and that was why I was there in the first place. He told me we would drive to my residence to collect some of the personal things I would need in the prison. We reached there and I prepared what I needed and after informing those with me in the flat we drove away together in Salih's car. That was how I got into jail. It was clear the police was not in picture at all.

In Kober, I found my friend, Edward Lino already there. I also found the entire political bureau of Fr. Philip Abbas' SNP, except himself for he was detained in a separate cell in the same prison, and his deputy Mr Ahmed El-Mahi who was not arrested at all. The rest from the S-G downwards were all there with me in the Eastern wing of Kober prison. In the same wing I met, for the first time Captain Kur Mica of the Central Reserve Police and two of his NCOs arrested in relation to the same alleged plot. Kur Mica hailed from Bor district in Southern Sudan. All the cells in the wing opened into the same compound and we shared the services. There were two each to a cell. I had private discussions with members of the SNP, some of whom I have met before, to satisfy myself of what was going on. The conclusion of these discussions was that they were all ignorant of any attempted coup or any plans for one. This was not the end of my investigation. Knowing the way Fr. Philip Abbas Ghabbush runs the party he could easily have acted alone without the knowledge of his political bureau. I needed to talk to him, but this proved to be impossible. He was incommunicado, at least for us under detention with him. Then I turned to the police officer and his NCOs. Their words were interspersed with expressions of bitterness of being treated the way they have been despite their loyalty to the service of the country. As days went by we organized classes where Edward Lino, Advocate Mursi Mursal and I taught the history of Sudan to the group.

Outside Kober prison my arrest hit the headlines of Khartoum's press. The NIF press which had always portrayed me as a communist, was convinced that I was involved in the "racist plot" and that I must face the full brunt of the law. The independent press was caught between incredulity and statements emanating from "responsible sources", the Attorney-General and other unnamed sources, to the effect that "the confessions" of the arrested soldiers confirmed my role in the plot. The NANS was firm: either the Attorney-General produced his evidence or I should be set free. I was visited in prison several times by delegations from KUTU and NANS. In all these meetings I had assured them in no uncertain terms of my total innocence and that the whole affair was a conspiracy against me and others for political motives.

The pressure of the NANS and KUTU continued to mount on Mr Omer Abdel Aatti, the Attorney-General, and he kept on setting a date after another when his "evidence" would be ready. The NANS had already given him a deadline when on the 21st of October 1985 a rally was organized by NANS in the University of Khartoum to celebrate the 21st anniversary of the October 1964 uprising. Mr Mohammed Ibrahim Nugud, the Secretary-General of the Sudan Communist Party, was among the speakers in the rally. Towards the end of his speech he commented on my arrest. He called upon Omer Abdel Aatti to set me free forthwith and that if innocent people were to be arrested at the whims of those in charge it would not be surprising that Omer Abdel Aatti might find himself in the same Kober prison one day. This statement provided the NIF yellow press with material for several weeks. "Nugud threatens the Attorney-General" ran the headlines of their dailies *"El-Raya"* and *"Alwan"*. They went on to write editorials, analyses and draw cartoons on the intentions of the Secretary General of the Sudan Communist Party. Turning to me, I was elevated from just being an ordinary member to the membership of the Central Committee of the Sudan Communist Party! The NIF continued harping on this nonsense even after the collapse of the Berlin wall when the communist-scare ceased to pay dividends any more. Interestingly, the communist daily newspaper, *El-Meidan*, did not at all bother to deny the claims of the NIF press about my membership in the party.

Under mounting pressure from inside the country and Human Rights Organizations abroad and in absence of any specific charges the Attorney-General had no choice but to set me free on the 23rd of October after having spent three weeks in jail. All this time I was interviewed by the police only once and none of the questions asked touched directly on the alleged coup plot. Dr Mum Kou Nhial, Lecturer in the Institute of African and Asian Studies, University of

Khartoum was arrested and joined us just a few days before my release. We left the Eastern wing together into freedom. We bade farewell to each other, those remaining behind and the two going, and I promised them to take up their case with the NANS.

As soon as I was out of Kober, I presented a written petition to the NANS in which I demanded that Omer Abdel Atti, as member of the TUA from the Bar Association, be summoned before the NANS to explain the circumstances of my arrest. It turned out that Omer Abdel Aatti issued the warrant of my arrest on an urgent request made by the Military Intelligence which promised to produce the evidence it had at a later date. This never materialized. But why he was making press statements without anything in hand remained unexplained. He did not want to appear before the NANS but apologized for the inconvenience. I raised the case of those still remaining in Kober prison and all the civilians were later released. Some days after my release I was visited by a representative of the International Commission of Jurists who interviewed me on my imprisonment and the conditions in prison, etc.

Since Nimeiri introduced Islam into the army in 1983 two departments of the army were particularly affected by the Islamic upsurge: the Morale Orientation Department and the Military Intelligence. Many Muslim Brothers found their way into these vital departments and eventually controlled them. Therefore it was hardly surprising that the Military Intelligence was in cahoots with the NIF.

The Sudan African Congress (SAC)

For the few months it had been in operation, the SSK had made a tremendous impact on the political scene in the country and especially in Khartoum. It was now time for consolidation before reaching out to other like-minded organizations. This meant looking into the issues of organizational structures, the change of name, etc. The Executive Committee was the only organ running SSK. It was composed of: the Chairman, Dr Walter Kunijwok Gwado, Vice-chairman, Mr

Stansilaous Kau Aping, Secretary-General, Dr Paul Wani, Spokesman, Dr Lam Akol, External Affairs Secretary, Dr Peter Nyot Kok, and Dr Akolda Man Tier, Dr Yongo-Bure, Mr Edward A. Lino and Mr Lumumba Kau Aping as members, the last represented the students. To discuss these matters the Executive Committee held a meeting in the house of Dr Akolda Man Tier. The change of name was agreed upon and many proposals for the new name were put forward. After careful consideration of the names proposed and how each reflected the objectives of the organization, the meeting adopted "Sudan African Congress" as the new name of the organization. This name was proposed by Mr Stansilaous Kau Aping. It was then resolved that the Sudan African Congress (SAC) shall be structurally composed of a General Congress, Central Committee and the Executive Committee. I was asked by the meeting to draft rules and regulations that will govern the functioning of these bodies.

I embarked on my assignment and consulted a number of relevant documents. Rather than produce one document as the Constitution of SAC, I settled for having two documents instead: The Basic Rules and the Internal Regulations. The reason for this was that Constitutions are difficult to amend and, therefore, those basic principles that need stringent conditions to be amended should be separated from the details that can be changed without affecting the basics. Hence, Internal Regulations are more or less details of the Basic Rules, the last requiring a two-thirds majority of the Congress to be amended. In two weeks, the documents were ready, copies made and distributed. Then a general meeting was called for to discuss the documents and approve the change of name.

The meeting took place in the University of Khartoum and the two documents were debated thoroughly and a number of amendments introduced. The approved draft of the Basic Rules and Internal Regulations were given to Mr Kuol Alor, from the Ministry of Foreign Affairs and a lawyer by training, to put them in the final legal form. This was duly done and the Sudan African Congress was ready to carry on with its programme. Copies of the documents were sent to Renk, Malakal, Wau and Juba for branch offices of SAC to be formed.

Sudan Rural Solidarity (SRS)

Since the 6th of April 1985, many political parties were revived or born. In the least developed areas of Sudan, the number of the political parties was too large for their own good. For example, in Southern Blue Nile alone there were three compared to two in the Nuba Mountains. The SSK, now SAC, has always felt that the best way for the least developed areas to make an impact was for each area to organize itself and then federate at the top rather than form one top-heavy African party that will not have a following on the ground where elections are won or lost. This meant that regional parties must enjoy the undivided support of their population, hence each area, such as the Nuba Mountains or Southern Blue Nile or Southern Sudan, for that matter, should keep their political parties to a minimum, one at best. Our efforts at first focused on trying to bring about unity between the General Union of the Nuba Mountains (GUNM) and the Sudan National Party (SNP), both from the Nuba Mountains. The Sudan National Party was newly formed and its leader, Fr. Philip Abbas Ghabbush, was the leader of the GUNM in the sixties and, in fact, most of the leading figures in the SNP were the same colleagues of Fr. Philip Abbas in the GUNM of the sixties. The GUNM of the eighties was led by Dr El-Amin Hamouda, Lecturer in the Department of Electrical Engineering, University of Khartoum, and the majority of its members were the Nuba intellectuals. Dr El-Amin Hamouda was a colleague and a friend and he assured me of his unconditional desire for unity. I had long sessions with Fr. Philip Abbas stressing to him that SNP and GUNM should really be one and relayed to him that that was the wish of the leadership of GUNM and everything rested on him. But I could discern that somehow Fr. Philip Abbas felt he was above the politics of the Nuba mountains and that his party was really 'national' simply because he has called it so! I had to abandon my attempts for the unity of the two parties but got assurances from Fr. Philip Abbas that he would cooperate with GUNM and the other African parties.

From there we proceeded to initiate talks on forging an alliance of the African parties. From the Southern Sudan there were two: the Southern Sudan Political Association (SSPA), that brought together some Southern politicians of the May regime, and SAC. The two organizations of the Nuba Mountains have already been mentioned. From Darfur was the Darfur Development Front (DDF). The three from Southern Blue Nile were: the General Union of the Ingessana Hills (GUIH), the General Union of Southern Funj (GUSF) and the General Union of the Northern and Southern Funj (GUNSF). These eight political parties held a series of meetings in order to form an alliance that will chart the course of their common action. It was finally agreed that they come together under the name of "Sudan Rural Solidarity" (SRS) and that the new alliance was to be launched in a mass rally to be staged by the parties to it in El-Mugran square in Khartoum towards the end of December 1985. Each political party was to mobilize its membership to attend in big numbers. The NANS was invited to attend the rally.

On the appointed date the square was full to capacity. The attendance was really big: the SRS was born with teeth. An introductory speech was delivered after which the Charter of the SRS was read out and the leaders of the parties came forward in turn to sign it. As they were doing so the crowd stood in standing ovation punctuated by ululations from the women. Dr Mamoun Mohammed Hussein, speaking on behalf of the TUA, gave a good speech of encouragement stressing unity of the masses. This was well received by the audience. It was a great day! When all the invited guests had dispersed that evening nobody was left in any doubt that the unity of the Africans was a great force to reckon with.

The Situation in Equatoria

The situation in Equatoria since April 6th 1985 deserves a special comment. As the TMC prevaricated on whether or not to cancel the Republican Order No. 1 that divided the South into three regions, the influential Military Governor of Equatoria, Major-General Peter Cirillo, effectively organized a strong lobby group that agitated for the continuation of Equatoria as a region on its own. This group, led by Mr Karlo Elia, a trade union activist, was shuttling frequently between Juba and Khartoum cautioning the TMC of the dire consequences of reverting to a one Southern region and that such a move would, no doubt, be unwelcome in Equatoria. The TMC listened to them with keen interest. On the other hand, the Southern politicians in Khartoum were pressuring the TMC to constitute a High Executive Council (HEC) so that the South is reunited again as one region. The TMC had a hot potato in its hands. Finally the TMC took a decision that satisfied neither side and which it could not enforce.

A High Executive Council, presided over by Major-General James Loro, member of the TMC, was formed comprising more than ten members. It was to have its seat in Juba. Major-General Peter Cirillo refused to recognize this body and made it known that he will not allow it to set foot in Juba. Eventually, the HEC got stuck in Khartoum without accommodation and it was Mr Peter Gatkouth Gual, the Minister of Transport and Communications, who found some space for the Regional Ministers in his Ministry. The HEC remained there in Khartoum for the whole transitional period as a living epitome of the lack of a clear policy on the South.

After scoring this magnificent victory, the politicians in Equatoria adopted some kind of a "splendid isolation." They embarked on forming parties exclusively for the Equatorians. The two that emerged with strong support were: the People's Progressive Party (PPP) and the Sudan African People's Congress (SAPCO). The PPP was led by Mr Eliaba James Surrur, from the Pajulo tribe and one of the most effective agitators for the division of the South in 1982/83. He has been a member of the People's Regional Assembly a number of times since December 1973. The party drew most of its support from among the Bari speakers of Eastern Equatoria Province. SAPCO, on the other hand, was led by Mr Morris Lawiya and drew most of its support from Western Equatoria Province. Of course, there were the Equatorian politicians who were opposed to the division of the South. They did not join these two parties but were a minority.

The Progressive Forces' Front

SAC was also a member of the "Progressive Forces' Front" (PFF) that brought together some parties of NANS with a national democratic programme. The Sudan Communist Party refused to join on the grounds that it cannot sit together in the same front with its so-called "renegades", a reference to some former members of the Communist Party who split away from the party in the late sixties, some of whom were leaders of the Union of the National Democratic Forces (UNDF), a member of the Front and the NANS. The pro-Iraq "Baath Arab Socialist Party" also refused to be member because its pro-Syria counterpart was included. The presence of all these parties together in the NANS was explained by the dissenting parties by reasoning that NANS was a country-wide alliance of political parties of all hues as opposed to a Front which was ideologically exclusive. They were for the first and against the second.

One burning issue that was of particular concern to all these groups, the SRS and PFF, was whether the elections should be conducted as scheduled especially when it became clear that the elections could not be carried out for insecurity reasons, in most parts of the South. It was strongly believed that partial elections would complicate the search for peace as the SPLA could not take part in such elections and would not certainly allow the carrying out of these elections in the areas under its control.

The NANS Medani Conference

In November 1985, the NANS convened a Conference of the forces of the Uprising in Wad Medani. It was one of the unsung success stories of the NANS. The effort put into organizing the conference was impressive. Delegates, representing political parties and professional and trade unions, came from all over the country to review the past months of the Uprising and to discuss the future of the alliance. In the conference I presented SAC's paper on the history of the South-

North relations; a paper I had earlier written and submitted by SAC to the organizers of the conference. Over tea outside the conference hall some Northern delegates felt free to tell me what they thought about the paper. 'It was good', they said, 'except that it was contributing to the opening up of old wounds'! The reference was to what came in the paper on the atrocities committed by the army against innocent law-abiding citizens in the South during the 17-year war. I answered them that for the proper treatment of rotten wounds they need to be opened up, and cleansed. All political groups in the North, regardless of their political persuasions, have always felt jittery against any criticism of the misconduct of the army in its war in the South.

In Wad Medani, I and my colleagues in SAC had useful discussions with a number of political groups one of them was the Intellectuals from Equatoria who had come from Juba. They were led by Mr Augustino Aremo. We drew their attention to the danger of isolating themselves from the other Southerners in the other two regions. Division or no division there were still issues that needed cooperation and coordination among the Southerners.

The General Elections

There was consensus in the NANS that the framework for resolving the conflict in the country was through a National Constitutional Conference (NCC) in which all the political parties and professional and trade unions would take part in discussing the problems of the Sudan to come out with an agreement on how to resolve them to the satisfaction of all. It was also the view of the SPLA as contained in the letter of Col. John Garang to the Prime Minister. The problem was: when, where and under what conditions would such a conference be held to ensure the participation of all concerned. It was for the transitional government and the SPLA, since they controlled the warring troops, to agree on the necessary arrangements that would make the convening of the NCC possible. But things went amiss right from the very beginning. The SPLA first wanted the TMC to resign and when this could not happen it declared that it would not talk to the TMC. The SPLA insisted on this position even after it became clear to it that the TMC was the accepted supreme authority in the country. A letter written by the Minister of Defence, Brigadier General Osman Abdalla, to Col. John Garang on peace talks well before Dr El-Jizouli's letter, was ignored, presumably because it was from one of the generals with whom the leader of the SPLA had vowed not to talk. The letter was delivered to the SPLA in Addis Ababa by the S-G of the SCC, Rev. Clement Janda. The NANS which the SPLA has chosen to have dialogue with did not control state power and there was no way of implementing whatever they agree upon with the SPLA without either ousting the TMC, which was out of the question and the NANS made this clear to the SPLA, or getting the consent of the TMC, which the SPLA has refused to negotiate with. No responsible government anywhere will just implement policies it is not party to their formulation. Therefore, the position of the SPLA of refusing to talk to the TMC led to only one obvious conclusion: the SPLA did not want the NCC to be convened during the transitional period, assuming, of course, it wanted it to be convened at all. Paradoxically, everybody including the SPLA, knew that the upcoming elections were going to bring into dominance political parties hostile to the SPLA.

On the other hand, the TMC was bound by an agreement with the political forces in the country to prepare for and conduct elections, then hand over power to an elected government after one year. For the TMC to deliver its part of the bargain it must carry out the elections on time. These elections cannot be anything but partial as the SPLA, whose participation would have made the elections general, has refused to have anything to do with the TMC. Hence, there was a contradiction in the logic of those who were calling for the postponement of the elections so that the NCC be convened first.

As time went by and there was no sign of any talks between the Government and the SPLA in the offing, the issue of the elections popped up into the centre stage of the political debate within and without the NANS. The Umma party, the DUP and the NIF were unequivocal in that the elections must be run on time so that, in their view, a strong government was elected to confront the rebellion; a reference to the SPLA. The voices within the NANS calling for postponement were construed as emanating from small parties not only sympathetic to the SPLA but are as well afraid to face the verdict of the masses they claim to represent. Hence such calls were brushed aside. After the promulgation of the electoral law and the formation of the Election commission all the political groups braced themselves to the reality and those which wanted to take part prepared to do so.

The Election Commission was composed of three members including the Chairman who was a judge and one member from Southern Sudan, Mr Manoah Majok, a senior local government administrator. The demarcation of the constituencies was to be based on the population census of 1983 which put the population of the country at 27 million. In that census, the estimate of the population, in millions, for the nine regions of Sudan were: Northern, 1.8; Eastern 2.4; Central, 4.9; Khartoum, 3.1; Kordofan, 3.9; Darfur, 3.9; Upper Nile 2.0; Bahr el Ghazal, 2.8 and Equatoria, 2.2. Except for Khartoum, each constituency was to have an average population of roughly one hundred thousand. The figure for Khartoum was less. When the number of the constituencies according to regions was announced it was evident that the three Southern regions and Darfur were allocated less constituencies than the population census would suggest. SAC presented a written complaint to the Election Commission against the decision. As far as the South was concerned, it argued that the three regions of the South, Bahr el-Ghazal, Equatoria and Upper Nile should have been allocated 28, 22 and 20 constituencies respectively. For Darfur, the DDF and the Umma Party protested demanding 39 constituencies for the region. The Commission was persuaded by the arguments presented and made the corrections accordingly. The number of the Graduates seats allocated for each region was to be one tenth of its Geographical constituencies. Hence, the total number of the Graduates seats turned out to be twenty eight (the Eastern region got three seats).

The parties forming the SRS held a number of meetings to consider coordination in the elections. Apart from putting up candidates at home constituencies there was the situation of the capital that needed close cooperation. The 1984/5 famine in Western Sudan and the war in the Southern Sudan, Nuba mountains and Southern Blue Nile have driven a large number of the population of those areas to the capital. They were made to settle in specific areas at the suburbs of the cities of Omdurman, Khartoum and Khartoum North. Some of these settlements such as Haj Yousif, Umbada, Mayo and others were delineated as constituencies. Added to this, there were the existing townships of the capital such as Fateihab, Rimeila, Oshash and others with a sizeable presence of Sudanese from the areas mentioned above from where the SRS draws its support. It was agreed that in the capital the SRS would field only one candidate in each of the constituencies in which it will contest elections, and that after the registration of voters was completed the SRS would sit again to consider the list of the constituencies to be contested and the candidates nominated by the SRS to each constituency.

When the time came, leaders of the SRS gathered in the office of the SSPA in Khartoum. Conspicuous by his absence was Fr. Philip Abbas Ghabbush, the leader of the SNP. The meeting had opened and reports about the state of the registration were being discussed when a representative of the SNP raised his hand. He said he was sent by Fr. Philip Abbas to inform the meeting that the SNP would put up candidates in all the constituencies being considered by the SRS and as a national party the SNP would like the SRS to support those candidates!

Everybody was stunned by such a conduct. Attempts to persuade Fr. Philip Abbas to change his mind fell on deaf ears. The SRS had to give up and proceed without him but the damage had clearly been done. When the results of the elections were announced the SRS lost all the winnable seats in the capital except one in Haj Yousif. This one was won by Fr. Philip Abbas himself beating Mr Abul Gassim Seif El-Din, the leader of the DDF and the official candidate of the SRS in the constituency.

Outside the capital, the Election Commission had declared 42 out of the 70 constituencies in the South as insecure for any elections to be carried out there. Even in the remaining ones in which it was decided that elections could be carried out, the registration was very poor amounting to just a few hundreds in some constituencies. The leaders of SAC, SSPA or SRS in Khartoum could not, for security reasons, travel to the South to campaign for the elections there.

SAC also attempted to get the PFF and the Sudan Communist Party into having one list of candidates for the elections. The latter politely turned the offer down saying that after many years of underground work the party needed to know its real weight among the people of Sudan. I have always been a member of SAC delegations to all these contacts. Soon after that the SCP requested a meeting with me as a representative of SAC. I agreed. Its side was represented by Mr El Tijani El Tayeb Babiker and Dr El Shafie Khidhir, the representative of the SCP in the NANS. Mr El Tijani El Tayeb introduced the subject as having to do with the upcoming elections. He said the party was considering nominating some democrats, who may not necessarily be communists, to be added to the list of the SCP candidates for the Graduates seats. He wanted to know whether SAC and I in particular would accept to be part of this arrangement.

I thanked the two for their confidence in me and my organization. But told them that I would be speaking for the whole leadership of SAC to tell them that such an arrangement would run contrary to our commitment to bringing about a broad national democratic front which we hoped the SCP, given its wealth of political experience, would lead. Unhappily, I added, it was the SCP that did not want to cooperate opening the door for the Islamic-based sectarian parties to have an easy win over the progressive forces. We continued discussions on other issues and parted as friendly as before. Needless to say the PFF and the SCP put forward separate lists of candidates for all the Graduates seats in the North.

Voting in the General Elections took place in April. When the results of the elections became known, the NIF had captured all the Graduates seats in Northern Sudan, a clean sweep. Looking at the voting figures the effect of the split vote was very clear especially in the capital and the central region. It was in Bahr el-Ghazal region in the South that the SCP won one of the Graduates seats, the other two went to the SSPA and the NIF. In Upper Nile, the two Graduates seats went to SAC and the NIF. It was only in Equatoria that the NIF failed to win a Graduates seat, all the two were captured by the People's Progressive Party (PPP).

The final election results showed the state of the political parties, in terms of seats won in the Constituent Assembly, as follows: Umma, 101 seats; DUP, 63; NIF, 51; People's Progressive Party (PPP), 10; SAPCO, 8; SSPA, 8; Sudan National Party, 8; Sudan Communist Party, 3; Sudan African Congress (SAC), 2; Beja Congress, 1; Sudan People's Federal Party, 1 and Independents, 3.

It is noteworthy that of the northern political parties which were members of the Sudan Rural Solidarity only the Sudan National Party of Fr. Philip Abbas Ghabboush was able to send members to the Constituent Assembly. Curiously, the Darfaur Development Front did not put up any candidate in Darfur region!

CHAPTER 4

In the SPLA

The Journey to Addis Ababa

THE PLANE my wife, Rebecca Joshua Okwaci, and I took for Athens, left Khartoum airport on May 1, 1986. We just got married on the 18th of March and so most of my friends took it for granted that we were going on a honeymoon in Greece. Why not, the country was full of historical monuments and many exciting things to see! But this was not quite what was in our thinking. We were heading for Addis Ababa to join the SPLA. We spent a few days in Athens and then flew off to Addis Ababa.

In Addis Ababa we were warmly received by a number of comrades in the SPLA, all familiar to me, who took us to the place of our accommodation. We chatted with them and others who joined us there. It was a great moment and a turning point in my life, a new chapter has just begun.

In the evening I was taken to see the Deputy Chairman and Deputy C-in-C, Lt. Col. Kerubino Kwanyin Bol, who was in town. I knew him before when he was serving in Malakal and met him again during the Koka Dam Conference in March. We greeted each other warmly and entered into a long informal conversation. Finally, he said the Chairman and C-in-C, Col. Dr John Garang, has been informed about my arrival and that all are delighted about my decision to come to the field leaving behind all the comfort of a University professor! I felt this came deep from his heart and I assured him that nothing could be equated to freedom, that the tree of freedom can only be watered with blood and that he had led the way and we professors and the like must follow the call of the struggle.

My decision to leave Khartoum had nothing to do with any security considerations or anything of the sort. It was purely political.

I had taken stock of the political landscape in the country and how one could best contribute. I appraised the situation since the uprising, the state of play of the political forces, the most probable outcome of the elections to the Constituent Assembly, the likely attitude of the democratically elected government towards a just peaceful settlement of the conflict, the internal situation within the SPLA in light of one's involvement with it, etc. In my assessment, it was clear that the Umma Party was going to emerge with most seats, but it was not obvious whether or not it was going to get the majority of seats in the Assembly. The DUP would come a close second. The government that would be formed by the Umma party, either on its own or in coalition with the DUP, given the attitude of both parties during the transitional period and their election programme, would not be seriously seeking a political settlement to the conflict. The forces of the NANS committed to peace would, in a game where only arithmetic and not consensus mattered, be marginalized. My conclusion was that under such conditions my contribution would be more effective in the field of combat than in Khartoum. The question that remained to be answered was in relation only to the most appropriate time to leave. A conversation at Koka Dam in March 1986 crystallized my thoughts on the matter.

It was just after midnight when I was awakened by a knock on the door of my room. I got up from bed and went to the door to find out who was there. It was 1st Lt. Mario Muor Muor who told me that the Chairman wanted to see me. I changed my clothes and went with him to meet the Chairman. I found Col. John Garang together with Kerubino, Arok and others. All of us shook hands and greeted each other warmly and I joined them. We chatted for some time and Col. John Garang called me to another room where we were alone. He started the conversation by thanking me and my colleagues for the good work we were doing inside the country and that it was a vital contribution appreciated by the movement. He then wanted to hear from me my assessment of the political situation in the country after the upcoming elections to the Constituent Assembly. I briefed him in detail and concluded that, given Sadiq's bellicose pronouncements during his election campaign rallies, the prospects for a just peaceful settlement in the near future were very slim. After that he told me that he deliberately chose to have the meeting with me without the other two (Kerubino and Arok, who were two of the five permanent members of the High Command of the SPLA. The other two: Lt. Col. William Nyuon Bany and Major Salva Kiir Mayardit were not at Koka Dam) for maximum secrecy. He elaborated on the point in a dramatic way. He held out his left hand with three fingers bent and two stretched out and pointing at the two fingers he said that a secret between two persons may reach to eleven (11) and stretching out a third, continued: "and between three may reach to 111 people", still stretching out a fourth he went on: "and between four may reach 1111 people", and so on.

Col. John Garang continued and came to the point as to why he wanted to see me that night. He said I held a senior position in the NANS (I was by then the Assistant Secretary-General of the NANS as the representative of SAC) and that if I declared my defection to the SPLA there and then it would be a tremendous blow to the TMC and would be a big boost to the SPLA as such an announcement would be carried by world media in their news bulletins (there was a good number of correspondents that went to Addis Ababa by then to cover the Koka Dam Conference). As to my position in the SPLA, he went on, he was going to appoint me as an alternate member of the Political-Military High Command and Zonal Commander of Northern Upper Nile. And to stress the urgency of the matter, he elaborated that the troops to go with me to Northern Upper Nile were towards the final stages of training and were expected to be graduated by the end of the month (March) and that the assignment of a Zonal Commander was basically political and hence there was no need for me to get military training before going there.

I found the talk interesting and it raised in my mind some serious questions on the organizational structure within the SPLA. I thought I was a member of the Central Committee, what is this body called the High Command? How are they related? How is the selection or election made? etc. But I suppressed these thoughts preferring to address first things first. I told Col. John Garang that whatever propaganda value my defection to the SPLA would make, it was going to be transient. Furthermore, it was not going to be a blow to the TMC. On the contrary, the TMC and their allies the NIF, would rejoice that the event confirmed a belief they have held all along that the NANS was in cahoots with the SPLA and this would strengthen their hand against the NANS and SAC in particular. I reminded him of my earlier briefing to him about the political situation in the country and that what I did not tell him was that I had already decided to join the SPLA in the field and that what was left undecided was as to when this would take place. I politely told him that I could not possibly do what he had asked me to do for a number of reasons. Apart from any commitments in the University by then, I must report back to both SAC and the NANS on the proceedings of the Koka Dam Conference, I had also to brief my cell and make a formal hand-over of my previous responsibilities. All these needed me to go back to Khartoum. I concluded by drawing his attention to the fact that it was my intention initially to be in the field but it was him who suggested otherwise. Therefore, by the same token, I cannot hesitate to be in the field when the leadership of the SPLA deems it fit.

He saw the point and asked me as to the earliest possible time I could make it to Addis Ababa from Khartoum. I told him that it would be sometime within the first two weeks of May. He said that was all right with him. We bade each other farewell. It was bout 3.00 a.m. when I was escorted back to my room by the same officer.

Back in Khartoum, I continued with my normal schedule while making preparations to leave. All the election results had come in. As expected the Umma Party got 101 seats (short of absolute majority which was 130 seats), followed by the DUP with 63 seats. However, the scale of the NIF's score, 51 seats, astounded the pundits. They were expected to do better than the last elections in 1968, when they had only two seats in the Constituent Assembly, but none of the best estimates contemplated even half the number they got. This result meant that the Islamic-based parties (all of them called during the election campaign for an Islamic Constitution) had among them more than 80% of the total number of seats in the Assembly. The strong showing of the NIF reinforced my assessment referred to earlier.

When the arrangements were complete, I packed the most essential of my belongings and boarded that plane which took me to Athens to arrive Addis that morning.

In the field for the first time

In Addis Ababa, Col. John Garang sent a radio message, in reply to Kerubino's, that I should go to join him in the field. In a few days, I left for Gambela to meet him. We drove together to Bonga Training Centre where he issued me with military uniform. On the 25th of May 1985, Col. John Garang and I were flown by a helicopter to Makuac village, near Bilpam, where we found recruits waiting to be graduated by the Chairman and C-in-C that day. We were received by Lt. Col. William Nyuon Bany who greeted me warmly. We knew each other well in Malakal.

The force about to be graduated was trained together at Bilpam as two battalions named Madhlum 1 and Madhlum 2 (*Madhlum* in Arabic could be translated as "treated unjustly"). The first was composed of young men from the Dinka sections (Dingjol, Ager, Nyiel and Abilang) east of the Nile northwards of Malakal, and the second was composed of the Collo boys. These areas, in addition to Ngok Dinka and the Dinka sections between Atar and Wunlam, form what the SPLA termed "Northern Upper Nile Zone". The recruits were cheering and singing as we arrived the parade ground where they were assembled. After the other formalities were conducted, it was time to address them.

I was given a chance to address the recruits. My speech was brief. I told them that they were held in high esteem by the people in the country for offering their lives in a just people's war, that they must maintain this by observing both military and self-discipline, and that they must respect the people they will be in contact with and should not in anyway violate their values and properties elaborating on the familiar "fish-water" example of guerrilla war.

Finally, it was the turn of the Chairman and C-in-C to speak. Col. John Garang explained to them that they were called *"Madhlum"* because the people of Northern Upper Nile (N.U.N.) did not receive just treatment both in the Government of Sudan and in the SPLA and that this must be rectified. He went on to enumerate military victories of the SPLA closing this part by saying that the SPLA had chased away Field-Marshall Nimeiri and then pushed out General Siwar ed-Dahab and it cannot be Sadiq al-Mahdi the *"Malaki"* (meaning civilian) in *"Jalabia"* (meaning the loose dress worn by Muslims), who does not know to cock a Klashnikov who could present a problem to the SPLA. The crowd cheered and sang in appreciation for some minutes. The C-in-C now turned his attention to administrative matters. He said the battalions were to be renamed as Madhlum and Fashoda, the last name replacing Madhlum 2, that the first would be commanded by Major Daniel Deng Alony and the second by Captain Oyai Deng Ajak. He finally announced that the overall commander of these two battalions and the other forces in Northern Upper Nile will be Dr Lam Akol Ajawin pointing at me beside him, and added that I was not going to go with them then but would follow later. As to the mission of the two battalions, he said that N.U.N. was the gateway to almost all the areas where the SPLA was fighting the enemy and that it was their mission to close this gate. Finally, the C-in-C ordered the troops that as they go to N.U.N. they must clear out the *Nyagats*[1] they find on the way! They were to be issued with military equipment in the morning of the next day.

That evening we had time with the Chairman and the C-in-C to discuss a number of issues ranging from the situation in the country to the situation within the SPLA and the effect of the external factors on both. In the morning the whole place was busy issuing uniform,

---

1   The word "Nyagat" is probably derived from the Nuer word "gat" meaning "to loot". Nyagat, therefore, acquired the general meaning of a bandit. It has been used in the SPLA derogatively to refer to the Anya-nya-2 and their supporters.

rifles, support weapons, ammos and other military equipment to the troops. We started with Madhlum and then with Fashoda. That day I also received an AKM rifle, my first ever. After that the troops were given orders to march on.

We followed the troops to Mangok, towards Jekou on the Sudan border, and from there we drove back to the refugees camp in Itang. There I met a lot of intellectuals and a good number of officers of the SPLA, most of whom I knew before. We exchanged views on many issues and I learnt a lot from them on the situation within the SPLA.

After a couple of days in Itang, I left with the Chairman for Gambela to take a helicopter to Tiergol (opposite Akobo on the Ethiopian side of the border) where Major Arok Thon Arok was. Major Arok had just defeated a siege on his forces at Tiergol by a force of the Anya-nya 2. Having overrun Bukteng on the first week of May, the Anya-nya 2 (A-2) thought they would do as well in Tiergol. They were mistaken. When we were approaching Teirgol we could see from the air dead bodies littering the periphery of defence. We landed and were received by Major Arok who greeted us warmly and we congratulated him on the victory he had scored. He then took us to his hut where he briefed us about the engagement with the A-2. Then the Chairman briefed him about the graduation of Madhlum and Fashoda battalions and their commands and that he had announced to the forces that I was their overall commander. Major Arok was surprised and his comment was that he was aware of my contribution and conscious of my position but he thought the announcement was too soon. This was the clearest indication yet that the Chairman's decision was without consultation. The concern of Major Arok was quite genuine. As we shall see later, in a highly regimented organization such as the SPLA, the soldiers would not understand how a civilian without a rank or a defined capacity be made senior to a Major or, for that matter, any officer. I think he had in mind to get things formalized first.

Major Arok took us around the defensive area in Tiergol where the dead bodies of A-2 soldiers were still scattered all over the place. After completing the walk, the Chairman took him aside for a private conversation at some distance from where I and the officers stood. After about half an hour they came back and we took off back to Gambela.

We caught up again with Madhlum and Fashoda at Adura (Thiayjak) and at Kuanylou. At the last point we again met Lt.Col. William Nyuon Bany. He was coming from Bukteng where a force under his command composed of these two battalions and some other units had driven the A-2 out of Bukteng. The two battalions were now within Sudan and on march to N.U.N. Zone.

While in the field, the Chairman had asked me to record a statement to be broadcast over Radio SPLA on my decision to join the SPLA. I prepared the statement and showed it to him. He was very much impressed and said so. It was then recorded in both English and Arabic languages and the tape sent to Addis Ababa. In this statement I had outlined the political problems facing the country, the frustration of the wishes of the Sudanese people when the Uprising was nipped in the bud and called for the convergence of the armed struggle with the political struggle in the towns of the country as the only way to bring about a genuine change in Sudan.

The statement went on air on the 11th of June 1986. It was the first news in Khartoum about my decision to join the SPLA. The reactions of the political forces in the country were immediate with many stating that my decision was a great loss to the democratic process in the country. As was to be expected, the NIF press had a field day. According to their media, they were not surprised and in their view there still were other "reds under the bed" and "fifth - columnists" within the NANS just waiting for the right moment to do the same. This matter occupied Khartoum's mass media, for or against, for a couple of weeks.

It was now mid-June and the Chairman advised that it was time for me to go to Addis Ababa. There were a couple of things to be done there. He was going to deliver a speech to the Sudanese people over Radio SPLA on the movement's position following the last general elections after which Sadiq al-Mahdi was elected Prime Minister. I was to be a member of the Committee to draft the Chairman's speech. There was also need to make preparations for the upcoming OAU summit scheduled to take place in Addis Ababa in July. My contribution in the preparations was, according to the chairman, essential. When I was leaving for Addis Ababa the Chairman informed me that he would be following shortly. I left for Addis Ababa soon after the conversation.

In July, my friend and colleague at the University of Khartoum, Dr El-Wathiq Kemeir, was in Addis Ababa for a follow-up meeting between the NANS and the SPLA as stipulated in the Koka Dam Declaration. He prodded me into writing a statement in the form of an open letter explaining the reasons why I chose armed struggle as opposed to purely political means of the struggle. The open letter was to be published in one of the daily newspapers in the Capital so that my point of view could be read by many inside the country. He had in mind the SCP's newspaper, "*El-Meidan*". I wrote the statement in Arabic, signed it and handed it over to Dr El-Wathiq. I asked him to deliver it personally to Mr El-Tijani El-Tayeb Babiker, the editor of "*El-Meidan*". Dr El-Wathig read it and applauded it. The statement, however, was not published in El-Meidan. It was "*El-Siyasa*" newspaper which published it in full. Dr El-Wathiq later explained that he had to resort to "El-Siyasa" because the communists dragged their feet on publishing the statement. I was not surprised!

The committee to draft the Chairman's speech sat in Addis Ababa under the Chairmanship of Major Arok Thon Arok. We had a copy of Sadiq's policy statement which he delivered before the Constituent Assembly on July 7, 1986. In that statement, Sadiq was constantly using the phrase "imported violence" in reference to the SPLA. We had other documents of the Umma Party to consult. The Committee discussed the proposed skeleton of the Chairman's speech, areas of stress and the approach to peace from the SPLA's perspective. The draft speech was ready within a week. It was in the course of preparing the draft of the Chairman's speech that I came to discover the state of disorganization in the SPLA's office in Addis Ababa. The documents were carelessly thrown about in the office, singly and in heaps, some in cupboards without locks! With people coming in and out it was horrifying to handle sensitive information in that way. In addition, it was almost a nightmare to get the information one needs in such a maze.

Back in Khartoum we used to hear complaints from people who had to deal with the office that matters discussed were not followed up or that documents were lost. We had our headaches too in the SPLA cell of inexplicable failure of communication on urgent matters. In my discussions with the Chairman, I also found out that he had not read or been briefed on some documents which were sent to Addis months before. Here lay part of the explanation. There was no filing system of any sort. I asked the permission of Major Deng Alor Kwol (he was promoted in December 1985), who was in charge of the office, to allow me to sort out these documents and arrange them in some order for easy reference. He readily consented. It took me a week of hard work to accomplish the task. That was the first filing system ever in the SPLA office in Addis Ababa.

In the fourth week of June, the Chairman arrived to Addis Ababa.

Appointment to the High Command

On the morning of the first of July 1986, an extraordinary event took place that opened my eyes in a direct way into the inner workings of the SPLA. A number of us were in one of the three rooms that together with the foyer formed the SPLA office in Addis Ababa. Captain James Wani Igga was busy packing some items into a bag in preparation for a trip as member of a two-man delegation to Kinshasa led by Major Elijah Malok Aleng. Captain Atem Yak Atem, Dr Justin Yac Arop and I were conversing informally. Then the door opened and Captain George Maker Benjamin of Radio SPLA, came in excited. He saluted and said "Congratulations!" extending his hand to me and then to Captain James Wani. Both of us shook hands with him astonished. We asked him what was the good news. He said that both of us plus Major Riek Machar Teny, Captain Yousif Kowa and Lt. Col. Daniel Awet Akot were appointed to the High Command of the SPLA! Dr Justin Yac fuming with anger left the office immediately and entered the other office where the telephone was. Captain Atem Yak and the others who were present congratulated us abundantly. Neither Captain

James Wani nor myself was informed about this development although the Chairman was in town! In fact, I was with him the night before and I was to see him at ten that morning in order to go with him to meet President Mengistu Haile Mariam.

Captain George Maker Benjamin was coming from the studio where they had just recorded the news to be broadcast at 3.00 p.m., Sudan local time. The appointments to the High Command were one of the items in the news. When the time was approaching ten o'clock I left the office for the house of the Chairman. I met him and did not indicate having heard anything. He said nothing on the subject. After a while we went into the saloon car that was to take us to the President's office. His bodyguard was sitting in the front seat and we sat next to each other at the back . We were about to drive out of the gate when 1st Lt Marhum Dut Kat entered. He congratulated me. He was also coming from the studio. I asked him what was on and he related the same story I have already heard from Captain George Maker Benjamin. As soon as he finished talking, the Chairman extended his hand to me saying: "since it has become public knowledge now, congratulations!" I took it coolly. We then drove off for our meeting.

In the car I was silent. It was the proximity of the President's office and the presence of his bodyguard that warded off making my reaction known there and then. I was wondering as to why the Chairman did not inform us in advance. Was he taking us for granted? It is true he opened up the topic to me in passing at Koka Dam but it was in a different context and that could not have been the way to conduct such serious matters anyway. In the case of the others, none was informed; two were in the front and Yousif was outside Sudan and Ethiopia, Wani who was present admitted honestly that he had no idea and I believed him on the evidence of what I saw him doing. In my case, I was commissioned as a Major in the SPLA before getting the military training, was I in the meantime, going to conduct myself as a soldier or as a civilian? The biggest question for all of us was: What are the rules and regulations of the High Command?

The OAU summit

The OAU summit opened in the fourth week of July. The Chairman had a heavy schedule of meetings with Heads of state in Africa taking part in the summit. Sometimes the meetings would go on up to the small hours of the morning. For convenience, the authorities in Addis found him a guest house for accommodation and for making meetings with those heads of state who would prefer to have meetings outside their embassies or hotel accommodation. I was with him in all the meetings taking notes and hence, I was given a room in the guest house. He had also arranged that other members of the High Command present in Addis Ababa by then (William, Arok, Wani) be part of his delegations to these meetings in an alternating manner.

It was in the guest house that I had time to discuss seriously with the Chairman the question of organization within the SPLA and the necessity of it at an early stage. There, I came to know definitely that there was not any structure in the SPLA other than the high command, that the high command itself had no rules or regulations, that no code of conduct for the leadership, etc. These, of course, confirmed what I have already been told since I arrived Addis from Khartoum. The Chairman's justification for all this was that the movement started with a bang and hence attracted people of diverse political persuasions; the majority of them reactionary. That time was needed for socialist cadres to be developed in order to take up assignments within the structures to be made. In other words, the development of cadres was a condition for the structures to be set up! This is an argument I would rather want to postpone for another chapter in this work. Anyway, the Chairman finally gave me a folder to read and comment on. It was the programme of action written during the formation of the SPLA but was brushed aside. It sets out the definitions and functions of the specialized committees of the Movement, such as: Military, Political and Foreign Affairs, Administration and Justice, Finance, etc.

I studied the document for two days and made copious notes. I recommended to the Chairman the reorganization of the committees contained in the file into committees the number and functions of which I defined and that these be adopted as soon as possible. When he read it he had only one problem: he did not like the use of the word "committee" and wanted it replaced by the term "commission". I agreed. What was in a name if the functions were the same! I never heard anything again on the subject.

During my presence in the guest house, the Chairman informed me that he had wanted me to attend Shield 4 officers training course but he had managed to find places for three of us (Wani, Yousif and I) in a reputable military college in Latin America and that we will be joining it in September.

The Chairman meets the Prime Minister

The 31st of July saw the historic meeting between the Chairman and the Prime Minister, Sadiq al-Mahdi. Days before the meeting, there were conflicting reports on whether or not the Prime Minister was going to come to Addis Ababa to attend the OAU summit. It was only on the 29th of July that we were informed that the Prime Minister was definitely coming. Apart from the Chairman, the SPLA delegation was composed of Lt.Col. William Nyuon Bany, Major Arok Thon Arok, Major Lam Akol Ajawin, Major James Wani Igga and Major Yousif Kowa Makki. The last had come back to Addis a few days before. The day before the meeting the Chairman issued a press statement that he was meeting Sadiq al-Mahdi as leader of the Umma party but since he was also the Prime Minister there was no way of separating the two capacities he represented. He also insisted that members of the NANS be present in the meeting. It was eventually agreed by the two sides that the meeting would be in two sessions: the first one would include the full delegations plus members of the NANS who will be there, and the second session would only be between the two leaders with at most one more person with each to take notes, if necessary.

The procedural matters were settled and the meeting started in earnest in the morning. Sadiq opened his speech by stating that he had come to explore possibilities of bringing the war to an end, that he was committed to the spirit of the Koka Dam Declaration but as to the letter of it he gave a number of reasons why there was need to look again into the matter. First, the Koka Dam Conference was held at a time when the political forces were busy with the elections and could not devote much attention to the conference. Second, the delegates of the Umma Party to the conference were not mandated to sign the final outcome without going back to Khartoum. Third, the DUP with which the Umma Party was in coalition government was not a signatory to the Declaration. During the discussion a fourth reason emerged: Sadiq was frank that no Muslim leader of Government in the North would ever repeal the Islamic laws. So, in plain man's language, the Prime Minister came to negotiate a new deal with the SPLA outside the framework of the Koka Dam Declaration.

The SPLA side could not buy the argument of the Prime Minister. He was advised to stick to agreements and improve on them when necessary. The SPLA delegation argued that the DUP needed to be brought into the peace process by the Umma Party, its partner in government. The Prime Minister was reminded that if he continued to be afraid of the reactions of the DUP and the NIF to the implementation of Koka Dam Declaration he would end up doing nothing and a military coup d'etat may eventually topple him. The SPLA refused to be drawn into discussing any arrangement outside Koka Dam Declaration.

The second session was short. I was the one left with the Chairman on our side. We went over a summary of positions discussed in the first session. May be the only new addition was the restatement of the SPLA's position in a more explicit way by the Chairman when he told the PM that peace demanded both of them to take bold decisions, elaborating that Sadiq declares a repeal of the September laws and he, simultaneously, declares a cease-fire. As expected, Sadiq could not agree to this. The meeting ended in the evening after a total of nine hours of deliberations.

The meeting ended, rather unfortunately, on an acrimonious note. Most of it was the PM's doing by attempting to present an inaccurate analysis of the situation inside the country especially in relation to the

South, but part of it, honestly, was our own. There were some remarks, observations and comments which could have been put in a less provocative manner or avoided altogether. The PM left for Khartoum not long after the meeting. When asked by the press to comment on his meeting with Col. John Garang, he commented that Garang had an inflated opinion of himself and needed to be reduced to size!

A civilian plane shot down over Malakal

The plane incident over Malakal on the 16th of August, tragic as it was, provided the PM with the excuse he was looking for to absolve himself from any commitment to a peaceful settlement of the conflict with the SPLA. He immediately issued directives banning any contacts with the SPLA describing it as a "terrorist" organization. He further announced a general mobilization to fight this "imported violence."

There is another aspect to this disastrous event that I ought to explain. The media in Khartoum have held me personally responsible for the downing over Malakal of the civilian plane that fateful day with the NIF press carrying sensational headlines such as "University lecturer downs a civilian plane." The truth is that I had nothing whatsoever to do with either the order of downing or its execution. Actually, I was informed about the shooting down of the plane by a friend, Mr Collins, whom I knew as a freelance journalist in Khartoum. He was in Nairobi and wanted to confirm the news he had got about the incident and so he rang up the SPLA office in Addis Ababa. I spoke with him over the phone and he asked me whether I heard anything like that. I told him that I did not but promised him to enquire about the incident. After our conversation was over, I informed Major Arok Thon Arok about what I had heard from Mr Collins.

The confusion must have arisen from the announcement over Radio SPLA on the 1st of July of the order of appointments to the High Command referred to earlier. The order, in my case meant three things in one: a commissioning, an appointment and an assignment.

I was commissioned to the rank of Major in the SPLA, appointed as alternate member of the High Command and assigned as Zonal Commander of N.U.N. It was assumed that I took up my assignment immediately and since Malakal fell within N.U.N. Zone then I must have been the one commanding the troops there. In fact, I did not take over as Zonal Commander of N.U.N. Zone until on the 1st of July 1987. That is, after exactly one year since the announcement was made over Radio SPLA!

The NAM Summit

In September 1986, the Non-Aligned Movement (NAM) Conference was to be held in Harare, Zimbabwe. The Chairman formed a two-man delegation led by me with James Wani Igga as the second member, to go there so as to lobby the delegations to the conference on the situation in Sudan. We prepared a paper that we were going to distribute to the delegates, and then took off for Harare the day before the conference was to convene. According to the arrangements made at the Zimbabwean Embassy in Addis Ababa, we were to be granted entry visas at Harare airport. On landing we found very tight security arrangements at the airport and we were denied entry visas. Our explanation as to what we were promised by their embassy in Addis Ababa and repeated pleas could not help and we had no choice but to take the first plane back. We landed in Dar es Salaam and distributed the same documents to the relevant embassies there! When this was done we went back to Addis Ababa.

I spent the period from the 26th of September to the 21st of December 1986 undergoing military training. Training centres are always secluded places and, therefore, there was no way I could have been giving press statements or appearing physically in any other place. My disappearance from media coverage in that period became a subject of speculation in Khartoum and there were suggestions in the media there that I was liquidated.

Delegations to Europe and North America

Since early 1984 when the SPLA sent a delegation to Europe the only other delegation sent there again was in 1985 during the transitional government in Khartoum. There have been a lot of developments since then and it was necessary to have people from the field go to strengthen the work of the SPLA offices there in putting across the point of view of the movement. Important as it was, no SPLA delegation ever visited the U.S.A., although the situation in regards to the U.S.A. was not as straightforward as with Europe. Khartoum's accusations of the SPLA as communists and apparent reluctance from the SPLA leader to meet with some important policy-makers in the U.S.A had the effect of the latter adopting a cool attitude towards the SPLA. After the 1986 elections, pressure was mounting on the movement from its supporters and sympathizers to mount a diplomatic offensive in Europe and North America. A democratically elected government in Khartoum would be listened to more keenly in those countries than a military one and hence it was in the movement's interest to seize the diplomatic initiative.

In September 1986, the Chairman formed two delegations: one to Europe led by Major Arok Thon Arok and another to U.S.A led by me. Funding for the two delegations could not be obtained in time and the one to the U.S.A. was called off. The delegation to Europe took off in September.

In December the Wilson Centre in Washington, which was organizing a Conference on Sudan in February 1987, extended an invitation to the SPLA to send representatives to attend the conference. Other political parties in the country were also invited. As a result of this invitation, the idea of sending a delegation to the U.S.A. was revived in January. I was still to lead the delegation with Major James Wani, Major Yousif Kowa and Dr Justin Yac Arop as members. Three of us were in different locations in the field and our directives were to meet in Addis Ababa and go from there to join Dr Justin Yac, the SRRA Secretary General, in Nairobi. The four of us would then leave for Washington from there. I was with the Chairman in Pochalla when he made the decision and he briefed me about these arrangements as well as on what to do and not to do there in America. He then added an additional mission. Lt.Col. Martin Manyiel Ayuel was to join the delegation in Addis so that together we deliver a letter to President Daniel Arap Moi of Kenya. After that the delegation would proceed to the U.S.A and Martin returns to Addis. Lt. Col. Martin had been appointed in October, together with Lt.Col. Kuol Manyang Juuk, as an alternate member of the High Command and assigned as the manager of the office of the Chairman and C-in-C in Addis Ababa.

The letter to President Moi was an apology to him from the Chairman for being unable to visit Nairobi as requested by the President, the reason he gave for the difficulty was that he was fully engaged in military operations. The failure of the Chairman to visit Nairobi up to that time is a long story on its own and had caused constant embarrassments to SPLA representatives abroad who have been handling the matter. Parenthetically, since the trip of Nimeiri to Nairobi in December 1983 he had made it known that he has requested President Moi to help end the war in Sudan. It is known that since 1984 the Kenyan authorities have been making contacts with the SPLA so as to arrange a meeting with President Moi in Nairobi. In fact, in 1985, Mr Mark Too was sent to Addis by the President with a special message on the subject to the SPLA leader. He was accompanied by Mr Ambrose Kot, an SPLA member in Nairobi. They met Col. John Garang in Addis Ababa. Other Kenyan officials were also involved in the contacts. Even during the OAU Conference of 1986 the invitation was renewed. The crux of the problem, however, was that some SPLA officers of the neo-Marxist trend who formed a clique around the Chairman by then, created a myth that Nairobi was a CIA centre full of CIA agents looking out for Col. John Garang to cause him harm! Their story was supported by a self-appointed adviser to the Chairman in Nairobi who claimed the same ideological predilection. He was lecturing in the University of Nairobi and had not seen Southern Sudan or any other part of the Sudan since 1965. He committed himself to writing on this theory. Absurd as it is, they talked about it with absolute conviction. Sardonically, the professor was living in Nairobi and the comrades, at least two of them, were several times in and out of Nairobi over the same period and no harm befell them from the CIA. I was in a meeting between the Chairman and President Mengistu in Addis Ababa when the latter told the former that even if the CIA were to be looking for him he did not think that President Moi would allow something like that to take place in his country. Yet, the first visit of the Chairman to Nairobi could not take place until the second half of 1987 and only in the company of a delegation of the Union of Sudan African Parties (USAP) that came from Khartoum to hold talks with the SPLA.

The Chairman handed me the letter to the President and I left Pochalla for Addis Ababa. There I briefed my colleagues about our mission and we started working on the paper which we were going to present at the conference. It was already February and the travel papers of James Wani and Yousif Kowa were not ready. Hence, Martin and I had to leave for Nairobi to carry out the first mission while they continue processing their papers. At Nairobi airport we were received by Dr Justin Yac. In the hotel we were visited by Mr Mark Too and we briefed him about our mission and requested him to arrange an appointment to see the President. Late in the evening, Mark informed us that the President had agreed to see us at about 7.00 a.m. the next day.

Martin, Dr Justin and I met the President at the appointed time. I informed him that we were sent by the Chairman to deliver a letter to him and then handed him the letter. He read it through and shook his head in appreciation. Then we briefed him about the situation in Southern Sudan, especially the plight of the civil population. The meeting went very well. Back in the hotel when the three of us were alone in my room, Dr Justin rhetorically asked: "is this the kind of man who can kill the Chairman?" His voice was full of bitterness. We understood what he meant.

Two days before the opening of the conference my colleagues were still in Addis and hence Dr Justin and I decided to leave for Washington and asked them to follow us. They arrived Nairobi on the last day of the conference but were denied entry visas at the American Embassy in Nairobi on the grounds that the conference which was the reason for their application for a U.S visa was over. In Washington, we met Mr David J. Fischer, an aide of the Assistant Secretary of State for African Affairs who was attending the conference, and we requested from him an appointment with his boss or any of his assistants. He came back the next day to inform us that an appointment had been arranged and the time fixed. We thanked him for that and started to prepare ourselves for the meeting. The following day, however, he came back to say that the meeting has been cancelled by higher authorities! No reason was given. Dr Justin and I looked at each other in disbelief. Sudanese individuals in the conference, were going to and coming from the Department of State and meeting Mr Chester Crocker himself as frequently as they wished, why is it that the Department of State cannot listen to representatives of an armed movement that has a role to play in the future of Sudan? Anyway, we thanked him again for his efforts.

We have always known that the USA administration viewed the SPLA as a communist organization due to its association with the regime of Mengistu Hailemariam and the propaganda emanating from Khartoum, but we never thought that they would not meet an SPLA delegation in Washington. Efforts were exerted by some friends so as to persuade the Department of State to have a meeting with us on a low level. These efforts were successful and we later met in a restaurant over dinner with Mr Harlan Robinson of the Sudan Desk, U.S. Department of State, who was also attending the conference. We had useful discussions with him on the situation in Sudan and the attitude of the U.S. government towards the SPLA.

At the conclusion of the conference at the Woodrow Wilson Centre, we discussed with Dr Dominic Akec Mohamed, the SPLA representative in the U.S.A., arrangements to organize a visit to some parts of the U.S.A. where the SRRA was active. We concurred to go to California, the mid-west and Chicago. We also decided to pay a visit to Canada and from there to New York and then back to Washington on the way back to Africa.

In California, we met the SRRA committee headed my Mr Lako Tongun and Mr Moses M. Akol. We briefed them about the situation in the country and Dr Justin Yac spoke to them at length on the relief needs of the civil population and what was expected of the SRRA in efforts to alleviate their suffering. I also gave a lecture on the war and peace in Sudan at the Berkeley campus of the University of California.

In the mid-west, we visited Iowa and Wisconsin. There we met Mr Martin T. Kenyi and Mr Akuei Malwal, two young men full of energy, who managed against all odds to get the SRRA registered in the state of Wisconsin. Martin took us to Dubuque where we spent two days in his house and were interviewed by the local press there. Mr Timothy Chanaud of *The Telegraph Herald* newspaper published an article on my interview in the issue of Friday, March 13, 1987, of the paper. Martin also organized a lecture at the University of Wisconsin which I addressed.

Akuei Malwal drove us (Dominic, Justin and I) in his car to Chicago where we met a group of influential Afro-American Congressmen and media people. We gave interviews to the local radio stations and the press on the situation in Sudan. The zenith of our presence there was when we met Mr Jesse Jackson just before entering a hall where the Rainbow Coalition was waiting for him to address them. We shook hands and, despite the tight schedule, Mr Jackson kindly gave me two minutes to address the gathering. That was a great moment. In the time specified, I told them about the suffering of the Africans in Sudan, why the SPLA had to take up arms and appealed to them to stand by the struggle of their brethren in anyway they can. There was big applause from the audience.

The first part of our trip to the USA came to an end and we flew to Canada. We first landed in Winnipeg, Mannitoba. There we held meetings with Canadian NGOs, notably the Mennonite Central Committee, and impressed upon them the need to assist the needy population in South Sudan and to support the SRRA to enable it meet its obligations to serve the people efficiently. We also had useful discussions with a number of Southern Sudanese who were staying there. They did not know much about the SPLA.

In Ottawa, Mr Manok Acuil Lual, the SPLA representative in Canada, had organized a programme of engagements for us. We held meetings with the NGOs such as Oxfam Canada and others. We also had audience with the Head of the African Desk at the Ministry of Foreign Affairs. Meetings were arranged with representatives of the political parties in Canada and we had a most useful discussion with the spokesman on Nationalities in the New Progressive Party, the third largest party in Parliament by then.

We visited Montreal where we were joined by Mr Paul Odiong, a staunch Southern nationalist, who was self-employed in that part of the world; a testimony to his hard work and strong determination. The most memorable occasion in Montreal was our encounter with a panel of Quebecan journalists. They were not impressed by the SPLA's call for a united Sudan and urged us instead to be true to ourselves and work for the secession of the South.

Our trip to Canada ended in Toronto where I had an opportunity to deliver a lecture at the University on the situation in Sudan. There was a sizeable number of African students in the University of Toronto and they made their presence felt in that lecture. There I met my friend and former colleague in the University of Khartoum, Dr Taisier M. A. Ali. He had gone there for some research work.

From Canada we flew to New York city. There we visited the African American Institute where we had discussions with Mr Frank Ferrari, the Vice President of the Institute. I also gave an interview to Ms. Margaret Novicki, the editor of the magazine being issued by the Institute. The interview was published soon after. In New York, we also organized and held a meeting with the Southern Sudanese who were studying there. We briefed them about the situation in the country and answered the questions they raised on the same.

CHAPTER 5

Northern Upper Nile

A Long Trek to the Zone

I CAME BACK from my trip to the U.S.A. and Canada in March. I met the Chairman in Gambela, briefed him about the trip and presented a written report on it. After that he informed me that the force that I would command to N.U.N. was in Bilpam but that we would not be taking the direct route. That the force under me and those under Wani and Yousif would be going through Pibor to defend it against the enemy as Sadiq had vowed to retake it from the SPLA. The battalion under Wani and the battalion under Yousif were both to start off from Bonga. The first R.V. was to be Pochalla. I left for Itang the next day to see through some necessary arrangements for my movement to the front. I spent a couple of days there and what could be done was done and then went back to Gambela with some officers, NCOs and men who will be moving with me. On the 31st of March 1987, Khorfulus Bn started marching towards Pochalla. Two days after I took a car to Abola where I met them and spoke to the officers and informed the troops that I would be joining them in Pochalla and from there we would be marching together to N.U.N. I saw them leave before I returned to Gambela. After a couple of days I flew to Pochalla in a helicopter now ready to start a truly bush life.

The first groups of Khorfulus Bn were beginning to arrive when I arrived Pochalla. The place was buzzing with activity. Other forces that came ahead were there in preparation to leave for their missions. There was no time to be wasted. I sat down with my deputy, Col. Majur Nhial Makol, to plan. In Pochalla there were also a number of officers who had just completed the officers training course but were not yet deployed. Some days after my arrival the Chairman arrived. I informed him that my force was ready to move and he agreed on the date I proposed for the movement.

On the appointed day, I organized the movements in such a way that Task Force 2 commanded by Capt. Edward Makuac Kuol, was ahead to be followed by my HQ and lastly by Task Force 1 commanded by Major Elijah Maduk Yuang. We were all ready. The group to be ahead has begun marching when I went into the fence where the Chairman was to bid him farewell. We shook hands and he wished me good luck. I was turning to go away when I heard him say: "By the way," I stopped, turned towards him and saluted. "Captain Dhol Acuil is going with you." He ordered. I said that was all right and asked if there were any other instructions. He replied there wasn't any and wished me good luck once more. Outside the fence, I informed Col. Majur Nhial about the new orders and ordered him to go and inform Capt. Dhol Acuil that he was moving with us. Col. Majur did this and we started our march. I saw Dhol following us putting on a long face.

A few days before, Captain Dhol Acuil was brought down from a helicopter ready to take off for Gambela by Capt. Bior Ajang Duot, the commanding officer of the Chairman's bodyguards and the officer in charge of Pochalla. Dhol had no permission to travel to Gambela. The story spread in Pochalla and it was rumoured that Dhol was attempting to escape to Gambela where he was going to surrender himself to the United Nations authorities there. Whether this was the intention of this officer when he boarded the plane is a matter of speculation but he should have known that no military personnel, whatever his rank, is permitted to move from one location to another outside the area of his deployment without a valid Departure Order. In this case it would have been Captain Bior Ajang Duot to issue it. The Chairman was not in Pochalla when this incident took place but he must have definitely been informed about it. Nonetheless, it cannot be stated with any degree of certainty whether or not there was a connection between the incident and the last-minute deployment of the officer in question.

Our force spent the night at an area known as Adok-bar on the Oboth river not very far from Pochalla. It was not inhabited nor was there any buildings, but there were herds of antelopes in the area and we decided to camp for some days so that the soldiers can get some meat to supplement their diet. Fresh from the training centres, most of them looked haggard and weak. We organized hunting teams, and also a rehearsal programme for the whole battalion. They rehearsed tactics, weaponry, drill, etc.

At Adok-bar we were joined by Task Force 1 of James Wani's Shakush Bn commanded by Major John Koang Nyuon. The final destination of the battalion was Equatoria west of the Nile. There was a sizeable number of Nuer boys in Shakush Bn and a good number of them deserted at Adok-bar to their homes. Major James Wani delayed in Bonga with the other task force and his HQ. John Koang has been sending messages to him, through my radio, for directives but up to the time we left the place a week later he had received none.

The rains became heavy and the wild animals moved far away towards the east. It was time to continue the march. The two task forces moved on foot and I with my HQ followed on a car until after several days we reached our place of deployment in defence of Pibor on the Nanam stream some 55 km west of Likwangoli. It was the only water point in the area by that time of the year and was occupied by an enemy reinforcing force in February during the battle for Pibor. There I found Major Salva Kiir Mayardit with his HQ and Lazim Bn commanded by Major Hakim Gabriel Aluong. We took our positions on the defence perimeter and settled for the constant state of alertness.

The place was quite inhospitable. It was very hot by day and there were no trees to provide shelter. It was a desert as it were. Nothing alive that one's eye can fall on except the herds of Murle cattle with which, together with non-edible birds, we shared the pool. The water was muddy, or it was rather a watery mud, and smelling. I improvised a way of minimizing the mud but not the smell by digging holes not very far from the pool at night, in the morning a good quantity of water would have trickled into the holes. The food problem added to the difficulties. The heavy rains at the shadow of the Ethiopian mountains (in the areas of Pochalla, etc) cut off the road to Pochalla and with it food supplies. At the same time, it was inadvisable for political reasons to take cattle rations from the Murle tribe.

In a week or so since I arrived, Major Salva and Lazim Bn moved to Akobo area to reinforce Major Arok who was preparing to fight an enemy convoy on the way to reinforce Akobo enemy garrison. I remained alone with my force. I redeployed the force around the pool and prepared for hard times ahead should the enemy or the rains fail to come soon enough. It was already in the middle of May and it has not rained yet. May be the "rains battalions" were this time on the side of the enemy! Fortunately, as the water receded in the pool, fish appeared in good quantity. We were to live on this fish up to the 29th of May 1987 when we moved out after having received orders the day before from the Chairman and C-in-C to do so. We were heading to Kuanylou through Wiclual (Tiergol). Major Salva left Akobo about the same time for Boma.

According to the plan of the enemy, the convoy going to reinforce Akobo was the same one to proceed to retake Pibor. In deed, the enemy convoy did manage to reach Akobo but not before getting tough fighting from the SPLA. After entering Akobo, the convoy was ordered to move back to Malakal. It was decided not to proceed to Pibor.

We arrived Wiclual on the 31st of May. There I met Major Arok Thon Arok and the other officers who were with him in the Akobo fighting. Most of the forces that were there had deserted and only small units were left. In the early morning of the 1st of June we received a radio message from the Chairman that Jekou was captured by the SPLA forces the night before. We celebrated the victory with great joy. There was something special to it; Jekou, that small spot, has claimed several thousands of lives since SPLA started fighting there in 1984.

I left Wiclual on the 3rd of June and arrived Bukteng on the 6th. My directives were to camp in the area opposite Kuanylou and wait for ammos before proceeding to N.U.N. Zone. There were also remnants of Shemis Task Force and Daneil Chwogo Task Force to be added to the force moving with me. These two task forces were trained to go to N.U.N. but got committed in the Jekou operations. Many deserted during the fighting and what remained of them was less than one full task force. These were in Kuanylou under the command of Lt.Col.

Jeremy Kinmoi Afrika. I gave them orders to cross to Bukteng as their location of deployment. Task Force 1 of Khorfulus Bn was deployed at Mandeng and Task Force 2 and my HQ at Makak between the two locations. This time there was no fighting with the A-2. Reconciliation talks were going on between them and the SPLA and a cease-fire has been agreed upon to create a conducive atmosphere for the talks. These efforts to bring about reconciliation and possible unity between the SPLA and A-2 were out of the initiative of Captain James Hoth Mai, commander of Yony Bn in Kuanylou, ably assisted by 1st Lt. Michael Manyuon Anyang, the political commissar of the Bn and a lawyer by training. They were able to establish regular contacts with the leader of A-2, Gordon Kong Chol, himself related by marriage to James Hoth, and his force in Pananyang and Jokmiir. Both Gordon Kong and James Hoth come from the *Cieng Laang* sub-section of the section of the Nuer tribe around Nasir known as the Jikany. Except for the officers, the entire Yony Bn, which Captain James Hoth commanded, are sons of the Jikany Nuer. Gordon Kong's A-2 forces in the area were similarly composed. Hence, the grassroots urge for peace.

A few days after my arrival, the Chairman and Lt.Col. William Nyuon Bany flew in to Kuanylou and we held a meeting on the military situation in the area after the fall of Jekou. The Chairman read to the meeting intercepted enemy messages from the Commander of Nasir enemy garrison, all indicating his desperate military situation. He suggested that Nasir be attacked and captured using the force I was commanding. Captain James Hoth was the first to speak. He reminded the meeting of the stiff opposition of the A-2 to any attack on Nasir now before their forces in Malakal could get out from the enemy garrison. In addition, he thought it would take time to organize the attacking force. I mentioned to the meeting that Nasir may be a target of opportunity but it was important to keep in mind the primary mission of my force. The force was poorly armed in terms of support weapons and the fight for Nasir was not going to be just a runover, it would take days and possibly weeks. In the meantime, the forces I have, composed of the sons of N.U.N. zone, would desert leaving me with no force to go with me to N.U.N. zone. I also added my voice to the consideration raised by Capt. James Hoth, a breakthrough with the A-2 was of paramount importance. William Nyuon averred that Nasir must be attacked and he would provide my force with support weapons and the ammos immediately as soon as he flies back to Mangok and, in his usual way of underrating the enemy, concluded that it would be a matter of days and Nasir would be in our hands whether the A-2 like it or not. The meeting ended on this note. It was now an order to attack Nasir.

After both of them were gone, James Hoth told me that from his experience with William he would bet that William was not going to send a single support weapon. I also had a meeting with D.K. Mathews and David Dak Gai, who had just joined the SPLA and were sent to Kuanylou to help with the peace efforts with the A-2, on their request. They cautioned that an attack on Nasir would be construed by the A-2 as sacrificing their forces to the enemy and would shatter the reconciliation effort and push the A-2 back to the enemy. I told them that all the views will be weighed carefully before a decision is taken. Both of them were not in the meeting and I assumed they were unaware that a decision has indeed been taken.

As James Hoth correctly predicted, nothing came from William Nyuon. Then soldiers from Khorfulus Bn, for the first time since they left Bilpam on the 31st of March, began to desert to their homes. This created a new situation that demanded urgent solution. I flew to Gambela and briefed the Chairman about the situation and recommended that the ammos be rushed there so that we move to N.U.N zone. He agreed and in a few days I was back with different types of ammos. They were distributed to the troops and we started our march to N.U.N zone. The fruits of the cease-fire with the A-2 were evident. We were never shot at throughout our journey.

While in Gambela I came to learn about a problem developing between the Chairman and his deputy, Lt.Col. Kerubino Kwanyin Bol. The latter was using the long-range radio sets to talk in open uncoded language to senior officers on his grievances against Col. John Garang. It was baffling why he had to express his grievances to the people he chose to talk to and, when he did, why he chose the way he did it. He no doubt was aware that what he was saying could be listened to by anybody, including the enemy, who cared to tune to the same frequency. In Gambela, the signalists at the HQ of the Chairman were recording on a magnetic tape all his conversations. I advised the Chairman to call him for a meeting either with him or with the High Command. He retorted that somebody in such a frame of mind was suspicious and would not accept to come.

Assuming the Command of the Zone

The forces with me arrived Chwai, the first village on the eastern border of N.U.N. zone, on the 1st of July 1987. There the Chairman sent a message to all the battalion commanders in N.U.N zone that with effect from that date he has handed over the command of the zone to me, that they will fall directly under my command and as such all their messages should be addressed to me and that it was me who will address the C-in-C on the affairs of the Zone. Before that the zone was divided into independent areas each reporting directly to the C-in-C.

While on move I was informed that the enemy in Malakal were sending a convoy of cars to reinforce Nasir town. We prepared to fight it. I sent the engineers ahead to join a company of Fashoda Bn, commanded by Major Oyai Deng Ajak (he was promoted in May), the battalion commander, so as to advise them on the most appropriate locations to lay mines. This force was in Anakdiar area. We continued our journey. In Abwong we met Capt. Moses Dhieu Kiir, the commander of Abushok/Sobat Bns. We spent two days where I received his report, and had an open discussion with the troops to brief them about the situation and to listen to their problems. I also met the civil population. After that the forces in the area were reorganized into two separate battalions: Abushok and Sobat. The last being commanded by 1st Lt. Daniel Chwang Michar. Captain Moses Dhieu would continue to command Abushok Bn which would be deployed in the Ngok area whereas Sobat Bn would go to the area between Atar and Wunlam.

The first engagement

We arrived Anakdiar at about mid-day. At about 4.00 p.m., we heard an explosion and a rising smoke on the Malakal-Anakdiar road. I sent somebody to go and find out what the matter was. He went and at about 7.00 p.m. he came back with a report that it was our landmine that hit a car from the enemy convoy, that the enemy was burying their dead and that he had gone near enough, using the cover of darkness, to listen to their voices. This must be the enemy convoy to Nasir. We attacked them that night and attacked them again the day after. On the third day the convoy had to go back to Malakal, it could not proceed to Nasir. I later came to learn from intercepted enemy messages that the car hit by the landmine was an APC carrying the commander of the force. The enemy's retreat was followed by a night raid on Malakal town itself.

The food shortage was very acute in Anakdiar and so there were no enough rations for the soldiers. They began to desert in sizeable numbers. We decided to move to west of the Nile where the food situation was slightly better. Before leaving, I met with the population in the area to brief them about the policies of the movement and to hear their views.

After our first engagement with the enemy at Anakdiar, I received a letter from Gordon Kong Chol, the leader of A-2, writing from Doleib Hill asking me to withdraw to the "frontiers" - this is the word he used - otherwise I was not a party to the peace process! I called a meeting with the officers from the rank of Captain and above to discuss the letter. We agreed to reply it. I wrote to Gordon acknowledging the receipt of his letter and that I have referred it to the joint peace committee between the SPLA and the A-2. I concluded my letter with the following words:

"While we await the reply of the joint peace committee, I caution you that never again give orders to an SPLA officer. As an SPLA officer, I receive my orders from the SPLM/A Political-Military High Command".

I sent Gordon's letter by radio to Captain James Hoth Mai and to the permanent members of the High Command and I sent the original copy by a messenger to James. Gordon did not directly respond to my letter in anyway. When I met James Hoth in 1988, he told me that when he asked Gordon about the letter, Gordon had first denied having written one but when James showed him his signature he turned around to say that it must have been the adjutant who wrote it that way!

Period of Reorganisation

We camped at Orieny, the HQ of Fashosa Bn, and took some rest after the long journey. The forces with me had to be reorganized and deployed. Khorfulus Bn has now shrunk to one task force commanded by Major Elijah Maduk Yuang and deployed around Kodok town. Shemis TF under the Command of Capt Aciek Anot was ordered to proceed to Kaka and Daniel Chwogo TF commanded by 1st Monylang Agok deployed at Bhol area. Fashoda Bn had done a good work in collecting the deserters who arrived its area of operations. These were sorted out and every soldier made to join his unit. After this we still had two battalions to reorganize: Madhlum and Koryom. The first was deployed east of the Nile with HQ at Ajopic near Melut and the second had its HQ in Tonga.

Koryom Bn comprised the Collo soldiers trained with Koryom division who had deserted from their various units to the Collo area. They were collected from their villages by Major Alfred A. Akwoc and organized into a battalion commanded by him.

I left for Tonga in August. That was the first time for me to see for myself the degree of devastation wreaked by the A-2 upon the Collo area in February 1987. Whole villages were razed to the ground including Nyilwal village where the venerable shrine of Nyikang[2] once

---

2   Nyikang Okwa is the founder and first *Reth* of the Collo nation who reigned in the first half of the sixteenth century.

stood. Only a few homesteads remained in the area extending from Oweci to Ayie (in Tonga area). It was quite an ugly sight. I spent a number of days in Tonga meeting the officers, the troops and the civil population. 1st Lt. Acuil Amum became the new commander of the battalion, now renamed Bilpam. Major Alfred Akwoc was to report back to the GHQ of the SPLA for further directives. From Tonga, I went back to Orieny. There I sent a radio message to Lt. Col. Daniel Deng Alony to assemble his battalion at Ajopic so that I meet the soldiers there.

I went to Ajopic through Kaka where Shemis TF was. The villages from Detwok northwards were almost empty until one reaches Nyiwudo and Nhon. The famine has hit the area for two consecutive years and this has caused population movement to the nearby areas of Kordofan region such as Dengor and Abu-Jibaiha. Life begins to pick up again from Akurwa village at the edge of the forest to just a little north of Kaka station. Then from there no human being one can come across until Wad-Akon. The people in these villages are nearer to Renk and Kotsi in the North and moved there for the same reason. At Akurwa,where according to the Collo history Nyikang had disappeared into thin air, I was taken to the shrine of Nyikang together with the force with me for blessing. In this part of the Collo area, although the population has moved away, their huts are still intact, the A-2 have not set foot here.

Across the river the story was the same, if not worst. You find people in the Dingjol and Nyiel areas (Akoka, Kaidin, Panom Dit, etc) and at a small village called Mabek near Melut. The rest of the land from there up to Renk was without any human being. The great villages of Paloc and Abayath of the old good days were gone. Of course, there was an enemy garrison in Jalhak but there were hardly any civilian there.

At Ajopic I met the officers and then the NCOs and men and discussed with them the affairs of the movement and of the N.U.N zone. Since Lt. Col. Daniel Deng Alony was the third most senior officer in the zone, he had to join the Zonal HQ and Captain Kur Akol took over as the commander of Madhlum Bn. The reorganization of the forces was now complete. In my HQ, the senior officers were: Col. Majur Nhial Makol, Deputy Zonal Commander, Lt. Col. Daniel Deng Alony for Operations, Lt.Col. Jeremy K. Africa for Administration and Captain Dhol Acuil Aleu, the Judicial officer.

In November, the Chairman issued an order to all units of the SPLA in which the officers ranking system was changed. The lower ranks of 2nd Lt, 1st Lt. and Captain were not affected but the rest of the ranks from Major up to Major-General (the highest rank we had) were lumped together into a new rank to be known as "Alternate Commander", A/Cdr. The next rank, also to be the ultimate in the army, was to be known as "Commander", Cdr. Thus, the gradation in the officers ranking was now limited to only five steps instead of the eight we had, a system which was open-ended. The order also stipulated that the promotion from the rank of Captain to that of A/Cdr would be not according to seniority but in recognition of outstanding merits. It was silent as to how and by whom would the "merits" be determined. Finally, members of the Political-Military High Command (both permanent and alternate) were to be given the rank of Cdr. The order dealt with other issues as well.

The mission of the forces in N.U.N. was to block the routes the enemy uses in order to move troops and military hardware into his garrisons in the South. This means blocking the river route along the Nile, frustrating movements of convoys on land and closing Malakal airport to military flights. This was a difficult mission and required enormous resources in terms of manpower and military hardware. In the first place, N.U.N is an open country and it is almost impossible to organize ambushes on enemy convoys moving on land because such ambushes can be bypassed easily by avoiding the road and driving cross country in the open dry land. To be able to follow them, the attacking force must have the same resources which, of course, cannot be got by a guerrilla movement. This was a problem for which no immediate solution was available. Second, even with enough force available, fighting the steamers requires enough support weapons especially anti-tank weapons (more sophisticated than RPG-7) and long-range GPHMGs such as 14.5mm or 12.7mm. These were within what the

SPLA can do. Third, and more important, enough manpower was needed. Any sensible military appreciation would suggest that most of the forces should be concentrated to defeat the enemy as far away from own territory as possible. Since N.U.N was the main entry point (the others were W.U.N and N.B.G zones) the bulk of the SPLA should have been here.

The situation as I arrived the zone was as follows. The hunger situation in the entire zone has meant shortage of rations and consequently desertion of a good number of soldiers. Desertion was a chronic problem in the SPLA as a whole and was not limited to any one area or zone. Thus, the available force I had was far less than what was required for the mission. Since there was no population around, there was nowhere to recruit from. There was an additional problem. The zone is inhabited by the Collo and a number of sections of the Dinka tribe and the soldiers were unwilling to cross the boundaries. Hence, the shifting of troops from one place to the other was difficult as the soldiers in Atar, for example, would not go to Kaka or vice versa. Even the soldiers at Ajopic just across the river would not cross and stay in Kaka. This meant that the concentration of the forces, quite necessary for such operations, within the zone was not possible even for very short periods of time. The armament in the zone was very poor. Even the RPG-7 launchers were in small numbers. The force that came with me was not any better armed than what I got. Apart from the two SPG-9 guns that I carried with me, its armament was worst than the Bns I found. There was not a single GPHMG in the whole zone. This area of armament could have been improved as the SPLA had enough at the rear areas. As to Malakal airport, the enemy had learnt his lessons from the last Cessana plane shot down over Malakal towards the end of 1986 and closed access to it. None was shot down ever since although attempts did continue. The enemy had since established a ring of garrisons around Malakal town to make access to the airport (within the range of anti-aircraft guns) impossible.

Therefore, the mission remained to fight the river steamers which was what I set myself to do. In August 1987, a military steamer moving from Malakal to Kodok was engaged by Fashoda Bn and Daniel Chwogo TF at Bhol and after heavy fighting was forced to return to Malakal. February/March 1988 saw the biggest engagements between our forces and an enemy convoy of steamers numbering up to thirteen. They were engaged at four ambush points along the river route from Renk to Malakal. The enemy sustained heavy casualties in manpower and material but the convoy fought its way to Malakal. The A-2 accompanied these steamers and fought fiercely on the enemy side. They were led by William Reath Gai and James Duoth Lam who later joined the SPLA. Since it was dry season, the enemy used tanks to break through some of our ambushes.

In the period I was zonal commander, only one convoy of steamers passed without a fight. This was in September 1987 when the convoy was moving from Malakal to Kosti. The steamers were not detected in time due to a failure of the company of Daniel Chwogo TF that was deployed in the forward position (toward Malakal) to carry out its duty. Major Oyai Deng Ajak and his force that was to launch the attack at the ambush site discovered the steamers after having passed. The convoy was not shelling as they always do. According to a message I received from the Chairman, this incident was used in Itang as a subject of agitation by some people. The agitators claimed that I had reached an agreement with my father-in-law, who was acting Governor of Upper Nile state by then, on the enemy side to allow the steamers to pass!!

In addition to my military duties, I had the responsibility of mobilizing and organizing the population in support for the movement. It was decided to maintain the local administration under the chiefs. In the Collo area there was no much difficulty as they are organized under the Reth. In the other areas there have been a lot of changes made by military commanders. In some areas, Chiefs were being changed arbitrarily and in some, such as in the Dingjol area, the chiefs were superseded by the militia who were seeing cases. There was need to establish a system of selection/election and accountability of the chiefs in the Dinka areas. It was imperative to discuss the matter with the population first before adopting some rules on the issue. I have already met the population in the Ngok area and I was to meet the population in Dingjol and in Atar. I went to Kaidin and Akoka in the Dingjol area in December 1987 and then to Atar in January 1988 to discuss this issue with the population. The meetings went very well and there was near unanimity on two points: maintenance of the old chieftaincy boundaries and elections of the chiefs. I informed them accordingly, to prepare for elections in December 1988. The elders in all these areas knew my late father very well and they were confident I would emulate him and serve them with diligence and self-denial, the way they knew him.

There was another reason for my going to Atar at the time. I was to proceed to the HQ of Cdr John Kulang Puot, alternate member of the High Command and Commander of Fangak and Ayod Area, in Fangak area. I had some issues to discuss with him. Cdr John Kolang and his deputy, A/Cdr Isaac Galuk Rik, have been constantly interfering with the administration of the troops and the civil population in the areas of Pawiny, Thoi and Luac (Khorwac) which fall under my command as part of N.U.N. zone. John Kulang and his officers have been claiming that these areas have been part of Fangak district according to the borders established by the Government of Sudan (this is true) and hence should fall under the Fangak and Ayod Area under the SPLA (which was not true). In this claim, he was being supported by Cdr William Nyuon Bany, the Chief of Staff, who hails from the same area as John Kulang. When I met John Kulang I told him that there was nothing to quarrel about, I just needed a written order ceding these areas to his area of command and I would comply and that what William should do is not to instigate him to violate the Chairman's order but for him (William) to persuade the latter to issue a new order to his liking. The matter was left at the status quo, all the outstanding issues resolved and we signed an agreement on all these. We were both happy with the outcome of the meeting. It was also an occasion for the two of us, as alternate members of the High Command, to exchange views on the political developments within the movement and outside it.

First Meeting with the Reth of Collo

The Reth was not in the Collo area when I arrived the zone in July. On my way to the Dingjol area in December 1987, I had made arrangements to visit Reth Ayang Aney Kur at his village *(Pare-ben)*. His Majesty received us warmly and we spent a good time there.

I had private audience with the Reth in one of his huts where he related to me the discussion he had with the Prime Minister, Sadiq al-Mahdi in Khartoum a couple of weeks before. The PM had invited him to the capital and encouraged him to form pro-Government militia in Collo land. The Reth rejected the idea flat arguing that the role of the Reth was that of reconciliation and as such should be seen to be impartial in relation to the parties to the conflict. The PM then questioned why he (the Reth) used to entertain the 'rebels' in his village. He told me his answer was that this stemmed from the fact that he looked at the antagonists in the civil war all as his children and could not favour one against the others. He reminded the PM that he also welcomes and entertains Government officials and army when they visit him. All this had to do with his impartial role in the conflict. There were other related issues the PM raised with His Majesty.

The Reth concluded that when the PM finally failed to recruit him (into forming a militia force) or find a special connection between him and the SPLA, he awarded him the "Order of the Two Niles, Second Class"!! The Reth showed me the decoration with a grin.

It is noteworthy that Reth Ayang is a grandson of Reth Kur Nyidhok who was reigning at the time of the famous 'Fashoda incident' between the British and the French in 1898.

This account of the discussion between the Reth and the Prime Minister confirmed the policy followed by the Government of Sudan of using tribal militias to fight the war in the South by proxy. Started by Nimeiri and developed by the transitional military council of Siwar ad-Dahab, this policy continues up to the present. In Upper Nile region, where most of the fighting between the Government and the SPLA raged, Sadiq al-Mahdi for the entire term he held office made it a point to appoint as Governor only persons of known allegiance to the Anyanya-2 militia or the *friendly forces* as they are officially termed. These appointments were in complete disregard to the democratic spirit of representation in the Constituent Assembly where Anyanya-2 did not have a single member whereas the other southern political parties had many including from the Upper Nile region itself.

Engaging the enemy steamers

In January, I received reports on the enemy's preparations to move a convoy of steamers laden with military hardware and troops from Kosti to Malakal. In October I had personally reconnoitred some possible ambush sites and my deputy went up to the northernmost site. On the basis of the reconnaissance and the constraints discussed earlier, we made a tentative plan then. We discussed this again in January and agreed on the final plan. The forces were deployed immediately thereafter. The steamers did not come till February and the first engagement took place on the 18th of February 1988 on the west bank of the Nile. In the second, east of the Nile, our troops were under the direct command of the Deputy Zonal Commander. Both engagements were north of Kaka. The third was just north of Kodok and the fourth was near Lul. It was here that the enemy landed tanks to fight our troops on land. This enemy convoy entered Malakal in March 1988.

On the 14th of March 1988, the Chairman sent a message to all the units of the SPLA that Cdr Arok Thon Arok, permanent member of the High Command, was arrested on a number of charges contained in the message. But the main charge was that he had an unauthorized meeting in London with the Chief of Staff of the Sudanese army and some of his assistants. However, the message promised that investigation would be carried out. I briefed the officers about the message. Nobody commented on it. Earlier in late 1987, the Deputy Chairman and Deputy C-in-C, another permanent member of the High Command, was arrested. The officers must have been wondering as to how permanent the permanent membership of the High Command was.

Some administrative problems

Some of the administrative problems that I faced in the zone are worth mentioning. The hunger situation referred to earlier was the most disturbing and had to be solved if any progress were to be made politically and militarily. In my discussions with the population, they had suggested that reopening Kaka market would help a great deal in solving the problem of hunger. In the market, traders from Kordofan sell dura, drugs, clothes and other essential commodities. It was closed in late 1986 when Fashoda Bn confiscated eleven lorries of these traders when one of its soldiers got killed in Kaka by somebody who went there on one of these lorries. The market had resumed on a small scale in 1987 but no dura was being sold as no lorry would risk coming. When I was in Kaka, I met some of the owners of these lorries who related what happened and expressed willingness to resume work if their lorries were returned to them. I asked Fashoda Bn Commander for his version of the story and what should be done. I was able to establish that the killer was a friend of the victim since their childhood. In fact, the former used to go to the military camp and go out with his friend to have drinks. This happened several times and it was in the last of such outings that the soldier got killed by the person in question. After killing the soldier this man ran away back to where he came from taking with him the AKM rifle of the dead soldier. There he gave the rifle to his father who handed it over to the army. The traders were blameworthy for having allowed a stranger on a car going to SPLA - controlled areas. Fashoda Bn was also to be blamed for having been lax on security measures. It was unusual for a stranger to frequent a military camp and go out several times with an SPLA soldier. Finally, I decided that the lorries be returned to their owners except one which will serve as some compensation for the lost rifle and that the owners of the ten lorries released resume trading and also to pay money to the owner of the detained car for him to buy another lorry. This formula was accepted by the traders and ten of their lorries were returned to them. Although some of them did not come again, the market flourished in Kaka and people were able to buy dura and other commodities. The population also sold out some items of trade. Strict security measures were made and financial regulations enforced.

There was also the issue of leaves and permissions for the officers. The Chairman had issued an order in March 1987 to all commanders cancelling all leaves and prohibiting giving any until further notice. Despite this some officers continued to ask for permission. Capt. Dhol Acuil was one of the most persistent on this. He applied for permission at Adok-bar, just a few hours walk from Pochalla, and again in Nanam. Coming so soon after his deployment, I took his application of leave to be another way from him of refusing to execute the order of deployment. I told him that I will not consider giving any permission to anybody, except on medical grounds, until we first reach N.U.N. zone. When we arrived Orieny he asked again permission to go to Nairobi where his family was. I replied him that as zonal commander, I can give permission up to Itang only. To go anywhere abroad would require the approval of the Chairman. He retorted that his destination was Nairobi. On that understanding I wrote a message to the Chairman requesting him to grant him permission. The reply of the Chairman on 4/10/87 was unequivocal that no officer should be given permission before completing at least one year in the zone and even then there would have to be strong reasons for that, and perhaps to reassure Dhol, the Chairman added that he had met the wife of Capt. Dhol Acuil in his last trip to Kenya and she was now a member of the Executive Committee of the Sudanese Women Association in Nairobi and she had told him (the Chairman) that they were doing well. I briefed Dhol about this and he was very much disappointed. Again, when I was leaving the zone in May 1988 he wanted to leave with me. My answer was that this could not be since he was left with just two months to complete the year but promised that I was going to talk to my successor about his case. I could read in his face that he did not believe me. But I kept my word and my successor granted him permission in July 1988 to go to Itang. He had to seek the consent of the Chairman to be able to go to Nairobi, exactly as I told him before.

In the gossip-infested SPLA I later learnt that Capt. Dhol Acuil was unhappy with me because he was "mistreated" - this was the word used

- by me in N.U.N. zone. I know of no mistreatment. As a matter of fact, I had all my meals together with him and the other senior officers in my HQ and I never ever interfered in his work as the zonal judicial officer. The "mistreatment", therefore, must be for having kept him in the field for just one year.

If Dhol Acuil had complained of mistreatment in Pochalla when he was deployed at the very last minute (actually, he was ordered, as explained earlier, to literally join a march) he would have had a valid point. But then the complaint would have been directed elsewhere and not against me. In naked terms, Dhol was a disgruntled man way back in 1986 if not a bit earlier. His disaffection can be traced more to blighted hopes than to anything else. Dhol joined the SPLA in 1984 at the time when the "politicians" were falling out of favour with the Chairman. This situation will be discussed more fully in Chapter 9. Of relevance here is the fact that when Joseph Oduho and Martin Majier Gai were "parked" in Nazaret, the Chairman was moving around in Addis Ababa with Dhol Acuil by his side ostensibly as his right-hand man. This special treatment may have given Dhol the impression of being close enough, in hierarchy, to the Chairman. Later in 1985, Dhol (still a civilian) led an SPLA delegation to Europe and Egypt which membership comprised senior Captains (Elijah Hon Top, Mark Maciec, Daniel Kodi, etc.) He again led another delegation to Kinshasa which included a Major (Elijah Malok). In the highly regimented SPLA, this could have meant only one thing: that Dhol Acuil was senior in rank to all these officers; most probably a member of the highest political organ of the movement. In December 1985, the Captains who were members of Dhol's delegation were promoted to the rank of Major and Elijah Malok was promoted, together with his batch, in July 1986 to the rank of Lt. Colonel. Yet, when Dhol Acuil completed his military training in March 1987, he was commissioned a Captain!! The only one person in the SPLA who can explain all these twists and turns was the Chairman. Rather than confront reality, it was much easier to look for scapegoats!

When Dhol Acuil was transferred from the SRRA office in Nairobi, he did not conceal his displeasure with the decision. He made his feelings known to the committee of three (Lt. Col. William Nyuon, Major Salva Kiir and Captain Nhial Deng Nhial) that the Chairman sent to Nairobi in 1986 to inform him about the transfer and to arrange a handing over of the office to Dr Justin Yac Arop, the new SRRA Secretary-General. Since then, Dhol has let his imagination run wild that the Chairman was out to liquidate him. Some small incidents with the instructors in Bonga Training Centre (where he went from Nairobi) helped solidify this belief in his mind. But what he kept talking about with bitterness as indisputable evidence was an unfortunate incident which occurred in Boma in 1986 when Dhol was still the SRRA Secretary-General. A small plane he was on was shot at by the SPLA in Boma. Thanks to God, it was missed by all the anti-aircraft guns which opened fire to shoot it down. The commander in Boma who, incidentally, hails from the same area, Tonj, as Dhol was then under orders to shoot down any hostile plane or any other which was not cleared by the SPLA. Had the commander in Boma exercised his sense of judgement, he would not have ordered shooting down a small non-hostile plane which was clearly landing in Boma. But that is entirely another matter. Technically, he was executing standing orders.

I was in Addis Ababa when Dhol Acuil asked Major Deng Alor Kuol, the office manager of the Chairman, for the clearance of that plane to fly from Nairobi to Boma. Two days later, Dhol enquired about the clearance and Deng assured him that he had informed the Chairman and that Dhol's plane was cleared. It was on the basis of this assurance that Dhol set off on the specified date. It turned out that Deng Alor did not communicate with the Chairman on the matter and the Boma base was unaware of Dhol's flight that day of the incident. Cdr. Arok Thon Arok and I were in Addis Ababa by then and carried out on our own some investigation on the matter. Deng Alor first claimed that he had written a radio message to the Chairman on the clearance of the plane and that it must have been the signalist who must have failed to send it. When the signalist, Lt. Deng Yie Thanypiny, confronted him with his radio message book with no such message in it, Deng Alor had to admit that he must have forgotten to write the message! Therefore, it was established that it was Deng who did not arrange any clearance and misled Dhol Acuil on the subject. The Chairman, however, did not take any measures against Major Deng Alor on this gross negligence which would have had tragic consequences. This behaviour could rightfully arouse suspicion. However, this was not the first time that the Chairman did not reprimand Deng on gross negligence in performing his duty and Dhol knew this fact quite well. So, it cannot be used as proof of conspiracy to kill him. If the Chairman wanted to do that, why would he risk international anger (if nothing else) by shooting down a plane and a pilot when the plane was landing in Boma anyway?

During my last days in the zone I had a problem with my deputy but it was of a different kind. On the 16th of May 1988, he had written a radio message to the Chairman which was repeated to Cdr William Nyuon submitting his resignation from the movement. The reason was that Cdr William Nyuon had taken his three cows for himself and gave A/Cdr Majur Nhial three other cows presumably of lower quality as replacement! I was then in Atar and Majur was east of the Nile. Hence he sent the radio message with somebody to the nearest radio set to be sent to me. When the commander of Fashoda Bn, who had the radio set read the message he was alarmed and since he knew I was going to come back from Atar soon, he kept it to hand it over when we meet. Indeed, I came back and got the radio message. I was shocked. I sent for him to leave whatever he was doing and come immediately. We met at the zonal HQ. When I asked him about the message he admitted that he did write it. Then I told him, jokingly, that when I saw the date of his message and to whom it was addressed I assumed he was congratulating the Chairman on the fifth anniversary of the revolution (the Bor incident). He was not amused. Then I made another joke that William was known for taking herds of cattle for nothing in return and that he was lucky his three cows were replaced. He was still very serious. Then I decided to take the matter seriously. I told him that resignation was no small thing and when it is on what I consider as trivial one gets concerned. I advised him that there were many options still open for him: first, he would have to establish the veracity of the reported exchange of cows, second, if proven then he can raise the matter directly with William, third, if this fails he could then raise a complaint to the Chairman against William, fourth, if the Chairman failed to solve the problem then he would be free to consider other options including resignation. He replied that the source that informed him about the cows was reliable and hence he was very much convinced the story was true. He insisted I send the message. I, finally told him that he would have to go with me to the General HQ where at least he would confirm for himself and do whatever else he wanted to do next.

A/Cdr Majur Nhial Makol went with me and in Abwong I related the story to A/Cdr Hakim Gabriel Aluong and asked him to try to dissuade Majur from his decision. Hakim tried hard but to no avail. Then one day I was talking with him on a different matter when he suddenly shouted at me that he would have been free of such problems if I was not sabotaging his resignation from the movement. I asked him to withdraw his words but he refused. This was in the presence of A/Cdr Hakim Gabriel Aluong. I had no choice but to order for his detention. When Cdr Martin Manyiel Ayuel arrived Abwong, he pleaded with me to set him free. I agreed but on condition that he apologised. Martin went to him and asked him to apologise but Majur was adamant. He went to Bilpam under detention. It later transpired that his three cows were intact.

Another "problem" was brought to my attention by my colleague, Martin Manyiel, at Abwong. He told me that the talk in Itang was that I transferred A/Cdr Oyai Deng Ajak, the commander of Fashoda Bn till the last week of January 1988, out of jealousy of his outstanding military success (as if a senior commander could succeed without the junior ones succeeding!). I related to him the whole story. In brief, Oyai was the security officer at the HQ of the Chairman until he made him the commander of Fashoda Bn in May 1986. When I was going to N.U.N. zone, and in my last meeting with him in Gambela, the Chairman ordered me to send the officer back to him as soon as I arrived the zone. When I arrived the zone and after having met all the commanders whom I found there I decided that I needed to keep Oyai Deng Ajak for at least a few more months precisely because he was an excellent officer and has impressed me and my deputy a lot. I wrote to the chairman on 20/7/87 a message that I would still need Oyai up to such time when the reorganization was complete. He agreed and the matter was laid to rest. Then on the 11th of January 1988 he wrote to me another message reminding me to send the officer to him. I informed Oyai Deng Ajak accordingly and directed him to hand over to his deputy. Before he left I called a big parade in front of which I extolled the performance of A/Cdr Oyai Deng Ajak in the zone concluding that his achievements in the zone were a challenge both to the others and to himself. To others because they will find it hard to equal and to himself because he had raised expectations about what he can do to the extent that anything less, although still outstanding, would not be acceptable. I closed by saying that I was confident he will be up to the expectations wherever he went. These could not be actions and words of a jealous person. The messages exchanged between me and the Chairman on the transfer of Oyai are included in the appendix.

Recalled to the HQ

On the 22nd of May 1988, I received a radio message from the Chairman that I was to report to the General HQ for an urgent assignment and that I hand over the command of the zone to Cdr Martin Manyiel Ayuel till I return. The nature of the assignment was not specified in the message. When I received the message I started wondering why I was called back at this time when I have just laid the foundation for what really needed to be done. The rains were coming and the agricultural programme I have mobilized the troops for would be interrupted. A host of other issues sprang to mind. My only hope was that since the assignment was urgent it was more likely that it would not take long before I was back. I was mistaken; I never set foot to the zone again.

At the zonal HQ, I prepared copious handing over notes and in June I moved to Abwong where I was to meet Cdr Martin Manyiel Ayuel.

He did not arrive until July. He himself had no idea what the "urgent" assignment was. In my discussion with him I discovered that things were not well between him and the Chairman (remember, Martin was his office manager in Addis Ababa.) I also discovered that he was suspicious that I may blindly support the position of the Chairman as opposed to his. I briefed him on the zone for two days and was ready to go on for a third day if it were not for his appreciation of what he had already got. We then went carefully through the written handing and taking over notes which both of us finally signed. On the third day we held a parade where I introduced him as the new zonal commander of N.U.N. zone. He addressed the troops then I concluded the gathering with a speech. After that I started my trip to Bilpam ignorant of what I was going to do there.

July was not quite the good time to travel between Abwong and Nasir especially on the side nearer to Nasir. By that time most of the low ground is flooded by water. In 1988 the rains were a bit more heavy than average and some of the places that were usually crossed at knee level were already to the waist and higher up. At these spots, we had to wade through the water and the tall grass for hours and hours. En route we passed through camps where the SPLA and the former A-2 were stationed together. In January, a unity agreement between the SPLA and the A-2 was announced over Radio SPLA but no text of the agreement has ever been released even to the High Command members. In any case, as a result of that agreement the leader of the A-2, Gordon Kong Chol, was commissioned as Cdr in the SPLA and appointed alternate member of the High Command and Zonal commander of Nasir and Maiwut area. His Deputy, Stephen Duol Chol, was commissioned as Cdr in the SPLA (the first non-High Command member to get the rank). Some other fifteen or so A-2 officers were integrated into the SPLA rank of A/Cdr. Except for these few, the rest of the A-2 officers were not integrated into the SPLA ranks and held the old ranks they had which were conventional ranks such as Major, Lt.Col., Col, etc. A joint committee to integrate the A-2 officers was formed in May but it never sat for its members were so scattered; some in Asosa area in the north, others in Equatoria in the south and some in between the two points. In those stations we passed through tension was already developing between the officers of A-2 on how to determine the seniority between those already integrated into the SPLA and those who were senior to them in the A-2 but were not yet integrated into the SPLA. For this they blamed the SPLA.

In Jokmiir, I met Cdr Gordon Kong Chol, Cdr Stephen Duol Chol and some of their officers. We discussed some of the problems including the pressure growing on them from the A-2 officers to hurry up with the integration process. I also got the same feeling from Captain Michael Manyuon Anyang (he was promoted in December 1987) who briefed me in more details about this and other issues.

We arrived Bilpam on the 30th of July and on the 31st I was picked up by a helicopter to Gambela. There I met the Chairman, William Nyuon and Salva Kiir. The last was the chairman of the joint committee on the integration of the A-2 into the SPLA ranks. We greeted each other and chatted for quite some time. Then I briefed the three of them about the situation I just saw regarding the integration adding that the whole process may unravel if the committee does not commence its work as soon as possible. I suggested that members of the committee who were far away be replaced by officers who were nearby. They looked a bit surprised about the scale of feeling among the A-2 and accepted the suggestion. They immediately went ahead to propose names. When I proposed Captain Michael Manyuon to be member, William objected strongly. I insisted stating that I was, in the first place, surprised that he was not in the committee given his remarkable role in starting the peace process between the SPLA and the A-2. William continued with his opposition giving no reasons. The other two kept quite, so I shut up. They may know something I did not know!

Eventually, they came up with some names and Cdr Salva Kiir was given instructions to start his work forthwith. The new persons whose names got added were in Itang. We reverted to informal conversation after that. It was not till about ten at night, after the other two had left, that the Chairman was ready to introduce the subject of my trip to his end.

The Chairman started by affirming that it was the rainy season and, therefore, the enemy activity would be minimal and this was why he had decided to make use of me on some matters which were important but should be through on or before December so that I was back to the N.U.N zone in time for the dry season. The main reason for calling me was to look into the cases of the arrested High Command members, Kerubino and Arok, and the officers detained with them. This, he said, was necessary to stem negative propaganda in Itang and elsewhere that we were detaining people without trial. He went on that the investigation into the case of Kerubino and the officers with him was complete but investigation into the case of Arok and those with him had just started and will take some time to finish, a month or so. In the meantime while this investigation was going on, the Chairman continued, I would lead an SPLA delegation to hold talks with the DUP which had requested to meet the movement in August. That, while in Addis Ababa, he advised, he wanted me to help organize the SPLA office there adding that "Deng is committed but lazy."!

I had quite a load on my plate! I thanked the Chairman for having thought about the case of the detainees. As a matter of principle, justice must be done so that we are seen to be what we say we are: a revolutionary people's movement striving to fight injustice and oppression. I assured him that I would try my best on this and the other matters he mentioned. I closed by reminding him that I was in the zone for less than a year and I needed time to build on the foundation I had just started. It was about mid-night, our meeting was over and I was shown where to spend the night.

Next morning I briefed him about the zone and gave him a copy of the handing and taking over notes signed by me and Cdr Martin Manyiel Ayuel. After that he gave instructions for a car to be found for me to go to Addis as soon as possible. Then we left together with him and the other two to the airport where he was taking a helicopter to somewhere else. After that I left for Itang in the car given to me.

In Itang, I met a stream of officers and as usual we discussed the affairs of the movement. In general the discontent was noticeable in the way they spoke. One person, however, who did not hide his feelings towards the Chairman was A/Cdr Alfred Lado Gore. We met alone in one of the rooms in the compound of Cdr William Nyuon in Itang. He said that he was now convinced the man was not what he claimed he was, a Marxist, but just a tribalist and that his flowery language will not fool anyone any more. He went on to say that the Chairman has betrayed what he stood for when he unleashed his warlords on the progressive officers. When I told him of what the Chairman had told me was my mission and that I would be going back to N.U.N. before the end of the year, he advised me to be careful and with absolute certainty he told me that I will never see N.U.N. zone again adding that success in executing missions and assignments has become a problem with the Chairman! He concluded that he was thrown into Itang and deployed with Cdr William Nyuon but he did not doubt that this was just a ploy to get him detained. We discussed a few other important matters before we parted.

I left Itang for Addis Ababa early morning on the 2nd of August 1988 on the car that the Chairman had arranged and I arrived there in the evening of the same day. I met my wife for the first time since March 1987 and it was a good opportunity to be together again after that long time apart. I also met the other friends in Addis. I then prepared for the expected meeting with the DUP delegation.

CHAPTER 6

OCER, COPS and OLS

Meeting with the DUP

OUR MEETING with the DUP delegation was the first ever between that party and the SPLM/A since the overthrow of Nimeiri. It will be recalled that the DUP was a member of the NANS but later withdrew under pressure of the NIF propaganda which portrayed the NANS as communist - controlled and opposed to the implementation of the Islamic Constitution in Sudan. As such the DUP did not take part in the Koka Dam Conference and expressed its total rejection of the Koka Dam Declaration signed in March 1986. The delegation of the DUP was a high-level one. It was led by Mr Sid Ahmed El-Hussein, Deputy Secretary-General of the party and the Minister of Interior, and membership of Mr Mohammed Tawfiq Ahmed, the Minister of Information and Culture, General (R) Yousif Ahmed Yousif and Mr Abdel Hakam Taifur, MP. The SPLM/A delegation was led by myself and included A/Cdr Deng Alor Kwol, Captain Nhial Deng Nhial, Captain Edward Abiei Lino and Captain Abdel Aziz Adam El-Hilou. We knew each other well with Mr Sid Ahmed El-Hussein and all the members of his delegation before and, hence, I was no stranger to them nor were they to me. Despite this fact, however, the talks were not at all easy.

From the outset, our delegation discerned the sensitivity of the DUP delegation towards the Koka Dam Declaration. The DUP did not want any mention of it. It did not need us to crack our minds hard to find out why. The DUP wanted to have an agreement with us that sounded "new" and/or described as such so that it gets the political credit for having initiated new inroads towards the achievement of peace in the country. We played along, tabling all the provisions of the Koka Dam Declaration without mentioning the term. Our delegation also noticed the reluctance of the DUP delegation to sign any joint statement on the talks, they wanted this done by Sayed Mohammed Osman El-Mirghani, the leader of the Khitimiya sect and the patron of the party. They needed his religious clout to ward off the anticipated accusations of heresy from the NIF and other Islamic bigots once an agreement is reached with the SPLM/A. The leader of the DUP delegation did not hide his contempt for Sadiq al-Mahdi and his mercurial character.

Most of the negotiation was done in this first round of talks and the text agreed upon then did not differ much from the final document signed in November under the rubric: "The Sudanese Peace Initiative." We adjourned to consult our principals and agreed to meet again on October 15, 1988.

In September, I left Addis with two members of my delegation, Captains: Edward Lino and Abdel Aziz Adam El-Hilou, to go and brief the Chairman on the first round of talks with the DUP. The Chairman was then in Eastern Equatoria. We took a car to Dima refugees camp where we were supposed to get an SPLA car to where the Chairman was. The camp manager was A/Cdr James Hoth Mai who was also a member of the Investigation Committee the Chairman had set up to investigate the two High Command members under detention and the officers arrested with them. A/Cdr Martin Mawien, the chairman of the Investigation Committee, was also there. In my discussion with both of them they informed me that it was not within their terms of reference to investigate Cdr Kerubino and Cdr Arok, only the other officers, and that the committee to investigate the officers with Cdr Arok has not yet sat as its members were scattered with some, such as A/Cdr Galerio Modi Hurnyang, in Equatoria where I was going to. They asked me to help in getting Galerio to come quickly.

We spent about a week in Dima waiting for the car but there was no sign of it coming. Finally, the Chairman sent instructions for us to walk to Raad on the river carrying that name which forms the border between Ethiopia and Sudan. We did walk to Raad and there I met A/Cdr Galerio and a number of officers waiting for a car to take them to Dima. I chatted with them and passed to Galerio the message from

Martin Mawien. The next day, A/Cdr Galerio and the officers with him left on foot for Dima.

A car eventually arrived and we had a difficult drive until we reached where the Chairman was. He and the officers with him were preparing to launch an attack on the enemy garrison in Keyala. The day after our arrival, all the officers were called for a sandtable discussion of the plan and execution of attack on the garrison. We all attended and contributed in the discussion. All this was normal military procedure. The Chairman, however, made a statement which I was hearing for the first time in that gathering. He said that the objective of that particular operation was to capture Keyala as part of the movement's strategy to capture the territory of Southern Sudan east of the Nile and South of the Sobat rivers and then declare a government. The Ethiopian border to the east and the Kenyan and Uganda borders to the South were the other limits of this territory. As a member of the High Command I did not know of a decision of the SPLA to form a government at any stage. But since the statement was made by the Chairman before more than thirty officers it had to be believed.

My colleagues and I briefed the Chairman on our talks with the DUP delegation and outlined to him the points of difference and what compromise terminologies could be acceptable. I further advised him to send a summary of these points to the other members of the High Command to send in their views on them so that the delegation can take these views into consideration in the next round of talks. He made comments and observations which we noted.

The second round of talks with the DUP

The second round of talks with the DUP started on the 15th of October. Our delegation came back with more or less the same draft document agreed upon in August. The DUP delegation sought some amendments. According to them they had consulted the Prime Minister so that he is involved from the very beginning. Thus, it was necessary to incorporate some of his observations. Our position was that although we would very much like unanimity of the Government on the issue, Sadiq and his party were committed to the Koka Dam Declaration, and that when the SPLM/A leader met Sadiq on 31/7/86 his excuse for the failure of his party to implement the Declaration was that the DUP, its partner in government, was not part of the peace process. We reminded the DUP delegation that if that comment from Sadiq in July was correct, it was not the case now since the DUP and the SPLM/A were talking peace. We were ready to discuss any point within the framework agreed upon.

At the end of this round, the DUP delegation went back happy. They had secured a particular mention of the party in the draft document. In addition, they persuaded the SPLM/A side to agree on a "freeze" rather than "repeal" of the Sharia laws (September Laws). Last but not least, the agreement was termed an "initiative", and not Koka Dam II or modification thereto, exactly as they wanted from the beginning of the talks. The two sides finally agreed that the leader of the SPLM/A and the patron of the DUP meet in the first week of November to sign the agreement reached in Addis Ababa.

The Signing of the Sudanese Peace Initiative

The SPLM/A Chairman and C-in-C, Dr John Garang, arrived Addis Ababa some days before the appointed date. He came with Cdr Salva Kiir. Cdr Yousif Kowa Mekki, who was on a tour to West Africa, also arrived. There was as well a flurry of activity from the side of Khartoum. Leaders of the NANS, the DUP and journalists flocked to the Ethiopian capital to witness this important occasion.

Dr John Garang called a meeting of our delegation that included the new arrivals to agree on the strategy of his first meeting with Sayed Mohammed Osman El-Mirghami. The Chairman opened the meeting by reading out the draft agreement mentioning that the delegation had consultation with him in September, that he had sent the contents of what was agreed upon in the first round of talks by radio to the High Command members for comments, and that he did not receive any response on the matter. As a matter of fact, the message (No. 209/10/88) from the Chairman to the High Command members on the DUP/SPLA draft agreement was not sent in September but on 22/10/88. Hence, the lack of response at that time was hardly surprising. He then invited opinions from all present.

The first to speak was Dr Justin Yac Arop, the Secretary-General of the SRRA based in Nairobi. He was not a member of the delegation that conducted the talks with the DUP and has visibly shown his unease when the Chairman was briefing the gathering. He pointed out that the document under discussion was not the same as the Koka Dam Declaration. This, in his view, should not have been the case. He then criticized the delegation for having agreed to the freeze of the Sharia Law instead of its repeal as stipulated in the Koka Dam Declaration. He concluded that the SPLM/A was up to a raw deal if it were to sign the document.

I took the floor to assuage the fears of Dr Justin Yac Arop. Firstly, I told the meeting that political situations are dynamic and can never be stagnant, that Koka Dam Declaration was signed 32 months ago under different local, regional and international conditions and cannot be expected to be a model agreement for all times, and that it would be expecting too much for the SPLM/A to require from any political group it wanted to negotiate with to just sign the Koka Dam Declaration. Secondly, I explained the background of the talks and the reason that led the SPLM/A delegation to agree to the document being discussed. I stressed that the document was not in substance very much different from the Koka Dam Declaration. As to the freezing, rather than repeal of the "hudud" in the penal code, I explained that, legally speaking, freezing of a law or repealing it meant the same thing as an act of parliament was required which must also enact the substitute law for there can never be a legal vacuum on such matters. But, politically, it was expedient to use the word "freeze" as this is what the DUP delegation preferred. I remarked that in serious negotiations one must always be conscious of the interest of the other side and that the whole exercise was to reach an agreement which each side feels will serve its interest. I concluded by saying that the delegation has tried its best in the given circumstances and ended my speech noting that the agreement was a historic step and politics in the Sudan will never be the same again henceforth.

Two or three others did speak all of them supportive of my position. Dr Justin Yac raised his hand again but the Chairman firmly stepped in. He said the discussion was useful and that the meeting had to come to a close. He concluded by stating that the draft agreement was satisfactory to the SPLM/A, that he was going to sign it and that the delegation has to be congratulated for a piece of work well done. Thus, the stage was set for the historic occasion.

Sayed Mohammed Osman El-Mirghani and his delegation did arrive Addis Ababa but not without problems. The night before he flew to Addis, his house in Khartoum was attacked by armed thugs, whose identity was not known but believed to be supporters of the NIF, in what was obviously meant to be an intimidation. In the same vein, an NIF controlled daily newspaper in Khartoum published the full text of the draft agreement about to be signed. How it leaked to the NIF remained unexplained properly. I took up the matter with Mr Sid Ahmed El-Hussein and he could only say that may be the leak came through their consultations with Sadiq al-Mahdi who was then close to the NIF which was partner in the coalition government.

Although Sayed Mohammed Osman El-Mirghani did not balk, the intimidatory tactics of the NIF began to show their effects on the DUP delegation in Addis Ababa. What was supposed to be just a signing ceremony turned into a new round of talks much to the surprise of the SPLM/A side. The DUP started to renegotiate the "draft agreement" and this went on for days on end.

Cdr. Salva Kiir and I had to leave Addis Ababa on a previously arranged visit to a number of African countries. I left the two sides still talking and when the "Sudanese Peace Initiative" was finally signed on November 16, 1988, I was in Accra, Ghana. I was not pleased that I could not see the whole exercise to the end but was heartened by the fact that our side stood firm on the original draft. There were minor additions relating to the procedural arrangements leading to the convening of the Constitutional Conference but these did not affect the substance of the document.

My two-month official trip took me to Accra, Brazzaville, Harare, Lusaka, Maputo, Gaborone, Harare (again), Dar es-Salaam, Harare (once more) and finally back to Addis Ababa. I arrived Addis airport on January 4, 1989. Only in Accra was our delegation composed of two members. In Brazzaville, we were joined by A/Cdr Elijah Molok Aleng, our representative in Congo, and for the rest of the trip Dr Barnaba Marial Benjamin, our representative in Southern Africa, was always with us.

In this tour we met Presidents: Denis Sasso Ngueso of Congo, Kenneth Kaunda of Zambia, Robert G. Mugabe of Zimbabwe and Joaquim Chissano of Mozambique.

The format in all the meetings in this tour was the same all through. The leader of our delegation always handed over the written message introducing me to explain our position on the issues raised in the message.

New Assignment

The year 1988 was characterized by high floods. Despite this fact, mobility of cars and heavy trucks should be possible by the first week of February 1989. According to the briefing the Chairman gave me in Gambela before coming to Addis Ababa, I was supposed to be back in Northern Upper Nile zone before the onset of the dry season. If I were to beat this time I should start movement from around the middle of January 1989. This was not to be. The Chairman had second thoughts.

It will be remembered that the main reason for calling me from the field was for me to look into the cases of the detained High Command members: Kerubino and Arok. I asked the Chairman twice about the progress of the investigations (the first time around Keyala in September and the second time just before his meetings with the patron of the DUP in November). In both cases I noticed his reluctance to discuss the matter. So, I adopted the attitude of wait-and-see. That was the end of it.

The other task of how to get the SPLM/A office in Addis organized, was a relatively simple matter. In fact, my ideas on the subject had sufficiently crystallized and it was just a matter of writing them up. This I did as soon as I was back in Addis Ababa from the trip referred to earlier.

Up to that time the SPLM/A office in Addis Ababa was called the office of the Chairman and the Head of the office was the Director of the office of the Chairman. To me this was a misnomer and had to cease. In the first place it was not the office of the Chairman, in fact he does not sit there even when he stays in Addis Ababa for extended periods. Secondly, its functions have nothing much to do directly with the Chairman. Therefore, I started by first defining what the office does and then draw up an organizational chart.

Functionally, the Addis office carried out Coordination with the field and also with the host country. In addition it was responsible for External Relations. This included contacts with the movement's offices abroad, contacts with foreign governments and NGOs and contacts with Sudanese political parties and groups. Thus, the most appropriate term to use was "External Relations" rather than "Foreign Relations". Given this dual function of the office the name that suggested itself was to call it: The Office of Coordination and External Relations (OCER). I adopted that. Organizationally, it was to be headed by a Director. Under the Director were heads of three departments: Administration and Finance; Publications and Documentations; and Radio SPLA. The office was to have an accountant and a cashier for the first time since its establishment in 1984. Both are to fall under the sub-department of Finance. The sub-department of administration was to take care of all members of the movement who are in Addis for one reason or the other, clerical work and general administration in the office. The head of Administration and Finance was ex-officio Deputy Director of OCER.

As the name suggests, the Publications and Documentations Department was in charge of publishing work and safe keeping of documents concerning or of interest to the SPLM/A. The movement was issuing in Addis the SPLM/A Newsletter which was supposed to be a weekly publication. Plans were also underway to issue a monthly magazine known as "New Sudan." This was not an easy task and needed a full time team. Radio SPLA, no doubt, was a vital organ of the movement and deserved special attention.

I completed my work together with the organizational chart and presented the proposed structure of the Addis Ababa office to the Chairman in Addis Ababa on Wednesday the 15th of January 1989. Two days later he was leaving for the field. As it is usually the case, I went to see him in his house so as to accompany him to the airport and also to get any directives from him. When we were alone in the room, he pulled out the chart from a file that was in front of him and with a red pen he started to fill in names against the blocks of the organizational chart. He wrote my name against that of the Director of OCER, A/Cdr Deng Alor Kwol's at Head of Administration and Finance, Captain Marhum Dut's as Head of Radio SPLA and Captain Nhial Deng Nhial's as Head of Publications and Documentation. He then handed me the paper. I was at a loss of what to say!

First, I was expecting a discussion of the ideas presented in the proposal. Second, if the proposal were to be approved as it was, I expected to be consulted on whom I had in mind to serve in the assignments suggested, at least the rung below the Director. Third, and most importantly, I expected the Chairman to really brief me as to why he had to give me a new assignment, particularly that he had promised me that I would be returning to Northern Upper Nile zone with the beginning of the dry season. Given my experience with him on the issue of the investigations, I saw no point in asking. Comrade Alfred Lado was right after all!

This was how I became the first (and the last) Director of OCER on January 17, 1989. I met the staff of the office on Monday the 20th and briefed them on the new structure of the office and what I expected from each person stressing the spirit of cooperation as the key to the success of any teamwork. I remained in this assignment up to January 6, 1990. All this period, I spent in Addis Ababa a mere 126 days. At one point, from the 17th March 1989, I was out of Addis for about three consecutive months.

The Ambo Workshop

The workshop which was held in Ambo, Ethiopia, as from February 4, 1989 hit the headlines mostly because of the adverse reaction Sadiq's government displayed towards it and the actions it took against those from Khartoum who participated in it. This is not to downplay in anyway the importance of the workshop and the issues discussed. By all standards, it was a magnificent achievement for all who made preparations for it and a great victory for the diplomacy of the SPLM/A. In all fairness, the workshop could not have been possible without the cooperation of the SPLM/A.

The idea of holding such a meeting germinated within the Trade Unions Alliance in early 1988. Dr El-Wathiq Kemeir, Lecturer in the University of Khartoum and member of the KUTU, was given the task of discussing the matter with the SPLA. When I met him late 1988 he was a disappointed man. He told me that he had met Dr John Garang on the matter which the latter welcomed and did instruct Deng Alor in his (Wathiq) presence to make the necessary arrangements in preparation for the meeting. Deng Alor did absolutely nothing and was evasive on the matter. The second cause for Dr Wathiq's disappointment was the attitude of the Sudanese Communist Party towards such a gathering. The party was adamant that it would not take part in a meeting that will be understood as a platform for the left.

After ascertaining the fact from Dr John Garang I assured Dr El-Wathiq Kemeir that the SPLM/A supported the idea and that I will personally take charge of the preparation for the meeting. I there and then wrote an official letter to the Secretary-General of the Sudanese Communist Party inviting the party to participate in the expected seminar. I mentioned in the letter that we were looking forward to benefit from the wealth of political experience the party has accumulated over more than forty years of struggle. I handed the letter to Dr.El-Wathiq Kemeir to take personally to Mr Mohammed Ibrahim Nugud or to Mr El-Tijani El-Tayeb Babiker. Indeed the letter was received but the party chose to stay away all the same.

Apart from the blessing of the Chairman all decisions on the preparation for and the holding of the Ambo Workshop were entirely mine. The paper presented by the SPLM/A at the workshop was formulated by me and I gave the ideas and notes to Captain Nhial Deng Nhial to write it up. I kept in constant touch with the NANS in Khartoum through Dr El-Wathiq and the date for convening the meeting was agreed upon by both sides.

The Ambo Workshop went on for four days and more than 30 participants took part in it including representatives of the SPLM/A, professionals, trade unionists, academicians and politicians. The participants from Khartoum flew back on February 9, 1989. As soon as they arrived Khartoum airport they were arrested, interrogated and thrown in jail on orders from the Minister of Interior, Mubarak Abdalla El-Fadhil. The Minister did not stop at that. He addressed the Constituent Assembly accusing them of treason and calling them names. He made full advantage of the parliamentary immunity to impugn the nationalism of these patriots with impunity. All the hullabaloo for no reason other than that they met the SPLA! Less than six months later, now in the doldrums, the very uppish Mubarak El-Fadhil not only met the SPLA but signed with it a "strategic agreement" to overthrow the regime in Khartoum as we shall see in Chapter 7. This tells a lot about how the country has really gone to the dogs.

The Bergen Forum

On February 21, 1989, I left Addis for Bergen, Norway, for a seminar organized by the Centre for Development Studies of the University of Bergen. Professor Abdel Ghaffar Mohammed Ahmed and Dr Gonnar Sorbo were in charge of organizing the seminar. Key political parties in the Sudan were invited to attend. I represented the SPLM//A. Others present were Prof. Hamad Omer Bagadi for the Umma Party, Gen. (R) Yousif Ahmed Yousif for the DUP; Dr Ali El-Haj Mohammed for the NIF; Dr Hunud Abia Kuduf for the General Union of the

Nuba Mountains, Mr Eliaba James Surur for the PPP, Mr Joseph Ukel Abango for the SSPA and Mr Joseph Modesto for the Sudanese Communist Party. Non-partisan contributors to the conference from Sudan included Dr Francis M. Deng, Dr Mohammed Ahmed Salih and Mr Taha El-Roubi, the Honorary Consul General of Norway in Sudan. There was a high attendance from the Nordic countries. The theme of the seminar was "Management of crisis in Sudan: Alternative Models for Action".

The SPLM/A and the NIF were identified by the organizers as of most "extreme views" and Dr Ali El-Haj and I were given chance to have a live TV debate on the issues of the war and peace in Sudan. The representative of the NIF was pushed to a corner and could not put up a coherent defence as to how the chopping off of hands for pilfering and stoning to death for adultery could be justified in any civilized society. His outfit (white gown and white turban) in the middle of Bergen made matters worse for him. The SPLM/A came up on top of things.

The forum issued a joint statement which urged that food must not be used as a weapon and called on the parties to cooperate with international organizations in the delivery of food to all the affected areas of the country. It also urged all the political forces to cooperate towards convening the National Constitutional Conference as soon as possible and to make all necessary preparations towards that end, including arrangements for a cease fire.

It was during the seminar that we heard of the petition presented by the army High Command in Khartoum to the Head of State on the state of the army and what needed to be done to rectify the situation giving an ultimatum of one week to get their demands met. The conclusion among us at the seminar was that such a move cannot be anything other than a military coup d'etat. The events were to prove us wrong.

At the conclusion of the seminar, I flew off to London on my way back to Addis Ababa which I reached on March 4, 1989.

Operation Lifeline Sudan

In 1988 the United Nations Secretary-General, Javier Perez de Cuellar, named Mr James P. Grant, the executive director of UNICEF to take charge of organizing a special relief operation in Sudan. This decision was taken on the backdrop of repeated media reports[3] of many lives lost as a result of war induced famine. For Southern Sudan, the figure was put by some sources to as high as 500,000 persons mostly children and the elderly. Mr Grant organized a conference on the matter to take place in Khartoum. The conference was to be attended by representatives from the United Nations, donor countries, relief NGOs and the Sudan government. The SPLM/A was not invited to attend. This "International Conference on Sudan Emergency Relief" opened in Khartoum on March 8, 1989. Mr Grant made it known that he would want the parties to the conflict to agree on a six-month cease fire so that the period is used to stock food on site for the needy population.

The Chairman was then in the field and he was informed about the development. He immediately sent a radio message on the 8th which he asked me to put in the form of a letter addressed to Mr Grant and dispatched to Khartoum by fax. After some editing the message was typed and faxed to Khartoum the same day. The letter commended the concern of the international community and their wish to help the needy people in Sudan and stressed that the SPLM/A had called for relief assistance to reach these needy people but Khartoum had been reluctant to help them. The letter affirmed:

"It is, therefore, to be reiterated that the movement is very keen to seek ways and means to ameliorate the situation and it is our wish that

---

3   See, for example, *The New York Times*, January 24, 1989; Colin Campbell and Deborah Scroggins, *Atlanta Journal and Constitution*, January 27, 1989 and the well researched article "Reporter at large: Famine", by Raymond Bonner which appeared in the *New Yorker* of March 13, 1989. Television journalists also tried their best to publicize the famine. For instance, Mr Gary Strieker of the Cable News Network (CNN) broadcast reports on Sudanese famine in July, September and October 1988.

this conference will come out with concrete proposals and practical suggestions so as to do what is possible in the sixty days left of the dry season. The needs are immense and time is almost running out."

The letter asked the conference to devote attention to the situation in the SPLA-administered areas and to earmark assistance to them according to the population size in those areas which constituted more than 90% of the population in Southern Sudan. It promised that:

"The SPLM/A is willing and ready to discuss all the above with the organizations and agencies now meeting in Khartoum either as a group in a conference similar to the one now being held in Khartoum or singly."

The letter concluded by wishing all concerned to have the will and determination to bring about the success of this humanitarian undertaking. Whatever the purpose of Dr John Garang was in sending that letter, the reactions and events which it engendered got him completely unprepared.

Mr James P. Grant took the letter seriously and as soon as the conference closed in Khartoum, he flew to Addis Ababa to discuss the issue as the letter promised. I met Mr Grant on March 10, 1989 at the Ghion Hotel in Addis in the company of two of my assistants. That was the first time for me to meet him and he impressed me as a first-class communicator who loved what he was doing. Mr Grant started the meeting by briefing us on the deliberations at the conference and, rather excitedly, added that the letter of Dr John Garang was well received in the conference. He apologised that they did not anticipate the difficulty involved when they were preparing for the conference. Finally, he outlined the issues he would like to get the agreement of the SPLA on. Apart from the six-month cease fire which was to facilitate the relief work, a massive relief operation was envisaged over this period which entailed delivering food into South Sudan by land, air and river from across the borders of its neighbours: Ethiopia, Kenya and Uganda. I gave my initial response to Mr Grant but promised him that I will convey our discussion to the Chairman so that a firm stand on the matter is made. We agreed to meet again.

I communicated to Dr John Garang what transpired in my meeting with Mr Grant. He ruled out a cease fire for any length of time but instructed me to continue dialogue on the relief operation suggested. He pointed out that the agreement of the neighbouring countries needed to be secured by the UN for any cross-border operation to be possible. I could see I was on a "mission impossible" but accepted the challenge.

I informed Mr Grant and the U.S. embassy in Addis that the SPLA was not prepared for a cease fire but was ready to explore other modalities as the target population were our people and we could only be too glad to see them assisted. From there on we got locked into a series of meetings with the staff of the U.S embassy led by Mr Bob Frasure, the DCM, to explore those modalities. At the final stage Mrs Julia Taft, a senior official of the US Office of Foreign Disaster Assistance (OFDA) in Washington, joined in the talks. She was an intelligent, unassuming and firm person. She did not stick to formalities but selected her words carefully. She impressed me a lot.

The hurdle that needed to be circumvented was: how could the operation be carried out without a cease fire? Finally, I came up with a suggestion that if the routes of the expected relief assistance could be identified it may be possible for the SPLA to consider cease fire along those routes for UN convoys as opposed to a blanket cease fire. This should address the concern on the land and river routes through which the bulk of the relief assistance was to be delivered. The air routes required further discussion but to me this did not pose much of a problem as the land and river routes. To my surprise this suggestion seemed to be what everybody was waiting for. It was a deal! Mr Bob Frasure termed those cease fire axes "corridors of tranquillity" a phrase which continued to be used up to today. This was its origin.

I did not consult Dr John Garang before hand on this suggestion but I was convinced it was the only way to get somewhere. I later briefed him extensively on the matter and stressed to him that the credibility of the movement was at stake if this arrangement just agreed upon were not carried through. I then strongly recommended that he approves it. The Chairman expressed some reservations but he trusted my judgement and gave his approval. It was a turning point for the SPLM/A.

I was instructed by the Chairman to represent the movement on the discussion and implementation of the relief operation. I left Addis for Nairobi on Friday the 17th of March. There I met Mr James P. Grant again to conclude the agreement on the operation . The Chairman also charged me with the responsibility to reorganize the SRRA to cope with the expected inflow of relief which was code-named: "Operation Lifeline Sudan" and officially launched on April 1, 1989 when Mr Grant flagged off in Nairobi the first convoy of trucks taking relief food to Kapoeta and Torit through Lokichoggio.

The operation aimed at getting sufficient food aid into Southern Sudan to feed approximately two million civilians. The plan was to get 100,000 tons of food into the region over a six-week period before the rainy season made the roads impassable. The cost of the operation was estimated at 132 million U.S. dollars.

Before that and on Monday, the 27th of March, a U.S congressional delegation was received by the Chairman at a location near Torit. The delegation comprised Senator Gordon Humphrey, and congressmen: Frank Wolff and Gary Ackerman. The purpose of their visit was to discuss the ways and means of reaching relief assistance to the needy. I was present in the meeting. The Chairman assured the visiting delegation of the commitment of the SPLA to unhindered relief assistance and pointing at me, added that he had decided to send Dr Lam Akol, member of the High Command, to be stationed in Nairobi to oversee the implementation of the relief operation underway. The U.S. delegation was happy with this and when they flew back to Nairobi later that afternoon they immediately held a press conference in which they declared that the SPLA has given its full support to the UN-sponsored relief operation.

Prior to meeting the U.S. congressmen, the Chairman was making a tour of flag-raising ceremonies in the towns recently captured from the enemy in Eastern Equatoria. He went to Nimule, Talanga, Katire and Torit. I joined him in the last two. The congressmen joined us in Torit after having been driven by car from Kapoeta where they had flown in from Nairobi. They spent the night at Torit and all of us who accompanied the Chairman assumed that the meeting with the congressmen was going to take place early in the morning of the next day after the military parade. This was not to be. The Chairman probably wanted them to have a feel of what things in the bush looked like. They had to be driven to the meeting spot. Before reaching there they had to walk across a stream a knee-high of water. Mr Frank Wolff, in fact, complained during the meeting of - to use his words - "the inconvenience of crossing the stream".

The meeting of the Chairman with the US congressmen was broadcast over Radio SPLA in the afternoon of the same day. Curiously, the Radio bulletin concluded the very item of news by adding that the Chairman, Dr John Garang, started on that day a tour of a number of African countries expected to last for three weeks. Of course, there was nothing of the sort. Dr John Garang was on the same spot and did not have plans at all to leave South Sudan at that time. After having listened to Radio SPLA, I asked the Chairman as to why he saw it necessary to add such untruth. He explained that the congressmen were going to talk and describe where they met him and this will reach the ears of Sadiq al-Mahdi who will then send his planes to bomb the place and as such it was necessary to keep Sadiq guessing as to his whereabouts!

The main purpose of my presence in eastern Equatoria that particular time was to brief the Chairman on my meetings in Addis Ababa and Nairobi on the UN-sponsored relief operation. We started the discussion in Katire but could not finish. This was continued after the meeting with the U.S. congressmen. I suggested that with the expected relief input it was about time to think in terms of a wider structure of the movement to coordinate the assistance provided, especially the non-food component, and tie it up with initiating production and providing services in the liberated areas. By then there was the SRRA, the relief wing of the movement, which was receiving relief assistance that hardly had any long-term objective. Then there was a fledgling National Economic Commission (NEC) which was to organize internal and border trade. But that time, neither trade took off. Finally, there was the refugees centres in Itang, Pinywudo and Dima which generated good income from contributions of the Sudanese refugees. The idea was to organize the three (SRRA, NEC and the Refugees administration) under one body so that they can be self-supporting to sustain production while providing services to the people in liberated areas and the refugees centres. This was agreed upon and the Chairman named the umbrella body the "Commission to Organize Production and Services", COPS, for short. COPS was to be led by a Head with the three Secretary-Generals of the three constituent organizations as members. I was there and then appointed the Head of COPS and given the task of organizing the SRRA, NEC and the refugees administration. I promised the Chairman that I will try my best and he retorted by saying that if I do not do it nobody else can. I felt flattered but did not underrate the challenge ahead.

I went to Nairobi, therefore, not only to take charge of the SRRA and international aid coordination, as many thought, but to initiate what could be rightfully called a civil structure of the movement. I understood my role to be supervisory and directing policy. The Chairman gave me powers to take decisions on the spot, only to keep him informed of such decisions as soon as they are taken and that I should render regular reports to the High Command on the work of COPS.

I flew back to Nairobi from Kapoeta in time for the launching of "Operation Lifeline Sudan" referred to earlier. The UN convoy of fourteen trucks left Nairobi on the 1st of April carrying 120 tons of food and arrived Kapoeta without a problem. When it left Kapoeta for Torit on April the 18th, disaster struck. The convoy was attacked by armed Taposa tribesmen. The casualties of the attack were: five killed, one lost (unaccounted for) and four wounded (two of them SPLA soldiers and two drivers). Among the dead was Mr Akau Gai Deng the SRRA official who was escorting the convoy. The incident made bad publicity to a highly publicized operation. It caused a jolt but this was quickly smoothed over following SPLA assurances that it was an isolated incident.

On April 23, 1989, I accompanied Mr James Grant for him to meet Dr John Garang at Panyigor (Kongor) in Upper Nile. The purpose of the meeting was for Mr Grant to be reassured about the position of the SPLA towards Operation Lifeline Sudan. The discussion centred on road, river and air routes; particularly those that started from and ended in Government held towns but passing through SPLA-held territory. There were the Muglad - Aweil rail and Kosti - Malakal river routes. At the meeting the SPLA spelt out its position that these rail and river routes would be allowed to deliver relief items provided that no military escort to accompany the convoys, they should include no commercial or military freight, relief items should be off-loaded to civilian populations at specific SPLA - controlled intermediate points along the route, the SPLA had the right to inspect all shipments to verify their contents. The SPLA had suggested that the total amount of relief items delivered on such routes to the Government and SPLA - held areas were to be in the proportion of the population in each area. The Government could not agree to this, as it controlled less population, and the SPLA finally agreed on a 50:50 ratio.

Mr Grant and his delegation left Panyigor for Nairobi at about 4.00 p.m. the same day. I remained behind to meet the Chairman and share with him a couple of matters. He could only stay for only 30 minutes. According to him, this was the reaction time needed before "Sadiq's bombers arrive to bomb Panyigor". He took off together with Cdr Lwal Diing Wol to Poktap. Since I had already made arrangements with the OLS to pick me up the next day, I had ample free time. I decided out of nostalgia to drive to Bor town, which had been captured by the SPLA just a week earlier. It was my first time since 1964 to see the town where I had my intermediate schooling. There I met Cdr Kwol Manyang Juuk, alternate member of the High Command (just like myself), for the first time in my life. Both of us were appointed to the High Command in 1986.

I flew back to Kapoeta from Panyigor on April 24, 1989 to continue my meetings with the newly formed 15-man SRRA Secretariat. The overhaul of the structure of the SRRA was not only dictated by the UN-sponsored relief operation but it had earlier been decided to look into the working of the SRRA office in Nairobi. This was in February and the main reason of my trip to Nairobi on the 17th of March was precisely to see this through. This issue will be dealt with more fully under a separate section.

The SRRA Secretariat was headed by the Secretary-General assisted by coordinators in the fields of: health; agriculture, education, veterinary, construction, stores and equipment, accounts, religious affairs, public relations, projects formulation, water drilling, field coordination, and the press. These were to be stationed in Kapoeta. The other member of the Secretariat is the liaison officer who was to be based in Nairobi to liaise with the UN and the NGOs there on the relief programmes as approved by the Secretariat. He was to visit Kapoeta as frequently as was possible to attend Secretariat meetings, to brief it about his work in Nairobi and to get any new directives.

I explained at length to the newly appointed members of the SRRA Secretariat the background to restructuring the SRRA,the new structure, the functions of each, the importance of cooperation and coordination, the collective responsibility of the Secretariat, and what I expected from each and every one of them. After having cleared all their questions, I told them that the challenge facing them was great as the expectations of our people have been raised by the publicity associated with Operation Lifeline Sudan and urged them to pull their straps. I then, flew back to Nairobi.

In Nairobi, I briefed Mr Vincent O'Reilly, UNICEF representative in Kenya and the Coordinator of the OLS, about the SRRA as the counterpart of the OLS and its work in facilitating relief assistance. We discussed the areas of cooperation and I requested that the OLS looks into building the capacity of the SRRA to enable it carry out in an effective manner its relief functions. Mr O'Reilly promised to take up the matter with Mr Grant and would feedback. Indeed, the contact was done and Mr Grant responded positively but there were issues to be ironed out first. Eventually in May, the OLS extended assistance to the SRRA in terms of office support, training, provision of cars for the use of the Secretariat in Kapoeta and one for use in Nairobi, air transport on OLS planes, etc.

The advent of Operation Lifetime Sudan provided the opportunity for the SPLA to "open up", so to speak. It was the first time that the leadership of the movement, in the person of a member of the High Command, had presence for an extended period abroad outside Addis Ababa. I found myself inundated with many questions which called for answers from the SPLA. What did the SPLA stand for? What was it doing in the liberated areas? Was it under the thumb of Mengistu? etc. These and other related questions came from diplomats, journalists, relief workers, political figures, businessmen, etc. Questions which seem to have accumulated over the years. I found myself the spokesman of the movement without being officially assigned to be so; the official spokesman of the SPLM/A was and remained to be the Chairman himself.

Before concluding this section on the OLS, it is necessary to highlight the basic principles on which it was based. The following terms formed the basis of the operation:

1 The UN has to deal with all the parties to the conflict that control ground through which relief items pass or to which they are delivered.
2 The parties to the conflict commit themselves to the safe and unhindered passage and delivery of relief items to the needy population.
3 The UN, as a neutral body, was to co-ordinate the operations with the parties to the conflict.

There was no written agreement between the parties to the conflict (the SPLA and the GOS) with the UN when the OLS came into being on April 1, 1989. None was required. It was only the express commitment of the parties to the above terms that kept the operation going. Although the UN does not confer recognition of any kind to the SPLA, it had to deal with it in order to be able to reach the needy population. Indeed, the choice of UNICEF as the UN agency to lead the OLS was in part - as Mr Grant put it - to stress non-recognition of the SPLA while dealing with it on this humanitarian undertaking.

Whereas Kenya and Uganda readily agreed to allow their territories to be used for cross-border relief operations, the Ethiopian government did not give its consent. Therefore, the cross-border operations (river and land) envisaged through Gambela were shelved. Lokichoggio was chosen as the main relief centre to serve the SPLA-administered areas of Southern Sudan especially by air. Before OLS, Loki housed the ICRC centre and hospital at Lopiding. The hospital treated war wounded from Southern Sudan. The ICRC was also active in some areas of Southern Sudan since 1988.

One final point related to the conception of the OLS deserves some space here. Given the donors' acquiescence in Khartoum's obstruction of relief assistance to the South since 1986, it has been suggested by some observers that Operation Lifeline Sudan arose as an attempt by the donors, especially the U.S.A., to gain leverage on the SPLA in order to exert pressure on it later to make peace with the GOS. Indeed, such 'pressure' was expected and the Chairman and I had a discussion on the matter on March 30, 1989 following the visit of the U.S. Congressmen to Torit. However, that pressure never came. But this is not to say that it was not on the cards. The circumstances must have had their influence on the development of events.

A possible explanation could be that the situation in Khartoum then placed the SPLA on a higher moral ground than the GOS and rendered any pressure on it unnecessary. By that time, Prime Minister, Sadiq al-Mahdi, was losing international credibility for his opposition to the DUP/SPLA peace initiative and was seen to be the one who needed to be pushed on the peace front. In mid-March, Sadiq had made a U-turn by endorsing the peace initiative and was, thus, able to form a new broad-based government that put peace on the top of its agenda. Although it had a promising start, the new government did not have enough time to prove its actual commitment to the realization of a peaceful settlement of the war. It was overthrown in an NIF inspired coup d'etat on June 30, 1989. Things might have been different had the military takeover not taken place at the time it did.

Problems in the SRRA and SPLM/A Offices in Nairobi

In June 1988, Dr Justin Yac Arop was removed from office as the Secretary-General of the SRRA and Dr Richard K. Mulla was appointed to replace him. For the first time, an SPLM/A representative in Nairobi, in the person of Captain William Bior, was appointed. The two left Addis Ababa for Nairobi immediately to assume their respective offices. A few months later, persistent reports were being received to the effect that there was lack of cooperation between William and Richard. As time went by the friction developed into confrontation. By that time the two were directly answerable to the Chairman and hence he was the only person who can do something about the situation in Nairobi.

In February 1989, the Chairman received a message from the Kenyan authorities expressing dissatisfaction with the conduct of Dr Richard K. Mulla and wanted him out of Kenya as soon as possible. The Chairman requested from the Kenyan authorities to postpone any action they would want to take until he (the Chairman) sends to them a member of the High Command to deal with the matter on the spot. I received directives in the middle of February to proceed to Nairobi to look into the above problems. In addition, I was to look into the work of the SRRA in general and come out with recommendations for improvement. My trip to Nairobi was delayed by the Bergen Forum and by my discussions in Addis Ababa with Mr Grant in the second week of March.

I arrived Nairobi on Friday, March 17, 1989. I met Captain William Bior and Dr Richard K. Mulla together the next day and informed them that I was in Nairobi to look into the problems facing their two offices and would want a briefing from each of them stressing that I expected a written presentation from each. They complied. I discussed with each of them the written presentation on the subject. I also interviewed the SRRA office staff as well as the other members of the movement who were in Nairobi such as Dr Justin Yac Arop and A/Cdr Joseph Kuol Amum.

All the statements given with the supporting documents were carefully analyzed and I came out with specific conclusions on the matter. For the good names of those involved most of these conclusions shall not be divulged here. Suffice it to state that the evidence against Dr Richard K. Mulla was overwhelming. I also discovered that Captain William Bior was not helpful either. Instead of containing the problems created by his colleague, he was blowing them out of proportion compromising the secrecy required on such matters. I decided that both of them be transferred to Kapoeta. One other conclusion I acted upon was the financial mismanagement in the SRRA Nairobi office. I decided to form an audit committee to look into the accounts of the SRRA.

At the end of my mission to Nairobi, I proceeded to Eastern Equatoria and briefed the Chairman on my findings. This was during Easter and at about the same time the U.S. Congressmen visited him as discussed earlier.

The case of the detained Bishop Paride Taban

One of the most immediate problems I faced in Nairobi was the issue of the Catholic Bishop Paride Taban, the bishop of Torit diocese. He was put under detention by the SPLA on the capture of Torit in February 1989. The churches and other concerned individuals and groups were exerting a lot of pressure for his release. His arrest and subsequent release is a story in which a number of players and factors were involved and is worth recounting.

I was in Stockholm, Sweden, on my way back from Bergen when the news of the fall of Torit became known. In fact, I got the news in one of the studios of the Swedish Radio where I went for an interview. After the radio interview I contacted Addis Ababa by telephone to confirm the good news. I was given more details about the capture of the town including the detention of Bishop Paride Taban. The reason given for his detention by the Chairman and C-in-C was: "to protect the bishop from being harmed by the SPLA soldiers who were very angry over the negative statements he has been making before the fall of the town"!

Torit town has been under siege by the SPLA for a long time. This started when Bishop Paride Taban was in Juba town. He entered Torit on July 1, 1988 in a convoy escorted by government soldiers. This convoy had to fight its way through a number of SPLA ambushes and when it finally reached Torit, a distance of about 100 miles from Juba, the journey had taken one month. This is a measure of the stiff resistance made by the SPLA. In Torit, the clergyman was shocked by the state of hunger and disease he found the civil population in. Quite naturally, he began to make statements and send out appeals to the outside world imploring a rescue of the town. These appeals were widely publicized by the government and the international media and won the bishop the wrath of the Chairman and C-in-C of the SPLA. The appeals of Bishop Paride Taban found listening ears. Mr Jan Erichson, the Head of NCA in Oslo who knew Torit and its people very well, approached me at one time in Addis with what seemed to us at that time a rather desperate proposal requesting the SPLA's approval for the NCA to do some air dropping of food in Torit. He summarized his feelings by the following words: "it is bad already when one hears people are starving, it is unbearable when the people starving are known to you by name." I was deeply touched. Our meeting was over dinner in the Hilton Hotel. When we were leaving, I confided to my colleagues who were with me that Mr Erichson made a strong case. In Bergen, Mr Haylor Aschjem of the NCA who attended all the sessions of the seminar made sure that every time we had some moments together the situation in Torit was always in the discussion. Needless to say, nothing materialized in rescuing Torit the way the Bishop and the NCA wanted it and, in his mysterious ways God delivered the town to the SPLA and the bishop was detained. He was held with a number of his assistants (Fr. Leo Traynor, Fr. John Lohito and Fr. John Le Vachier) at Kidepo camp. No visits were allowed.

I visited the camp in March and met the Bishop and his colleagues there. I found the conditions under which they were being kept unacceptable. I instructed the officer in charge to treat them in a special manner and give them good accommodation and better services. After our meeting with the U.S. congressmen, I raised the issue with the Chairman when we visited Kidepo camp. I questioned the wisdom behind the keeping of the clergymen, especially on the reason cited arguing that if it was the reaction of SPLA soldiers that was being feared the best solution would have been to allow the clergymen to go abroad where there was no single armed SPLA soldier. Cdr Lwal Diing Wol, who was part of the discussion, supported the continued detention of the clergymen pointing out that when Torit was captured it was found out that Bishop Paride Taban had dug a foxhole in his house. He rhetorically asked: "if he was not militarily involved why did he do that?" I did not want Cdr Lwal Diing to run away with this point and immediately replied that every commander who has ever been involved in active operations always advises the civilians as well as his soldiers to dig foxholes to give them some protection from flying shrapnels of air bombing. The discussion ended inconclusively. I lost this round.

During Easter, Mr Bethuel Kiplagat handed to me in Nairobi some gifts to be given to Bishop Paride Taban for the occasion. Before that he had a long talk with me advising the release of the bishop. I took the gifts and handed them over to the Chairman. It was another opportunity to revisit the issue. I added the concern of friends like Kiplagat. The Chairman was not moved. I began to wonder whether I really was effective in conveying to the Chairman the strength of feelings abroad towards the release of the Bishop or just the Chairman had other plans. I thought it was time to have a respite.

Another man who got directly involved in the issue of Bishop Paride Taban was Fr. Renato Kizito Sesana, of the Comboni Brothers and editor of the catholic "New People" magazine. He is a remarkable man. Soft spoken and intelligent, he is a man you have to respect. In addition, he is a journalist of the first order. He put these skills into good use when the news broke out that the Bishop and his colleagues were being kept by the SPLA somewhere near Torit. He and a colleague visited Kapoeta with the hope of being allowed to pay a visit to his comrades-in-catholicism. This was denied by the commander of Kapoeta in line with the official policy. But the commander decided to keep them for a while in Kapoeta. They were not under arrest but were not allowed to go beyond some few metres from where they stayed. Yet when Fr. Kizito went back to Nairobi he knew exactly where the Bishop and his colleagues were being kept.

In Nairobi Fr. Kizito looked me up and through a mutual friend, Mr Joseph Ngala, we agreed to have lunch together at the Jacaranda Hotel Pizza restaurant. There, outdoors, we had a relaxed atmosphere to discuss the issue at hand. Fr. Kizito was frank. He started by relating to me his experience in the visit he just had to Kapoeta and concluded that although the SPLA was strong militarily, his impression was that it lacked adequate political consciousness. He contrasted it with his experience with the situation in Guinea Bissau and other liberation movements. The two were surprised when I conceded the point without argument. My contribution was more to what was being done to correct this situation. I told them that the SPLM/A was reaching out politically and diplomatically and things will never be the same again, although it would take some time. They raised the issue of the Bishop and his colleagues. I told them to be patient but promised Fr. Kizito that he will be the first person to meet Bishop Paride Taban when he gains his freedom. I kept my promise and Fr. Kizito and I became friends since then and remain so up to today.

In May 1989, the Chairman sent me a message that he was planning to visit Germany, Geneva, U.K. and the U.S.A and that I contact the Kenyan authorities to inform them about this. He did not intend to come to Nairobi as his flight was taking off from Addis Ababa. The visit was in response to an invitation extended to him by the Chairman of the Foreign Affairs Committee in the German parliament (Bundestag) which had a hearing on Sudan. Similar invitations were extended to the GOS, Sudanese political parties and human rights groups.

I contacted Mr Kiplagat about the expected visit of the Chairman to Europe and the USA. He welcomed it but requested that he should pass through Nairobi before going there. I conveyed this to the Chairman. I also seized the opportunity to put a final case for the release of Bishop Taban. I wrote to the Chairman that this was his first visit ever to Europe and the USA as Chairman of the SPLM/A and therefore the visit had a special significance and must achieve its objective. For this to be possible it had to be a political and diplomatic offensive. Finally, I advised that the continued detention of the bishop was going to detract the importance of such a visit and, in my view, it was time to set him free. On the 23rd of May, I received the reply of the Chairman that I go public that the bishop was now a free man. I phoned Fr. Kizito, broke to him the good news and issued him with a pass permit to go to Torit to meet the bishop there. When I contacted the BBC correspondent in Nairobi, Ms Lindsay Hilsum, about a piece on the release of Bishop Paride Taban, her response was unjournalistic. She thought this was SPLA propaganda which should be disseminated not through the BBC but through Radio SPLA! Of course, the VOA, Deutsche Welle and other radio stations carried the item on their bulletins. She must have regretted having missed a scoop.

The bishop and his colleagues were released in Torit on the appointed date. He elected to stay there for some time. The Irish father was flown to Nairobi. The French Father had been set free earlier to be able to see his very old mother, in his country. Thus closed the curtain on the captivity of the clergymen of Torit diocese.

A surprise cease-fire

I spent most of the period from March 17 to June 7, 1989 in Nairobi and some of the time shuttling between it and Southern Sudan. It is in Kapoeta that I stayed most of the time to oversee the work of the new SRRA Secretariat. Generally, they picked up quickly and their performance was satisfactory. The only exception was none other than the Secretary-General himself, Pierre Ohure Okerruk. He turned out to be a real embarrassment. Not only did he fail to control his drunkenness on duty but because of that he became a menace to the few cars the SRRA had. In a span of two months he put four brand new Toyota cars, donated by the OLS, out of road because of driving while drunk. I talked to him several times to be conscientious of his duty and to seek improvement but to no avail. I must admit it was the first time in my life to tolerate a misfit. The reason was purely political. We had decided early that the position of the Secretary-General was to be filled by an Equatorian. There were not many in the SPLA senior enough with the required educational background to qualify. His predecessor, Dr Richard K. Mulla, was under investigation for misconduct and financial mismanagement over the span of less than a year (from July 1988 to March 1989) he spent in the office. I only hoped against hope that something will make Pierre change his ways.

The most dramatic event that made news over that period was the one-month cease fire declared by the Chairman and C-in-C of the SPLA, Dr John Garang, to take effect on May 1, 1989. It took many by surprise not least within the SPLA itself. It came at the wake of a string of SPLA victories which left the SPLA in control of the whole of Equatoria east of Bahr el-Jebel and the whole of Upper Nile south of the Sobat and east of the Bahr el-Jebel except for two garrisons only: Zeraf Mouth (New Fangak) and the Canal Mouth. The last government garrison to fall into SPLA hands was Waat; the enemy troops withdrew from it under the cover of darkness on the night of April the 30th. Having captured good quantity of military equipment, the morale among the SPLA soldiers was rocket-high and they were poised to advance on the two remaining enemy garrisons. It was at this moment that the C-in-C declared a cease fire. The question in everybody's mind was: why now?

In Nairobi and Kapoeta a number of SPLA officers mustered courage to discuss the matter with me as candidly as they could. (Yes, courage, for it needed a lot of courage those days to talk to High Command members.) Several versions were proffered as possible explanation to the declaration of cease fire. But one "theory" has been forwarded repeatedly and passionately that it deserves a mention here. It will be recalled that military operations that saw the SPLA capture one garrison after another in Eastern Equatoria and south-east Upper Nile started at Keyala in September 1988. There, the Chairman and C-in-C declared that the strategic objective of those military operations was to declare an SPLA government in the areas captured; i.e, the area of Southern Sudan east of Bahr el-Jebel and south of the Sobat river. I was present when the Chairman made this pledge as mentioned earlier . Up to here, this is no more than a statement of fact. The "conspiracy theory" picks up from here as follows. When the Chairman conceived the strategy, he had in mind that the process of liberating the areas concerned was going to take not less than two years and more likely more. The speed of capturing the enemy garrisons took him by surprise and, since he did not want to declare an SPLA government by 1989, he decided to halt the process just short of the last two enemy garrisons. End of theory. I leave it here without comment.

The reasons for the declaration of the ceasefire have to be found in the local and international situation at that time. Some of these were said in the statement of the Chairman on the cease fire announcement.

Locally, two situations have to be distinguished: in the SPLA and in Khartoum. Within the SPLA itself, politics aside, I do not think that it was militarily possible to have captured the two remaining garrisons at that time using the military equipment available. For one thing, the rains were soon coming and this was going to render any mobility of the "technicals" impossible, thus denying the SPLA considerable military superiority in materials. It needed this factor if the momentum acquired in Eastern Equatoria was to be maintained. For another, with the deep penetration of the SPLA close to the Nile, its supply line especially for fuels and lubricants, was overstretched. Time was needed to straighten this out. These points must have been at the back of the mind of the Chairman and C-in-C when he was considering declaring a cease fire.

In Khartoum, the impact of the DUP-SPLA agreement of November 1988 continued to reverberate. As it is well known, this agreement was enthusiastically supported in Khartoum by the masses of the people, trade unions and political parties, except Sadiq al-Mahdi and the NIF, the third coalition partner in Sadiq's government by then. Sadiq chose not to reject the agreement outright but to strangle it by buying time and lengthening the procedures needed in discussing it until a new situation that will bypass the urgency of its implementation imposes itself. As a result, the DUP withdrew from the coalition government on Wednesday, December 28, 1988 when all its ministers submitted their resignations to the Prime Minister. On the 1st of February 1989, Sadiq al-Mahdi announced the formation of a new coalition cabinet with the NIF which excluded the DUP for the first time. That was the practical confirmation of Sadiq's total rejection of the DUP-SPLA agreement. For all practical purposes the agreement was dead and buried, or is it?

The Sadiq - Turabi cabinet in Khartoum was met with the string of SPLA victories referred to earlier. Confronted with a series of military defeats the army High Command in Khartoum petitioned the Head of State with a 21-point memorandum. The Prime Minister was on Monday, February 20, 1989 served with a copy of it in the evening. Paragraphs (18) and (19) of the memorandum are relevant here and are reproduced *verbatim*[4] (the translation is mine and thus, unofficial).

> 18. The prosecution of armed conflict is inseparable from managing balanced state policies. Therefore, the state must aim at breaking the economic and military siege imposed on us from the Western and Eastern blocks. This aim can be achieved by adopting balanced policies which enable us obtain the economic aid and the military assistance we need today.

> 19. The coherence and unity of the internal front demands the implementation of a national outlook devoid of political manoeu-vrings, conflicts and conspiracies. This calls first and foremost for a wider participation in the government to get over this difficult stage."

This was a clear indication that the army top brass was not happy with the narrow-based Sadiq-Turabi alliance and were out for wider participation in the government to break the siege and isolation the country was in at that time. By then, the Netherlands and a number of other countries had stopped development aid to Sudan and made its resumption conditional on progress on the peace front. After some manoeuvring, Sadiq al-Mahdi declared on March the 5th that he has accepted the idea of widening participation in the government but the new cabinet was not made public till March 22, 1989. The formation was made possible by Sadiq's endorsement on March the 16th of the

---

4   *Alwan* newspaper, 25 February 1989.

DUP-SPLA agreement, after exactly five months of prevarication. The NIF decided not to participate in this government.

In its first meeting on March 26, 1989, the new cabinet formed a ministerial committee known as "the Peace Committee" chaired by Mr Sid Ahmed El-Hussein, the 1st Deputy Prime Minister and Minister of Foreign Affairs. The committee included three members from outside the cabinet. These were: General (R) Yousif Ahmed Yousif (DUP), Prof. Hamad Omer Bagadi (Umma) and Dr Taisier Ahmed Ali, Lecturer in the University of Khartoum. All the four were known for their tireless efforts to bring about a negotiated peace settlement with the SPLA. This move augured well for peace and the SPLA was duty bound to reciprocate.

On April the 3rd, the Constituent Assembly voted by a majority of two-thirds to endorse the Sudanese Peace Initiative. This opened the way for fresh peace talks with the SPLA. Indeed, the three non-cabinet members of the government Peace Committee were in Addis Ababa in the first week of April for a meeting with the SPLA to prepare for the first round of peace talks between the new government and the SPLA. This is the climate under which the one-month declaration of cease fire was made.

Internationally, there was the upcoming trip to Bonn on May 26, 1989 to address the Bundestag the timing of which was out of the Chairman's control. He was very keen to attend it and capture every moment of it to great advantage. This trip was also dovetailed with an invitation from the ICRC in Geneva for the chairman to meet its representatives there early June. It was definitely expedient to carry out these diplomatic contacts in an atmosphere of peace at home.

So much for reading between the lines. The lines of the statement itself are there for every interested person to read. One final note on the issue is that I had the privilege to get a hint from the Chairman on the forthcoming declaration of the ceasefire. This was in Panyigor on April 23, 1989. When he was prepared to drive away, I was close by to salute him off. He called me to get closer and while seated in the car he dropped the hint. As the car was about to take off, I snapped to attention and saluted the Chairman. The car sped away and I kept the matter to myself.

A couple of days after declaring the ceasefire, the Chairman was picked up by a helicopter from Akobo to Addis Ababa. The enemy troops in Akobo withdrew from the garrison without a fight in the small hours of April 12, 1989 and joined their brethren in Waat garrison. The SPLA commander around the town, A/Cdr Peter Panom Thanypiny, then sent a radio message to the Chairman reporting that "Akobo town has fallen into the hands of the gallant SPLA forces after seven days of heavy fighting"! Such false claims are not uncommon among SPLA field officers and have on several occasions caused great embarrassment to the superior command.

The First talks with a Government Delegation

In Khartoum, the reaction of the Prime Minister to the cease fire announcement was typically non-specific. He was quoted in a newspaper as saying: "for every one step taken by the SPLA we will reciprocate by taking two steps." He pointed out that the army would observe the cease fire but affirmed that it would remain vigilant. Furthermore, he proposed setting up a joint committee to enforce the cease fire. This proposal was rejected by the SPLA on the grounds that the committee would only be relevant when the government implements the DUP-SPLA agreement.

In Addis Ababa, the SPLA sent a message on the 25th of May to the Peace Committee in Khartoum proposing to meet it in Addis Ababa on Saturday, the 10th of June. This was agreed upon.

I flew to Addis Ababa on Wednesday the 7th of June to prepare for the meeting with the Ministerial Peace Committee. I had been earlier appointed the leader of the SPLA delegation to the talks. These talks had a special significance as it was the first time for the SPLA to hold peace talks with the Government of Sudan. All the previous talks have been held with political parties and trade unions, either as a group, such as the Koka Dam Conference and Ambo workshop, or singly such as meeting with the Umma Party in July 1986 and with the DUP in 1988. As a matter of fact, the two sides to the talks were led by the same persons who led the two delegations in the DUP-SPLA discussions leading to the Sudanese Peace Initiative signed on November 16, 1988. This was considered by many as an encouraging sign and raised the hopes for a positive outcome to emerge from the meeting.

The peace talks convened in the afternoon of Saturday the 10th of June. In the opening session, I addressed the meeting on behalf of the SPLA pointing out that peace was the wish of the Sudanese people stressing the movement's position that should the Government implement the provisions of the Initiative, there would be no problem in achieving peace. For the Ministerial Peace Committee, Mr Sid Ahmed El Hussein addressed the meeting reaffirming that peace was the wish of the whole Sudanese nation saying that the talks would naturally take time and hoped that all participants would be patient, understanding and tolerant so that final agreement could be reached. The meeting also received a message from Dr John Garang, who was then in Washington, wishing the meeting success. He urged the leaders in Sudan not to miss this opportunity to do their best to achieve peace.

The two sides were agreed that the Sudanese Peace Initiative was the basis of the peaceful settlement to the conflict. The SPLA side was insistent on the fulfilment of the pre-requisites contained in the Initiative so that the National Constitutional Conference which will resolve all the outstanding problems is held. Therefore, the meeting was for the government side to report on the steps they had taken so far towards the implementation of the Initiative.

The discussions centred on the abrogation of the military pacts between Sudan and other countries, specifically with Egypt and Libya. The Government side maintained that the Libyan agreement already expired. Signed in Tripoli on June 29, 1985 by Brig. Osman Abdalla Mohammed, the then Minister of Defence in the Transitional Government, the military protocol for mutual defence facilities was to last for one year. On the defence pact with Egypt, the Government side explained that the Prime Minister, Sadiq -al-Mahdi, had written to the Egyptian Prime Minister asking for the abrogation of the pact by mutual consent and that the latter had replied in writing giving his agreement to the abrogation.

On the "hudud," the Government side stated that the Government had decided that sentences involving "hudud" would not be implemented, although the courts continue to hand down such punishments. The SPLA side saw this as miscarriage of justice and that what was required was to strike out "hudud" punishments and replace them with other appropriate ones. In this sense an act of parliament was required.

The talks went on late into the night and resumed the next day. In the afternoon of June 11, 1989, the meeting ended and the two delegations issued a joint press statement on the talks just concluded. In their statement, the two delegations agreed that the steps taken by the governments of Sudan and Egypt for the abrogation of the Joint Defence pact by mutual consent were positive and that what remained was its ratification by the Constituent Assembly. In regard to the Sudanese-Libyan protocol, the two delegations differed. The Ministerial Peace Committee considered the steps taken by the Council of Ministers as satisfying the purpose of this provision whereas the SPLM/A delegates believed otherwise. Both sides, however, agreed to resolve their difference on the issue in a meeting between them to be held later. The Ministerial Peace Committee delegation and that of the SPLM/A differed on the provision relating to the freezing of the hudud. The Ministerial Peace Committee considered the steps already taken as satisfactory whereas the SPLM/A delegation underlined the necessity of an act by the Constituent Assembly to effect the freezing of the hudud. The statement concluded that both sides agreed to meet again on July 4, 1989 to follow up the implementation of the provisions of the Sudanese Peace Initiative and fixed September 18, 1989 as the date for convening the National Constitutional Conference provided that the prerequisites stipulated in the initiative have been implemented to the satisfaction of both sides. That afternoon, the Government delegation was packing to leave for Khartoum with a lot of hope and great expectations. At long last, it seemed the light of peace was beginning to emerge at the end of the dark tunnel of war. If a week is a long time in politics, then three weeks must certainly be very long indeed. The meeting scheduled for the 4th of July did not materialize; it was overtaken by serious developments in Khartoum five days earlier.

Visit to Kampala

Colonel Muamar El-Ghazafi of Libya has been depicted as flamboyant, capricious, etc. Some quarters even call him names. But like any human being, he has lasting impressions. One of these, in my view, is his respect for Dr John Garang. When the latter, heading a high-level SPLA delegation, met Col. Ghazafi in Tripoli in March 1984, he left a deep impression on the Libyan leader. Ghazafi has held him in high esteem ever since. It is true the two differed when Nimeiri was overthrown on April 6, 1985 but this is a story on its own. What is important to underline here is that Ghazafi did not change his personal opinion about Dr John Garang. For example, Sadiq al-Mahdi, who held strong ties with Ghazafi, invited the Libyan leader to Khartoum to attend Independence Day Celebrations in 1988. The occasion was held at the Khalifa square opposite the Mahdi tomb in Omdurman. As was to be expected, Sadiq's speech was full of abuse of the SPLA in general and its leader in particular. When Ghazafi spoke he had words of praise about Dr John Garang to the great embarrassment of his hosts. After the events of 1985, Ghazafi has been wanting to meet Dr John Garang but the latter has been unwilling. He did not feel safe in Tripoli. I personally know that since late 1986, messages have been received through the Libyan ambassador in Addis Ababa, Mr Khalifa Bazelya, who not only arranged the first visit to Tripoli but was instrumental in and saw through the period of cordial relations between the SPLA and Libya. First, Ghazafi wanted Garang to visit him in Tripoli for talks. This was turned down and Garang suggested Addis Ababa as a venue instead. Diplomatic niceties aside, Dr John Garang should have known that this was a non-starter for the simple reason that the relations between Libya and Ethiopia were by then at the lowest ebb. In fact, I do not remember Ghazafi visiting Addis at that time even for the yearly OAU Conference. From 1988 when relations between the SPLA and President Yoweri K. Museveni began to warm up, Ghazafi proposed Kampala as the venue for him to meet with Dr John Garang. There was an exchange of messages, the only one I got involved in was in May 1989.

I was in Kapoeta when I received instructions from the Chairman to leave for Kampala as soon as possible to meet President Museveni. The purpose of the meeting was to apologise to President Museveni that he (the Chairman) could not turn up for the meeting with Col. Ghazafi that had been arranged in Kampala. The reason for not being able to attend was-according to the Chairman - "that he was a thousand kilometres from the Ugandan border" and thus could not have made it in time. This explanation of his whereabouts was untrue. But this was not what struck me most about the affair. My real surprise was that, as Director of OCER, I was unaware of the arrangements for a Kampala meeting between the Chairman and Col. Ghazafi and could not have possibly known were it not that he wanted to use me to play the unsavoury role of conveying unconvincing apologies.

All the same I formed a delegation there on the spot. It comprised: A/Cdr Bior Ajang Duot, the commander of the Chairman's bodyguards and Chief of logistics in the Kapoeta - Torit area; Captain Edward Abiei Lino, the Civil-Military Administrator of Kapoeta, Captain Locho Lokunen, the Military Commander of Kapoeta and Captain William Kong Tut, the Military Commander of Ikotos. We drove from Kapoeta through Ikotos to Kitgum. There, we were picked up by a helicopter to Kampala.

In Kampala we were met by the commander of the Ugandan Army, General Salim Salih; a tall young man in his thirties. We got introduced and he took us for lunch at the Nile Hotel. Recently renovated, the hotel was very impressive and contrasted sharply with the surrounding area which still looked dilapidated from the effects of war that ended in January 1986.

At lunch, the general talked a lot about this war and his role in it. He showed us a big scar in his arm which he said was a result of a wound he sustained in combat and added that he commanded the force that stormed the Uganda Radio station on victory day. He prided himself of being the youngest General in the world! I heard some people say he was President Museveni's brother but I did not confirm this; I was not interested to know. After lunch we were taken to a military camp at Bombo where we spent the night.

The next day the General came early in the morning and took us to the Market to buy us some clothes to be in an acceptable appearance to meet the President. We very much appeared "bush-like". I thanked him on behalf of the group for the hospitality and his generosity. Each of us bought a full suit, a shirt, a tie, one pair of shoes, a pair of socks and underclothes. We were now ready to see the President. Before he bade us goodbye that evening, the General told us that he is not a politician, only a loyal military officer. Whatever orders the President gives him he will execute in full. Therefore, he concluded, we should ask for everything we want from the President. We appreciated the advice.

General Salim Salih accompanied us to Sate House in Entebbe in the morning to see the President. After some waiting he ushered us in and quickly withdrew. The President was sitting in the courtyard of the Palace and we took our seats on the chairs which had already been made ready for us. Without much introduction, the President asked a direct question: Where is Dr John Garang? Pretending not to have understood the motive behind the question, I gave a direct answer that he was in the Southern Sudan and precisely in Upper Nile but quickly added that he sends his best regards and had instructed me to pass an urgent message to him. I saw him beckoning to me to go ahead. I spoke about how thankful the Chairman was for his tireless efforts to see that a meeting takes place between him and their mutual friend Col. Ghazafi and that at the end of the day it was the SPLA that stood to benefit, that the Chairman was keen to come and that when he realized that he could not make it in time, he saw it courteous to send a senior member of the movement to explain the reasons and hear from the President what can be done next.

The President had his doubts. He replied that John should understand that he is a guerrilla leader and not a head of state. A guerrilla, he said, should knock at every door he could find. He stressed that he knew Col Ghazafi wanted to assist the SPLA if he can only meet Dr John Garang. If Garang had his fears about Tripoli, he should feel at home in Kampala. As he saw it, Garang had nothing to lose. The worst that can happen, he averred, was for them to disagree here and each goes back to where he came from. But, he affirmed, from what he knew about Ghazafi such an outcome was unlikely.

I thought this statement by the President was an eye-opener for us and what was needed was to assure him that we were going to convey to the Chairman his invaluable advice and add our voice for the necessity of the meeting to take place as soon as possible. Then Captain Edward Abiei Lino dropped a gaffe. He said given the state of relationship between the SPLA and Tripoli it was, to quote him: "necessary to break the ice" through a lower level meeting first before the two leaders could meet. I could see the face of the President change. He retorted: "Ice? What ice? You are talking like diplomats and not like guerrillas." He continued that a guerrilla should not care about diplomatic niceties but go straight to the crux of the problem, that as far as he was concerned, the crux of the matter here was for Dr John Garang to meet Col. Ghazafi. He gave an example as to how, in the Nairobi Meeting between him and the Okellos, some of his guerrilla colleagues wanted to make a fuss about in front of which delegation would the Ugandan flag be placed. He had to stop that nonsense, he stated, by ruling that the flag must be in front of the Okellos as they were then the sitting government in Kampala. Then it began to drizzle and we had to change position. The President led the way and we followed close by.

We were now sitting under a tent. The interregnum must have rekindled the ice-issue in the mind of the President. He started by asking what each of us was doing before joining the SPLA. I answered for the whole delegation pointing at the person concerned as I spoke. I told the President that I was trained as a Chemical Engineer and was lecturer at the University of Khartoum for six years before joining the SPLA; A/Cdr Bior Ajang Duot was a teacher at the Primary level, Captain Edward Abiei Lino was a student in the Faculty of Law in the University of Khartoum, discontinued in the second year and took up a number of jobs before joining the SPLA; the other two were students. Looking at Edward, the President said: "I see, so you had a legal training! This is why you talk more like a diplomat than a guerrilla." He then revisited his insistence on the importance of the meeting and that he will not be visiting any place outside Uganda for the whole month of June and, firmly concluded: "I expect Dr John Garang to come here to meet Col. Ghazafi."

This is what I knew it will come to. I assured the President that the point was well taken and we were going to inform the Chairman straightaway. I then proceeded to brief him on the political and military situation in Sudan and ended my speech by putting to him some requests to assist the movement.

The President began to discuss the strategy and tactics of the war being prosecuted by the SPLA. Among what he said, he questioned the wisdom of taking the war to North Sudan (Kurmuk, etc) and that he had raised this point with Garang before. He also felt the SPLA needed to concentrate on civil and political structures. On recruitment, he advised that the leadership of the SPLA should be able to estimate in advance the maximum number of recruits it can get adding that this was not difficult to arrive at as we had no factories and other institutions, like the government, which absorb some youths. Without this, he went on, it does not make sense to talk of a protracted war. He made some other interesting remarks.

At the end of the meeting, General Salim Salih was called in and he took us to the Nile Hotel where we waited to be taken to Kitgum. In the afternoon, the General informed us that he was hosting a party that evening in honour of a number of Tanzanian military instructors who were training his officers but their term of service had expired and were on their way back to Tanzania. He then asked my permission for him to invite the youngest two officers in my delegation (whom he called his agemates) to the party. We looked at each other in astonishment but finally agreed to his request. In the evening when the General sent his ADC to collect the two (Cap. Locho Lokunen and Capt. William Kong Tut) we cautioned them to behave themselves and not to take any alcoholic drinks. In the morning the two officers informed us that the General had gotten dead drunk in the party and that it were the two of them who literally carried him into his car!

We flew back to Kitgum on a helicopter the next day. There, we got our cars ready and drove back to Kapoeta where we prepared our report about the visit. We unanimously agreed to recommend to the Chairman that he goes to Kampala in June as proposed by President Museveni. I sent a summary of our report to the Chairman by radio. A day after, he replied that Kampala was not safe as "Ghazafi's hitmen are freely roaming the place", that in his last visit to Kampala a bomb exploded in the hotel he was in just a few hours from the time he checked out, and that he will not be able to go to meet Ghazafi there.

A/Cdr Bior Ajang Duot was in the delegation of the Chairman in the visit to Kampala referred to in his message and since I did not hear before the story of this bomb that had just missed the Chairman, I decided that A/Cdr Bior was the right man to ask. While chatting one day and without indicating as to where I heard the story from, I asked A/Cdr Bior Ajang Duot what he knew about it. His answer was a categorical expression of ignorance and added that the story must have been created by "agitators" against the Chairman! I did not disclose to him my source but informed him and the other members of the delegation that our recommendation for a Kampala visit in June was not acceded to by the Chairman for security reasons.

In Addis after long absence

My presence in Addis Ababa during the peace talks was the first opportunity to take direct charge of the affairs at the OCER HQ in Addis Ababa after three months absence. So I thought. During that period, it was the Head of Administration and Finance, A/Cdr Deng Alor Kwol, who was the acting Director, especially on the coordination part and the actual immediate administration of the affairs in the office. I found that the directives I had left with him in March were not implemented. The accountant, Isaac Kot, was sent to the refugees camp (Itang) for no good reason and the A/Cdr had relapsed to his old method of doing everything alone exactly as he was the Director of the office of the Chairman. Capt. Deng Alor Kwol had taken over as the Director of the Chairman's office in Addis Ababa from Major Riek Machar Teny in September 1985. He remained in that office ever since except on one occasion when he became Deputy to Cdr Martin Manyiel Ayuel, who became Director of the Chairman's office in October 1986. Cdr Martin did not stay long in that office for in late 1987 he was transferred to Itang and then to the field. A/Cdr Deng Alor Kwol then became again the Director. As already mentioned when the office was reorganized and changed role to OCER the Chairman appointed him the Deputy Director. All in all, Deng Alor Kwol has been continuously in Addis Ababa since 1985 and remained there up to the time the SPLA was asked by the EPRDF government to pack up and leave in May 1991! One would expect a person staying for such an extraordinarily long period in one place to have exceptional qualities of leadership and administrative skills. Not at all, he is lazy, incompetent and has no sense of public accountability (he dishes out public cash from his pocket without the slightest sense of remorse!). He hides his incompetence behind forgetfulness. As it will be recalled such forgetfulness almost cost us the life of comrade Dhol Acuil Aleu, that of a pilot, who has been a friend of the movement for long, and the plane itself over Boma in 1986. On the personal level, he is quite sociable and a "jolly nice fellow." But that is all there is to the man. Very few in the SPLA took him seriously.

The weakness of A/Cdr Deng Alor Kwol on official matters were obvious to all and sundry in the SPLA. On many occasions his behaviour caused the movement embarrassment with diplomats and political allies. The Chairman himself admits. Yet, there was and still remains a sense of personal loyalty between the two that eluded comprehension by others. This is the only explanation available for keeping Deng in such a sensitive position for so long despite everything else that did not work for him.

I set out to enforce discipline in the office and get things back to gear. However, I was on the move again. As soon as the talks with the Ministerial Peace Committee were over, I was instructed by the Chairman to fly to Cairo through Nairobi forthwith. I did this on the 13th of June; less than a week from the moment I arrived Addis on the 7th.

The First Trip to Cairo

Our delegation to Cairo was led by Cdr. William Nyuon Bany who joined me in Nairobi with the other members of the delegation. These included Capt. Michael Majok Ayom, Capt. Dau Aleer Abit and Capt. Justin Yac Arop. Before flying to Cairo, the delegation delivered a written message from the Chairman to President Daniel T. arap Moi of Kenya.

In Cairo, we were received by Mr Hilmy Namar, the Minister of Public Security, Mr Mohammed Abdel Salam, the Under-Secretary and other staff of the Ministry. We held several meetings in which we discussed the situation in Sudan. The Egyptian authorities urged us to be flexible in the peace talks with the government of Sudan which were expected to resume on the 4th of July. Our delegation also paid a courtesy visit to Mr Boutrus Boutrus Ghali, the State Minister for Foreign Affairs, in his office at the Ministry. We also had an opportunity to address the Southern Sudanese students in the African Society Centre in Cairo.

Before we left Cairo, a tour was organized for the delegation to visit the Suez Canal area, especially the Barlev line, and Port Said free port.

I was in Cairo when the mass media carried on June 21, 1989 news on a foiled coup attempt in Khartoum. SUNA carried a press statement made by the Minister of Defence, General (R) Abdel Magid Hamid Khalil, that afternoon which claimed that the coup attempt was masterminded by elements loyal to the former Nimeiri regime who had succeeded to persuade some elements in the army to take part. The Minister disclosed that 25 civilians and military personnel were arrested in connection with the coup attempt. When I met President Hosni Mubarak he asked me what I made of the news of the attempted overthrow of Sadiq al-Mahdi. I replied in Arabic that in my view Sadiq was crying wolf and related to him a fable, famous in the Sudanese elementary schools, about a certain shepherd and a tiger. The shepherd while looking after his sheep one day sounded alarm to the village shouting that his herd was attacked by a tiger. The men in the village rushed to the scene only to find out that the tiger never attacked! They admonished the shepherd and went back to the village. Another day the shepherd raised the false alarm again and the villagers being keen to save their son and sheep, could not ignore him. They rushed once more to the scene but to find out again that they have been hoaxed. Some days after, the tiger attacked the shepherd himself and his cries for help were ignored by the villagers. The tiger killed him and that was his shameful end. I told the President that by raising this false alarm Sadiq al-Mahdi is running the risk of being left to his fate when the real coup d'etat takes place. The President laughed heartily.

I left Cairo for Addis on the 27th of June. On the 30th Sadiq al-Mahdi was overthrown in a military coup. That morning Mr Ahmed Izzat, 1st Secretary in the Egyptian embassy in Addis Ababa who was in charge of SPLA contacts, was desperately looking for me. We met in the afternoon and he told me that he had received an urgent message from Cairo instructing him to find out from me who the coup makers in Khartoum were. When I expressed ignorance, I could read signs of disbelief in his face. Could he or his boss in Cairo have been told about my conversation with the President?

A day before I left Cairo, I gave an interview to Mr Salah Abdel Latif of the Middle East News Agency (MENA), in which I commended the positive role Egypt was playing towards the resolution of the conflict in Southern Sudan as Egypt had led wide diplomatic efforts in mediation between the SPLA and the Government. I also welcomed the abrogation of the Sudan-Libya military protocol and the freezing of the September Islamic laws by a resolution of the Constituent Assembly. I concluded my interview by confirming that the follow-up meeting between the SPLA and the Government was to take place in Addis Ababa on the 4th of July, expressing optimism on the prospects for a peaceful resolution of the conflict and adding that at the moment I spoke there was no fighting taking place in the South because of the observation of cease fire that was still effective. These statements were carried in the Egyptian papers on June 27, 1989.

A Coup d'état in Khartoum

On Friday June 30, 1989, a group of officers headed by Brigadier Omer Hassan Ahmed al-Bashir took over power in Khartoum. Little was known about the political affiliation of al-Bashir except some reference made in 1985 in an Arabic magazine "EL-DASTOUR" that he was by then planning a coup d'etat on behalf of the Muslim Brotherhood. The paper itself, an organ of the Arab Baathist Party of Iraq, is not reputed for accurate reporting and the piece did not attract the attention of many of its readers. It was only now, four years on, that it made sense.

On July the 2nd, the third day after the takeover, the Junta sent a delegation composed of three officers to Addis Ababa with a letter to the Chairman and C-in-C of the SPLA. The three officers were: Brig. Babiker Nasar, the military attache in Addis Ababa, Brig. Kamal Ali Mukhtar, Deputy Director of military intelligence and a confidant of al-Bashir, and Col. Mathiang Malwal of the military intelligence. The letter expressed the willingness of the coup makers to hold immediate peace talks with the SPLA. The Chairman issued strict orders to us in Addis that the delegation should not be met nor should the letter be received. The Khartoum delegation spent three days in Addis Ababa making desperate attempts to contact the SPLA office but to no avail. At one point, Col. Mathiang Malwal got Capt. Edward Abiei Lino, his brother-in-law, on the telephone and wanted to pass their message. The latter told him that unless he had some family matters to discuss, their conversation would have to end. The delegation returned to Khartoum baffled.

Some of us were at a loss as to the wisdom of such a hard line position. After all, it was the declared policy of the movement to talk peace to the government of the day in Khartoum. What was wrong in receiving the letter and telling the delegation to give the SPLA time to study it? Well, orders are orders and we had to comply. As it is now known, the SPLA met a delegation of the Junta in August 1989 and again in November/December 1989 to talk peace.

On the 2nd of July, the Chairman sent a radio message to all the

High Command members on the change of government in Khartoum and that any person who had ideas to contribute on the matter was welcome to send them to him. By then there were three High Command members in Addis Ababa: Cdr William Nyuon Bany, Cdr Lwal Diing Wol and I. When I received my message, I contacted the other two and impressed on them the need to discuss together the message from the Chairman. Cdr William agreed and we had a meeting under his chairmanship, in the office that evening. I explained to the meeting that the change of government in Khartoum and its effect on the situation in the country was a serious matter that required a full meeting of the High Command to consider. Sending ideas to the Chairman was not the best way because it was a one-way communication. It lacked the interactive process provided by a meeting in one place, in which somebody may be persuaded by the arguments of others to change his views and adopt new ones. William pointed out that some High command members were far in the field and could not possibly come in time for a meeting. I retorted that there was a good number of them not very far away: Cdr Salva Kiir was in Pibor area; Cdr James Wani Igga was in Dima; Cdr Kwol Manyang Juuk in Torit; Cdr Gordon Kong Chol in Nasir and Cdr Galerio Modi Hurnyang in Kapoeta. All of them had access to various means of transport and could be in Gambela where the Chairman was within a few days. These five, the three of us and the Chairman would make a total of nine out of the thirteen members of the High Command. The nine should meet, I continued, together receive the responses of the other four and discuss the issue at hand to come out with the true position of the SPLA. The meeting agreed to my proposal and Cdr William Nyuon sent a message to this effect to the Chairman. The next day the Chairman responded summoning us to Gambela. Significantly, the message stated: "since the meeting cannot take place in Addis Ababa, the three of you are to come to Gambela"!

We left Addis Ababa for Gambela by car on Tuesday, the 4th of July. When we arrived there on the 5th we were directed to proceed to Pinywudo where the Chairman was. We arrived there in the evening. In the morning of the 6th we were taken to address a parade of the

"Red Army". In the afternoon we drove back to Gambela. We were now five for Cdr James Wani Igga had arrived from Dima. Two more days passed without a meeting and when we finally met there was no sign that the others were instructed to come nor were there responses from them on the first message of the Chairman soliciting their views on the coup in Khartoum.

At the end of the meeting, Cdr. James Wani and I were asked to draft the policy statement which the Chairman will deliver over Radio SPLA on the position of the movement on the situation in the country following the coup d'etat. We completed our assignment within 24 hours after which we reported back to the Chairman. He told all of us who were present in the meeting that he would not make his speech soon as it "would provoke the Junta into military action when the SPLA was not yet ready"! Such a statement was a surprise to me for if there was no such hurry to make the statement why was he reluctant to call for a meeting of all the members of the High Command? Regarding the provocation of the Junta, I do not know what could be more provocative than the way their delegation in Addis was treated!

I left Gambela for Addis Ababa by car on July 11, 1989 and from there I flew to Nairobi on the 16th.

As it turned out, Radio SPLA had the onus of announcing a date for the expected speech just to cancel it some days later. The speech was not delivered till August 14, 1989, after a month from our meeting, with the contents substantially altered. It was redrafted by Dr Mansour Khalid. The frequency of putting off the broadcast of the speech sent rumours flying as to what might have befallen the Chairman, the wildest of which was that he was in the plane of the U.S. Congressman Mickey Leland which crashed in the mountains near Gambela in July killing all on board.

The last postponement in delivering the Chairman's speech, however, had nothing to do with him nor with the SPLA in general. It was due to the Ethiopian Security. The Chairman was going to the studio on the morning of August 10, 1989 to get the speech recorded when the security officer in charge of the SPLA informed the Chairman that he had orders from his boss, comrade Andarge, that he would like to go over the speech first before it could go into the air. It was a disconcerting demand. First, it was unprecedented and, second, it came at a most inappropriate time, in a couple of days the Chairman was to fly to Havanna and from there to Managua, Nicaragua. Should the visit be delayed? A copy of the speech was served to the Security Chief and we waited for two more days for his green light to come. It did not! What could be happening? We wondered. Could the Ethiopians have struck a deal with the Junta behind our backs? But the Chairman had just met President Mengistu who concurred with him on the analysis of the situation, or could this be a part of "dividing the roles"? Many more questions sprang to our minds. Whatever the real position of the Ethiopians was, we hoped they would not interfere with the arrangements for the trip to Latin America. We therefore, decided that the Chairman was to record his speech on tape and leave it with us behind to be played whenever the Ethiopian Security gives its consent. Should they go to the extent of suggesting amendments, then these would be made and the speech to be read by somebody else on behalf of the Chairman. Thank God, the Ethiopians allowed the trip to go ahead and the Chairman left for Havanna as scheduled. Not long after that, the Security gave its consent for the speech to be broadcast without amendments and so the tape left behind by the Chairman went into the air on the 14th and 15th of August 1989. By that time, he was thousands of kilometres away from the continent.

Radio SPLA had an immediate problem more disturbing than just the inconvenience of announcing a date and putting it off. It had to run its programmes for a month and a half without an official policy of the movement towards Khartoum! This may be easy in the case of a City Radio running pop music, call-in programmes or anything of the like. But inconceivable in case of a mouthpiece of a rebel movement in which all programmes are geared towards political propaganda and agitation. This was the most drab period for Radio SPLA. Most of the time was spent broadcasting statements issued against the regime by the proscribed political parties and trade unions, newspapers and magazines writings critical of the regime, lists of those detained by the regime, etc. After all this could the Junta in Khartoum be so daft not to deduce where the SPLA stood?

When the speech was finally broadcast those mostly surprised were in the SPLA for the speech had given undue emphasis on the issues of "separation" and "democracy" out of proportion.

Meeting with the Government Delegation

It was generally considered that Egypt had helped lever al-Bashir into power in Khartoum. Of course, it was common knowledge Sadiq al-Mahdi's relations with Cairo were very cool. Whatever the truth is about this assumption, it must have been fuelled by the alacrity with which the Egyptian establishment received the coup in Khartoum. The Minister of Security, Mr Hilmy Namar, visited Khartoum on July 1, 1989; the second day of the coup. President Mubarak took upon himself the duty to do the public relations for the Junta in Khartoum when he was meeting the heads of State and government in Paris on the bicentennial anniversary of the Paris Commune. Also, during the OAU summit in Addis Ababa in July he never lost a moment to talk well about the officers who had just assumed power in Khartoum describing them as untainted by partisan politics and being "clean officers". He said this much to the Chairman and our delegation that met him in Addis Ababa during the summit. I had very much wanted to see President Mubarak that day but I could not as I was down with severe malaria.

Given the good disposition of Egypt towards the Junta it continued its role to broker peace between the SPLA and the government in Khartoum. Contacts were made with Addis Ababa and it was finally agreed that the two sides were to meet on August 19, 1989 to talk peace. The two delegations arrived Addis Ababa on time for the peace talks to begin. On the SPLA side, I was the leader of the delegation and the other members were: Cdr Lwal Diing Wol, Dr Mansour Khalid, Cdr Stephen Duol Chol, A/Cdr Deng Alor Kwol, Capt. Nhial Deng

Nhial, Capt. Justin Yac Arop, Capt. Mohamed Saeed Bazaraa, Capt. Abdel Hameed Abbas, 1st Lt. Zamba Duku and 1st. Lt. Yasir Saeed Aarman. Except for Dr Mansour, we were in full military fatigue and had a press team equipped with a video camera. The government delegation was of the same number and was led by Col. Mohammed El-Amin Khalifa, member of the Revolutionary Command Council. It included: Brig. Babikar Nasar; Brig. Kamal Ali Mukhtar; Prof. Muddathir Abdel Rahim, lecturer in political science in the University of Khartoum; Dr Abdalla Idris, Dean of the Faculty of Law, University of Khartoum; Ambassador Osman Nafie, the Sudanese ambassador in Ethiopia, Mr Ali Nimeiri and others. There was not a single Southerner on the delegation! Before the start of the meetings I had asked the permission of Col. Khalifa to allow our pressmen to record the proceedings of the talks by video and he agreed. So the SPLA had it all on tape.

In the tradition of the previous SPLA peace talks, there was no mediator in these talks. The sessions were chaired by rotation between the two leaders of delegations. I chaired the first session. I told the meeting that the gathering was due to a request from Khartoum and it was, therefore, in place to give the first opportunity to Col. Khalifa to put to the meeting the proposals they came with in order to bring about peace to the country.

Col. Khalifa took the floor. He gave an introduction on the pathetic state the country was in and why it was necessary for the "Salvation Revolution" to take place to lift the country from the abyss. On the peace process, he said that when they talk about peace their concern was about the soldiers in the trenches and that the issue of peace in the previous regime had become a matter for political manoeuvrings. He went on that war does not solve a problem and what was needed was to face the reality head on in order to achieve peace. He affirmed that they as a revolution were serious to attain peace through dialogue and urged that the two sides should seize the initiative to resolve the problem. He then outlined their position as comprising three stages as follows:

First Stage: to conduct a preliminary meeting to discuss the following:–
1. Ceasefire arrangements
2. Continuation and expansion of relief assistance
3. Cessation of press hostilities against each other
4. Establishment of direct communication channel(s) between the two sides.

Second Stage: convening a conference in Khartoum. The conference to be attended by the SPLA, the Government, national figures and Foreign personalities (if the two sides agree to have them).

Third Stage: measures to return life to normality in the three Southern provinces.

In conclusion, Col. Khalifa described the speech of the Chairman of the movement as negative and they did not intend to respond to it but hoped that their peace proposal will find positive response from the SPLA.

Our side concentrated on the contents of the speech of the Chairman just broadcast over Radio SPLA, copies of which were distributed to members of the government delegation before the meeting officially opened. We lambasted the Junta for having overthrown a democratically elected government; banning political parties and trade unions; detaining leaders of the parties and the unions; cashiering thousands from the army, police, prisons and wildlife services; and generally for making life hell in the country. The claims of the Junta that their move was a salvation revolution were ridiculed. Finally, the other side was told that if they had come to Addis Ababa to solve the "Southern Problem", they must have missed the road for they left the Southerners in Khartoum and other towns in the country. The SPLA was a national movement only interested in the resolution of the "National Problem."

Then followed what could be described as a tongue-lashing match of accusations and counter-accusations, challenges and counter-challenges in which the real issues were lost sight of. The first day of the talks ended on that note.

The second session of the talks opened at exactly 10:15 a.m. on Thursday the 20th of August. Col. Khalifa was in the chair. He opened the meeting by referring to what he termed negative aspects which emerged in yesterday's discussions. He hoped these will be avoided henceforward appealing to the participants to note that they were in the final analysis Sudanese whether there was war or not. He again reiterated their three-stage programme for bringing the war to an end. Next to speak was Ambassador Osman Nafie who said that the idea of the National Constitutional Conference advocated by the SPLA was neither clear nor specific. He, therefore, suggested that the SPLA should accept taking part in the Conference they proposed to take place in Khartoum. Should the idea be acceptable to the movement he would suggest that the conference be held without delay on October 1, 1989 and that the resolutions adopted by the conference be put to a referendum for ratification. Dr Abdalla Idris followed. He opined that the discussion needed a common language as it could not proceed if the legitimacy of one side is questioned by the other. He called upon the SPLA side to acknowledge the fact that there was a government then in Khartoum that it has to do business with. He went on to say that it would not be helpful to the discussions to talk about detentions and trade unions. He concluded by stressing that their side had presented specific proposals adding that if the other side was serious in the search for peace it should suggest alternative proposals.

I took the floor to respond to the points made by the Government side. I affirmed that the SPLA was serious to arrive at a peaceful settlement to the conflict by negotiations and assured the other side of the fact that we recognized them as the government of the day and that was why we were talking to them. I drew their attention to the fact that the search for peace did not just start with the coming to power of the Junta on the 30th of June, there was a wealth of previous experience to draw from. I concluded by reiterating that the SPLA believed that the Koka Dam Declaration and the Sudanese Peace Initiative constituted the framework for the peace process and it would save the country more time and lives to start from where the others stopped.

Two others spoke on our side elaborating on the points I made. Then Col. Khalifa gave Dr Justin Yac Arop the chance to speak. He spoke for more than half an hour which seemed to us like a year! Dr Justin spoke only about South Sudan and for him the SPLA was ready to discuss the Southern Problem with the Junta if they were serious. As this was contrary to the official position, I drew his attention in a slip of paper I passed to him. He read it but it did not seem to have made any difference; he went ahead all the same! Col. Khalifa enjoyed the talk and did not care about the long time the speaker took. After all, this was what they wanted and what could be more gratifying to them than to "see the SPLA showing its real colours"! The boredom (on our side, that is) was broken by a laughter when Brig. Kamal asked Dr Justin about what he meant by the word *"Ingaza"* that came repeatedly in his speech. *"Relief!"* replied Dr Justin. Brig. Kamal thought Dr Justin meant *"Ingaz"* which is the Arabic word for "salvation". He was disappointed because, as it turned out, the speaker meant *"Igatha"*, the Arabic word for "relief".

Another disappointment that day was Cdr Lwal Diing Wol. His speech was punctuated by constant use of the word "WE", when he dealt with the issues under discussion. When the other side asked him about what he meant by "WE", his answer was: "The Southerners". It appeared the Southerners were not left in Khartoum after all! They were right there in Addis Ababa talking to the Government delegation.

Our side found it difficult to accept the government's three-stage programme as it overlooked fundamental issues, especially the necessary prerequisites for holding a meeting in Khartoum in which the SPLA is expected to take part. But we did agree to the establishment of a direct communication channel between the two sides as necessary to pass messages on peace talks. The person agreed upon was the Sudanese ambassador in Addis Ababa. We then presented to the government side our four-point programme for peace as a substitute to their three-stage programme. The government side promised to study our proposals. Thus, ended the first round of peace talks with the new regime in Khartoum.

The SPLA four-point programme presented to the delegation of the Junta was contained in the speech of the Chairman which was broadcast on the 14th and the 15th of August. It is summarized as follows:

1 Establishment of an interim broad-based government of National Unity free of the various sectarianism (racial, religious, tribal or any other politicized localism) that have plagued and bled our country for the last 33 years of our formal independence.
2 Establishment of a national, non-sectarian, non-regional army from both the SPLA and the regular army.
3 The convening of the National Constitutional Conference by the interim government of national unity to resolve the country's fundamental problems based on the Koka Dam agreement and the Sudanese Peace Initiative.
4 Preparations for elections, holding those elections, ratification of the constitution by the elected constituent Assembly and the establishment of an elected government.

It is interesting to note that the first point excluded the Umma party, the DUP and the NIF, since they are religious sectarian parties, from participation in the broad-based government! As mentioned in Chapter 4 of this book, these three parties mustered more than 80% of the seats in the elected Constituent Assembly dissolved by the Junta on June 30, 1989. What then was the criterion for the broadness of the base of government? It is a question our delegation has always found difficult to answer. A member of the government delegation, Brig. Babiker Nasar, put it to us bluntly during the talks when he said:

"The dissolved parties: Umma, DUP and NIF are the majority and will continue to be so for 200 years to come."

The Junta holds a Conference:

On the 9th of September, the Junta convened what it called "The National Dialogue Conference on the Issues of Peace". The conference was chaired by Col. Mohammed El-Amin Khalifa with General (R) Joseph Lagu as one of two deputy chairmen. The membership included prominent non-partisan personalities, such as Dr Francis M. Deng and Mr Abel Alier, and members of the political parties the regime had just banned on "individual capacity". Mr Abel Alier declined from participating in the conference. The Junta also made it known that it had invited the SPLA to send members to the conference and that it would take all the necessary security measures to guarantee the security of the SPLA delegation in Khartoum. I was not aware of an official invitation of the sort but clearly the regime wanted to score propaganda points.

The Chairman's response to Khartoum's claim of having invited the SPLA to its conference was total denial stressing that even if Khartoum were to make such an invitation, it would have been rejected by the SPLA because the conference was Khartoum's business to which the SPLA is not party. This was the official SPLA position regarding the conference in Khartoum which went on up to the 21st of October 1989. During this period, I remember an incident in which a difference in interpretation of this official position between me and the Chairman would have left the listeners of Radio SPLA at a loss as to what was really the SPLA's stand on the issue. I was in Addis Ababa and wrote a commentary on the Dialogue Conference which was broadcast over Radio SPLA, in both English and Arabic. In the commentary, I concluded that the conference was a farce and called upon all the supporters and sympathizers of the movement and the democratic forces in the country to boycott it. The Chairman was in the field and did listen to the commentary. The name of the contributor was not mentioned by Radio SPLA but he definitely knew who he was. As the radio was tightly controlled by the Chairman very few in the SPLA cared to contribute pieces to its programmes.

The Chairman reacted by writing his own commentary in which he called upon the very political forces I had wanted to boycott the conference to take active part in it and use it as a platform to expose the Junta! To complicate matters more, he sent his commentary by radio straight to Radio SPLA without a copy to me. Fortunately, the acting Director of Radio SPLA, 1st Lt. Chaw Mayol Juuk, was a journalist with experience. On reading the Chairman's commentary, he realized something was wrong. He brought the piece to the office for me to read and to give him final directives on what to do. Trying hard to suppress my anger, I thanked him for acting in the way he did and told him with absolute finality that the piece was not going into the air. I saw relief in his face. Indeed, it was not broadcast. I was expecting the Chairman to ask me about it but he didn't and that was the end of it. I could not understand how a self-respecting organization decides to boycott a conference and at the same time urges its supporters to participate in it. Worse still, how will others view an organization that contradicts itself within 24 hours on such a fundamental issue of policy? These were the implications if that piece was to be broadcast.

Khartoum's Dialogue Conference continued under a glare of publicity and its conclusion on the 21st of October was marked by the Junta with a celebration and sense of achievement. It produced a report which was translated into English and bound with a red cover. The English translation of the first copies, mentioned therein to have been done in the Ministry of Foreign Affairs, was horrible! Immediately after that the Junta embarked on a large-scale globe-trotting exercise to sell to the world the "solution" they have just found to the Southern problem. Delegations led by members of the Revolutionary Command Council were sent to Europe, U.S.A., Asia and the African countries. This publicity stunt went on up to late November. Khartoum did not bother to serve the SPLA with a copy of the report it was publicizing the world over despite our earlier agreement on a direct communication channel on the issues of peace. It could not have been an unintended omission.

The Cease-fire Collapses

On the military situation, the ceasefire had collapsed in October with renewed fighting on a number of fronts; mainly in Southern Blue Nile, Rumbek, Kajo-Kaji and the Nuba Mountains. It is to be noted that, all along, the ceasefire declarations have been unilateral. The SPLA was the first to declare a one-month ceasefire on the 1st of May. This was renewed in June. On seizing power in Khartoum, al-Bashir declared his own unilateral ceasefire on the 1st of July. There never has been an agreement to form a joint commission to monitor the ceasefire. The SPLA was averse to such an idea. Sadiq al-Mahdi proposed it in May and this was dismissed off hand. The same reaction met the proposal of the Junta's delegation in the meetings of August when they wanted ceasefire arrangements to be discussed.

The Chairman and C-in-C had planned a major military offensive which was to take place in September. The main thrust of the offensive was to capture three objectives at about the same time. These were: Kurmuk in Southern Blue Nile, Rumbek in Bahr el-Ghazal and Kajo-Kaji in Eastern Equatoria. To support the capture and maintenance of these objectives, operations were to be intensified in all the other fronts; particularly in Southern Kordofan. The Chairman himself assumed the overall command of the Kajo-Kaji objective, Cdr William Nyuon that of Kurmuk and Cdr Salva Kiir Mayardit the overall command of Rumbek. Such was the importance attached to this military offensive that it was commanded by the three most senior leaders of the movement. The necessary logistics and troops movements to execute the plan were well behind schedule. It was only the Kurmuk front that saw action in October. Kurmuk town was attacked and after fierce fighting fell into the hands of the SPLA. The momentum of this magnificent victory was kept and the enemy garrisons around Kurmuk (Geizan, Yabus, Chali El-Fil, etc.) were quickly overrun by the SPLA. The SPLA prepared to consolidate its victories in Southern Blue Nile while the Government in Khartoum vowed to retake these areas. The theatre of war was set for a bloody showdown. This was the background to the political moves of the Junta which it embarked upon as of the 21st of October. In the midst of the tension and out of a blue, emerged the "Carter initiative".

The Carter Initiative

The former U.S. President, Jimmy Carter, visited Khartoum in mid-November 1989. His visit must have been connected with his mediation efforts in the Ethiopian conflict. President Carter was arranging peace talks between the Ethiopian Government and its armed opponents; the EPLF, TPLF, OLF, etc. The leaderships of these guerrilla fronts were based in Khartoum. After consultations with the main actors there and in Addis, the former U.S. President secured the agreement of the Ethiopian Government and the EPLF for peace talks to be convened between them in November in the Kenyan capital, Nairobi. Many political analysts on the situation in the Horn of Africa subscribed to what has become known as the "linkage theory", according to which the attainment of peace in Ethiopia and Sudan were linked and that no peace can be achieved in one country without achieving it in the other. The validity of such an assumption is doubtful but there is no denying of the fact that there is a relationship between the conflicts afflicting the two neighbouring countries. Whatever the former U.S. President perceived to be the situation on this matter, he made use of his presence in Khartoum to contact the authorities there on a possible second round of peace talks with the SPLA. He was not disappointed. From Khartoum he flew straight to Addis Ababa.

President Carter met the SPLA delegation on Saturday the 18th of November in the house of Mr Robert G. Houdek, the U.S. Head of Mission in Ethiopia (he should have been "ambassador" were it not for the low level status of the diplomatic relations between the two countries). Our side was led by the Chairman and included A/Cdr Deng Alor Kwol and myself. Besides the President and Mrs. Carter, Mr Houdek and Robert Frasure were present.

President Carter opened the meeting by making points on the OLS which al-Bashir had closed in November. He praised the operation and appreciated what was achieved in six months. He said he had given an award to UNICEF for their good work especially in the immunization of children. He regretted the fact that the closure of the OLS inevitably led to the cutting of aid to Sudan. According to him, al-Bahir said there was no way he could open OLS as long as the war was going on. Then President Carter briefed the meeting about his meeting with al-Bashir in Khartoum in which they discussed the peaceful resolution of the conflict in Sudan. He said he was given a full report (the National Dialogue Conference report referred to earlier) a copy of which he would make available to the SPLA. He went on that the report outlined some good ideas, such as guarantees for religious freedom, the right of each state to opt out of the application of the Islamic law, etc. He added that there were obviously some things that may not be acceptable to us but the conference resolutions could serve as a proposal. He asked the Chairman if the SPLA was ready to meet a government delegation on December 1, 1989. Possible venues for the meeting were Cairo, Nairobi or Addis.

President Carter made it clear that he thought the issue of the Constitutional Conference and related ones were ironed out in the Dialogue conference. He admitted there might be omissions but all matters can be decided in the peace talks. He said he had asked al-Bashir about his military agreements with Libya and Egypt, his reply was that they get arms because the SPLA was getting them from Israel and the neighbouring countries ruled by Christians. He also asked al-Bashir if he (President Carter) could relay al-Bashir's ideas about the meeting. The latter agreed and informed him that their delegation would be headed by Col. Mohammed El-Amin Khalifa and composed of seven or eight persons. President Carter concluded that it was his opinion that it was good for the SPLA to meet the government delegation. He suggested that either President Mubarak or President Mengistu could chair the peace talks.

Mr Robert Frasure contributed by saying that the situation in Sudan was at the edge of an explosion which may take people to square one. He advised the protagonists in the war to learn from the South African experience where the 1985 proposals were rejected by all the parties only to come back and accept them three years later in 1988 after a bloody stalemate.

The Chairman thanked President Carter for his concern and tireless efforts to bring about peace in both Sudan and Ethiopia. He explained the Junta's ill-intentions, that they were feverishly preparing for war while trying to isolate the SPLA internationally. He cited as an example the fact that the Junta failed to serve the SPLA with the report just made available by President Carter at the moment they were publicizing it all over the globe. On the OLS, the Chairman asserted that the OLS agreement was reached during the height of fighting and, thus, saw no sense in what al-Bashir said in that respect. He said the needs of the population in Southern Sudan for food and non-food relief items was still great and there was need for the OLS to resume. On the government's readiness to talk peace, the Chairman expressed his willingness for another round of peace talks to be convened. He stated that he was convinced that the SPLA cannot be destroyed by the Sudanese army nor can the SPLA destroy the army. It was this reality, he added, that needed to be driven into the minds of the Junta to be sensible and take the peaceful option seriously. He agreed for the meeting to take place on the suggested date but expressed reservations about Cairo as a venue saying that he would have no problem with either Nairobi or Addis Ababa as the meeting place.

President Carter settled for Nairobi and said that he would first seek the approval of President Moi before making an announcement on the matter. He left for Nairobi early morning the next day, met President Moi in the afternoon and held a press conference afterwards in which he made the announcement on another round of Sudanese peace talks to take place in December, 1989. The news item was reported widely in the mass media. For example, the London Guardian of Monday the 20th of November reported the following:

Addressing a news conference on his arrival in Nairobi, Mr Carter said he had persuaded both sides to hold fresh discussions without preconditions. Asked whether he intended to mediate on the Nairobi talks, Mr Carter said: 'My understanding from both sides is that they think they can initiate the talks again without mediation. My guess is that when they get past initial phase, they'll need some mediation in the main talks, but I would prefer that someone else do that. And if they want a mediator, I will help identify one'.

In Nairobi, President Carter became engaged in his mediation effort in the Ethiopian conflict. In the Sudan, the fighting went on unabated. If anything, the announcement of another round of peace talks had the effect of intensifying the fighting as each side wanted to go to the peace talks from a position of military advantage. The enemy's counter-offensive to retake Kurmuk took off from Ed-Damazin and heavy fighting was reported on that front in the week preceding the talks. In the last week of November, Rumbek was attacked by the SPLA and there was a lot of action on the Wau-Tonj and Tonj-Rumbek roads.

The SPLA delegation was constituted headed by me and the membership of Dr Mansour Khalid, A/Cdr Elijah Malok, A/Cdr Patrick Ayitang, Capt. Daniel Kodi Angelo, 1st Lt. Joseph Agoth, 1st. Lt. Yasir Saeed Aarman, 1st Lt. Zamba Duku and Dr Barnaba Marial Benjamin. Patrick, Daniel, Joseph and Zamba drove from Kapoeta to Nairobi; Dr Mansour Khalid flew in from Europe and Dr Barnaba from Harare. The other two and I left Addis for Nairobi on an Ethiopian airline flight on Wednesday the 29th of November. This flight got delayed in Addis Ababa and as a result we missed a prearranged meeting with President Carter set for late that afternoon. We checked in at the Panafric Hotel. No sooner we settled down than we received the disconcerting news that the enemy had broken through our defences around Kurmuk and had entered the town in the afternoon of November 28, 1989. This blow could not have come at a worse time. These are some of the few moments in the war where some reverses on the military front have political ramifications more than comparable reverses, even greater ones, at different times. Although we put up a brave face to it, we entered the peace talks two days later with the spectre of Kurmuk haunting us. The elation on the other side was unmistakable.

Our directives on the mediation were very specific. There should be none. President Carter had facilitated the coming together for the talks but that was the end of his role. The talks were to continue without him. President Carter did not see his role that way and we had a problem right from the start. Our meeting with President Carter took place on the 30th of November. It took six hours, three on the positions of each side, two on whether he should be a mediator or not and one for lunch. President Carter was insistent on chairing the meetings. The Junta side went along with this while our side continued to reject mediation. President Carter was bewildered. He could not understand why we were so inflexible on what seemed a matter of no real significance on the outcome of the talks. He spoke to the SPLA delegation in our hotel that evening with the sense of being let down displayed on his face. He thought we were going to welcome his mediation with open arms. A compromise arrangement was worked out. President Carter would chair the first two sessions of the general discussions after which he would withdraw but would have one of his assistants present in all the meetings with audio equipment. We took this decision on our own and did not consult the Chairman. The Junta's delegation saw our insistence on the point as an opportunity to knock our head against that of President Carter who they accused of sympathy with the SPLA's point of view. They almost succeeded.

After this episode, we were having lunch one afternoon hosted by President Carter. He made sure the two of us were alone on our table. We discussed a range of issues connected with the peace talks with obvious concentration on how to overcome the hurdle of the Islamic laws. He thought he could involve President Hosni Mubarak and Omer al-Bashir to intervene personally in order to resolve this issue. Then towards the end of our discussion he asked me two leading questions. He first asked whether the rank and file of the SPLA included communists. My answer was that the matter did not occur to me at all nor to the other leaders of the movement because we do not ask the combatants as to their political affiliations before joining the struggle. We needed every person who can carry arms as the liberation struggle needed all to be involved. He then asked whether there were communists in the High Command of the SPLA. I answered that I did not know of any of the thirteen members of the High Command who has declared himself one. I left lunch wondering whether the NIF delegation might have fed President Carter with their too familiar propaganda nonsense that I was a communist. I shared this encounter with some members of our delegation.

The peace talks were formally opened on the 30th of November by the Kenyan Deputy Minister of Foreign Affairs who gave a speech on the occasion. President Carter also delivered a speech, then followed the leaders of the two delegations. The delegates then settled to business. The meeting worked out a nine-point agenda to deliberate on. In his briefing to me, the Chairman was clear that the peace talks should not take long. He did not expect progress and in view of the military operations underway the Chairman stressed to me that it was going to be bad publicity for war communiques to be in the air while the two sides were talking peace. I agreed with him.

Following the withdrawal of President Carter from the chair-manship of the talks as agreed upon, the meetings were chaired by rotation between the two leaders of the two delegations. It was Col. Mohammed El-Amin Khalifa who chaired the first session and I chaired the second. In two days, we were through with the points on the agenda. President Carter was alarmed with the speed the delegates disposed of the points on the agenda. At one stage, while I was chairing the meeting, he requested permission to be present. I agreed and he took a seat. He followed the discussions up to the end of the meeting.

Later that evening, I received a message from the Chairman that our forces around Rumbek had attacked the town and they were doing very well. According to the briefing he had received from Cdr Salva Kiir, the Chairman believed the town was expected to fall in two or three days time. He instructed that I try to drag on with the talks for a longer period until the SPLA captures Rumbek! Of course, it was too late to do anything of the sort, the meetings had practically come to an end. I told him so. Interestingly, the situation in Rumbek was quite the opposite of what the Chairman was made to believe. I did not know this by the time but got it later from the officers who took part in the operation. There were obvious errors in the planning and execution. As a result we suffered a lot of casualties.

The Nairobi peace talks broke down on December 5, 1989 on a number of issues including the status of the Islamic law in Sudan. Each side issued a press release stating its version of what led to the failure to reach an agreement. President Carter, in a press statement placed the blame on both sides, saying "neither side came to Nairobi prepared to take the difficult steps necessary for peace."

President Carter felt somehow that I was the obstacle or at least made things difficult for an agreement to be reached at the Nairobi peace talks. He indicated this much in a letter he wrote to the Chairman, Dr John Garang, on the matter. I read the letter without bitterness; the thought in my mind was: "I wish he knew"! I did not meet President Carter again until four years later under totally different conditions. His mediation role had expanded. In addition to that between the SPLA and the Government of Sudan there was another within the SPLA itself.

In Kapoeta Town

After the end of the Nairobi peace talks, I left for Kapoeta. Apart from briefing the Chairman on the Nairobi peace talks, there was a couple of other issues to address. I had just received the report of the audit committee into the finances of the SRRA for the period when Dr Richard K. Mulla was the Secretary-General. The committee concluded that Dr Richard K. Mulla, Capt. Mayom Kuoc Malek and Capt. Nyang Jok Juuk had a case to answer for. The last is related to Dr John Garang by marriage, the two are married to sisters. I recommended to the Chairman that an investigation committee be formed in order to initiate the legal measures against the three officers. The approval of the Chairman for such a step to be taken was needed because Capt. Mayom Kuoc Malek was deployed by him at the HQ of Cdr Salva Kiir who was senior to me.

I was also to follow up the work of the SRRA Secretariat and satisfy myself with the progress they were making since my last meeting with them on the 25th of October. In that meeting they raised complaints on a number of issues: lack of comprehensive planning due to inexperience, absence of information sharing, sluggishness in decision making, drunkenness on duty and interference by filed commanders in the work of the SRRA. Most of the complaints were directed against the Secretary-General. James J. Duku, the liaison officer, also came under criticism for exceeding his powers most of the times. One of the coordinators, James Ajith, described Duku as acting "like a co-Secretary-General." I had explained to them that experience had to be gained but what was a must was for one to know what he or she was doing. I asked each coordinator to put on paper as a proposal what he wanted to be done in his area of specialization. When individual proposals are ready, they were to be discussed together by the Secretariat to develop a comprehensive plan for the SRRA secretariat. The plan would then redefine the role of each coordinator within it and the coordination needed between coordinators. I made it plain that it was the duty of the Secretary-General to follow up the progress of the programmes of all the coordinators and to ensure discipline and teamwork. I had told them that any interference in the work of the SRRA must be reported to me without delay in order for me to take the appropriate corrective measures. I left with them some manuals on "Project Formulation" and "Proposal Writing."

Also in October, I had identified a building in Kapoeta to be turned into a library. I hoped, if nothing else, it would help combat drunkenness. I donated some of my personal books to be put there to get it started and promised the SRRA Secretariat more books when I had returned to Nairobi. Indeed, a good friend of mine, Mr Onyango Ogutu, who was working with the Heineman (East Africa) Books in Nairobi, was very generous and donated a good number of books on a wide-range of subjects. It was an unforgettable contribution for which one will always remain very grateful. I took the books to Kapoeta in December and the library became worthy of the name because of these books.

I met the Chairman again on December 11, 1989 at Khor Klansh outside Kapoeta where he chose to stay. Courtesies over, I briefed him extensively on the Nairobi peace talks with the delegation of the Junta in Khartoum. I also informed him that the Khartoum delegation had taken exception to the video recording made by the SPLA of the first round of the peace talks with them in Addis Ababa in August. Some of them described the copies smuggled into Khartoum as "tampered with" and not true recordings! As a result they were quite edgy about allowing even simple magnetic tape recording in the second round and that they only consented reluctantly when President Carter insisted. The Chairman in turn briefed me about the military situation, the disappointment at Rumbek and that other theatres were either quite or nothing spectacular worth mentioning was going on. He reserved much of his criticism to Cdr Martin Manyiel and what was happening in NUN zone. He sounded dejected. My response was immediate. I suggested to him that, in view of the fact that the Junta had stopped OLS, I felt I did not have much to do in the political and diplomatic arena and that I was ready to offer my services in the field of combat. I reminded the Chairman of my uncompleted programme in Northern Upper Nile zone. In hindsight, I now know that I made a mistake by adding the last sentence. The Chairman rather quickly retorted assuring me that the situation was not that bad to warrant taking such a measure and that my presence abroad was still necessary. Not long after this discussion and precisely on January 8, 1990, I was deployed in the field, not in Northern Upper Nile zone but in Southern Blue Nile.

Before I went back to Kapoeta that evening I handed the Chairman his copy of the report of the SRRA audit committee and he promised to read it so that we discuss the contents the next day.

I met the Chairman once more at about mid-day on the 12th of December. He profusely commended the professional work done by the audit committee, and turning on the chairman of the committee, Abraham Malak Lual, the Chairman and C-in-C confessed that he could not believe him when Malak said during the Chairman's first interview to him that he was a University graduate for he looked "shabby", and that he had to ascertain the claim from his contemporaries. I volunteered to inform the Chairman that I knew Abraham Malak Lual very well since the University days. He was two years my junior but we played cards together at the Khartoum University Students Union's

(KUSU) club during some of our leisure time in the evenings. True, he was a bit care-free about his dress and carriage, quite unassuming but was a bright student and finicky in carrying out his duties. I added that I had to get him from Jekou, where he was assigned, to do this work because I knew the man and what he was capable of doing. After this session of praise, the next thing I expected from the Chairman was to approve my application for an investigation committee to be formed in order to initiate the legal procedures against the officers the audit report accused of embezzlement. This was not to be. He said he will let me know in due course and that was the end of the whole affair. Cynics in the SPLA later told me that I was expecting too much. How can the Chairman act against his brother-in-law (Capt. Nyang Jok) and against the relative and friend of his protege Cdr Salva Kiir (Capt. Mayom Kuoc)? They added that it was the poor Dr Richard K. Mulla who had nobody "High up" to back him.

The Chairman was leaving for Torit the next day. I invited him to Kapoeta town to take him around to see some of the developments that had taken place in the town since the advent of Operation Lifeline Sudan. The best example was Kapoeta Hospital. Physically damaged during the fight for the town, the hospital was renovated, had an operation theatre, laboratory, a pharmacy and was admitting patients. Efficiently run by Dr Achol Marial, Kapoeta hospital became a referral hospital for all the liberated areas. Other places worth visiting were the offices of the SRRA, the new library, office of the NEC, etc. I took the Chairman that day around all these places. He was very much appreciative of the achievements made in so short a time. I passed on the commendation to my subordinates. In the new library, the Chairman stopped at John Reed's book "Ten days that shook the world". Skimming through some pages he admitted that he did not come across it before. I was surprised. The book is a familiar hand-out in the socialist ideological schools. Not that it offered any exposition of socialist principles and tenets; far from it. It was the first eye-witness account of the Bolshevik Revolution written by an independent journalist, an American for that matter. The book was seen as favourable in Moscow and thus became recommended reading.

After the tour, I accompanied the Chairman up to Kapoeta bridge where he continued with his trip to Torit.

In Kapoeta, I continued with my programme with the SRRA Secretariat. Things had improved noticeably except on the side of the Secretary-General himself. I issued directives that the Public Relations Coordinator shall, in addition to his other duties, be the secretary of the Secretariat; to be the custodian of the minutes of the meetings and arrange matters that need follow-up. He was to be in constant touch with the Secretary-General on these matters. I left Kapoeta for Nairobi.

The First Christmas Party since 1985.

I flew to Addis Ababa on the 23rd of December. I found Cdr William Nyuon Bany there. He had been there for quite some time. He told me he was in Addis to see through the repair of his cars. What was the Addis office doing, I wondered.

On the 25th of December my wife and I organized a Christmas lunch. Cdr William was the guest of honour. It was the first Christmas I ever celebrated since 1985. A sizeable number of SPLA officers who were around in Addis Ababa attended. It was a good opportunity for informal discussions. We had a nice time together.

On the 28th of December, Cdr William Nyuon finally left Addis Ababa for Asosa. I saw him off and bade him goodbye. He was in high spirits. It did not occur to me that he was in for difficult moments ahead.

CHAPTER 7

Southern Blue Nile

Disaster Strikes

THE YEAR 1990 opened with a tragedy in Southern Blue Nile, a tragedy which had a tremendous impact on the SPLA and traumatic experiences among the Uduk People. At the small hours of the morning of January 2, 1990, the *"Wuyane"* – the Ethiopian rebels – supported by elements of the Sudanese army launched a surprising three-pronged attack on the SPLA positions at the border stations of Geizan, Dul and Gatawarga. They quickly overran these stations and by about 1000 hours were at Agumbela inside Ethiopia. This was the rear base of the SPLA forces in Southern Blue Nile and contained the stores of military materials and foodstuffs. The SPLA forces there put on a stiff and fierce resistance but they could not match the accurate fire of the Sudanese army artillery and armour and the huge number of men the enemy has thrown against them. In the afternoon, the SPLA force which was mainly composed of the Red Army was annihilated and Agumbela fell into enemy hands.

The enemy maintained the momentum and exploited his initial successes and on the 3rd of January the Training Centre and the Refugees camp at Tsore (Longkuei) were under the control of the enemy. The Uduk refugees they laid hands on in the camp were slaughtered and the SPLA wounded heroes and disabled found there were brutally beheaded. They could not be given the honour of dying by bullet shots. Such was the degree of callousness and inhuman behaviour of the enemy. They were now poised to capture Asosa, the main town in the district. On the 4th of January the enemy had advanced to some few kilometres within Asosa. The town was shelled in the morning of the 5th and by mid-day it was under the control of the Wuyane and the Sudanese army troops supporting them.

Cdr William Nyuon Bany was in Tsore Refugees camp when the hostilities broke out. With the enemy's rapid advance, he got hold of the few cars available, loaded them with his personal belongings and hit the road to Asosa. The cries of some of the disabled imploring him to take them to safety with him were not listened to. As he withdrew to Asosa, the forces withdrew in disarray. Some of them headed towards the east but most crossed to Sudan together with the Uduk refugees. I got in touch with Cdr William Nyuon on the second day. He was highly demoralized. He complained that he has been trying to send a radio message to the Chairman but could not get through. I promised him that I will try from my end which I did but also without success. The signalists at the Chairman's HQ informed both of us that the Chairman was engaged in operations and had ordered that no messages should be received. I insisted that the situation was pressing and was an SOS. The signalists went and consulted the Chairman but the answer was a categorical 'No'. I agonised over the reply. Here is a situation where the Chief of Staff, the next man to Dr John Garang in the hierarchy, was in deep trouble and the C-in-C was not willing to listen to his predicament on the excuse that he was busy with the operations to capture Kajo Kaji. Was he a Commander-in-Chief or a local commander?

The Chairman and C-in-C off air!

The situation continued like this and even when Asosa fell there was no contact yet established with the C-in-C. Cdr William Nyuon was in desperate need for food and wanted to proceed to Addis Ababa. I advised him against this idea and suggested that he should proceed to Gambela instead. I had discerned hostility against him being shown by the Ethiopian authorities in Addis Ababa. They blamed him for what had happened.

I was summoned by the President on the morning of the 4th and asked to get in touch with the Chairman to convey to him a message on the grave situation around Asosa area. The message was as follows:

a) A joint force composed of Sudan army and the Ethiopian rebels have crossed the Ethiopian borders and are advancing towards Asosa town. they have overrun all the outposts between Asosa town and the borders including all the SPLA positions. These enemy forces have killed and displaced the refugees. It is now the Ethiopian forces that are fighting the enemy outside Asosa town.

b) The SPLA forces did not put up any resistance. They got dispersed and Cdr William Nyuon neither has control over the SPLA troops nor was he cooperating with the Ethiopian army there.

c) The Ethiopian army did not amass forces in the Asosa sector because this was left to the SPLA to defend.

d) The SPLA has to mobilize a force to attack the enemy from behind. The SPLA should not count on Cdr William, a fresh force was needed.

e) Whatever the SPLA is doing on other fronts, should be relegated to this serious situation which should receive priority consideration.

I summarized these points together with my recommendation that Dr John Garang should come to Addis Ababa as my radio message No. 006/1/90 dated 4/1/90. I handed it over to the signalists to be sent to the Chairman whenever he can be reached and I proceeded to try my luck if I could secure some food items for Cdr. William Nyuon.

I went to the Ministry of Defence and discussed the matter with Brigadier – General Gismu. Indeed, he was so kind to load an Ural truck with different types of foodstuff which I sent to Cdr. William Nyuon when he was at Nejo. I passed to him the pleading of General Gismu that the car must be sent back to Addis Ababa as soon as he (Cdr. William) was in Gambela. Despite his promise to do so, Cdr. William later hung to the car and refused to send it back!

On the same day I sent another radio message to the SPLA stations near the borders (Bilpam, Bonga, Gambela, Itang, Pinywudo, etc) giving them a brief information on the situation in Southern Blue Nile and ordering them to be on maximum alert.

In the morning of the 5th, I called for and held a meeting with the office staff and other officers who were around in Addis Ababa. The purpose of the meeting was to review the situation in view of the fact that the C-in-C was inaccessible. I informed the meeting that something needed to be done quickly not only to help Cdr. William but to rescue what can be rescued if the SPLA was to maintain a presence in the whole front of Southern Blue Nile. I gave an estimate of the situation where in relation to own forces the following were made clear. Our forces in Southern Blue Nile were in complete disarray but it was reassuring that the SPLA was still keeping Yabus and many soldiers were gathering there. At the rear, specifically in Zinc and Gambela, we had a force, commanded by A/Cdr James Hoth, which was part of the HQ force of the C-in-C and was well equipped. The other force in Bonga was collected from refugees camps and needed some reorganization to put it in combat gear. I suggested that before the enemy could think of advancing to Yabus, it was prudent for us to take a fresh force there in order to maintain it to give the SPLA the opportunity to reorganize the retreating troops. I stressed that as the most senior officer in Addis Ababa, I was ready to take immediate action in light of what transpired in the meeting. They agreed to the suggestion and that I should do what I can. I sent a radio message to the Chairman suggesting to him the course of action to be taken. I decided to leave for Gambela the next day to wait for his reply there.

When I reached home that evening, I got a message that President Mengistu had asked for me to see him at 8.00 a.m. the next day, i.e., the 6th of January. As mentioned earlier, I had met him on his request at 10.00 a.m. on the 4th and discussed the situation in the Asosa area. At the end of that meeting he had requested a meeting with Dr John Garang and I had replied him that he was around Kajo Kaji and that I was going to pass the message to him by radio. The meeting took place at 8.30 a.m. on the 6th and it was, as expected, on the situation in Asosa and what could be done to arrest the enemy's advance. I informed him that I could not, unfortunately, get in touch with the Chairman and that I was travelling to Gambela that morning and will continue contacts from there.

I left Addis Ababa by car at about 1.00 p.m. and spent the night at Jimma. I continued the journey in the morning of Sunday the 7th and arrived Gambela at about 3.00 p.m.

Change of Command

It was in the evening of the 7th that my message to the Chairman on the situation in Southern Blue Nile went through. We were informed that Kajo Kaji has been captured by the BSC forces commanded by the BSC commander on Sunday the 7th of January. We were elated but this fleeting moment soon relapsed into the sombre mood we were in over our immediate situation in Southern Blue Nile. On the 8th, the Chairman responded to my message. I was assigned as the new overall commander of Southern Blue Nile but he refused flat to allow me to have the force at Gambela. How I was going to command Southern Blue Nile without a force to go there with me was a mystery. The Chairman's message contained another important omission; it did not give any new assignment to Cdr William Nyuon Bany who was being replaced by me. William read presentiment into this and his sagging morale sank. The night after, he and his bodyguards sneaked into Gambela. A/Cdr James Hoth and I were staying in Zinc some fifteen minutes drive from Gambela. William's entourage passed our place in the small hours of the morning.

In the morning proper, we prepared to go and meet our chief of staff. James advised me to take one bodyguard only so that with him and the driver we would be only four. This, according to him, was the only way to reassure Cdr William Nyuon that we were not in possession of an order to arrest him! I agreed and so we went. When we arrived William's place we were seated outside and were kept waiting for more than fifteen minutes while his bodyguards constantly moved in and out of the room he was in. Finally, Cdr William appeared beaming. We hugged and embraced emotionally for quite some time. At the end of it all, he called the two of us in and we chatted. We made sure we did not touch on any embarrassing issue. A/Cdr James Hoth was absolutely right in his assessment of William's frame of mind. His meeting with us had an electric effect on his morale. Immediately after the meeting, he left for Itang.

The Debacle: was it justified?

It is worth pausing here to flashback and ask the question as to what went wrong on the first week of January as to make the enemy's surprise so total. All the officers and soldiers I had spoken to that time had only one story to tell and did not mince their words as to where to lay the blame on what had happened. It is to be recollected that Kurmuk town was retaken by the enemy on the 28th of November 1989. The SPLA troops in the area laid siege on the town and continued harassment actions against the enemy. SPLA patrols moved deep beyond Kurmuk on donkeys and on foot collecting information on the enemy and harrying his patrols and agents. Then, things changed suddenly. Sometime in December, just before he could leave for Addis Ababa, Cdr William decided to withdraw all the battle-tested forces around Kurmuk and Geizan to the training centre for "refreshment training" and were to be replaced by a newly graduated force. In so doing, he lacked tact when he addressed the soldiers to be retrained by giving the impression that they did not perform well in combat. This caused resentment and the soldiers started to desert in big numbers. William's reaction, yet another mistake, was to arrest a number of officers; all from the Dinka of Bahr el-Ghazal that formed the bulk of that force, for "agitating the soldiers to desert". He left them in jail when he left for Addis Ababa.

The fresh force was issued orders to move to the positions previously occupied by the old troops but William ordered that they should not be involved in harassment actions against the enemy without orders from him. This was not only a mistake but a grave blunder, more so when his deputy, Cdr Galerio Modi Hurnyang, was a High Command member and so could as well issue the orders William wanted to retain. With no harassment, the enemy relaxed and began to send agents into the Ethiopian side of the border. They took back very accurate information about the dispositions of the SPLA and the Ethiopian army. In the meantime, the contagion of desertion has reached the fresh forces being kept idle. Things went out of control. Hence, when the enemy launched the attack on the new year, not only did they have accurate information on the SPLA and preponderant manpower and armament but, in addition, a very small fraction of our force was ready to put up a fight. As mentioned already this small force fought valiantly.

The immediate consequence of the Chairman's decision not to approve sending a force to Southern Blue Nile was the loss of Yabus garrison to the enemy with no single bullet shot. Without any reinforcement in sight, it became untenable to maintain Yabus any longer. The soldiers that had gathered there were demoralized, exhausted and hungry. They had had a harrowing experience on their disorganized withdrawal. They carried some wounded heroes and some moved with their families. A fresh force was needed to lift their spirits and get them back into combat - worthiness. This was not to be. Therefore, the SPLA force in Yabus, had to withdraw on a long southward trek to Itang. Ten days from their withdrawal the enemy moved in and occupied Yabus which they still maintain up to today.

I have always found it difficult to grasp the military strategy and tactics adopted in the operations in Southern Blue Nile. Of course, such matters are not discussed by the High Command and it was the Chairman who decides on them and issues out orders to the rest of us to execute the missions which have been set. I remained unconvinced about the wisdom of approaching the area entirely from the Ethiopian side of the border. This approach, because of access to heavy artillery support, may give the advantage of a quick military victory in capturing the towns. But such victories are by their nature shallow and are easily reversible. Our own experience there bore this out clearly. When Kurmuk was captured in November 1987, it was retaken by the enemy within forty-five days. Again, when it was captured in October 1989, it went back to the enemy within a month. In addition to the reverse this time, the SPLA was driven out of the whole area after about a month from the time the enemy recaptured Kurmuk. In all these operations, we could not succeed to win over the tribes in the area around Kurmuk (The Watawit, El-Berta, Gumuz, etc). It was among the Uduk of Chali El-Fil, which is much deeper inland from the border, that the SPLA gained sizeable support among the population. Some of their young men joined the armed struggle.

What I thought should have been the best approach was to make full use of our presence in the Maban area. By then it was an Independent Area Command, just short of being a zone, under the command of A/Cdr Makuei Deng Majuc. In that area it was only Boiny (Maban town) which was in enemy hands. For some inexplicable reason, this garrison has always been ignored in all the operations in the Southern Blue Nile area. In 1987 and again in 1989, all the enemy garrisons in the area including Chali and Yabus, which are not far from Boiny fell into SPLA hands. But Boiny itself was never attacked. In 1989, Boiny garrison was used by the enemy as one of two launching pads to attack Kurmuk; the other was Dandoru. What I thought should have been done was to increase the size of our presence in the Maban area by supplying it with more troops and support arms. Then have the main thrust of advance into Southern Blue Nile take off from there. The attack from across the Ethiopian border could have been launched simultaneously to support the advance from within Sudan; not the only attack as has been the case. With Boiny out of the way, our rear would have been completely cleared of any enemy presence giving the movement more time to concentrate on the political work among the population, thus consolidating the victories and the SPLA force would have advanced deep into the Ingessana Hills. As it were, the SPLA never set foot into the Ingessana Hills at all.

My idea of holding to Yabus following the misfortune of 1990 stemmed from this consideration. In short, I was convinced that it was necessary to change the approach and win over Southern Blue Nile from within Sudan.

Back to Addis Ababa

As soon as Cdr William Nyuon left for Itang, A/Cdr James Hoth and I drove back to Zinc. There, I waited for any directives from the Chairman. He was still around Kajo Kaji. On the 14th, Kaya was liberated and I received instructions from the Chairman to go to Addis Ababa and await him there. I left Gambela on a car at 11.15 a.m. on

Monday the 15th on my way to Addis Ababa. On Tuesday, I received messages from Cdr Gordon Kong Chol who was in Abwong area that the enemy has, for the first time in the war, attacked his positions from South of Sobat and that the situation was very desperate indeed. The enemy had overrun Abwong itself and, with the help of the remnants of Anya-nya-2, was advancing towards Galachel and Aluel. He felt he could have halted the advance and driven the enemy out had it not been for the fact that he was running out of ammos. Such messages are normally sent to the Chairman and C-in-C, but I guessed Cdr Gordon Kong must have found difficulty of getting through to the BSC commander the way William and I did. I promised him to do what I can with the friends.

I contacted the office of the Chief of Staff of the Ethiopian Armed Forces and he kindly agreed to meet me at 4.00p.m. on Wednesday, the 17th. I explained the situation to him and urged for an immediate action to be taken to reverse it. He was very understanding indeed. He spread an operational map in front of him and I showed him the area in question and the possible locations for droppings. He gave his word that the matter was going to be taken care of within two days. Indeed it was. Gordon was also true to his word. Within a couple of days of receiving the ammos he flushed the enemy out.

In the same afternoon of the 17th, I made a courtesy call on my friend, Comrade Andarge in the Ministry of Interior. We met at 5.15p.m. He was eager to be briefed on the general situation but as usual, we afterwards slid into discussing political, ideological and organizational matters within the SPLA. Among the things comrade Andarge said that evening, he admitted to me that it was they (meaning the state security) who in 1987 arrested Cdr Kerubino Kwanyin Bol because they were misled into believing that the action was in the interest of the movement. They have realised now that it was a mistake and for sure, he went on, this will never ever be repeated. It was wrong, according to him, for the Ethiopian Government to pick up from among the SPLA commanders who is good or who is bad. This must be left to the SPLA to sort out on its own. I was flabbergasted. In spite of my acquaintance with comrade Andarge, he never went this far before. Of course, I could not help but commend his frankness and above all the new position of his government stressing to him that this was what we expected of it. As a friend, it can give advice but not to interfere in the affairs of the SPLA. I did not relate this conversation to anybody.

The timing of comrade Andarge's statement on Kerubino was interesting. Some days before, precisely on the 8th, the BBC "Focus on Africa" programme in its 15:15 GMT edition carried a piece about the SPLA titled "Sudan Rebels accused of victimizing their opponents". It was a report from Nairobi by Lucy Hanan on an interview she made with Capt. Bari A. Wanji who claimed to have "escaped from solitary confinement and came to Kenya on his way to Tanzania". According to the BBC report, Bari Wanji ".... escaped early December with the help of Ethiopian officials who sympathized with his case." The report went on: "Bari Wanji said he has been kept in isolation in very cold conditions with little food". Why was he arrested? The BBC report continued: "Bari Wanji was apparently arrested by the SPLA after composing a memo to the Ethiopian Government demanding the removal of the SPLA leader, John Garang. This memo was said to have been forwarded by a number of commanders in the field who complained of harsh policies within the SPLA towards the civilian population and the domination among the ranks by the Dinka tribe. He apparently complained of the forced recruitment of young boys and girls, of the rape of women and the burning down of vital crops and granaries...."

That the Ethiopian officials sympathized with him was true, but not with his case. The truth is that Capt. Bari A. Wanji was supporting Cdr Kerubino Kwanyin Bol in the latter's quarrel with Dr John Garang. It was him who persuaded Kerubino to abandon his trenches in the field and go to Addis on the assurance that he (Wanji) had persuaded the Ethiopians and the socialist comrades "to ditch Garang to be replaced by Kerubino." The memo addressed to President Mengistu and signed by Kerubino was drafted by Bari Wanji. However, things did not work as Wanji imagined and made Kerubino to believe. The Ethiopians did not crown him, they incarcerated him instead. They nonetheless rejected repeated requests from Dr John Garang to get Capt. Bari A. Wanji arrested. The Ethiopian security accommodated him full board in "Marabiti" hotel from November 1987 to December 1989 when he left Addis Ababa on his own volition. He did not need to escape because he was quite a free man enjoying the protection of the Ethiopian security. In fact, they provided him with the tickets. Addis Ababa can sometimes be cold all right, but there was a lot of food and beer at the Marabiti hotel which, far from being in isolation, was in the centre of a district buzzing with all sorts of activities.

The Chairman arrived Addis Ababa from Kampala on the 24th of January. As soon as he arrived arrangements were made for him to meet President Mengistu the next day. The Zairean embassy was also waiting for a reply from the Chairman to confirm the time of his going to Kinshasa to meet President Mobutu Sese Seko. This was fixed for Friday, the 26th of January.

The meeting with President Mengistu took place at 9.00 a.m. on Thursday the 25th. It discussed a wide-range of political and military issues. The Chairman briefed the President on the operations in Eastern Equatoria and his expected trip to Zaire. The President raised the situation in Asosa and the events that took place in the first week of the month. An outline plan of action was agreed upon and the President informed the Chairman that the Deputy Chief of Staff for Operations would be ready to receive us that afternoon to discuss the details. Indeed, we met him at about 2.00 p.m. for about two hours and our discussions resumed again at 12.30 p.m. the next day. All was set for action.

The Chairman's trip to Zaire

In the morning of the 26th, the Zairean embassy official organizing the trip of the Chairman to Kinshasa informed A/Cdr Deng Alor that a jet was arriving Addis Ababa that afternoon to collect the Chairman with up to seven other members of SPLA who may accompany him. When Deng came to the house of the Chairman with the news, the

Chairman was in his study. Capt. Majok Ayuen, the Secretary General of NEC, and I were in the sitting room. Deng proceeded to where the Chairman was to pass the information. He spent longer than we expected but eventually came back and joined us.

Deng told us about his conversation with the Zairean embassy official, that he had just passed the message to the Chairman and that it seems there was a snag which may stand against the journey that day. Almost simultaneously, we both asked Deng what it was. He said the Chairman wanted to have ten persons go with him and that none of them he could leave behind and since the plane can take only seven, he would rather postpone the trip until the matter was sorted out by the Zaireans. Majok and I looked at each other in amazement. Deng concluded that his instructions were to go and tell the poor Zairean diplomat that it was either ten or no plane at all.

Majok Ayuen, a man of integrity and forthrightness, could not take all this. He addressed both of us that the Chairman should be advised that he was dealing with a head of state and must be careful in the way he conducts himself. He said it was his considered opinion that the Chairman must go with the number fixed by the Zaireans as sending the plane back would be a serious diplomatic rebuff the consequences of which nobody can tell and which cannot under any circumstance be to the interest of the SPLA. I concurred with Majok and ordered Deng to wait until we had discussed the matter with the Chairman.

It did not take long before the Chairman joined us in the sitting room. After exchanging greetings and courtesies, I requested the permission of the Chairman to say something. I related to him what I heard from A/Cdr Deng Alor about the arrangements for the trip to Kinshasa and what Deng was supposed to take back to the embassy as our reaction to those arrangements. I told him I had a different view on the matter and that was why I had asked Deng to stay until I had shared it with him (the Chairman). I said that Mobutu, the proud man he knows, would take offence if we were to turn down his arrangements. I advised that the best we could do was to accept the offer and once the Chairman was there he would request from President Mobutu another plane to collect those left behind. I concluded that I thought

President Mobutu would feel flattered and send the jet. Majok nodded in agreement and so did Deng. The Chairman consented and asked Deng to act accordingly.

The jet touched on Addis Ababa airport at about 3.00 p.m. and the Chairman took off for Kinshasa at about 5.00 p.m. that afternoon. The plane had made a stopover at Goma passing through Rwanda. The Rwandese authorities made some noise that day about the plane's "violation of their air space" but that was after the Chairman had already met President Mobutu. This was the only nearest thing to a hitch in the whole trip. The next day, the same jet returned to Addis Ababa to take the bodyguards of the Chairman who were left behind the previous day. We were all delighted the way things turned out.

Juba town shelled:

On Thursday the 18th of January 1990, the Chairman decided to shell Juba town. He sent to us in Addis Ababa a message to that effect to be broadcast over Radio SPLA the same day. The message appealed to the population of Juba to evacuate the town so that they are not caught in cross fire. The public announcement went on air the same day. Following the broadcast, OCER was contacted by a number of diplomatic missions (notably the U.S.A and the U.K.), NGOs, the U.N. and ICRC so that they are given time to airlift their subjects and/ or personnel out of Juba town. They chose Mr Bob Frasure of the U.S. Embassy as their representative to discuss the matter with the SPLA.

On the 26th of January, A/Cdr Deng Alor Kuol and I held a meeting with Mr Bob Frasure to discuss the request and we agreed that Monday the 29th be the date of air evacuation as from 6.00 a.m. to 6.00 p.m. On this date, the SPLA undertook not to shell the town nor shoot at the planes evacuating the personnel concerned from Juba. It was also agreed that no military plane should fly into Juba within the specified time.

We issued a press statement on the 27th of January outlining what was agreed upon and appealing to the international opinion to pressure Khartoum to allow the population in Juba town who want to leave to do so. The airlifting operation went without incident but the Khartoum government did not allow the civil population to leave juba town. A number of them fell victims of the shells that fell into the town.

The Famous February Encounter

On the 14th of February, I left Addis Ababa for Gambela. On the way between Jimma and Metu, I met the Chairman who was on his way to Addis Ababa. I knew he was in Gambela after having come back from Zaire through Eastern Equatoria but I was unaware of his trip to Addis Ababa. We greeted each other and then drove together back to Addis Ababa. We spent the night in Jimma and continued our journey at about 8.00 a.m. the next day.

A meeting with President Mengistu was fixed for 2.00 p.m. on Friday the 16th of February. It was however, cancelled by the office of the President that morning.

Those days, Cdr Riek Machar Teny, Cdr James Wani Igga and Cdr Lwal Diing Wol, all members of the High Command, were in Addis Ababa. They were staying in one hotel; the "Tourist Hotel" in Arat Kilo. The hotel was between the office and the house I stayed in. I paid them a visit that Friday afternoon as I usually do almost on a daily basis. We chatted, shared field experiences and predictably, we touched on the politics and SPLA affairs. All of us felt that a lot of things in the movement needed to be set right and that the leadership of the SPLM/A should meet to review the progress of the struggle. I told my colleagues that I stayed closer to the Chairman more than most, if not all, of them and that the conclusion I had reached was that the Chairman was disinclined to convene a meeting of the High Command. I suggested that their presence was an opportunity for all of us together to go and talk to the Chairman in order to persuade him to call for such a meeting. The suggestion was accepted and it was agreed that I pass by the hotel in the morning of the next day for all of us to drive together in my car to the house of the Chairman.

On Saturday, February 17, 1990, I left the house early in the morning to meet my colleagues in the High Command as agreed upon the previous evening. All except, Lwal Diing were ready. The latter seems to have had second thoughts about the meeting. He said he could not go as he was waiting for some friends who were visiting him that day. Riek, the most senior among us, tried to persuade him telling him that the visit was a private matter which could be rescheduled but the meeting was very important. He was not convinced and the three of us decided to go without him.

We arrived the house of the Chairman and found him in the sitting room with A/Cdr Deng Alor. Greetings over, we were seated and were served with tea amid light conversation. The Chairman made jokes about his last trip to Kinshasa and how things were in Zaire. We seemed to be enjoying our time. After a while A/Cdr Deng Alor excused himself and left the room. Suddenly, the sitting turned into a formal meeting.

Without introduction, Cdr Riek who was sitting opposite the Chairman, told the Chairman that he had brought with him the report he was supposed to present to the Chairman with his briefing and that he was ready to proceed with the briefing. He did not wait for a word from the Chairman but went ahead to brief the meeting about his report. Had Cdr Riek allowed the Chairman to say a word, the latter would have told him not to proceed for it was his way of doing things to be briefed alone without anybody else being present beside the one or ones doing the briefing. There was unease in his face for such a breach of procedure. This briefing took about thirty minutes or so. When it was over, Riek immediately shifted gear to what we were there for. He started by stating that he has been in the field for a very long time and that many things in the movement have been going on without his knowledge. He talked about the detention of High Command members, the so-called "progressive officers" and other arrests in general. He specifically asked the permission of the Chairman to allow the wife of Capt George Maker Benjamin to visit him in jail. The Chairman squinted. Riek went on to talk about some administrative issues that needed to be addressed and concluded by requesting the Chairman to call for the first meeting of the High Command. This took him more than ninety minutes.

The Chairman turned to me asking if I had anything to say. I took the floor. I arranged my ideas on specific points. The crucial point, I told the sitting, was the activation of the High Command as the institution leading the movement. To me it did not exist adding that when the three of us in the room were appointed to the High Command on 1/7/86 none of us was served with regulations, procedures or rules of the High Command and that there was not even a code of conduct for members to abide by. I stressed that without collective decision-making many things were bound to go wrong, hence, the necessity to call for a High Command meeting as soon as possible. Having said this, I continued, the problems at hand must also be addressed. I spoke about the detention without trial and how I was called from Northern Upper Nile zone to look into some of the cases only to be assigned elsewhere without the slightest explanation as to why. I criticized the arbitrary promotions from the rank of Captain to A/Cdr which neither took seniority into account nor were the opinions of the direct commanders of the officers concerned sought. I gave as an example the last promotion of 17 captains made in July 1989. I also spoke about the need to curb the excesses of some senior High Command members and touched on other matters. When I looked at the clock on the wall it had taken me more than one hour.

The Chairman finally turned to Cdr James Wani Igga to make his contribution. Wani's reply was: "I have nothing to say since I do not know the topic under discussion." After about three hours of talking let alone our discussion of Friday night, Cdr James Wani still did not "know the topic"! This was unbelievable. We all sensed he was scared stiff.

The reply of the Chairman was short and sharp. He first underlined the fact that this was not a formal meeting of the High Command as we were only four which number did not make a quorum. On detentions, he said the "progressive officers" were not arrested by him but by Cdr Arok Thon Arok. As to allowing the visits of wives to their husbands under detention, he said, he had put an end to it because he had allowed it before for Martin Majier, Garang Deng Aguer and others but "this was abused; all the women came back pregnant"! He grimaced and as if to tell us: "How dare you forget", the Chairman said while pointing at the three of us: "when you were appointed to the High Command you were competing with those of Abu-Hadid"[5]. Then, rather quickly added that he would call a High Command meeting during the rainy season when the enemy activity was least and we would have the opportunity to repeat what we had just said. He then declared the meeting closed. We took permission to leave.

On the way back to the hotel, Riek queried James Wani on his strange behaviour during the meeting. The latter wanted to be left alone. We drove in silence for some ten minutes till we reached the Tourist Hotel. I dropped them there and proceeded home.

Our understanding of the purpose of this meeting was that it was a normal sharing of views with the Chairman. For me personally, I did not feel that there was something new I told the Chairman in that meeting that I did not tell him on several occasions before. However, in the gossip-ridden SPLA, numerous interpretations were made of the meeting. Some half-truths were advanced and even some conspiracy theories imputed to it. The first to hit out was none other than Cdr Lwal Diing Wol. While the meeting was still in progress, he told A/Cdr Deng Alor, Capt. Mario Muor Muor and a number of other officers in Addis Ababa that we had conspired to leave him out of the meeting. He swore that he was not informed at all!

I later came to learn, in early April, that the Chairman himself had given his close bodyguards, including A/Cdr James Hoth Mai, a doctored version of what was discussed in the meeting. He had told

---

5   Abu-Hadid, an NCO in the SPLA, was a bodyguard of Lt. Col. Kerubino Kwanyin Bol. The reference is to the consultations the Chairman made with Kerubino, William, Salva and Arok prior to our appointment to the High Command on July 1, 1986. By this statement he is suggesting that Kerubino preferred to have his bodyguard appointed to the High Command! By implication, it must have been the Chairman who prevailed to get us appointed instead. Hence, we should remain grateful to him.

them that he was "challenged" by Dr Riek and me and that both of us pressured him to release the political detainees including Cdr Arok Thon Arok without trial! As it will be remembered, A/Cdr James Hoth Mai was in the committee that investigated the officers who were arrested together with Cdr Arok Thon Arok in March 1988. The mention of Arok by name must have been meant to appeal to James' emotions that we did not appreciate whatever work he and his colleagues in the investigation committee had painstakingly done. It was then that I came to realize that the Chairman did not take our sincere advice in good faith. As soon as such stories begin to spread out from the HQ of the Chairman, the SPLA officers have come to learn through experience that such talk was a premeditated prelude for some action to be taken against the supposed challengers of the Chairman. The truth gets drowned in the sea of misrepresentation and distortion.

A good number of officers who heard such nonsense were concerned and took courage to ask me about what had exactly taken place in the meeting of February the 17th. I did not hesitate to give them the true story. Such explanation was viewed by the Chairman and his close associates as "agitation". Thus, the meeting acquired an importance it did not deserve at all.

On Monday the 19th, two days after the meeting, the Chairman ordered for me to go and see him on an urgent matter. I complied. He told me that a road was to be constructed between Gambela and Pagak to be used for transporting troops to Southern Blue Nile, that the work on the road has already started and that I was to go to Gambela to supervise the work. He added that there was a bulldozer at Bonga (not the famous Bonga, but another one on the way to Dima) which was just parked there for the lack of some minor spare parts. He wanted that bulldozer repaired and I had to go there personally to see what spare parts were required. I was surprised by this supervision business, especially the last one, but I chose not to discuss it. I assured the Chairman that his instructions will be executed as soon as practicable. The meeting ended on this note.

That afternoon, I summoned Lt. Chol Chiman and asked him what he knew about the bulldozer. He said he was already working on it and that what it lacked was just a battery and the hydraulic fluid for the hoses which manipulate the blade. He concluded that he had bought all these items and was just waiting for any car going that direction to take them to where the bulldozer was. This junior officer is in the HQ of the Chairman and handles sums in hundreds of thousands of Ethiopian Birr in Addis Ababa ostensibly to buy spare parts. By then one Birr was equivalent to one half of a U.S. dollar. This was being done outside the authority of the Addis office. When I appointed and took to Addis in July 1989, a new accountant to the OCER, 1st Lt. Alipio Mabuoc Guryuom, I had ordered some control measures to be put in place regarding the expenditure of such huge sums of money. I instructed that Lt. Chol Chiman deposits his money with the accountant and expends them against pro forma invoices. This system was followed for some time but during my extended periods of absence from Addis Ababa it broke down and the whole thing reverted back to what it was. It was because of this anomaly that I had to talk to the officer.

I decided to forget about the bulldozer and prepared to leave for Gambela. This I did on the 25th and arrived there about 8.00 a.m. on the 26th. But before hitting the road to Gambela, I had three important meetings in Addis Ababa.

The first, on the 21st, was with General Olusegun Obasanjo, the former President of Nigeria and Dr Francis M. Deng, a fellow at the Brookings institution in Washington D.C. The two gentlemen were involved since early 1988 in a mediation effort between the SPLA and the Government of Sudan. At one stage, they managed to arrange for a meeting to take place in Switzerland between the Prime Minister, Sadiq al-Mahdi, and the Chairman of the SPLM/SPLA, Dr John Garang. The summit did not materialize because Dr John Garang failed to turn up at the last minute. The reason given for this failure has never been convincing. The meeting took place in the house of A/Cdr Deng Alor. Our side was led by the Chairman and included Dr Riek Machar Teny, A/Cdr Deng Alor and me. The two ambassadors of peace informed us that they would like to revive their mediation effort and should this be acceptable to the SPLA, they would proceed to Khartoum to meet

Lt. General Omer Hassan Ahmed al-Bashir and his colleagues in the government. They got the green light to go ahead.

The second meeting was with Mr Salman, the adviser of the PLO's Chairman on Africa. I met him with Dr Mansour Khalid at the Hilton Hotel on the 23rd of February. We briefed him on the situation in Sudan, what the SPLA was fighting for and what role was expected of the PLO to play. Although the SPLA has been in contact with some factions of the Palestinians, this was the first time that an official close to Yasir Arafat ever met the SPLA on such a high level.

The third meeting was on the same day and in the same venue as the second. It was with Mr Ismail Bin Gadad, the Algerian representative in Namibia and adviser to the Head of State, Chazli Bin Jadid. Again, I was with Dr Mansour Khalid. After having briefed him fully on the war and peace in Sudan, we requested from him to arrange a visit by our Chairman to Algiers. He promised to convey our discussion to President Bin Jadid.

On Road Construction in Gamebela

In Gambela, I visited the road being constructed on the 1st of March. The construction of the Gambela - Jekou road was one of the projects undertaken by the Ethiopian government as part of the development of the extremely underdeveloped Ilubabor district, later to become Gambela region. The road was about a hundred kilometres long. The whole track was cleared and about half of it raised ready to be surfaced with Tarmac when the work suddenly came to a halt sometime in 1988/89. The road we were constructing (clearing, rather) was an offshoot of this main road branching off from some point in the Lara area extending to about twenty kilometres to Pagak. Then from Pagak it was to continue up to Maiwut. There was supposed to be two bulldozers working but only one was in operation. The SPLA soldiers guarded the equipment and secured the road. There were no surveying instruments or a surveyor for that matter; everything was done by intuition and improvisation. All said and done, we had, at the end, what could be called a track.

On the 3rd of March, the Chairman arrived Zinc at about 9.00 a.m. I briefed him about the progress on the construction of the road and some of the problems facing those involved in the work. He jotted down the points I made. He informed me that the Egyptian government has extended an invitation to the SPLA to send a delegation to Cairo around the 3rd week of the month and, to my surprise, added that I was to lead that delegation. I had assumed that my coming to Gambela was to prepare to move to Southern Blue Nile. Now, two months after my appointment as the commander of the zone there was no sign of moving into the area. I raised the matter with the Chairman. His only reply was that the forces were not ready. By now I have learnt not to ask too many questions. The Chairman also briefed me about other political and relief matters that required my attention while in Addis Ababa.

I left Zinc for Addis Ababa early morning on the 8th and spent the night at Metu. I continued my journey at about 6.00 a.m. and arrived Addis at about 5.30 p.m. on Friday the 9th of March.

The American Initiative and the Second Trip to Cairo

The first engagement I had in Addis Ababa was a meeting with Mr Jack Davidson of the U.S. State Department. It took place at about 1.00 p.m. on Monday, the 12th. We discussed the situation in Sudan and the prospects of a peaceful settlement of the conflict. At the end of the meeting, he delivered a peace proposal which became known as the "American Initiative". This important document deserves a detailed discussion and this will follow later. However, I found the choice of Mr Davidson for such a mission rather interesting. In the Nairobi Peace talks held in November/December 1989 he had accompanied President Carter when the latter called on our delegation in our hotel to discuss his mediation role in the talks. Mr Davidson had a verbal brush with A/Cdr Elijah Malok Aleng, the Secretary of our delegation, on Mr Davidson's position regarding the debate on the division of the South in 1981/82. Mr Davidson had visited

Juba that time and had met a number of Ministers and politicians of the Southern region including Mr Elijah Malok Aleng who was a member of the People's Regional Assembly representing Bor North Constituency. Elijah believed Mr Davidson's views lent support to Nimeiri's position. In Nairobi in 1989, A/Cdr Elijah Malok reminded Mr Davidson, in a rather undiplomatic language, that he (Elijah) had warned the Americans through Mr Davidson that if the South were to be divided they will fight. "Now", continued Elijah pointing to Mr Davidson, "you have come again and found us fighting". I, as leader of our delegation, did not intercede. I thought this was going to send a signal to the American side.

I prepared to leave for Cairo. Before I did, I had a series of meetings with Mr Michael Priestley who had taken over as the Chief of Operation Lifeline Sudan. Mr Priestley, an Englishman, was the UNDP representative in Khartoum. The meetings took place consecutively on the 16th, 17th and the 18th. The subject of discussion was to work out modalities for the resumption of OLS. He brought proposals from the Khartoum government on the new terms under which the GOS would allow the relief operation in Southern Sudan to be resumed. The whole thing amounted to renegotiation of OLS in Khartoum's favour, as if the Junta had to be rewarded for having stopped OLS in November 1989. Our side found the proposals difficult to swallow but agreed to continue the talks with Mr Priestley.

Our delegation flew off to Cairo in the afternoon of Monday, the 19th. Other members of the delegation were: Dr Mansour Khalid, A/Cdr Deng Alor Kuol and 1st Lt. Yasir Saeed Aarman. At Cairo airport we were received by some senior officials of the Ministry of Public Security.

On Tuesday, we held a meeting with the Minister of Public Security, Mr Hilmy Namar and his Under-Secretary, Mr Mohammed Abdel Salam. The Egyptian government wanted to mediate in bringing about a peaceful settlement to the conflict in Sudan. They wanted to know the opinion of the SPLA on this as well as on how to circumvent the sticking issue of the Islamic laws. It is to be noted that by then they enjoyed the best of relations with the Junta in Khartoum.

The two sides agreed on the role of Egypt as a facilitator of a new round of peace talks with Khartoum. But this turned out to be the only point agreed upon. We differed with the Egyptian side on the analysis of the setup in Khartoum and on how the issue of Islamic laws could be addressed. The Egyptian side could not buy SPLA's position that the Junta in Khartoum was inspired and controlled by the Islamic fundamentalists, the Muslim Brotherhood, organised in Sudan under the umbrella of the National Islamic Front (NIF). The SPLA's side could not agree to the Egyptian proposal that the movement accepts the exemption of the South from the application of the Islamic punishments as a way of resolving the difference with the GOS on the issue of the Islamic laws. The discussion continued over dinner the next day. We were joined by Mr Abdel Aziz Hind, Namar's deputy. Rather plump, Mr Hind was a man of great humour. He made the discussion enjoyable, the difference notwithstanding. After the dinner, we had a night cruise by boat around the island of Geiza while being entertained to sweet Egyptian music and traditional dances. Earlier in the evening Mr Namar had informed us that President Mabarak was ready to receive our delegation on Monday or Tuesday.

In Cairo, we had a busy schedule with the press. On Thursday, the 22nd, we had an interview with Mrs. Amina El-Nagash of the left-wing newspaper *El-Ahali*. The interview was published in the issue of the paper on 28/3/90. On Friday, the 23rd, we met Mrs. Saeeda Ramadan the columnist in *El-Wafd* newspaper. Mrs. Saeeda Ramadan had a full page in the paper every week devoted to Sudanese affairs. Although the paper belonged to "El-Wafd" party, she managed to maintain a considerable leeway of independence in the views expressed in her writings rendering the paper a favourite of the not insignificant Sudanese community in Egypt. The discussions she conducted with members of our delegation appeared in *El-Wafd* on 25/3/90. Our exposure to the media was not limited to the opposition papers, we also had an extensive interview with the government papers: "El-Ahram" and "El-Jamhoria". We met Mahfouz El-Ansari and Mohammed Murad together on Sunday, the 25th. The first was the editor-in-chief of "El-Ahram". Finally, we held a press conference with the foreign journalists in Cairo on Wednesday the 28th.

Our delegation also met some leaders of the opposition parties in Egypt. In the afternoon on Monday, the 26th, we had audience with "pahsa" Sirag el-Din, Chairman of "El-Wafd" party, Dr Nieman Juma, deputy Chairman and Ibrahim Faraq, the Secretary-General of the party. On the 28th we had a meeting with the leadership of the Unionist Alliance Party, the left-wing party that owns "El-Ahali" newspaper.

In addition to these meetings, our delegation met on the 28th with Mr Makram Obied, the editor-in-chief of "El-Musawar" magazine and the Secretary-General of the Egyptian journalists Union. On the same day, we met Mr Farouq Abu Eisa, the Secretary-General of the Arab Union of Lawyers. Mr Abu Eisa held a number of Ministerial portfolios under Nimeiri prior to the 1971 aborted communist-led coup d'etat.

Part of our brief as a delegation, was to discuss with the representatives of the Sudanese political parties and trade unions the Charter of the National Democratic Alliance which was issued clandestinely in, October 1989 in Khartoum. The Charter was signed by the Umma party, DUP, Sudan Communist Party, SAC and seven other political parties together with 31 professional associations and 51 Trade Unions. The signatories to the Charter had written letters to the SPLA requesting it to join the National Democratic Alliance (NDA) which objective it was to lead the struggle against the NIF regime in Khartoum in order to restore democracy, basic rights and freedoms to the Sudanese people. The SPLA welcomed the coming together of all the opposition forces against the regime but naturally wanted to renegotiate the wording of the charter to incorporate its views. This was what we set out to accomplish in Cairo. By then, the elements of the Sudanese opposition in Egypt were operating under considerable difficulties as the Egyptian government was still hand-in-glove with the Junta in Khartoum. This included the DUP; well known for its pro-Egypt inclinations. Our delegation had to request permission from Mr Mohammed Abdel Salam of Public Security to meet them. He granted this reluctantly.

The first meeting took place on the 24th of March in the house of Mr Mohammed El-Hassan Abdalla Yassin, a former member of the Supreme Council and a leading figure in the DUP. He led the DUP delegation. The meeting was attended by the representatives of the DUP, SCP and the Umma Party. The delegation of the Umma Party flew in from Tripoli and was led by Dr Suliman Dibeilo, a former lecturer in Gezira University. We knew each other well; for we taught together at the Faculty of Science and Technology in the Gezira University in 1982. I was teaching there as part-time lecturer. The SCP delegation was led by Dr Izz el-Din Ali Aamer. Our position on the Charter was put in writing and formed the agenda of the discussion. Considerable progress was made but the other parties wanted to be given time to make consultations before the final agreed upon points were to be signed. We agreed to meet again on the 27th. The discussions resumed that day and the proposed amendments of the Charter were approved and signed. The details of these amendments will be discussed later on in this Chapter.

In the evening of the 22nd, I received a telephone call from Addis Ababa to the effect that the Chairman had sent an urgent message from the field that I must report back to Addis Ababa immediately in order to proceed to the front. I asked the reason behind this and I was informed that the Chairman had said it was the military situation on the ground which dictated this step. My interlocutor added that the order of recall included Cdr Martin Manyiel Ayuel who was undergoing medical treatment in London and Cdr Riek Machar Teny who was on a mission to Kinshasa with Cdr Lwal Diing Wol. All were to cut short the visits and even medical treatment. Something big must have befallen the SPLA, I thought. I asked the comrade whether he had heard news of any major sally by the Khartoum troops. His reply was that he didn't. I cleared my throat and told him that he should get a pen and paper and write down what I was going to dictate to him over the phone. I asked him to inform the Chairman that his message was received but I could not come immediately as I have already got an appointment to meet President Mubarak on Tuesday, the 27th, and that only after that will I take the first available flight to Addis Ababa. I asked him to read over to me what he had written after which we bade each other goodbye.

There and then I decided to continue with the programme of the visit. I was in Gambela barely two weeks before. Then I was told the troops were not ready. I was in Addis just four days earlier, I never heard of any graduation of new troops. So, whatever situation which might have developed could certainly wait. The SPLA forces were jettisoned out of Southern Blue Nile almost three months to the day and we did nothing. What could be worse? There was no one convincing reason to rush back to the field.

Our delegation had another meeting with Mr Namar in his office at 10.00 a.m. on Monday, the 26th. It was a brief one. We agreed on a summary of the issues discussed and the need to continue the dialogue. At the end of the meeting he informed us that President Mubarak was ready to receive us the next day.

The delegation met President Hosni Mubarak on Tuesday, the 27th of March in the presence of Mr Namar, the Minister of Public Security. The President stressed the urgency of arriving at a peaceful settlement of the fratricide in Sudan and urged that dialogue must be maintained. He was briefed about the discussions that took place between the delegation and the Minister and his staff on the possible modalities of bridging the gap between the positions of the SPLA and that of the Government of Sudan. At the end of the meeting, the President renewed his invitation to the Chairman, Dr John Garang, to visit Cairo.

After the meeting, Mr Mohammed Abdul Moniem, the press officer at the Presidency, gave a statement to the press that the delegation had handed President Mubarak a written message from Col. John Garang, Leader of the "Southern Movement" and that the meeting was within the context of the efforts being exerted by Egypt to create a conducive atmosphere in Sudan for the realization of a peaceful settlement of the Southern problem between "Garang" and the Government of Sudan. This statement was prominently carried by the Government dailies, El-Ahram and El-Jamhoria, on Wednesday, the 28th.

It is to be noted that in all the interviews and material published by the Egyptian newspapers during our visit to Cairo one thing was consistent, the avoidance of calling the SPLM/SPLA by its name. It was variously referred to as "Garang's movement" or the "Southern Movement". The only exception in this was the "El-Ahali" newspaper.

The 28th of March, our last day in Cairo, was a busy day. In addition to the meetings referred to earlier, we held a news conference with the foreign journalists in Egypt. In this conference we briefed the journalists on our ten-day visit to Cairo and the results achieved. It was also an opportunity to explain the objective and policies of the movement. Our plane took off from Cairo airport at 8.30 p.m. to make a connection at Jeddah airport. Contrary to our expectations, Jeddah airport turned out to be a complete disappointment. There was no "transit lounge" deserving the name. What we found were some chairs to sit on and nothing more; no waiter, no services, nothing at all! We sat uncomfortably on those chairs the whole night up to the time our plane took off at 7.00 a.m. on the 29th bound for Addis Ababa. We arrived the Ethiopian capital two hours later.

In less than 48 hours from my arrival to Addis Ababa, I received yet another message from the Chairman ordering me, Riek Machar, Martin Manyiel to report to his end within 72 hours. I was to inform the other two (who were in Nairobi and London, respectively) "if they are not in Addis as yet", according to the message (No. 238/3/90 dated 31/3/90) of the Chairman.

I left Addis Ababa for Gambela on a car at 12.30 afternoon on April 1, 1990. With me was Cdr Riek Machar who had arrived from Nairobi two days earlier. We arrived Gambela on the 2nd and proceeded the next day to Maiwut through Itang reaching there at about 7.30 p.m. A/Cdr Oyai Deng Ajak found the two of us a small hut outside the compound of the Chairman and C-in-C where we spent the night.

In the morning of Wednesday, the 4th, we paid a courtesy call on the Chairman. Then without much delay he went into business. He first called Cdr Riek Machar alone to brief him on his trip to Kinshasa and Nairobi. After that the Chairman called me in, again alone, to brief him on my trip to Egypt. These separate briefings took between three to four hours. Later in the afternoon each of us was served with a typed and signed copy of an Operation Order dated March 21, 1990. The

Chairman instructed us to study the order carefully in preparation for meeting him early morning the next day. Our scheduled meeting with the Chairman took place in the morning of the 5th. He opened the meeting by asking if we had any comments to make about the Operation Order. Naturally, none of us said anything. Although there was a lot to be said about the Order, it is unmilitary to discuss an Operation Order signed by the Chairman and C-in-C. The Chairman then proceeded to tell us that the forces were ready (in fact, some of them have gone ahead), that we were leaving that afternoon to our respective sectors of operations and that the rest of the logistics will follow.

At 4.00 p.m. the Chairman accompanied the two of us to where the cars were waiting. Shortly after, we drove off. My destination was Dajo. We drove the whole night and arrived Paiteth village, a few kilometres from Dajo, at about 2.00 a.m. There we set up camp for a couple of days until I was joined by Cdr Martin Manyiel Ayuel.

Bright Star Campaign, Phase 2/New Funj Campaign (BSC Phase 2/NFC)

The Operation Order referred to earlier was about military operations in the areas of Northern Upper Nile, Nasir District and Southern Blue Nile. Geographically, this is the area bounded to the east by the Ethiopian border, to the south by the Sobat river and Bahr el - Jebel up to about 32 km before Lake No, to the west by the border between Upper Nile and Kordofan regions and to the north by the 12th parallel.

The term "Bright Star Campaign", BSC for short, was first used with the forces that fought in and around Kapoeta town in December 87/January 88. I, personally, heard the term for the first time when the liberation of Kapoeta on January 26, 1988 was announced over Radio SPLA. It continued to be used since then. On the other hand, the term "New Funj Campaign", NFC for short, was introduced on 21/9/89 when the Chairman and C-in-C issued Command Policy and Directives No. 3.

According to the Chairman's message No. 015/1/90 dated 8/1/90 (Command Policy and Directives No. 4), the BSC was divided into three phases with each phase sub-divided into a number of sectors. Additionally, BSC phase 2 was combined with NFC. This is the basis of the Operation Order under consideration.

As shown in the appendix, the Operation Order dealt with: task organization, situation, mission, execution, administration and logistics, and command and signals. There was ten annexes to the Operation Order, the most relevant of which is Annex A on command, staff and organization which is also shown in the appendix.

A. The Operations in and around Boiny (Maban Town)

The Operations on Maban town were part and parcel of BSC Phase 2/New Funj Campaign as detailed in the Operation Order No. BSC/ Phase 2/NFC/01 dated March 21, 1990 (referred to earlier). The execution of this particular mission was outlined under para 4(b) (4) of the Order. I, therefore, became the overall commander of the Combined Command of sectors 4, 5 and 6; Cdr. Martin Manyiel Ayuel my deputy and A/Cdr Makuei Deng Majuc the Operations Officer.

The D-day for all sectors, as per the Campaign Commander's message No. 081/4/90, was set to be 10/4/90. However, due to logistical transport problems, the set date could not be possible and the Campaign Commander, as per his message No. 104/4/90, ordered sectors commanders to inform him at least 24 hours in advance about their combat readiness to commence operations. This was necessary for the purposes of coordination between the sectors. The forces under the combined command were Zahjan TF 1, 3, 5 and 6; New Funj TF 1 and 2 and Maban TFs.

The Maban TFs were the forces already deployed in sector 6 (Maban Independent Area Command) under the command of A/Cdr Makuei Deng Majuc. According to the Operation Order these were to be three TFs (Maban TF 1 and 2 and Gojam TF). The reality we found on the ground was that these three "TFs" totalled less than 300 men, a mere one TF. Zahjan and New Funj TFs were to be moved from Maiwut which was the assembly area for the whole campaign. By the time I arrived Paiteth, most of the force had arrived but some were still moving on foot on the way. Dajo was being manned by a company from the commando which was later withdrawn when all the Zahjan and New Funj TFs arrived. The movements of troops, their reorganization, movements of supplies, etc, took many days. The supply of logistics was always behind schedule due to lack of cars at the rear.

Zahjan TF 6 of about 250 men was deployed to defend Dajo. The New Funj two TFs totalling about 590 men were deployed around Yabus enemy garrison. The other Zahjan TFs were moved towards Maban town to join the forces of the area in the attack on the town. I established my HQ at Keiweji. From there I sent recce teams to as close to the town as was practicable. All these were translated into a draft Operation Order which was discussed with all the officers through a sand table in the morning of the 24th of April. After thorough discussion the Operation Order was rewritten and I signed it as the overall commander on the 25th. I had initially set the D-day as the 26th to coincide with the first day after the Ramadan Bairam "Eid El-Fitr". However, this had to be adjusted because of the delay in the supply of some important items from the rear. The Zahjan TFs that had assembled at Keiweji were addressed by Cdr. Martin Manyiel and me in the evening of the 24th before leaving for Dhangaji for deployment around the town.

According to our Operation Order, the plan was to commence shelling the town on the 27th of April and on the next day, Zahjan TF 1 would attack and occupy northeast of the town. This is the area of the militia, school (used as an army outpost), police and prisons quarters and Malakia. In other words, the whole town with the exception of the army garrison were to be occupied that day. Following this, Zahjan TF1 was to dig in and defend the occupied positions so that support weapons could be moved there to continue shelling the army garrison in order to soften its defenses. Zahjan TF3, already deployed on the stream before shelling started, was to be the reserve force during the attack of Zahjan TF1 and on the accomplishment of the mission of TF1 as above, TF3 was to attack the enemy garrison and to occupy the primary defensive enemy positions. The final assault was to be accomplished by the rest of the forces on the third day or thereafter depending on the tactical situation.

Due to logistical problems, shelling started early morning of Saturday the 28th. Zahjan TF1 overran the militia, school, Malakia, police and prisons quarters with relative ease early morning of Sunday, the 29th. The enemy forces in these positions ran to the army garrison. However, our attacking force did not dig in as planned. Some of them were euphoric and continued pursuing the fleeing enemy up to the army garrison. There they were subjected to sustained enemy fire and suffered heavy casualties and when their ammos got exhausted they made disorganized withdrawal. Most of the force had remained behind bogged down by looting and could not either dig in or come to the rescue of their comrades under fire from the enemy in the army garrison. Eventually, the whole force withdrew in disarray to the stream carrying along their booties. The same day, the enemy reoccupied his lost ground despite the considerable efforts of our support weapons to deny them these positions.

On the same day, the 29th of April, Zahjan TF 3 and one coy of Zahjan TF 5 attacked the town; the same positions which were reoccupied by the enemy after the withdrawal of TF 1. Their battle was not as easy as the first. The enemy returned fire vigorously using all their weapons and our force suffered heavy casualties and made disorganized withdrawal. These joined Zahjan TF 1 beyond the stream looking after the cows, goats and sheep captured from the town. Soon after, the soldiers started to desert in big numbers.

On the 30th of April and the 1st of May, the HQs of sectors 4 and 5 plus one Coy from Zahjan TF 5 attacked the enemy main defensive positions but was met with stiff resistance and our force withdrew tactically to the stream. All this time, the shelling of the town was continuous. With the news of the advance of the enemy reinforcement towards the town, the shelling was stepped up on the 2nd of May. In this, the 120mm and 82mm mortars, 76mm AT gun and the ZSU-23 GPHMG were all used. The garrison was on fire and the enemy in absolute confusion. It was almost certain that the enemy would withdraw that night.

Prior to the attack on Maban town, our forces of sector 2 had attacked Sursuru on the 17th of April and moved back to Khor Far the same day. The enemy sent to the area a convoy code-named "Agbudh El-Harriri" to hunt down these SPLA forces that attacked Sursuru. The enemy convoy entered Khor Far on the 26th but did not find the SPLA there. It then pulled back to Ulu. When Maban town was attacked on the 28th, this convoy was ordered to move immediately through Chali el-Fil to reinforce Maban town. The convoy advanced from Chali on the 1st of May. It comprised ten cars including two tanks.

The bulk of Maban TFs and one coy of Zahjan TF 5 were deployed to block the Chali - Maban route. They laid ambushes at Jaberdida. As the enemy reinforcement advanced, one of its trucks hit a land mine planted by our ambushing force. The explosion was followed by a brief engagement then our force withdrew. The enemy occupied the positions previously occupied by our forces, reorganized and spent the night there. Meanwhile when information on the above engagement was received, most of the support weapons (two jeeps mounted with 14.5 mm GPHMG, one Ural mounted with 14.5 mm4B and the BM 122mm) were withdrawn from around Maban town and sent to the ambush site together with another coy of Maban TFs. The forces which were on the ambush site informed them that the enemy had withdrawn backwards from where the engagement had taken place that day. The new arrivals decided to spend the night and attack the enemy early morning the next day.

On the 2nd of May, while advancing on the reported enemy position, our force together with the support weapons unknowingly found themselves inside the enemy encampment. The enemy was equally off-guard but was the first to open fire. Our infantry withdrew without putting up a fight and the fighting was left to the support arms alone. They fought valiantly and managed to break through the enemy cordon. Unhappily, there was no infantry to complete the rest of a job well done. In the process these support weapons had to be withdrawn. The enemy regrouped again at Jaberdida and moved cross-country eastwards to reappear from the northeast of Maban town entering it at about 4.00 p.m.

While the fighting with the enemy convoy was taking place at Jaberdida, our positions around Maban town were being bombed by an enemy high-altitude Antonov plane. Since our forces on the stream around the town were already in a state of disorganization, the enemy reinforcement entered without significant resistance. The hopes of capturing the town that day were completely dashed. The next obvious course of action was to lay a long siege on the town. The food shortage, however, became very acute and the soldiers deserting increased in number.

Soon after entering into Maban town, the commanding officer of the enemy's "Agbudh El-Harriri" convoy asked for reinforcements to start combing the area and to destroy SPLA camps. He urged Damazin to send more forces quickly. On the 6th, the enemy planned to evacuate their wounded from Maban town. According to the intercepted enemy message (I.E.M), a force would leave Chali to meet at Nila the convoy carrying the wounded from Maban. At Nila the convoy from Maban will hand over the wounded to the Chali convoy and return. The first information was that the enemy would follow the straight Maban - Jaberdida route and our forces of Zahjan TF 1 and one coy of Maban TFs were deployed at Jaberdida to ambush the convoy carrying the enemy wounded.

Another information was then received that the enemy wounded will follow the Gismalla route and, again, another force comprising Zahjan TF 5 and the HQs of sectors 4 and 5 were sent to Gismalla to lay an ambush there while the first force remained in its position. On the 10th, the enemy advanced taking the Maban - Jaberdida route. Far from being ambushed, it was the enemy convoy which attacked our force instead and dispersed it. According to the commander of Zahjan TF 1 who was commanding the force, he did not expect an enemy coming from Maban town and hence had deployed his force expecting an attack from the opposite direction of Chali. A stupid excuse by all standards. It is worth mentioning that the enemy convoy was composed of only four cars. This should just have been minced beef for a motivated officer especially bearing in mind the fact that our ambushing force was composed of more than 400 men. This easy victory strengthened the belief of the commanding officer of the enemy's "Agbudh El-Harriri" convoy in his ability to clear the area from the SPLA. He asked for a quick reinforcement from Damazin so that he can clear the Maban area from the SPLA and advance to capture Dajo. Indeed, a convoy was sent and it entered Maban town on Sunday the 13th of May without any resistance.

On the 15th, the enemy came out of Maban town with the intention to clear SPLA forces around the town and to burn Dhangaji, Liang, Keiweji, etc. As this attack was expected it was planned to engage the enemy in the forest around the town in self-supporting ambushes. A force of about 500 men was deployed. However, the enemy was able to penetrate one ambush after another with little resistance as most of the soldiers took to flight with the first enemy shells. In the end it was the HQs of sectors 4, 5 and 6 supported by the support weapons that put up a desperate last fight along the stream (Khor Yabus). This stiff resistance checked the enemy's advance forcing them to retreat without crossing the stream as they had planned. The enemy suffered many casualties and one of their tanks was disabled but they managed to pull it along in their withdrawal. This was a golden opportunity for our forces to take revenge on the enemy but the soldiers just refused to fight. Again, the conduct of Zahjan TF 1 commander was blame-worthy. His force was to block the Maban-Piakeji route and to flank the enemy when they are engaged by the forces which were given the principal role in the action. The commanding officer of Zahjan TF 1 closed his radio and ceased contact with the HQ. The force deserted there and then while their commander remained out of contact for two days without reporting to the HQ.

After this followed massive desertions from among Zahjan forces and finally the total number of Zahjan TF 1 and 5 which remained was only one coy. Hence, the two task forces were amalgamated and put under the command of the TF 5 commander and sent to Bugaya where they stood a better chance of getting food from the citizens. Zahjan TF 3, now totalling about 150 men, had been earlier sent to the same area for the same reason. As of the 12th, in my capacity as the overall commander, I was holding a series of meetings with the officers and making parades with the forces to probe into the reasons behind the obvious reluctance of the forces to fight. Most of their grievances centred around the treatment they underwent when they were forcibly rounded up from the refugees centres (Itang and Pinywudo) and subsequently in Bonga training centre. We shall return to this point later. Apart from the sick, a good number of them were old men and youngsters who were still in school when they were rounded up. There were indications, however, that some irresponsible officers agitated negatively among the soldiers to make them desert but there was no material evidence to be produced against them.

After the engagements of the 15th, the enemy requested more reinforcements to continue with their initial mission. A convoy was sent from Damazin which entered Maban town on the 31st of May. On our side, it was necessary to keep pressure on the enemy by being aggressive through raids, shelling, etc. But as our forces were deserting the only way to do this was to shell the town by BM-21 rocket launcher to delay the enemy while our forces in Bugaya were on the move to reinforce us at Dhangaji (where I had moved to since the 29th of May). The shelling of the town took place on the 1st of June. On the 2nd, another enemy convoy entered Maban town and Damazin ordered the whole force to get out and clear the area of SPLA presence. Our forces planted anti-tank and anti-personnel mines around the town and north of the stream. By then the water in the stream was drying up and it was feared that the enemy tanks and equipment might cross the stream from where our cars used to cross into the town during the earlier operations. The Operations Officer was, therefore, ordered to plant anti-tank mines there. By the 2nd of June our force from Bugaya had arrived and our deployment was complete.

On the 3rd, the enemy got out of the town in the direction of Piakeji but returned at about 1200 hours noon without reaching there. There was no obvious explanation to this enemy behaviour except that the detonation of some anti-personnel mines may have led the enemy to conclude that there was a minefield ahead. This explanation reinforced the premise that the enemy may cross the stream at the suspected point.

Indeed, on the 4th, the enemy crossed their tanks and other equipment using wood logs as a bridge at the very point suspected that they might cross at. There were no anti-tank mines to detonate, for it turned out that the operations officer did not order the planting of any. The enemy was engaged by our forces between 1200 hours to 1600 hours. The enemy tanks dominated the fight. These would advance for more than 300 metres away from their infantry chasing the fleeing soldiers. This enemy superiority was dampened only by the two jeeps mounted with 14.5mm GPHMG which put up a courageous and tenacious fight. But, obviously, there was little they can do against tanks and with no infantry to be supported by them. Eventually, the enemy was able to burn Leka, Dhangaji camp and the villages around before he returned to the town in the evening. More soldiers of Zahjan TF 3 and New Funj TF deserted right from the battle ground. Our losses that could be ascertained were 18 KIA, more WIA and at least two captured by the enemy. The figures could be higher because desertion hindered making an accurate count.

By the end of these operations, the only force that remained was a total of about 450 men of Zahjan and New Funj broken down to 200 and 250 men, respectively. Most of those who remained in Zahjan were the NCOs who were nominated for the Cadet officers course but could not attend as they were said to have reported late for admission to the course. Since April, the two New Funj TFs were harassing the enemy around the garrison of Yabus. Some soldiers of TF 2 had deserted leading to the amalgamation of the two task forces into just one New Funj TF. This task force was called to participate in the last battle when the enemy in Maban town planned to get out.

Finally, another enemy convoy entered Maban town on the 27th of June making a total of five reinforcements since the operation started.

The enemy Antonov has also been active during the same period. It first dropped bombs on our positions around Maban town on the 2nd of May from 0810 to 0850 hours just before the enemy convoy entered the town. The Antonov was active again on the 8th from 1555 to 1615 hours, targeting Dhangaji with its bombs. The third bombing was of Keiweji on the 19th of May from 1410 to 1430 hours. The fourth was on the 31st of May around Maban town from 1000 to 1045 hours before the enemy reinforcement entered the town. Keiweji was bombed again by the Antonov on the 22nd of June. Fortunately, these air bombings were not quite effective; the only serious casualty was a citizen who got the fingers of one of his feet chopped off by a shrapnel.

B. The Troops used

A proper appraisal of the operations in and around Maban town could not fail to notice the ill-preparedness of the troops to the mission. These troops were mainly Zahjan TFs. What type of forces were they?

Zahjan – the Arabic equivalent of "irritated" or "annoyed" – was the name given to the units formed from soldiers forcibly collected from Itang and Pinywudo refugees camps in September/October 1989. On September 21, 1989, the Chairman and C-in-C imposed martial law in Itang and Pinywudo following bloody clashes which took place between the refugees and the Ethiopians accompanied by extensive looting of the properties of the latter. He appointed martial law administrators in both camps with extensive powers to impose the martial law. Para 4(G) of the order (Message No. 188/9/89) stipulates:

> Officers, NCOs and men in Itang and Pinywudo who have no assignment or units who are staying without proper documents are to report to Bonga with Departure Order from the martial law administrator.

This part of the order was used to forcibly round up any officer, NCO and men who did not carry the proper papers. Cars were ready to transport them immediately to Bonga. It was the "*Kasha*" in action. The "*Kasha*" which the SPLA has always been vociferous in condemning. In fact, the martial law administrators were honest and called it as such.

The soldiers so collected were certainly irritated or annoyed, if not downright disillusioned, as a result of the way they were treated. Their problems did not end with the lashing (both physical and verbal) in the refugees camps but the same treatment, sometimes worse, continued in Bonga for all the months they spent there. They told stories which have to be lived through to be believed. These Draconian measures against them had very negative impact on their morale.

These are the officers, NCOs and men who were organized in March 1990 into Zahjan task forces. The only exception was Zahjan TF 2 which was in Bilpam and composed of soldiers of the former A-2 from the Lou area. The other Zahjan TFs were the "fresh" forces to undertake such a major operation as the attack on Maban town.

C. Conclusions

The following remarks and conclusions can be made about the operations in and around Maban town in the period from 28/4/1990 to 27/6/1990.

1. The enemy was not expecting an attack on Maban town and our attack on the 28th of April took them by complete surprise. However, the enemy's reaction time was shorter than expected due to the presence nearby of their convoy code-named *"Agbudh El-Harriri"* referred to earlier.

2. The fighting spirit of our soldiers was at its nadir. On the first day of the attack, the main concern of the soldiers was to loot the town. After having looted what they could lay their hands on, they had no further incentive to continue fighting. Indeed, some made their own camps feeding on their looted cows, goats and sheep. The Zahjan forces were not combat effective as of the third day. The forces from Maban area were not any better.

3. Apart from the crew of the 14.5mm and ZSU-23 GPHMG, the training of the gunners of the other support weapons was wanting. Although these weapons fought with courage and determination, the fire delivered by these guns was not accurate enough. Therefore, the superiority we had over the enemy in support weapons could not be fully exploited.

4. The supply of logistics was always behind time. The lack of food in the area contributed much to the instability of the forces.

5. Some commanding officers made grave errors in the execution of their missions. For example, the operations officer did not plant the mines as ordered, Zahjan TF 1 commander deliberately severed contact with the HQ at the most critical moment, the commander at Jaberdida who did not know the exact location of the enemy on 1/5/90, the Zahjan TF 1 commander who made the wrong deployment on 10/5/1990, etc.

6. If our forces put up some resistance on the 15th of May as did the HQ, the enemy would have suffered even more casualties. By their own admission, as per the I.E.M. No. 69 dated 16/5/90, the enemy reported to Damazin that we forced on them a commanding siege. They were seeing our soldiers all around them in big numbers. What the enemy did not know was the fact that these soldiers were not willing to give battle.

7. The fight of the 4th of June, proved to the enemy that we did not have a jeep mounted anti-tank gun as they assumed on the 15th of May according to the same I.E.M. quoted above. This gave their tanks more confidence to be more aggressive than was tactically reasonable.

8. If we had a jeep mounted with anti-tank weapon the course of the battles on the 15th of May and the 4th of June would have been different.

9. The nature of the operations in and around Maban town demanded a quick capture of the town in order to proceed to the other objectives deep in Southern Blue Nile. This was not possible mainly because the troops deployed were ill-prepared for the mission. Hence, even if Maban town were to be captured early in May, the concrete situation was that the force we had could not have

repulsed an enemy counter offensive to recapture the town. We did not have a strategic reserve to resort to.

10. The enemy attaches great importance to holding Maban town in order to block the SPLA out of Southern Blue Nile. During the engagements, the town received five reinforcements and air strikes were quite frequent.

Initiatives on Peace and Unity of the Opposition

Two important political developments took place in March 1990 that deserve consideration on their own. These were: the American Initiative in searching for a peaceful settlement to the war in Sudan, and the SPLA's endorsement of the Charter of the NDA in pursuit of the unity of all the forces opposed to the NIF military dictatorship in Khartoum. They will be discussed in turn.

A. The American Initiative 1990

What became known as the "American Initiative" was a six-page document which was to have been issued as a "joint declaration" by the SPLA and the Government of Sudan. The document was titled: "Agreement on a Framework for the Peaceful Settlement of Sudan's Internal Conflict." As mentioned earlier, it was handed to the SPLA in Addis Ababa in March 1990 by Mr Jack Davidson of the U.S State Department. What was it all about?

The paper had three sub-titles: Basic Principles for the Settlement, the Process for a Settlement in Three Phases, and the Modalities for Disengagement of Forces in Sudan. The last appeared as an Annex and, as is clear from the title, it dealt with the military aspect of the conflict.

I was asked by the Chairman to draft a response of the SPLA to the proposal. I prepared my comments and recommendations in writing. These appear in the appendix. As it was for group discussion, many small details were left out to be covered in the meeting during the explanation of the response. Only four of us in the whole Movement were involved in this exercise. Apart from the Chairman and myself, the other two were: Cdr. Martin Manyiel and A/Cdr Deng Alor Kuol.

The American proposal was made up of two components: the political and the military. In the proposal, the military component appears as an annex. Although the proposal leaves a lot to be desired regarding the way it was written, I recommended that we adopt the political component as it stood without amendment. The points were reasonable and as far as I was concerned, fine-tuning the language was not the crux of the matter at such an early stage of the negotiation. It were the principles on which an agreement was to be based that mattered. It was also clear that the mediator or facilitator was interested in our stand on the principles.

It is the annex, or the military component of the proposal, which was quite off the mark and needed to be revised. However, it was positive to note that the annex affirms the principle of separation of forces. The issue was where to draw the line or lines of demarcation. This was a bold move. The Americans proposed the line made up of "the Bahr-el-Ghazal, Bahr-al-Arab, Nahr Sobat" as the northern border between the SPLA and the Government of Sudan troops. The use of the word *"nahr"* - the Arabic equivalent of the word "river" - was rather unfortunate. It strengthened some of the lingering suspicion from our side that the document was either Khartoum's or prepared in consultation with it. In any case, this line was arbitrary without any historical or political justification . I proposed instead the 12th parallel which marks the northern border of Southern Sudan. Inside the South itself, my recommendation was that all government forces be pulled out of all the garrisons and that the three main towns in the South (Juba, Malakal and Wau) be free of any military presence up to a radius of 10 km from the centre of the town. Outside this radius, of course, will be SPLA territory. Furthermore, the role of an appropriate African observer force was affirmed rather than being on "call" as it came in the original proposal. Finally, my recommendation on the appointment of civilian governors in the South was that they be chosen by the SPLM/A from amongst competent Sudanese who may or may not be members of the movement. This was the first time ever for the SPLA to consider sharing power with non-SPLA members. I expected eyebrows to be raised but I prepared myself for that.

Before handing over my draft to the Chairman, I shared the final version of it with Cdr Martin Manyiel who gave his full approval to it. When I met the Chairman on the matter, he made it clear that he very much welcomed the principles on which the American Initiative was based. In his words: "this will shorten the struggle and save us lives". However, he did not hide his fears about the connotation which may be read into it by others inside and outside the SPLA. The Chairman was wary that the endorsement of the initiative would be misunderstood to be an acceptance of separating the South and the North. I thought there was nothing to be apprehensive about. In any liberation struggle there are always two areas in the country concerned: the liberated areas under the administration of guerrillas and the "other area" under the control of the government. These areas are separate and distinct in the way each is being administered. It is true each side strives to bring the other area under its control but this is a protracted process in which the separateness of both gets consolidated with time. Therefore, depending on how soon one side imposes its will on the other or when peaceful settlement is reached, there can never be avoiding the de facto reality of a politically and administratively divided country. This was already the case in Sudan and the SPLA cannot shy away from the fact. I emphasized the fact that the de facto situation in this case would be by agreement with a definite timetable and stressed that this would exert pressure on the parties expected to participate in the Constitutional Conference, envisaged in the initiative, to be more serious in tackling the issues that divided the country. We agreed on this point.

On the line which separates the SPLA and the government troops, the Chairman suggested the line that passed through the most northern tip of the border of Southern Kordofan. The two of us actually drew this line on a Michelin road map of north-east Africa and measured it to be 12.76 degrees north which approximates to 13 degrees north. This was the origin of the 13th parallel which was later adopted in the SPLA position paper. I argued that the SPLA would be seen as realistic and score more points by insisting on the 12th parallel as a non-negotiable point because of the well known distinctiveness of South Sudan. The Chairman replied that the authors of the document (by then, he had his doubts that the Americans may have been negotiating on behalf of Khartoum) were expecting the line to be a point of haggling and that was why their proposal on it came the way it did. The Chairman went on: "this being the case, let us start from the 13th parallel". I conceded the point.

The Chairman also drew my attention to the phrase "pull out" used in relation to the second point in my proposed annex. He suggested that it be replaced by the phrase "disengaged to". This was quite a valid point which I readily accepted. Psychologically, the phrase "pull out" is too strong and could be construed to imply defeat which no side was ready to take. Finally, the Chairman added a new point which was not in the original proposal. This was in relation to the security of the national capital and that it should be the responsibility of the two armies. By this suggestion, he certainly wanted to allay the fears of those who may think that the Initiative was a "separation thing".

On the political component of the American Initiative, the Chairman agreed with the spirit of it but thought that precise wording was necessary in such an important document. Therefore it became necessary to elaborate on point 1 of the Basic Principles, the qualification of democracy as multi-party in point 3, and the use of the phrase "constructive disengagement" in point 4. A fourth phase was added to the process of achieving the settlement. It was on the formation of a broad-based government. I thought this could have been taken care of by the phase on the National Constitutional Conference since a broad-based government would definitely be one of the decisions to be taken by it, but the Chairman insisted that it be highlighted as a phase of its own.

The above gives an outline on how our response to the American Initiative (see the appendix) was developed. It is important to observe that, although the SPLA insisted on that the system in Sudan be multi-party democracy, it, at the same time, was selective on which parties are to take part in such a system. As such, Phase Two of the process for the settlement refers to "agreed representatives of relevant political parties" to take part in the National Constitutional Conference. This position was in line with what came in the Chairman's speech of August 14, 1989, when he ruled out the participation of the sectarian parties (Umma, DUP and NIF) in the interim broad-based government of national unity (see para 46(a) of the speech).

When it was ready, I personally delivered the response at the U.S. embassy in Addis Ababa. I did not hear anything again on the Initiative except that it fell through. How and when, I do not know. I am not quite sure either if Khartoum had ever given a written response.

B. The Charter of the National Democratic Alliance

One of the first decisions taken by the group of military officers who seized power in Sudan on June 30, 1989, was to issue a proclamation imposing a ban on the political parties which were operating under the democratic setup they had overthrown. These political parties were thus driven underground and continued to agitate against the military dictatorship.

On the 21st of October 1989, eleven political parties and more than eighty professional associations and trade unions signed a political Charter which committed the signatories to the struggle to overthrow the Junta promising a return to democracy. The choice of date was not without significance. It marked the 25th anniversary of the first popular uprising that brought down the military regime of General Ibrahim Abboud in 1964. Most of the organizations which signed the Charter worked closely with the SPLA before the coup when they were organized as the National Alliance for National Salvation. It was just natural, therefore, that they sought the involvement of the SPLA in the new move to forge a common front to fight the Junta.

The movement received the first official communication on the matter in January 1990. It was a letter dated the 1st of January and signed on behalf of the NDA by Mr El-Khatim Adlan of the Sudan Communist Party. It called amongst other things for the SPLA to sign the Charter of the NDA. The letter went on:

We do not just mean the literal sense of signing, which should be done whenever the circumstances allow, but we mean that you declare your agreement to the Charter through all the mass media available to you as you see fit. Of course, we do not rule out the possibility that you may have some additions, amendments or reservations. It is your right to express all these in the document which you will issue agreeing to the substance of the Charter, its basic problems and the direction it is charting for the future of our country.

The movement did not discuss the matter but in the same month the Chairman sent a three-man delegation to Tripoli. There, it met with Mr Mubarak el-Fadhil al-Mahdi where the two sides signed on the 29th of January an "Agreement of Alliance between the SPLM/SPLA and Umma Party". A clumsily written document, this agreement made ripples within the leadership of the SPLA, at least some of us who were in Addis Ababa by then, for it committed the SPLA to "making short-cut to the present war by taking power in Khartoum". This was contrary to the declared policy of the movement which was opposed to military coups. Furthermore, the document's claim of having agreed on a "political and military strategic alliance" between the SPLM/A and the Umma Party did not go down well with the members of the movement in Addis Ababa by that time. Although the Chairman did not express his objections to the document, he nevertheless, did not raise an objection when I, Dr Mansour Khalid and others insisted that it be revised and renegotiated if necessary. Indeed, the agreement was revisited and the final version of it was signed in Addis Ababa on the 22nd of February by Cdr. Lwal Diing Wol on behalf of the SPLM/A and Mr Mubarak El-Fadhil al-Mahdi on behalf of the Umma party as a joint communique. The two agreements signed in Tripoli and Addis Ababa on the 29th of January and the 22nd of February, respectively, are included in the appendix.

The relevant paragraph in the 22nd of February joint communique stipulated that:

> After a careful study of the Charter and programme of the National
> Democratic Alliance (NDA) signed on 31st October 1989 by the
> Confederation of the Trade Unions, Representatives of the regular
> forces and political parties, the SPLM/SPLA has agreed to the principles
> of the Charter with the reservation that it has the right to revise and/or
> amend the details of the Charter and programme which were worked
> out in its absence in a meeting of the signatories to the Charter.

It was in this context that the Chairman briefed our delegation to
Cairo charging it with the responsibility to meet the representatives of
the NDA there to discuss with them the membership of the SPLM/A
in the newly formed alliance.

In Cairo we had a close look at the Charter and prepared a
position paper on the amendments we saw necessary for the SPLM/A
to append its signature to the Charter and thus become a member
of the NDA. It was this position paper which we discussed with the
Sudanese opposition parties in Cairo. The paper was written in the
Arabic language. An unofficial, my own, rendering of it into English
appears as an appendix in this book.

Our first concern was that the preamble of the Charter was
written in a way which lacked the required self-criticism on the side
of the political forces which were in government for the three years
that constituted the third democratic era in Sudan. This did not
augur well for a fresh start with a clean slate. Secondly, there was a
conspicuous absence of any mention of the struggle to attain peace
in the country as part of the programme of "daily struggle" as came
in the Charter. Thirdly, the Charter was silent on the armed struggle
as one of the means of fighting the Junta in Khartoum. Fourthly, the
status of the SPLA troops during the interim period was not dealt
with. It was imperative to define this clearly because the issue of the
security arrangements in general and the Armed Forces in particular
have always been a contentious issue in the North-South relations.
Finally, it was our contention that one of the strong reasons that led
to the success of military coups in seizing power was the abuse of
democracy itself by the ruling parties. Thus, the Charter needed to

set out some guidelines in the exercise of democracy at least in the interim period.

The above points formed the core of our position paper presented for discussion with the representatives of the NDA in Cairo. The rest of the points were concerned either with the clarity of issues or putting forward a realistic attainable programme within the span of time targeted by the charter. The movement reaffirmed its commitment to the struggle for democracy and to being part and parcel of the NDA.

As mentioned under a sub-heading earlier in this Chapter, these points were discussed as from March 24, 1990, agreed upon and signed on the 27th. The parties issued a press statement after the meeting which stated, *inter alia*, the following:

1 The parties have agreed on all the issues raised in the position paper presented by the delegation of the SPLM/A on the Charter;

2 That the position paper just agreed upon be attached as part and parcel of the Charter;

3 The meeting recommends the incorporation of the SPLM/A's ideas as above into the Charter so as to produce one document that confirms the unity of the forces of the NDA.

The meeting reiterated the commitment of members of the NDA to continue with the struggle to overthrow the oppressive NIF military regime and to strive to restore democracy and to rebuild it on a sound foundation, the holding of the Constitutional Conference and to undertake to implement all the provisions of the Charter and its attachments.

Days of Tension

I was in Keiweji when I heard rumours towards the end of May that the Chairman was about to go on a trip abroad. It had become his habit to do so without informing members of the High Command.

He leaves instructions with his signalists to continue receiving radio messages from all SPLA units normally as if he was there.

I saw it necessary to immediately remind the Chairman about our discussion with him on the 17th of February in Addis Ababa where he promised to call for a High Command meeting by the end of June. The meeting was likely to be held close to the international borders and we had some members of the High Command as far away as in Bahr el Ghazal, Nuba Mountains and Northern Upper Nile. Hence, if there were to be a meeting by the end of June, they needed to be informed in May so as to give them enough time to be able to walk to the meeting place. It was the rainy season and there was no way of using cars in the areas concerned.

I wrote the reminder on the 1st of June in the form of a radio message addressed to the Chairman repeated to all members of the High Command. The message reads:

Top Secret

FM: Alpha Beta
To: Thunder

R: Spear	R: Hammer	R: Sennar
R: Merowe	R: Kush	R: Amara
R: Napata	R: Soba	R: Ivory
R: Yermuk	R: Matata	

001/6/90

1 Reference Thunder's 015/1/90 and 045/1/90 ordering all High Command members to be physically in the field to repulse the enemy's offensive in the dry season ending on 30/6/90. I suggest that a meeting of the High Command be convened as soon as possible after 30/6/90.

2 This is a matter of utmost urgency to discuss and take decisions on issues of strategy and policy in the conduct of our revolutionary war. As the movement enters its eighth (8th) year, many political developments have taken place inside the movement, in Sudan, in the region and internationally. These are bound to have an impact

on us and this calls for our collective consideration.

3   We have two (2) Cdrs and a big number of A/Cdrs. They can take command of the forces while the meeting of the High Command is in progress.

4   This is for your consideration.

This radio message was received by the HQ of the Chairman in the morning of the same day. I proceeded to prepare in a written form the issues I would like to raise for discussion in the expected meeting of the High Command. I typed the points on a portable typewriter I was carrying with me. This paper was titled "Towards Organizing the SPLM" and is reproduced as an appendix in this book. Four copies were produced. I sent one to the Chairman and one each to Cdr. Martin Manyiel Ayuel, who was with me in Keiweji, and to Cdr Riek Machar Teny who was around Melut area. I kept the last copy for myself.

On the 5th of June, Cdr Martin Manyiel and I moved to Rubub south of Keiweji. Martin had earlier requested permission from the Chairman to be allowed to resume his medical treatment which was cut short in March because of the operations. His message was not replied. In Rubub he contacted the signalists of the Chairman urging them to remind him of his case. It was then that we positively learned that the Chairman had gone on a visit abroad. We did not know how long the visit would take. Cdr Martin was really suffering. When he tries to walk for a few hundreds of metres his body heats up especially the feet which have to be soaked in water to get cooled.

I did not see any reason why he was being kept in the field with us, particularly that the operations were over. Even if the operations were still on he needed to be healthy to contribute effectively. When Cdr. Martin told me what he got from the signalists of the Chairman, I suggested to him that he should go for medical treatment. He advised me that we should wait for the Chairman but I prevailed on him to go. It is true we were both members of the High Command but at the same time he was my deputy and so I can exercise my own judgement on matters under my command. I gave him permission and Cdr. Martin Manyiel left for Itang on Saturday the 9th of June on a car. The next day I moved to Lool on Khor Dajo where I established my HQ for the rest of the period I spent in the area.

The first communication I got from the Chairman was announcing his arrival back "after 35 days away". This was on 22/6/90 in a message addressed to all High Command members and ten other senior officers. The full text of the message is shown in the appendix. The only briefing the Chairman could give the High Command about his 35-day visit was the following:

I arrived back yesterday 21/6/90 after 35 days away during which time I visited ten (10) countries and met their Presidents. The visits were very successful as we are or will be getting some military assistance from seven (7) of these countries.

Counting backwards, one can now say that the Chairman must have left for the visit abroad on or around the 17th of May. Who accompanied him in the visits? Which are the countries visited? Which among them offered military assistance? What is the nature of this military assistance? These and other related questions, the Chairman did not see necessary to brief his High Command about.

After the above briefing, the Chairman significantly added the following:

Above is for your information and also to allay fears of those under your commands who might have been concerned about the recent developments in Europe and the Soviet Union. The truth is that since 1983, Eastern Europe, Soviet Union, U.S.A. etc. of the big countries, none of these has ever given us any military assistance. The impact of the changes in the international situation on our military supplies is thus marginal and indirect. And to assure them there is no cause for alarm.

This is Dr John Garang at his best. It did not need much intelligence to discern that the Chairman wanted to "allay fears" of members of the High Command itself. Thus the call for a High Command meeting was an "alarm" unjustified by the fact that "the impact of the changes in the international situation on our military supplies is thus marginal and indirect". When I met my colleague in the High Command, Cdr. Lwal Diing Wol, in Itang later, the first thing he told me was that my message No. 001/6/90 has been replied by the Chairman's message above and hence he thought no High Command meeting will ever take place. He was right.

On receiving the Chairman's message above, I concluded that he was not yet prepared to call for a meeting of the High Command as I requested on the 1st of June. It was not until the 6th of July that he directly replied my request which he chose to term a "recommendation". It was terse and non-committal on the issue. It reads:

Top Secret

Date: 6/7/90
FM: Thunder
TO: Alpah Beta
INFO: Spear　　　INFO: Hammer
034/7/90
Ref. your 001/6/90. Whereas I agree with the recommendation, message is unprocedural. The repeated to all High Command members is at best unnecessary.

How informing "all High Command members is at best unnecessary" on a request for a meeting that involves them is mind-boggling. But he then chose to inform two of them; on what basis? Needless to say, there was certainly a disguised threat by using the phrase "at best" in the context.

It was imperative for me to explain myself frankly and politely. I sent him the following message:

Top Secret

Date: 7/7/90
FM: Alpha Beta
TO: Thunder

INFO: Spear   INFO: Hammer
017/7/90
Ref. your 034/7/90. I am glad that my suggestion for a meeting [of
the High Command] is accepted. As to the procedure, frankly, I am
not aware of the procedures of the High Command as a political body.
I was only relying on common sense. I am deeply sorry if informing
colleagues was unprocedural.

The Chairman did not respond to this message and the idea of a
High Command meeting was laid to rest. However, subsequent events
indicated that the Chairman took the episode with hard feelings. He
was together with Cdr. William Nyuon and Cdr. Salva Kiir when he
wrote his 034/7/90 and there can be no doubt he discussed with them
its contents, including his own interpretation of the idea of a High
Command meeting.

On the 31st of July, I requested from the Chairman permission
to go to Zinc/Gambela in order to meet him to discuss with him
the military situation in my theatre of operations: the lessons learnt
from the last battles and the way forward. While in Zinc, I was also to
coordinate certain logistical matters connected with my sector. Finally,
my presence in Zinc was also going to be an opportunity for me to
meet my wife. I explained to the Chairman that it takes no more than
five days to walk to Itang/Zinc from where I was.

The reply of the Chairman came on the 13th of August that there
was nothing urgent in what I wanted to go to Gambela for and that
he will not be in Gambela area but Cdr. Salva Kiir "may be there and
if so you brief him and discuss as came in your point B(1) of your
message." Knowing the way the SPLA works there was no purpose to
be served by discussing the matters at hand with Cdr. Salva. He can do
absolutely nothing without reference to the Chairman. Nonetheless, I
resolved not to provide an excuse and accepted his proposal to meet
Salva. I was given thirty days as from the 22nd of August to accomplish the mission as came in my message.

I was at Dajo as from the 13th of August and the last message of
the Chairman on permission to go to Itang on duty got me there. I left

Dajo at about 6.00 a.m. on the 25th and spent the night at Wadessa. In the morning of Sunday the 26th, I held a meeting with the chiefs of Wadessa area to discuss the problems facing them and to brief them on the policies of the movement. I left Wadessa early morning of the 27th and spent the night at Katen which I left on the 28th spending the night at Ngwankec. I left Ngwankec at 6.00 a.m. on Wednesday the 29th and arrived Itang in the evening of the same day. Thus, I spent five days on the way.

In Itang, I met Cdr. Salva Kiir before the end of the month and briefed him fully on the situation in Southern Blue Nile. I presented to him written reports on military and administrative issues pertaining to the area complete with my recommendations on what to be done. I waited for what he could do but as expected nothing materialized. Finally, I decided to go back to my sector on the 9th of October. Unfortunately, I could not wait for the well publicized (see Chairman's 448/9/90 dated 29/9/90) trip of the celebrated Sudanese singer, Mohammed Wardi, to Itang.

While in Itang, I volunteered to brief Cdr. Salva on the work of the Commission to Organize Production and Services (COPS) which I headed till the 4th of August 1990 when Cdr. Salva Kiir was appointed the new Head of COPS. The Chairman's message No. 033/8/90 dated 4/8/90 on the matter did not call for a handing and taking over process but for the interest of good work I thought it fit to do so to facilitate his beginning. According to the message (see the appendix), para 2(B) stipulates that Cdr. Salva Kiir "addresses COPS units with information to the Chairman and information to Cdr William Nyuon". I had differed with the Chairman on this point. I could not see how I can address my subordinates with information to my superiors. The claim in the message in the opening of para 2 that this was the channel of command before is simply not true.

During the same period, the Chairman picked up an issue out of a trivial matter. This was on buying draught animals: mules and donkeys, to be deployed in sectors (2), (3), (4) and (5). The matter was not discussed with us as the commanders of the sectors concerned and none of us has ever thought let alone recommend procuring these animals. The matter came to our attention in a message the Chairman was writing to Cdr Riek Machar Teny repeated to Cdr. Martin Manyiel and myself with information to Cdr. William Nyuon, Cdr. Salva Kiir and A/Cdr. Deng Alor. The message of the Chairman was replying a message written to him by Cdr. Martin Manyiel on 28/8/90 regarding the deployment of the new recruits being graduated at Bonga at that time where he stressed the need to consider sectors (2), (3) and (4) in the deployment. The suggestion of Cdr. Martin was supported by Cdr. Riek in a message he wrote to the Chairman on 29/8/90. As usual, the Chairman does the deployment of the recruits, all alone without consultation with the field commanders. The full text of the message is reproduced in the appendix but the relevant paragraph here reads:

7. Again our problem remains to be and will be transport. I discussed this problem thoroughly with Ebony [President Mengistu] in our last meeting some three weeks ago. I requested a fund to buy draught transport animals (mules and donkeys). He approved two hundred thousand (200,000) Birr for this purpose. The amount was received by Fire [A/Cdr Deng Alor Kwol] last week and a committee under Fire is now in the process of buying these animals. All will be deployed in sectors (2), (3), (4) and (5). These animals plus Equatoria (Yei, Maridi, etc) should solve the transport problem of the dry season plus, of course, draught animals we can find in these areas and trucks we will get when we reach the projects [in Kennana and Southern Blue Nile].

The message was dated 2/9/90 but I received my copy on 5/9/90. This was the first time I came to know of the project. Of the four sectors mentioned, two (sectors 4 and 5) fell under my direct command. In the reports I rendered to Cdr. Salva Kiir on the situation in Southern Blue Nile I had included a list of the spare parts needed to put the cars we had on the road, including one additional jeep given to me by the Ethiopian commander of the western sector to mount an anti-tank gun on. The total estimate of the money needed was less than 50,000 Birr (i.e. less than a quarter of the money earmarked to buy the mules and donkeys). Had the Chairman consulted me, I would have certainly advised against the animals and gone for the spare parts instead.

The argument for the draught animals was never convincing at all. In terms of initial cost, they cost more than the spare parts needed for the cars. Both the cars and the animals have their running costs and it cannot be said with any degree of certainty in advance which running costs are higher. Tactically, the argument for the animals falls through easily. The enemy was attacked using Urals, Jeeps and BM-21 vehicles. These are the means the enemy knew to be at our disposal. The enemy would prepare his armament and counter measures according to that knowledge and will certainly upgrade his means and weapons to match this challenge. It must be reiterated here that in terms of support weapons, we had a superiority over the enemy in the operations in and around Maban town. How would the animals fare in such a match? There are other arguments to be adduced against the idea of using the animals such as in relation to the terrain, control, etc. but the above are the most obvious ones.

To the best of my knowledge, none of us responded to the Chairman's project on the buying of mules and donkeys. In my meeting with Cdr. Salva Kiir in August, he had promised that the spare parts I had requested would be procured by the Itang Commander before the end of October. On the 21st of October, I sent a message to A/Cdr Deng Alor to use some of the money he had for mules and donkeys to procure the spare parts immediately and that he would be refunded later by Itang Commander. My message (No. 022/10/90) to Deng was with information to the Chairman and Itang commander. A/Cdr Deng Alor never bothered to make a reply. Eventually, neither the spare parts nor the animals did arrive. It was not till the second week of February 1991 that some mules and donkeys began to be seen in the Gambela/Itang area but none ever reached the field. The Chairman must have been brooding over the matter. On the 20th of February, he burst out. In his typically oblique way of addressing serious issues he wrote to Cdr Salva Kiir as follows:

Top Secret

Date: 20/2/91

FM: Thunder

TO: Hammer

INFO: Spear   INFO: Sennar   INFO: Alpah Beta   INFO: Wawat

277/2/91

1   As you must have found out in Gambela/Itang area, there is a lot of talk about alleged ill-advisability of buying draught animals: mules, donkeys, horses.

2   The money that was used to buy these animals was neither raised by any zonal or sector command nor was it collected in the refugees camp. This money was donated by the Friends' top man for this purpose. The animals are therefore an addition rather than a subtraction to what is deemed the best mode of transport.

3   It is alleged that there is no water, etc. for these animals when these vital items are available for other animals in the area such as the Gajak cattle, unless the grass and water escaped the area on the arrival of C-in-C's donkeys. Obviously, the donkeys, like support weapons, cannot capture garrisons. They must be managed to achieve the intended goal.

4   There are other areas where these animals can be effectively used, such as between Tambura and Busere, where incidentally the enemy is using a fleet of donkeys for transport. If you found the local commanders persuaded that the donkeys are useless, then they cannot possibly manage them. In that case you can send them to this end. If you can use them, of course keep them as they were meant for your end. I have ordered Amara [Cdr Daniel Awet Akot] to get mules, donkeys, horses and camels for Yambio, Tambura, Busere, Raga transport. With a drum of diesel now 800 Birr in Addis in the black market and difficult to find, we really have little choice but to use vehicles when we can and use animals when we must. As is clear in Gambela, even when there is money, there is no fuel to buy.

The Chairman has not been to the Gambela/Itang areas since August. That he was absolute about "a lot of talk" is in itself surprising. Of course, the "local commanders persuaded that the donkeys are useless" are none other than myself and possibly Cdr. Riek who commanded sectors 2 and 3. The most astounding aspect of the message was the solution proposed to the problem. The role of Cdr. Salva was just to find out if the local commanders were ready or not ready to use the animals. Depending on the finding the animals will either be withdrawn or kept. If the option were to withdraw the animals, what about the transport problems in the sector concerned? Fundamentally, if the issue was just between the Chairman and Cdr. Salva as the message suggests, why then serve us with copies of it?

On the 20th of January 1991, the Chairman issued a new directive on the command structure. According to the directive, the Chairman continues as before, to be the commander of BSC Phase 2/NF Campaign but unlike before when the sector commanders reported to him directly he introduced the position of the Deputy BSC Phase 2/NFC commander who was also the overall commander of sectors 4, 5 and 6. This assignment was given to Cdr. Salva Kiir. Cdr. Martin Manyiel (who commanded sector 5) and I (who commanded sector 4) were now "assistant commanders" under the Deputy Commander of the phase. As such, the chain of command demanded that I render my reports to Cdr. Salva Kiir and to nobody else senior to him. I observed this principle strictly. Therefore, I had no official capacity to write any messages to the Chairman thereafter. I had earlier ceased to be the Director of OCER and to be Head of COPS. These were the other official capacities where I was directly answerable to the Chairman. That I was not sending messages to the Chairman, surprisingly, became a subject of agitation and gossip within some circles in the SPLA. How could they have known about the fact?

The Third Trip to Cairo:

On the 31st of December 1990, I received the following message from the Chairman who was then in Addis Ababa. I was in Lool. The message reads:

Top Secret

Date: 31/12/90
FM: Thunder
TO: Alpha Beta
R: Fire
INFO: Spear   INFO: Hammer   INFO: Sennar
255/12/90

1. There will be a Seminar in Cairo on problems of the Horn of Africa from Jan. 7 to Jan. 10, 1991. It will be addressed by notables such as Herman Cohen, the U.S.A. Assistant Secretary of state for African Affairs. The movement is invited to send one participant to present our position.

2. Alpha Beta is here given the above assignment. The most senior A/Cdr commands in his absence and coordinates with Sennar.

3. Fire to process travel arrangements of Alpah Beta so that he proceeds to Cairo on arrival and on time.

4. Alpha Beta to start preparing the position paper while moving. Fire to prepare and make references ready.

The message was sent as "most urgent". The time scale was definitely too short for any meaningful contribution to the conference. That I could "start preparing the position paper while moving" was inconceivable in our circumstances. This would definitely be difficult in a comfortable car on a tarmacked road, how would it be in our case when it is the cars that make the roads? To write a paper in order to be presented in such a high-profile conference required that the theme to be addressed be clear and definite. "Problems of the Horn of Africa" is a title too general to guide an author especially one in the "middle-of-nowhere" away from reading materials. Furthermore, the Chairman knew too well that A/Cdr Deng Alor Kuol is the last person to be charged "to prepare and make references ready." Such an intellectual exercise is simply not his cup of tea. I was also faced with an immediate problem which the Chairman well knew about. I replied the next day as follows:

Top Secret:
Date: 1/1/91
FM: Alpha Beta
TO: Thunder
INFO: Spear   INFO: Hammer   INFO: Sennar
INFO: Fire
002/1/91

A. Ref. your 255/12/90. In view of the time element, it will not be practically possible for me to make it to the conference in time. I have no car with me and from where I am it takes not less than five days good walk to Itang. I, therefore, suggest that rather than miss the opportunity, somebody else can go to represent us.

B. This is for your information and directives.

In less than three hours from the moment this message was sent to Addis Ababa, my signalists were already in receipt of the reply of the Chairman to it. This was a record time in our communication network. The Chairman's message was insistent. It reads.

Top Secret

Date: 1/1/91
FM: Thunder
TO: Alpha Beta
R: Piankhi   R: Fire
INFO: Spear   INFO: Hammer   INFO: Sennar
002/1/91

1   Ref. your 002/1/91. I have already sent your name and Fire will receive tickets tomorrow in your name. It would be confusing to make the substitution.

2   Piankhi is in Gambela. He has one of my HQ toyotas with him. I
     will order him to send you this early morning tomorrow, 2/1/91.
     This means that you can be in Gambela next tomorrow, 3/1/91,
     and proceed to Addis to arrive on 4/1/91 or 5/1/91. Your booking
     for Cairo is on 6/1/91.

Indeed, the Car was sent on 2/1/91 and arrived late at night the same
date. I left my HQ for Itang at 8.00 a.m. in the morning of Thursday
3/1/91. I arrived Itang at 10.00 p.m.

Parenthetically, the eagerness of the Chairman to see me in Addis
Ababa contrasted sharply with his reluctance to, if not avoidance of,
meeting me on a more serious matter in August, i.e., to brief him on
the military situation in Southern Blue Nile. On the basis of this fact,
I was advised by a good number of officers at my HQ and in Itang not
to proceed to Addis Ababa. They thought the Chairman was luring me
to Addis Ababa to be arrested in the same way he did to Cdr. Kerubino
Kwanyin Bol in 1987. I explained to them that there were no similar-
ities between then and now and that the very arrest of Kerubino and
the other two members of the High Command (Arok and Kulang)
were a hot potato in the hands of the Chairman so much so that he
would rather solve than aggravate the problem. In any case whatever
was in the mind of the Chairman, I knew exactly where the Ethiopian
security stood on the issue.

I arrived Addis Ababa at about 10.00 a.m. on Sunday 6/1/91. A/
Cdr Deng Alor was not in town and those in the office knew nothing
about the mission except that I was expected that day and will be
proceeding on a mission abroad and that it was Dr Mansour Khalid
to brief me on it. I did meet Dr Mansour Khalid in the evening and
he told me that the tickets and other travel arrangements should have
been made by Deng Alor. It turned out that, contrary to the assurance
of the Chairman, there were no tickets and no booking made. As the
plane to Cairo was leaving on Monday, the 7th we had no alternative
but to try our luck at the airport.

As soon as I arrived Addis Ababa, I sent a car to Debre Zeit to
collect Dr Peter Adwok so that we may share ideas on the situation in

the movement. During our conversation, he informed me that A/Cdr Dhol Acuil Aleu had informed him that he (Dhol) had read a paper I had written for the High Command meeting, a paper which Dhol thought was a good basis for structuring the movement and putting the struggle on the right track. According to Dr Peter Adwok he did not see the paper which A/Cdr Dhol Acuil said was with Cdr. Martin Manyiel. I apologized to him that I did not carry with me my copy of the paper referred to but I briefed him on its contents. Some minutes before 6.00 p.m. A/Cdr Deng Alor arrived to take me to meet the Chairman. I had to cut short my conversation with Dr Peter Adwok but we agreed to continue with it once I was back from Cairo. He was taken back to Debre Zeit and Deng drove me to the house of the Chairman.

We arrived the Chairman's house a little after six. He was already dressed up ready to leave the house any time. He told me that he and his wife were invited for dinner by Dr Mansour Khalid and they will have to leave the house just a little before eight. Since I had a lot to raise, I took a hint and readied myself for the briefing about the mission after which I would raise my points. The Chairman elaborated on the contents of his message and stressed the importance of being present there. But he did not have much to say as to the arrangements made. He also added that while in Cairo, I would be meeting the Egyptian authorities who he expected should be more sympathetic to the SPLA as Khartoum had exposed its real colours as NIF in addition to its position on the situation in the Gulf which supported Iraq.

I informed the Chairman about my findings since I arrived Addis Ababa and that it was uncertain whether I was going to travel the next day. There was no tickets, no booking, no exit visa on the passport and of course no "references ready". By the time I was about to start discussing the other issues, the Chairman was already looking at the clock on the wall. It was something to eight, his time to leave. I told him that since nothing was in order regarding my travel, I would have no time to see him in the morning as we will be going straight to the airport. He promised that we will have more time when I come back from Cairo. He wished me a nice trip. We said our goodbyes and I left.

We went to the airport on Monday morning. Deng Alor and A/Cdr. Nhial Deng Nhial were with me as they were travelling on the same plane; something the Chairman did not tell me about the previous evening. The two were on their way to Libya through Cairo. A return ticket was bought in the airport and, with the help of some Ethiopian friends, I was booked a seat and my passport was stamped for exit. Thus, I was able to take off for Cairo at noon that day. The three of us sat next to each other in the plane. Mr Mohammed Abdel Salam, the Under-Secretary of the Ministry of Public Security, was informed the same day by Dr Mansour Khalid about my trip. Although the information was at short notice, he kindly made the necessary arrangements for the reception of the "delegation" at the airport and our accommodation at Cairo Meridien Hotel.

The Conference

I arrived Cairo at about 3.00 p.m. on Monday the 7th of January. The conference had opened earlier in the morning. On arrival I met Mr Frank Ferrari, Senior Vice President of the African-American Institute and the conference convener. I knew him since the Wilson Conference on Sudan held in Washington in February 1987. Mr Ferrari informed me that the invitation to attend the conference was extended to the SPLA in mid-November 1990. He also added that on Saturday 5/1/1991, he was informed by the Egyptian Ministry of Foreign Affairs of their objection to the participation of the SPLA in the conference and that he thought it fit to involve Mr Bona Malwal to make the necessary contacts with the Egyptian authorities in an attempt to make them drop their objection. Mr Bona Malwal's efforts with Dr Boutrus Boutrus Ghali, the State Minister for Foreign Affairs, whom he knew very well were fruitless. Mr Bona Malwal, with disappointment in his face and voice, briefed me on what had transpired between him and the State Minister for Foreign Affairs. I thanked him and Mr Ferrari for their efforts and told him that I will take up the matter with the Egyptian security.

I met Mr Namar, the Minister of Public Security, in the presence of Mr Mohammed Abdel Salam on Wednesday morning. I raised the matter with them. They expressed complete surprise promising to straighten up things straightaway. Indeed, I was informed in the afternoon that the "misunderstanding" has been cleared up and that I was welcome to attend the conference. Hence, I was only able to attend the sessions of the 9th and 10th of January.

The conference, titled "The 21st African-American Conference", was co-sponsored by the Institute for Diplomatic Studies, Cairo, and the African-American Institute, New York. It was to discuss a number of issues under the following heads:

1 The Horn of Africa.
2 Liberia
3 South Africa
4 Social and Human Resources Development Needs
5 Special Needs of Women and Children
6 Technology, Agriculture and the Environment
7 Refugees
8 Media Perceptions
9 The Need for Building a Constituency in the United States.

There were no written papers prepared by the participants for presentation and discussion as was to be expected. The format was that a panel of speakers is chosen for a particular topic, each is given a reasonable time for presentation and then, after all of them have spoken, discussions from the floor follow. The conference was attended by Africans and non-Africans including ministers, ambassadors, academics, etc.

Given the long list of topics discussed, four days were not enough for any of them to get the special intensive consideration required.

Contacts Outside the Conference

Outside the conference hall, I had a recorded interview with Miss Jihan El-Alai'ili, the BBC correspondent in Cairo. Among other questions, she asked me a direct one on whether the contingent of SPLA fighters had arrived Kuwait then. It is to be recalled that the Chairman had made a statement reported by the mass media that the SPLA was contributing a task force of its fighters to be sent to Kuwait to take part in the liberation of Kuwait from Iraqi occupation of the country. This SPLA task force was to fight side by side or shoulder to shoulder with the allied forces contributed by the Western countries and some other countries of the world. We, in the SPLA knew that the Chairman's statement was nothing more than just PR; no such force was being prepared. My answer to the BBC correspondent was that the force has not reached Kuwait because the SPLA, unlike governments contributing to the allied Forces, lacked resources and movements were on foot. I reminded the correspondent that since the time Kuwait was occupied on August 2, 1990 up to the end of January 1991, it would be still rainy season and no vehicular movement was possible. This is just one of several occasions where one finds himself skirting round the truth for the sake of the movement's image to outsiders.

While in Cairo, I had a number of meetings with individuals, groups and the Egyptian authorities. Sayed Mohammed Osman el-Mirghani was in Cairo at about the same time, on the invitation of the Egyptian government. I paid him a courtesy visit in his hotel. We exchanged views on the situation in the country but he did not tell me anything about his mission in Cairo.

Meeting the "Legitimate Command"

I also had a meeting with the three members of the "Legitimate Command", General Fathi Ahmed Ali, Lt. General Abdel Rahman Saeed Abdel Rahman and Brigadier-General El-Hadi Bushra Hassan. They were respectively, the C-in-C of the Sudanese Armed Forces, the Deputy Chief of Staff for Operations and the Head of Public Security, when the Junta of Omer al-Bashir overthrew the government in June 1989. The three briefed me fully about their meeting with the Chairman in Isoke, Southern Sudan, in December 1990. In addition to a two-page statement on the meeting, they gave me a 15-page document on the discussions. The issues discussed comprised: the relationship between the SPLM/A and the Legitimate Command of the Sudanese Armed Forces, the Charter of the NDA, Co-ordination in the political and military spheres both within and outside the country, the POWs and cease fire. It was the first time for me to know all these details. I never got a briefing from the Chairman on the matter. So was the case for the other High Command members who were not with the Chairman in that Isoke meeting.

Meeting with the Egyptian Authorities

My meetings with the authorities in the Ministry of Public Security took place on the 9th and the 15th. The discussion centred on two main issues: the situation in Sudan and the co-operation between the Egyptian government and the SPLA.

On the situation in Sudan, my impression was that the Egyptians appear to have given up any hope of influencing the Junta in Khartoum against implementing an Islamic fundamentalist programme. Omer al-Bashir had announced in December that his government would implement the provisions of the Islamic Laws with immediate effect. Since Egypt was involved in trying to bring the two sides to the conflict into agreeing on a peaceful settlement, I enquired from the Egyptian authorities as to how they would proceed on the peace front. The only answer they could give was that the situation had been complicated by the regime's recent announcement on the implementation of the Islamic Laws.

Despite the new position of Egypt on the Junta in Khartoum regarding its fundamentalist orientation, which in fact concurs with the position of the SPLA, the attitude of the Egyptian authorities towards the SPLA was cooler than previously. The incident regarding the movement's participation in the conference may have been due to lack of co-ordination between Foreign Affairs and Public Security but correlated with other events they all point to a trend.

Given Khartoum's internal and external isolation and its support to Iraq's aggression in the Gulf, the attitude of the Egyptians was difficult to understand. Could Egypt be grooming a pro-Egyptian group to take over in Khartoum? As mentioned earlier, the Sudanese opposition in Cairo were since June 1989 under severe restrictions in their political work. It was significant this time that the Egyptian government was hosting Sayed Mohammed Osman el-Mirghain, Chairman of the DUP and a leading opposition figure.

The Beja Congress (Revolutionary Movement)

A four-man delegation of the Beja Congress (RM) led by its Secretary-General, Mohammed Tahir Abu Bakr, met me and A/Cdr. Michael Majok Ayom in Cairo. The delegation was preparing to go to Addis Ababa to discuss with the SPLA leadership areas of co-operation between the two organizations. They said the following about themselves:

1 Their programme was basically that of the Beja Congress but with a new dimension added; that is the commitment to armed struggle.
2 The people in the Beja area are prepared and willing to undertake armed struggle.
3 The problems of the Sudan cannot be solved without recognizing the Beja as an entity.
4 There are objective reasons for the Beja Congress (RM) to operate as a separate organization, at least for the time-being. What was needed is co-operation.
5 Their resources are very limited and would request the help of the SPLA to train their youth who, after military training, will go back to fight in the Beja area.

6 One of their sons, Lt. Tahir Mohammed Adam, is a POW with the SPLA. They request that he be released in order to help them in their work.

We discussed at length how recruits could reach the nearest SPLA controlled areas. As some of them own boats, they preferred transporting them by sea using these boats up to Assab. We argued for land movements up to Gadaref and Matema. We agreed that they should give this matter more serious thought and inform the SPLA accordingly on what was practical. Our side made it clear to them that the SPLA could not be of any help in the Red Sea. I promised them that I would convey the discussions to the Chairman which I did in a report dated January 17, 1991.

I left Cairo at about 3.30 a.m. and arrived Addis Ababa at 8.30 a.m. on Tuesday, January 15, 1991.

Back to the Field

I did not get the Chairman in Addis Ababa, for he had earlier gone on a foreign trip that took him to Kenya and Zaire. I was instructed to wait for Cdr. Salva Kiir in Addis Ababa to follow up on some matters together. While in Addis Ababa, I had opportunity to have an informal discussion with A/Cdr Elijah Malok Aleng. He was coming from Congo, where he was previously the SPLA representative, on his way to join the Chairman in Zaire. After exchanging views on the situation in general terms, I interrupted the course of the conversation to tell Elijah why I wanted to talk to him. I told him that although my message to him will definitely touch on official issues, I was talking to him in his personal capacity in the hope that, given his experience in politics, his contribution may influence things positively. I briefed him about my repeated attempts to persuade the Chairman to call for a High Command meeting so as to discuss the problems facing the movement, that not only were these attempts fruitless but it appeared the Chairman was offended by the thought, and that I have given up on trying again. I concluded that my message to him was brief and in confidence: since he concurs with me on the urgency of a High Command meeting, I would like him to talk to the Chairman on the matter. He thanked me for having placed my confidence in him and agreed to raise the matter with the Chairman when the two of them meet soon.

It was not only for his previous political background that I chose to entrust A/Cdr. Elijah Malok with the task. He hails from the same village as Dr John Garang (as a matter of fact, some say he is John's uncle) and has of late become one of the few in the SPLA who had the Chairman's ear. I did not meet Elijah again until July 23, 1991 when, now as the Executive Director of the SRRA, he accompanied Mr James Jonah, the UN Under-Secretary General for Humanitarian Affairs, to Nasir. The group arrived Nasir at 8.00 a.m. to discuss with Riek and myself the corridors of tranquillity and security guarantees for the UN convoys. Elijah did not tell me anything about the assignment I had given to him six months earlier. However, in October in Nairobi, under different conditions altogether, he informed me that he had passed my message to the Chairman. I did not ask him as to when he did so.

Those days, the situation in the Gulf cast a shadow on the political scene. The deadline given by the Allied forces for Iraq's withdrawal from Kuwait had expired at midnight of the 15th of January Washington time and all were braced for the commencement of open hostilities. Indeed, the Allied forces started bombing Iraq from the air in the small hours of the next day. A big number of planes from many countries were used in the air strikes. These strikes went on for more than a month. In Ethiopia, the government was under considerable pressure from its rebels. The news we were getting never made good reading to the government at all.

I left Addis Ababa for Itang on Tuesday the 5th of February and arrived there at 9.00 p.m. the next day. In Itang and Gambela we had a series of meetings with Mr Thokwat Pal, the party secretary and governor of Gambela region, and party officials on issues of mutual interest. Cdr. Salva Kiir and I also held a meeting on the 4th of March with the SPLA commanders of Itang, Pinywudo, Bongo,

Bilpam and Zinc to brief them on the situation and to plan together what to do.

I left for Pagak on the 11th of March and proceeded to my HQ at Lool. I arrived there in the afternoon on the 15th. I held a meeting with the officers on the 17th to brief them about the situation and my visit to Cairo.

Events began to move quite fast. On the 22nd, Radio SPLA carried the cheering news that Maridi town has been liberated. But early morning the next day the BBC announced that the Ethiopian authorities have expelled two Libyan and two Sudanese diplomats for "engaging in activities incompatible with their diplomatic status." They were asked to leave the country within four days. The four were in fact, alleged to be aiding the "rebels". On the 2nd of April, Nkempte, a regional capital, was captured by the Ethiopian rebels from the government. It was a significant victory for the rebels and they kept the momentum ever since.

We had information that the enemy was preparing to break out from Maban town to attack our positions in Dajo, Maiwut and Pagak with the objective of capturing Itang to disperse the refugees there. The force given this task was to move simultaneously with another from Renk that will attack Nasir and Jekou in order to link up with the force from Maban in Itang or just before it. Therefore, Itang was the target and, with what happened in Tsore (Longkuei) refugees camp still fresh in our minds, the information could not be taken lightly. We prepared to defend ourselves.

Indeed, on the 19th of April, an enemy convoy attacked our force at Chetta early morning. Our force put up a stiff resistance but was overwhelmed by enemy's superiority in numbers and armament. By late afternoon, Chetta had fallen to the enemy and occupied it. The only other force we had (New Funj TF) was at Bugaya and if the enemy were to keep the speed with which it attacked Chetta, Bugaya would fall on the 20th or the day after thus exposing Dajo and the rear completely. We did not have a big force in Dajo. I briefed Cdr. Salva Kiir of the situation and urged him to send the force promised for the area to Dajo immediately and that I would meet these troops there.

The reinforcing force did not leave Pagak till the 28th. Hence, I left Lool for Dajo on the 29th. Between the 27th of April and the 1st of May, it had been raining heavily in the area. This brought succour to us. The enemy convoy having advanced towards Bugaya found it impossible to continue the advance because of the rains. The convoy decided to go back into Maban town which it entered on the 1st of May. The "Rains Brigade", has done its job. We now had no enemy to worry about until next January.

I continued with my journey to Dajo. I left Buldit in the morning of the 2nd and arrived Dajo in the evening. I received the new task force there, reorganized it and then dispatched it to Bugaya.

CHAPTER 8

Out of Ethiopia

The Gambela Situation and the Evacuation of the Refugees

THE INFORMATION I was receiving from Itang was that Cdr. Salva Kiir and Cdr. Riek Machar were busy making arrangements for the defence of Itang refugees camp against any possible attack from within Ethiopia itself. Troops were organized and sent to Dembidolo as the first defence line.

My new assignment, as per the Chairman's directive issued on 2/4/91 (his message No. 011/4/91), was the Chief of Servscom (Service Support Command) of BSC phase 2. This meant that I would be stationed at the rear to facilitate the provision of logistics for the whole phase. Now that the enemy threat was over, it was time to take up my new assignment. I had to go back to Lool first to brief the officers there about the change and to ensure that everything was in its proper place. I left Dajo for Lool on the 3rd of May and left the latter for Pagak the next day. I spent the night at Maiwut and arrived Pagak on the 5th. I left Pagak on the 8th arriving Itang at about 2.15 p.m. the same day.

Since around the first week of May, the Chairman was in Addis Ababa. Cdr. Riek and I suggested to Cdr. Salva Kiir that it would be a good idea for the Chairman to come to the Itang/Gambela area to acquaint himself with the developments taking place around the area. Salva gave us the impression that he liked the idea and promised to write a message to the Chairman urging him to come. Rather than come to Itang/Gambela, the Chairman ordered Cdr. Salva Kiir to join him in Addis Ababa instead. The Chairman left Addis Ababa for yet another foreign trip around the middle of May. Salva remained there until the developments of the military situation in Ethiopia forced him to return to Gambela on the 23rd of May.

In the face of the steady rebels' advance towards the capital, President Mengistu Haile Mariam relinquished power and left the country on the 21st of May. The "three Tesfais" took over the helm of state in what was rumoured as a palace coup. While his plane was bound for Harare, Zimbabwe, the event was making the headlines in the international radio stations and other mass media. This had a very devastating negative effect on whatever morale was left in his troops. Brigades were surrendering *en masse* without a fight. This was the case in Dembidolo where the SPLA troops were deployed. The SPLA officer commanding these troops was foolhardy enough to think that with a few hundred soldiers under his command he could reverse the tide. The movement paid dearly in manpower for such an act of folly. The force was put to rout and the survivors, including the commander, had to follow difficult routes that avoid the main road to Gambela. They began arriving Gambela in ones and in twos on the 24th.

I had already moved to Gambela on the 22nd and when Cdr. Salva Kiir arrived on the 23rd he got me there. I immediately raised with him the issue of transferring our logistics from Zinc stores to Pagak and informed him that I have already made ready the cars to carry out this task. I was dumbfounded by his analysis of the situation. He thought that the new leadership in Ethiopia were in firm control; that the advance of the "*Wuyane*" will be checked, and that should the worst come to the worst the SPLA would defend Gambela and keep it. Such a simplistic presentation was not worth any discussion. I reminded him that I was the Servscom Chief and hence it was within my authority to transfer the ammos and other logistics to Pagak. He retorted that whereas he agreed with what I said, the Chairman had ordered him that the ammos be taken to Pinywudo. I replied that the Chairman was far away; what did he think as the most senior person on the spot? He didn't budge and we left it at that.

On the 25th, the withdrawing Ethiopian soldiers together with elements of the rebels were gathering in noticeable numbers in Gambela town, especially on the Southern end of the bridge. They were poorly clad and it was difficult to tell who was a guerrilla and who was not. Significantly, they were gathering in small groups with their guns on both sides of the main road that leads to Addis Ababa. I visited Cdr. Salva Kiir at Zinc that morning and we drove back to Gambela together in the afternoon. I drew his attention to those soldiers pointing out that they must be bent on doing something; otherwise they should have collected themselves in the barracks or just dispersed to their homes. He did not comment.

On the 26th, I could not stand the inaction of Salva any more. I put it to him that there was no useful purpose to be served by the presence of the two of us in Gambela and hence suggested I would rather go to Itang to take charge of the situation there. He readily agreed. Hence, I left Gambela for Itang at about 4.00 p.m. By the time I was leaving Gambela, the situation was extremely tense. Later that evening, the force at Tharpam guarding Itang, evacuated the place but not before carrying out some demolitions. They were certainly destroying some of the equipment they could not carry, but the sounds scared the refugees. The Uduk, who had experienced the 1990 disaster, withdrew that night. In Gambela there was shooting for the whole night.

In Itang, I met Cdr. Lual Diing Wol and discussed with him the situation of the refugees and the directives to evacuate them. The plan of movement was agreed upon. The force of Itang was to be the vanguard followed by the bulk of the refugees and then my HQ together with all the support weapons we had were to be the rear. All were to withdraw to Nasir town from where it would be easier to move to other places if need be. Cdr. Lual Diing was to join me in the morning to supervise the movement and move with me to Tharpam in the evening. I summoned Itang commander the same evening and instructed him to distribute whatever food items are left to the refugees early morning so that they start movement without delay.

In the morning of the 27th, Cdr. Lual Diing was nowhere to be seen. Itang Commander executed the orders to the letter and the refugees started a long trek back to Sudan. As there was a lot of rains that time, the roads were flooded and the refugees had to wade their way through. When the last refugee had left Itang, I moved to Tharpam in the evening where I spent the night. It turned out that, contrary to our agreement the evening before, Cdr. Lual Diing had gone to Bilpam. I was later informed that soon after we parted that evening he had agitated the Dinkas among the refugees not to head toward Nasir but to move to Pinywudo instead. Some heeded his call.

The refugees moved along two axes: one along the Gambela-Itang-Jekou road and the other along Itang-Makuac-Mangok-Jekou route. It was a big and difficult operation. The refugees were overloaded with the items they had to carry and most of them were accompanied by children. The weather was unkind. It rained continuously adding to the water to struggle through. Additionally, there were roving bands of armed Gajak tribesmen who had an eye on something to loot. They attacked twice but were repulsed. They did not attack again. Despite all these difficulties when the refugees had reached Jekou in Sudan, our casualties in the hazardous movement were only four; three dead and one wounded. In Jekou itself, on the 31st of May, an enemy Antonov plane dropped bombs on the refugees. The thunderous sound of the explosions was frightening but luckily enough no one was hurt. This cowardly act by the enemy clearly proved that the innocent civilians were their prime target.

In the afternoon of the 27th, I received a radio message from Cdr. Salva Kiir who, it will be recalled, had insisted to stay in Gambela. The message reads:

Top Secret

Date: 27/5/91
FM: Hammer
TO: Spear
R: Thunder   R: Alpha Beta
171/5/91

1. Ref. my previous messages about the security situation in Gambela. The town has fallen to the enemy after very fierce battle. Almost half of the force that I committed sustained wounds, some very severe.
2. Equipment in Zinc is not evacuated nor exploded. Details will reach you.

Wishful thinking was finally over and reality had to prevail. The "very fierce battle" is doubtful but that is beside the point. The real disaster is the loss of tons of military hardware in Zinc, especially ammos of various types. I did not receive any of the messages he refers to but one hoped he had the courage to admit that the loss of equipment was entirely his responsibility.

I left Tharpam in the afternoon of the 28th and we rested for the night in one of the villages on the way. There, we received news that Addis Ababa has fallen into the hands of the EPRDF. Thus, a new regime has taken charge in Ethiopia.

I arrived the Lara junction on the 30th of May and spent the night there. I decided to go to Pagak first before continuing with the journey to Jekou. I left Lara at about 12.00 noon and arrived Pagak in the evening. In the morning I briefed the base commander and the officers on the situation in the refugees camps. I instructed the base commander to take good care of the logistics he had as there was none to hope for from Zinc or somewhere else. I took a list of all the items in Pagak store and left for Lara at about 7.15 a.m. on the 4th of June arriving there at about 11.30 a.m. Having rejoined the group that I left there four days before, we continued our journey to Jekou at 4.30 p.m. We spent the night at Mading cattle camp. We were received warmly by the Gajak there in sharp contrast to some of the things our refugees have gone through. We left Mading at about 10.30 a.m. on the 5th arriving Jekou in the afternoon.

By the time I arrived Jekou, most of the refugees had already arrived Nasir. There, they were settled in camps along the Sobat river and Khor Wako. The places selected for them were: Man-deng, Kwerenga, Pananyang, Noar, Dhuor Diing, Koat and Torpot. The problem then was how to feed them. The number that finally arrived Nasir area was estimated at around 150-200 thousand. It was difficult to get an accurate figure as some of the former refugees melted into the society there (being relatives or friends) and some proceeded to their homes in other areas of Upper Nile.

Finally, I left Jekou for Nasir on a motor boat on the 8th of June arriving there in the evening. The plight of the returnees in Nasir was already attracting attention abroad. An OLS team had visited Nasir while I was still in Jekou to assess their needs.

John Garang Speaks

The tumultuous events in Ethiopia took place while the Chairman was on his trip to a number of African countries. No doubt he must have been getting briefing from Addis Ababa and Nairobi where the movement kept radio contact with the field. The first communication from him was on the 1st of June in a radio message (No. 002/6/91) to all the High Command members. The message informed the High Command members that:

> I arrived back to Mercury country [i.e., Kenya] yesterday 31/5/91, after fifteen days during which I visited this country, Zambia (twice), Namibia, Nigeria (twice), Ghana (twice) and Zimbabwe (from where I just came).

To assure us that he was as much concerned about the situation in Ethiopia, the Chairman went on:

> I have been following the developments in Ethiopia over the media as all of you have been doing with great concern. I decided to extend the visits in view of these developments so that we secure in some of these countries the necessary ammos to defend and extend our gains. Despite the adverse situation in Ethiopia, I am glad to inform you that I was able to get 800 tons of ammos of various types from some of these countries. These include fifteen million rounds of AKM (about 10,725 big boxes). The main problem is now air transport which I am working to solve.

He elaborated on the specifics of how the transport problem was being solved and gave dates to the delivery of the ammos. Says he:

The total number of freight flights using a (727) Boeing is (20) trips at a cost of about 50,000 U.S. dollars. I have already secured money for three trips and hope to get today for another six trips. So we will be able to transport half of the ammos before June 15. I am still working to transport the remaining half so that everything is at Napata's RVs [Eastern Equatoria] before the end of June.

As if they needed to be reminded, the Chairman now turned to assure his commanders of imminent victory over the enemy. He averred:

The above means that we will not have problem of ammos in the immediate future. Our people need not be worried, demoralized or panicked. We will turn the tables on Beshir despite the Ethiopian situation. All commanders are to keep up the morale of our people. We will win. Victory shall sooner than later be ours, and the current celebrations in Khartoum by Omer's Junta will turn to sorrow and mourning.

In the same vein he concludes:

All commanders are to start mobilizing as great a number of forces as possible, as we shall have no ammos problem, so that we give a final deadly blow to Omer El Beshir and as soon as possible. SPLA Oyee. Aluta Continua and Victory is certain.

After having written the above message, soothing as he thought, it must have dawned on the Chairman that the problem of ammos and some sloganeering were not the only concerns of the members of the High Command, the supposed highest political and military organ of the movement. His next message No. 003/6/91 dated 1/6/91 addressed to the same persons sought to redress the omission. It opened thus:

1. Ref. my 002/6/91. The developments in Ethiopia are of course a very serious development. The situation demands our collective thoughts and decision making.

2. As soon as practical I will call a meeting of the political-military High Command to review our situation in the light of the developments in Ethiopia.

Thus, at long last and after the loss of Ethiopia, "our collective thoughts and decision making" was discovered to be necessary. Despite this late recognition of an obvious fact, the Chairman was still non-committal as to when he would call a meeting of the High Command. Few, if any, believed he would.

Nothing was heard from the Chairman again for more than 45 days. On the 18th of July, in his message No. 021/7/91 addressed to the High Command members and repeated to all units of the SPLA, we were informed that since he arrived Nairobi on 31/5/91, the Chairman did not come to the field. He had continued with his trip now extended to include the U.S.A. and U.K. The message states:

1. I left Addis Ababa on 17/5/91 and went on diplomatic mission to Southern and west Africa. On 12/6/91, I was joined by Cdr. James Wani Igga, Cdr. Daniel Awet, A/Cdr. Deng Alor and A/Cdr. Richard K. Mulla. The five of us plus a security officer continued the diplomatic mission to West Africa, USA, UK, West Africa again and Southern Africa again.
2. The delegation arrived back to Nairobi two days ago on 16/7/91, on our way back home.

There is one positive aspect to the Chairman's delegation as from the 12th of June. It included two members of the political-military High Command. This was the first time ever since 1984 that a delegation of the Chairman to any African country, Europe or the U.S.A included a High Command member. He always travelled in the company of bodyguards and junior officers of his HQ.

The Chairman's message went on to brief us on the many developments and events which have occurred in the last two months. These events were:

The friendly Mengistu regime collapsed completely and a new EPDRF (sic) based government, currently hostile to the SPLA, took over in Addis Ababa. Their first act was to close down Radio SPLA and to expel our Addis Office and to force the evacuation of all refugees and all SPLA presence in Ethiopia.

The Chairman stated that this was why he stayed away for nearly two months so as to seek solutions to the most serious problems created by the events in Ethiopia. He informed the addressees that he has "raised the necessary funds to purchase a powerful radio broadcasting station of our own that will cover the whole Sudan and beyond," and that he has "been able to acquire more ammos than at any other one time before". Of course, it is not true that the new regime in Ethiopia forced the evacuation of the refugees in Ethiopia. The evacuation was Garang's decision.

The message also briefed the commanders in the field about the two ill-fated major offensives the NIF Junta had launched in early June. According to the Chairman, "the one from Wau has been halted, contained and is under destruction." As to the second offensive from Juba to Yei, the Chairman continues: "The enemy managed to reach Yei ...... Now the forces that were in Yei and the new arrivals are in deep crisis."

Curiously the Chairman's message contained the following paragraph:

What we need now is more manpower and for the majority of the SPLA forces to converge now on a decisive objective, and with more commitment, more dedication, so that we, like the guerrillas in Museveni's Uganda, Eritrea, Ethiopia, Somalia and Tchad achieve a decisive military victory. All soldiers are to move according to orders (from their commanders) immediately beginning from today 18/7/91 to that objective. Victory is certain and near. SPLA Oyee.

It was absolutely strange that, in a message addressed to all units of the SPLA, the Chairman was actually issuing orders to the soldiers to move to "the objective" which was unknown at the time to their commanders. It was my first time to be informed about a "decisive objective". What it was and how it could be decisive, only the Chairman knew. The broader issue of whether the guerrillas listed in the Chairman's message achieved a decisive military victory because they captured a decisive objective is open to question and a debatable matter. Whether what happened in Somalia could be considered "a decisive military victory" to be emulated should have been obvious to the Chairman by the time he was writing; more than six months after the collapse of the regime of Siad Barre in Mogadishu. Whatever the case may be, all will, however, agree that if the guerrilla movements referred to in the Chairman's message were just military machines devoid of political structures and lacking firm organization deep-rooted among the people "decisive military victory" would have been just a chimera.

To recapitulate, the Chairman has explained what he has been doing in the two months extending from the 15th of May to the 16th of July in the three messages referred to above. He made assurances and gave promises. Notably, he promised to call for a meeting of the High Command although he did not say when. However, whether his recent conversion to the belief in "our collective thoughts and decision making" would be taken seriously by the top commanders, the subsequent events are the best judge.

CHAPTER 9

THE SPLA:
In Search of a Strategy

Victory depends on active support of the population, mobilized by a revolutionary party or movement. While many have learned that "Political power grows out of the barrel of a gun", far too many would-be revolutionaries anywhere have failed to heed Mao's corollary injunction: 'The revolutionary war is a war of the masses; it can be waged only by mobilizing the masses and relying on them.'

Richard Gibson, *African Liberation Movements*, Oxford University Press, 1972, page 12.

Introduction

GUERRILLA WARFARE is a weapon of protest employed by insurgents to bring to an end real or imagined wrongs meted out on a people either by a foreign invader or by the ruling government, but it has also been used in an offensive role, in both ancient and modern times. It may be employed independently or to complement orthodox military operations. In the latter definition, the guerrilla force first fights independently and later grows into an orthodox insurgent army. Since the Second World War, guerrilla warfare had played an integral role in revolutionary warfare, people's wars or wars of national liberation in many countries of Asia, Africa, Europe and the Middle East.

The issue of strategy and tactics is of paramount importance in any guerrilla warfare. According to Encyclopedia Britannica[6]:

---

6   *The New Encyclopedia Britannica,* Vol. 29, 1983, p. 691

The broad strategy underlying successful guerrilla warfare is that of protracted harassment accomplished by extremely subtle, flexible tactics designed to wear down the enemy. The time gained is necessary either to develop sufficient military strength to defeat the enemy in orthodox battle (as did Mao Zedong in China and Ho Chi Minh in Vietnam) or to subject him to internal and external military and political pressures sufficient to cause him to seek peace favourable to the guerrillas (as did the Algerian guerrillas to France and Angolan and Mozambican guerrillas to Portugal). This strategy embodies political, social, economic, and psychological factors to which the military element is often subordinated – without, however, lessening the ultimate importance of the military role.

Thus, this strategy is that for a morally strong and materially weak. Through protracted war, the guerrillas, a seemingly weak force, can defeat a strong enemy by gradually reducing that enemy's advantages and aggravating his shortcomings. This is not an easy task and it demands a lot of brain, brawn and courage from the leadership at all levels of the guerrilla structure.

The political goal is fundamental in motivating people to action. The importance of this point has been stressed by Mao Tse-Tung, an authority on guerrilla warfare. He wrote[7]:

> Without a political goal, guerrilla warfare must fail, as it must if its political objectives do not coincide with the aspirations of the people and their sympathy, cooperation, and assistance cannot be gained.

The political goal of a guerrilla movement must correctly be determined and defined. However, as equally important is the method of carrying out the struggle to achieve the goal set. Therefore, victory depends primarily on both a correct political goal and a correct method or methods of waging the struggle.

---

7   Mao Tse-Tung, *On Guerrilla Warfare*, trans by S. B. Griffith, Frederick A. Praeger Publishers, New York, 1961.

Methods or forms of struggle are undertaken to defeat the enemy in the most advantageous way so that the objectives of the struggle are attained as quickly as possible. The choice of which method or form of struggle to follow demands creativity as there is no unique formula for waging the struggle suited to all countries at all times and under all circumstances. The choice is determined by the concrete historical conditions of the country concerned. For sure, the wealth of experience of other nations must be studied, made use of and adapted to the peculiar situation in one's country. In the course of the struggle, the movement must always and constantly assess and improve upon the experiences gained in the struggle, and also study the experiences of similar struggles waged elsewhere. This activity is, therefore, a continuous and vital process which cannot be delayed or relegated to any other.

Organization is a decisive problem of the struggle. A people's war is a work of the masses of the people. Only by organizing them will conditions be created for educating them and learning from them. All the activities and actions that form the various tasks of the armed and political struggle can only be carried out effectively through a clear organizational structure.

In the light of the above tested principles of guerrilla warfare, we shall examine in the following paragraphs the struggle being waged by the SPLA since its birth in 1983.

The Birth of the SPLA

Most guerrilla movements have their origin in a political party agitating the population to take up arms in revolt. The party militants spend considerable time among the population preparing for the revolt and when it actually takes place, the party assumes the leadership of the armed struggle. This was the case, for example, in Guinea-Bissau and other countries. In the case of the SPLA, the story was different.

The events in Sudan and particularly in the South have by early 1980s reached a stage where the people were already in rebellion.

The discontent in the South centred on the failure of the regional government in the South to meet the expectations of the Southerners, especially the former Anya-nya officers. These grievances were successfully used by Southern politicians, organised under several groups, to incite rebellion against the May regime of Jaafar Mohammed Nimeiri. They were most successful among the soldiers of the former Anya-nya (but not the absorbed officers) and the students. However, there was nothing like a united political, or even military, group that directed these activities nor was there, of course, a clear strategy guiding the revolt if and when it happened. The events leading to the Bor incident of May 16, 1983 could hardly have been planned actions by a group bent on waging a revolutionary war. The battalion in Bor had mutinied when it disobeyed orders to be transferred to northern Sudan. Like the case in any army, they must have known that it was just a matter of time before their mutiny was put down by force. Yet, they waited to be attacked.

The events leading to the Bor, Pibor and Pochalla incidents followed by Ayod's mutiny have been outlined in Chapter 2. Here, we intend to shed more light on the efforts exerted to reorganize the withdrawing forces. Before battalions 104 and 105 were dislodged from their garrisons to the bushes, there were already a number of guerrilla organizations active in the bushes of Southern Sudan and the Ethiopian border. There was the Anya-nya 2 of Vincent Kuany Latjor and James Bol Kur that mutinied in Akobo in 1975; there was the SSLM under Lokurnyang Lado; there was the Anya-nya 2 in Bentiu area under several commands; and there was the Melut Liberation Front which attacked Akoka garrison in 1982. All these groups were in Upper Nile region. There was also Anya-nya 2 operating in Bahr el-Ghazal under many generals since 1982. Apart from the name, the Anya-nya 2 groups mentioned above had nothing in common organizationally.

Col. Dr John Garang was in Lang Bar, an outpost of Bor garrison, with its commanding officer when the force of Major Kerubino Kwanyin Bol was attacked by the army unit sent from Juba. He did not take part in the battle on either of the opposing sides; quite an abnormal conduct for a military officer under such circumstances. The next day, Col. Dr John Garang put his wife and two children into a Land Rover car and drove away towards Malakal town. With them was his uncle, Chagai Atem Biar, and Mr Maker Deng Malou who was formerly an Anya-nya officer and was later to become Col. Garang's ADC. In the SPLA Chagai Atem Biar was in fond of boasting that he was the one who persuaded Dr John Garang to join the rebellion of Kerubino instead of going to Malakal where he might get arrested. Whatever the truthfulness of this claim may be, Dr John Garang told me personally that he drove towards Malakal with his leave certificate ready so that he can instantly show it to any army unit he may meet on the way. According to him, the plan to attack Bor involved two battalions: one to come from Juba and the other from Malakal. Just before Abwong town, Dr John Garang's car, which he drove himself, abandoned the road to Malakal and turned east. He continued driving east until the car had to be abandoned south of Sobat river not far from Ulang. From there he started his walk to the Ethiopian border. He caught up with Mr Samuel Gai Tut and Mr Akwot Atem, two veteran politicians, on the way where they continued their journey together. At Kurmayom, Samuel Gai Tut's village, the group enjoyed his hospitality for a couple of days.

The withdrawing forces arrived Itang in Ethiopia in June 1983 and Dr John Garang and the group with him arrived in July. Discussions to organize a movement to wage the armed struggle started soon after. Samuel Gai Tut wanted Akwot Atem to become the leader of the movement and Col. Dr John Garang to be the chief of staff of the army. Garang did not like the suggestion as he wanted to be the leader himself. William Abdalla Chuol, a former Anya-nya officer, also expressed an interest in the leadership. Garang moved among the officers inciting them to insist that the active military officers, as opposed to the politicians, should assume the leadership of the movement. He was counting on the fact that, being the most senior army officer, his leadership will be assured should the officers accept his line of thinking. Garang won the crucial support of Major David Atali, an Anyuak, who was the only one by then with organized forces under his command. This was the force which joined with the Ethiopian contingent to attack the group opposed to Garang in September. This attack resulted in the dispersion of the civilians who were in Itang forcing them to withdraw to Lara area near the Sudan-Ethiopia border but still within Ethiopia. After he has driven out his opponents in Itang, Garang organized a force under the command of William Nyuon and the Anya-nya 2 force in Bilpam was attacked, dispersed and their cattle seized. The force of Anya-nya 2 in Bilpam was under the command of Gordon Kong Chol. It never showed any hostility to the group in Itang. On the contrary, it was willing to co-operate with them.

Despite Garang's resort to force, Samuel Gai Tut insisted on reconciliation and managed to persuade the others with him to go back to Itang for talks with Garang's group. He went with a force estimated to be 8,000 of armed and unarmed men. In Itang, Lt. Col. Michael, the Ethiopian commander of Gambela and a good friend of Samuel Gai Tut, issued ammos to the group against the directives of his government which supported Garang to the hilt. The trucks carrying ammos for Gai Tut passed through the check-points manned by Garang's supporters as a food convoy. The ammos were laid underneath the sacks of maize. Gai Tut's group waited but there was no sign of any efforts from the other side to meet them. On the contrary, rumours were ripe that Garang was not interested in genuine reconciliation and that his only aim was to eliminate the leaders of the opposing group and absorb their followers into his own force. Under such uncertainty and with the memory of the previous unprovoked attack on them by Garang still fresh in their minds, Gai Tut's position on reconciliation was overruled and the group withdrew from Itang under the cover of darkness. Two days after, the advance force of the group arrived Adura (Thiayjak) and attacked Garang's unit which was stationed there. Garang's unit was dislodged and the station occupied by Gai Tut's force.

Garang sent a reinforcement from Bilpam to Adura which mounted a counter attack driving out Gai Tut's group. Samuel Gai Tut himself was killed during the fighting. This was on March 30, 1984. His body was not discovered until two days later. On receiving the news, Dr John Garang and Kerubino Kwanyin Bol flew by a helicopter to

Adura where Kerubino lashed the decomposing body of Gai Tut fifty strokes while Garang looked on in appreciation. The body by then was beyond recognition were it not for the characteristic finger of Gai Tut. Soon after, Garang wrote to the London office of the SPLA that Samuel Gai Tut was buried "with full military honours"! Following the death of Gai Tut, his supporters withdrew to Sudan and regrouped under the banner of Anya-nya 2. Then followed a period of bitter interfighting among the Southerners (between the Anya-nya 2 and the SPLA) which was to continue for four years. The lives lost in the process were more than the number lost in fighting the enemy over the same period. Naturally the enemy exploited the split and supplied the Anya-nya 2 with arms and ammos to fight the SPLA.

Rather than seek dialogue and reconciliation, Dr John Garang was adamant that the Anya-nya 2 must be crushed. "There must be no compromise with the '*Nyagats*'," was the order to all SPLA units. That compromise came years later at the cost of several thousand lives. Despite their small size (the estimated size of soldiers was around 300 armed men), the Anya-nya 2 could not be defeated militarily as they enjoyed the full support of the population (also armed) in the areas of their operation. It was only through dialogue that this fratricide was brought to an end in 1988. This laudable effort in reconciliation was the initiative and work of some small SPLA officers as pointed out in Chapter 5.

Therefore, the SPLA started off with interfighting among the Southerners. Contrary to Garang's later propaganda, the first bullet was not shot at the separatists but at competitors over power and the top position in the movement.

The Provisional Executive Committee (PEC)

Before the discussion on organizing the movement could turn violent, a political structure of the SPLM had been worked out.

It was agreed upon that the highest organ of the movement was to be known as the "Provisional Executive Committee" of the SPLM which was to be headed by a Chairman. Falling under the PEC were a number of specialized committees, such as the military, political, foreign affairs, finance, administration and justice. Each specialized committee was to be headed by a Chairman with the Chairmen of all the specialized committees constituting the membership of the Provisional Executive Committee. By virtue of his office, the Chairman of PEC was also the commander-in-chief of the SPLA.

Thus, the PEC was to lay down the political-military strategy for the conduct of the war against the enemy. It was to lead the building of a revolutionary movement which would mobilize the masses of the people in order to lead the armed struggle to victory.

Mr Akwot Atem, a veteran of the Anya-nya war of the sixties and a former regional minister in Juba, was elected the Chairman of PEC with the support of Mr Samuel Gai Tut. The latter wielded considerable following among the Southerners in Itang by then and could have taken the leadership himself if he so wished. He, however, chose otherwise despite his impressive credentials. This tells a lot about his humility and commitment to the unity of Southerners. Gai Tut was a senior commander in the Anya-nya and was in 1972, after the conclusion of the Addis Ababa agreement, absorbed into the Sudanese army as a Lt. Col. when Dr John Garang was absorbed as a captain. Gai Tut later joined politics and was elected several times as member of the Regional Assembly representing Waat constituency and served as regional minister in Juba several times. He thus combined experience in both practical politics and the military.

Other positions of PEC were as follows: Samuel Gai Tut, Chairman of the military committee, Joseph Oduho, Chairman of the Political and Foreign Affairs committee; and Martin Majier Gai, Chairman of Administration and Justice Committee. Col. Dr John Garang was elected the chief of staff in charge of the SPLA. Dr John Garang rejected the outcome of the election and this was the reason behind his resort to use force to seize the leadership of the movement.

Contrary to the claims made by Alier[8] in his book, Samuel Gai Tut neither allied himself with the Sudan government nor was he "determined to defeat John Garang." As we have seen, he died within the Ethiopian territory soon after the split.

The Demise of PEC

Following the ousting of Akwot Atem from the chairmanship of the PEC, Dr John Garang instituted himself as the Chairman. Thereafter, the military committee dominated the scene. The "politicians" were being condemned openly in official meetings and public rallies. It was being propagated that the political work was quite unnecessary and that it was only the military might that was needed to bring about victory. The movement took a sharp turn to militarism.

The brutal murder in Addis Ababa in September 1984 of Mr Benjamin Bol Akok, the London representative of the movement, under the orders of Dr John Garang, perilously hammered the point home as to the fate awaiting the "politicians." The assassination shocked the Southern Sudanese to the marrow for they have not known murder as a means of settling political difference of opinion. Mr Benjamin Bol Akok, a graduate of Oxford University, was formerly the deputy speaker of the first Regional Assembly in Juba (1973-78) and a former regional Minister of Agriculture (1978-79). He hailed from the Dinka Malwal, the most numerous section of the whole Dinka tribe. It was reported that Dr John Garang entertained fears about Bol's leadership ambitions.

Not long after this tragic incident, the only two civilian members of the PEC - Mr Joseph Oduho and Mr Martin Majier Gai - were stripped of any powers they had and were made to stay idle in Nazaret town, some 100 km south-east of Addis Ababa. They were finally detained in March 1985 on trumped-up charges. Their arrest sealed

---

8   Alier, A. *Southern Sudan: Too many Agreements Dishonoured*, Ithaca Press, Exeter, 1990, p. 252.

the fate of the PEC and nothing was heard again about it[9]. Thus, the last symbol of any semblance of collective leadership in the movement was gone. The military committee took control and changed its name appropriately to be known as the "High Command." The first decision they took was that every person joining the movement, regardless of his age, must undergo military training and be commissioned. This was to ensure absolute submission to the orders of the military institution. The curtain fell on any hopes of organizing a strong popular movement.

By taking such a step, Dr John Garang chose to ignore a cardinal requirement of a revolutionary armed struggle: a strong political movement to mobilize the people. It was a leap in the dark. The problems which afflicted the movement afterwards stemmed from this attempt to overlook political work in a people's struggle.

The High Command

This body came into existence to supplant the PEC which to Dr John Garang and the career military officers around him was "too political". It was not meant to function democratically or as an organ of the movement where decisions are taken collectively. It was a glittering facade behind which Dr John Garang would run the movement alone unquestioned while at the same time hoodwinking the world into believing that the movement was run on a democratic basis. The High Command had no law defining its authority nor rules and regulations governing the conduct of its business. The Chairman and C-in-C became the final authority in the day-to-day running of the movement's affairs. Political and military decisions were taken by him alone. He may choose at times to seek opinions of some or all of

---

9   For external propaganda purposes the name of PEC continued to be used outside the movement. For example, Lt. Col. Kerubino Kwanyin Bol signed Koka Dam Declaration as "Deputy Commander in chief of the SPLA and Deputy Chairman of SPLM Provisional Executive Committee." There was no SPLM Provisional Executive Committee at that time.

the High Command members, separately, but this process was never formalized and, hence, whatever was proposed could not be binding on him.

An interesting example is worth mentioning here. When Nimeiri was overthrown on April 6, 1985, Lt. Col. Kerubino Kwanyin Bol, the Deputy Chairman of the High Command, was in Itang. On hearing the news he got excited and euphoric. He shot some bullets into the air to express his happiness with the fall of the dictator. Other officers, NCOs and men who were in Itang by the time, and there were many, followed the example of their commander. As a result Itang turned into a scene of live fireworks for almost one hour. An eye-witness later opined that the volume of fire used in this celebration was enough to liberate a town from the enemy.

It will be recalled that Garang's propaganda has made it plain that the enemy was only Nimeiri and his regime. Hence, it came as no surprise that everybody in the movement, may be except him, believed that the exit of Nimeiri would mark the end of the war. In fact, Kerubino said this much to the officers who had gathered in his house that day to listen to his briefing on the situation. Yet, three days later, on the 9th of April, Dr John Garang addressed the world over Radio SPLA to say that he would have nothing to do with the generals in Khartoum and vowed that the war would continue unless they resign within a week. Who took this serious decision? To the best of my knowledge, the High Command did not meet to discuss the matter. In 1986, in what was meant to be a snide about Arok, Dr John Garang told me that Major Arok Thon Arok, who was in Bor area by then, had written a radio message to him advising that the movement should talk peace with the army generals who had taken over power in Khartoum. I have no reason to disbelieve the substance of the information. On the basis of it and Itang episode above, one can conclude that at least two members of the High Command – Kerubino and Arok – preferred that the SPLA conducts dialogue with the new regime in Khartoum. The point is, with this different point of view from at least two members of the High Command (they were five in all), wasn't a meeting necessary to have a consensus of opinion on the course of action to take?

In August 1985, to give another example, William Abdalla Chuol Deng, the leader of the Anya-nya 2, was killed by a group of soldiers who had just deserted the HQ of Major John Kulang Puot, the SPLA commander in Fangak area. On getting the information, John Kulang immediately sent a radio message to Dr John Garang informing him that at long last he had managed to get the head of William Abdalla Chuol. This was big news to Dr John Garang and without consulting anybody, he decided to appoint Major John Kulang as a member of the High Command. When the announcement came out, the High Command was to have two new members: Major John Kulang Puot and Major Nyachugak Nyachiluk. The reason cited for the appointment of the first was that he killed William Abdalla Chuol, and for the second it was that he had captured Boma Hills in April 1985. However, the listeners to Radio SPLA when the appointments were being broadcast noticed something else: the two new comers to the High Command were to be "Alternate Members". Since that time, the five members who first constituted the High Command became "Permanent Members" while the others who were co-opted after-wards were "Alternate Members." There were no rules or regulations or anything on paper defining the difference between these two tiers of membership. Only Dr John Garang knew.

A parallel system where the two-tier membership is common is to be found in the socialist parties. In the political organs of these parties one finds "full" and "alternate" members. But whereas there may be good reasons in the socialist parties to have "full" and "alternate" members, no single convincing reason could be adduced to justify the application of the concept to the High Command. Let us explain.

The structural organization of a socialist party is such that the General Congress is the highest organ of the party (or movement). It is convened once every four or five years and its membership is always in thousands representing all parts of the country. The General Congress elects the Central Committee which is the highest organ of the party between General Congresses. The Central Committee is usually convened once every year or two and its membership in hundreds. The Central Committee in turn, elects from amongst its members the

Political Bureau of the party which number of members usually, but not always, ranges between 10 to 40 persons. This is the executive organ of the party and would meet as frequently as desired according to the constitution, rules and regulations of the party concerned.

Since it is the General Congress which elects members of the Central Committee, it follows that if, for any reason, there was to be a vacancy or vacancies in the latter body, then the General Congress has to be convened again to elect new members to fill the vacancies. Surely, this could be a very costly business as the exercise involves the transportation and accommodation of thousands of members from all over the country. To avoid this unnecessary expenditure, it was thought fit that the General Congress in electing the Central Committee includes in the list a given number of the runners-up (in the order of votes scored) as some kind of a reserve list. Should a vacancy arise in the membership proper, then this is filled from the reserve list without the need to convene a General Congress just to elect one or a few members to the Central Committee. The reserve list is what is known as "alternate" members to distinguish them from the "full" - not permanent - members who have won the election. It is implicit that the number of the alternate members is a small fraction of that of the full members. In some parties where the membership of the Central Committee is large or/and its meetings infrequent, this procedure similarly applies to the Political Bureau and one gets "full" and "alternate" members of this organ of the party as well.

In all such parties, the alternate member attends all the meetings of the Central Committee (or the Political Bureau, if applicable) and participates fully in the discussions and debates within it. However, an alternate member has no right to cast a vote when voting is called for. Hence, the alternate member is, more or less, in a training process to prepare him to become a full member should a vacancy arise. It is, therefore, a transitional stage of membership. How can all this be relevant to the "High Command" of the SPLA? Not in anyway at all.

First, it is only Dr John Garang who appoints all members of the High Command. Therefore, the element of cost does not arise as he can do the appointment any time he likes as he has no Congress to convene. Second, the training aspect is redundant since the High Command does not meet anyway.

It is common knowledge that the High Command has no fixed number of members, so creating two tiers of membership cannot stand up to reason. Worse still when the alternate members outnumber the "permanent" members by a ratio of 3 to 1. Even if, for argument sake, this arrangement were to be accepted, it did not follow its own logic. Since March 1988, the permanent members of the High Command dropped from five to three following the detention of Kerubino and Arok and actually dismissing them from the High Command (see message No. 115/3/88 dated 14/3/88). No alternate members were appointed to fill the two vacancies. This could only mean that permanent membership, which proved not to be as permanent as it was first conceived, was an exclusive club of a select few.

Being "permanent members" however, was not enough to keep the members of the High Command quiet for Dr John Garang to run the movement as he wished. As he was a permanent member and the C-in-C, they wanted titles too. These members, especially Kerubino and William, forced a meeting to take place towards the end of 1985. This was in Bonga training centre and it was a stormy one according to the participants in the meeting and eye-witnesses. Each went to the meeting with a good number of bodyguards armed to the teeth. Dr John Garang cleverly avoided a confrontation and in fact won the day. He dished out the titles they wanted which made them extremely happy to the extent that none raised the more fundamental issue of the definition of powers within the High Command. As it turned out, that was the first and the last meeting of the High Command and the issue was laid to rest. The other four permanent members emerged from the meeting triumphant: Kerubino was now the Deputy C-in-C, William, the Chief of Staff, Salva, the Deputy Chief of Staff for Operations and Security, and Arok, the Deputy Chief of Staff for Administration and Logistics. Things, however, never changed. The Chairman and C-in-C continued managing the affairs of the movement alone. When in 1987 his deputy protested that he was kept out of picture on the movement's affairs, he ended up in jail. A few months after, Arok, another "permanent member" followed him in gaol. The positions they held in the High command were never filled; another testimony to the fact that they were after all just empty titles.

The High Command continued to be a useful instrument for the Chairman to employ in his public statements. His own statements would variably be issued as a "resolution of the High Command" or as from "the spokesman of the High Command" or simply from "the spokesman of the SPLM/A". This was the reality which every SPLA officer knew. This attitude of the Chairman was explained off by some well-intentioned persons that he had no choice as the High Command by then lacked "quality", in terms of well educated members in its ranks. At face value, this argument would appear to be reasonable. Apart from Arok , who was a graduate of the military college, one of the other three was illiterate and the remaining two had only primary school education. However, the situation did not change when in the second half of 1986 seven new members with well founded education and experience were co-opted as alternate members of the Political-military High Command. Therefore, those who thought quality was the problem must have been disappointed greatly. The Chairman had other considerations in mind.

In fact, as time went by, it became more consolidated in the Chairman's mind what a rubber-stamp the High Command was supposed to be. For instance, when the elected government of Sadiq al-Mahdi was overthrown in a military coup d' etat on June 30, 1989, the Chairman and C-in-C sent a radio message to all the High Command members on 2/7/89 (message No. 006/7/89 in the appendix). Far from calling for a High Command meeting to deliberate on this serious development in Khartoum and its impact on the movement, the Chairman had decided what ought to be done. To him "the coup is a symptom of the last kick of the dying Old Sudan" and what was required was "to exploit the coup militarily and politically to make the situation worse for the new regime and thus to accelerate the birth of the New Sudan." The only contribution the Chairman needed from the members of the High Command was their "ideas and advices" on the above "urgently and from time to time as events develop."

The Sudanese political groups, the diplomatic missions and relief organizations which had to deal with the SPLM/A in Addis Ababa and Nairobi in the second half of the eighties could not have failed to notice the unnecessarily long time it took to get a feedback on the matters they raised with the movement. Every single decision had to be made by the Chairman some hundreds of miles away. The situation appeared to be improving in 1989 but not without problems as some of the previous chapters have made clear.

Political Strategy

In 1983, the newly born SPLM published two major documents: the Manifesto of the Sudan People's Liberation Movement[10] and the "Punitive Provisions for the Conduct of the People's Revolution No. 1"[11]. The first, as the title suggests, outlined the principles and policy of the movement. The second was the law to govern and regulate the behaviour of members of the SPLM and the citizens within the SPLA operational areas. Interestingly, however, it contained important political provisions. For instance, section 21 of the "Punitive Provisions ....." defined the SPLM as a "Marxist - Leninist Movement". Although the two documents refer to a Programme of Action of the SPLM, none was published. The Manifesto, however, in section 23 presented some points it claimed to be contained in the Programme of Action.

The two documents were short-lived, at least the high-pitch Marxist-Leninist provisions in them, for a mishap took place shortly after their publication. At that time, Col. Pio Yukwan Deng, a former Anya-nya officer, was the military commander of the enemy garrison in Nasir. As pointed out in Chapter Two, the Chairman sent a letter to Col. Pio in an attempt to persuade him to cross over and join the SPLA. The letter was accompanied by the two documents (the Manifesto and the Law). Col. Pio Yokwan Deng passed over the documents to Jaafar

---

10 The Manifesto of the Sudan People's Liberation Movement, 31st July 1983..
11 Punitive Provisions for the Conduct of the People's Revolution No.1, SPLM, 1983.

Mohammed Nimeiri, the President of the Democratic Republic of Sudan and the C-in-C of the People's Armed Forces. Nimeiri must have thanked his lucky stars; the documents arrived like manna from heaven. He put them to good use, both at home and abroad, drumming up propaganda that the SPLM/A by its own admission was a communist movement and that it was planted and supported by the communist bloc to gain a foothold in Sudan in order to consolidate their presence in the region. The implications of a communist takeover in Sudan were at that time very grave to the West, especially the U.S.A. Sudan had become a strong ally of the U.S.A when it supported the Camp David accords, the only country of significance in the Arab League to do so. Sudan was also the missing link for the Aden Axis states (South Yemen, Ethiopia and Libya) to have continuous geographical territory. If Sudan were to become communist then Egypt, a staunch ally of the U.S.A, would be isolated and cut northwards by a communist belt extending from Yemen to Libya. There was no way the U.S.A could have taken such a possibility lying down. Nimeiri, the wily old bird, must have mused over all these when he played the communist scare to its limit. Soon after that, he paid a visit to Washington where he met President Ronald Reagan.

The Manifesto also referred to the successive regimes in Khartoum as "pseudo-Arab." This as well did not escape the notice of Nimeiri and he used it in the Arab world to portray the SPLA as anti-Arab and thus a racist movement.

The reaction of the SPLM/A to Nimeiri's propaganda was categorical denial. It was affirmed that the movement was neither communist nor racist. What about the reference in the documents to the movement being Marxist - Leninist? The SPLM/A's answer was to disown the documents and accused Nimeiri of having invented them. The SPLM/A immediately set to work on amending these documents which have caused all that embarrassment. Soon later, there appeared new versions of the documents. The words "Marxist-Leninist" were expunged, the phrase "pseudo-Arab" replaced by "minority clique", the word "bourgeoisie" modified to the rather unwieldy expression: "bourgeoisified bureaucratic elite", etc. Apart from the modifications, however, there was no substantial change in the text of the two documents. We now know that even this last version of the Manifesto was amended in Tripoli in March 1984 (see later) but, curiously enough, the date of publication to this day still remains to be 31st July 1983. The laws were finally amended in July 1984 and renamed "Penal and Disciplinary Laws of the SPLM"[12].

The debacle over the Manifesto and the Law could not have come at a worse time. So early and so soon, the credibility of the SPLM/A was put to test and was found wanting. In spite of the cosmetic change, it was still obvious to any serious reader that the new version and the one in the possession of Nimeiri must have been written by the same person (or group of persons). To many observers, one thing the hurried change proved was probably that the SPLM was unprincipled and could change colours if and when the going gets tough.

The communist jargon was not the only controversial provisions in the Manifesto. The Sudanese society and the world at large were divided in absolute terms into two camps: the "real and potential enemies" of the SPLA/SPLM and the "real and potential friends". In the first camp was placed: The Northern and Southern Sudanese bourgeoisified and bureaucratic elite; religious fundamentalism; the Anya-nya-2 reactionary commanders; African and Arab reactionary countries; and Imperialism. In the second camp we find: Workers, peasants and their mass organizations; students and revolutionary intellectuals; progressive elements within the Sudanese Armed Services; Socialist and progressive countries in Africa; Europe, Asia and Latin America; and other countries, national and international organizations and agencies sympathetic to the aims and objectives of the SPLM.

Of particular concern to the Southern Sudanese was the way the Manifesto looked at the history of the Southern struggle. The Anya-nya movement which led the 17-years struggle (1955 - 72) was dismissed as one whose "objectives and aims centred around jobs and job titles", the Torit mutiny in August 1955 which triggered off the Anya-nya struggle, was "precipitated by the unfair distribution of colonial jobs

---

12 Penal and Disciplinary Laws of the SPLM, SPLM, 1984

between the Southern and Northern bourgeoisified bureaucratic elites" and the historic Addis Ababa Agreement of 1972 "was a deal between the Southern and Northern bourgeoisified bureaucratic elites. The Northern elite dictated the terms while the Southern elite compromised the interests of the masses in return for jobs which had long been denied them."

Since this study is about political strategy of the SPLM, we shall henceforward concentrate on the specific stipulations of the Manifesto and the law in this respect. Section 21 of the "Penal and Disciplinary Laws of the SPLM 1984" on the establishment of SPLM and SPLA stipulates:

1   There shall be established a Socialist Revolutionary Movement to be known as "The Sudan People's Liberation Movement" which shall be the sole political organization established in the interest of the oppressed masses of the Sudanese people in order to liberate the country from the oppressive, corrupt and undemocratic clique system of Khartoum.

2   The Sudan People's Liberation Movement shall have an armed component to be known as "The Sudan People's Liberation Army" which shall at the initial stage of gradual transition from civil war to total takeover of the whole country, exercise executive and judicial authority with assistance from the SPLM Provisional Executive Committee.

Curiously, the definition of the SPLM and SPLA is not contained in a constitution but in a penal and disciplinary law! More surprising still is the reversal of roles in subsection 21(2) between the SPLM and SPLA. The army is to exercise executive and judicial authority whereas the political arm, the SPLM Provisional Executive Committee, was just to give "assistance". In other words, the political element is subordinated to the military. This was quite a novelty in the history of revolutionary movements.

The Manifesto discussed the formation and objectives of the SPLA and SPLM in Chapter seven. The relevant sections and parts are reproduced below:

Section 20. ...Although the Movement has started by necessity in the South, it aims eventually at engulfing the whole country in Socialist transformation. The SPLA is fighting to establish a United Socialist Sudan, not a separate Southern Sudan.

Section 21. The immediate task of the SPLA/SPLM is to transform the Southern Movement from a reactionary movement led by reactionaries and concerned only with the South, jobs and self-interest to a progressive movement led by revolutionaries and dedicated to the socialist transformation of the whole country. .....

Section 22. ...This imminent, latent and impending disintegration and fragmentation of the Sudan is what the SPLA/SPLM aims to stop by developing and implementing a consistent democratic solution to both the nationality and religious questions within the context of a United Socialist Sudan.

Incidentally, the word "democracy" is not mentioned anywhere in the whole Manifesto. The nearest reference to it is the use of the word "democratic" as in section 22 above.

On the basis of the above stipulations, the SPLM was proclaimed to be a Socialist Revolutionary Movement which shall be the *sole* political organization to liberate the country and establish a United Socialist Sudan. True socialism must be predicated on democracy, both internally within the party or movement and in the whole country. But since the Second World War, the world has seen many totalitarian regimes which claimed to be socialist. Dictatorship is antithesis of socialism and one-party systems always end up as one-man enterprises and thus dictatorial. Thus, for the SPLM to proclaim itself socialist and at the same time the sole political organization in the country was a contradiction in terms unless it wanted to follow the example of the travesty of socialism in vogue those days. The silence of the Manifesto on even a mention of democracy tends to throw doubt on the Movement's socialist credentials let alone democractic pretensions.

Subsequent to the publication of the Manifesto, the SPLM had made public statements that it was against liberal democracy. It even signed a joint statement with the Nasserite Arab Socialist Party reaffirming their opposition to liberal democracy. This was in the first few months of the Uprising in 1985. Which type of democracy then, did the SPLM stand for? The SPLM also declared that it would not talk to the sectarian parties: the Umma party and the DUP. The SPLM cell in Khartoum was astonished by the Movement's policy and pronouncements on the two related issues (liberal democracy and refusal to talk to sectarian parties) and advised a review. On the sectarian parties, the concrete reality in Sudan was that the Umma Party and the DUP enjoyed the most popular support in the North and the two parties have formed, either singly or in coalition, all civilian governments in Sudan since 1953/54. There is no way they can be wished away and in any democratic setup they will always emerge on top for quite some decades to come. Like them or loathe them, the movement would have to deal with them as long as it is committed to democracy. As to liberal democracy, it is the only type of pluralistic democracy acceptable to the Sudanese political spectrum. The Chairman appears to have heeded the advice on the sectarian parties and accepted to have dialogue with them as well as with all the political parties in the country regardless of their colours. As it turned out, not only did the movement engage these sectarian parties in talks but both the DUP and the Umma Party signed agreements on "strategic alliance" with the SPLM/A.

It is the issue of democracy which remained tricky. The wind of democracy which swept Sudan with the March/April Uprising had its effects on the public relations of the SPLM/SPLA. The movement became vociferous in its propaganda and political agitation about its commitment to democratization within the movement and to multiparty democracy in the country. The Chairman went as far as to claim publicly that the movement has organs on the grassroots level which deliberate on matters of policy. In his famous letter to Dr El-Jizouli Dafallah, the Prime Minister after the March/April Uprising, the Chairman wrote the following[13]:

---

13 Letter from the Chairman and C-in-C, SPLM/SPLA, to the Prime Minister, September 1, 1985..

> The letter [El-Jizouli's] had to be discussed in various committees of the Movement, a necessary democratic process that culminated in the final resolutions by our highest organ, the SPLM/SPLA Politico-Military High Command.

Everybody in the SPLA knows that no such organs did exist and that the movement had no political institutions other than the dummy "High Command". Hence, none was convened to discuss anything, let alone the Prime Minister's letter. In fact, most senior officers in the movement, including High Command members did not come across the Prime Minister's letter to the SPLA leader nor the latter's reply to it. The High Command itself never met and the "resolutions of the High Command", as came in the letter, were conceived and written by the Chairman alone. The movement got stuck with these pre-conditions in all its peace talks ever since. Cdr. Martin Manyiel Ayuel told me in 1990 that the Chairman did not even think of replying the Prime Minister's letter and that it was through his repeated promptings together with his colleague, Major El-Tahir Bior, that the Chairman finally agreed to put pen to paper. This is a more plausible explanation for the delay in replying the letter than due to being " discussed in various committees of the movement", as stated in the Chairman's letter to the Prime Minister.

Thus, although the SPLM/A was making the right noises about democracy, these were nothing more than expediencies meant to impress outsiders but never to sink and establish roots within the movement itself. Nothing had changed since the demise of the PEC before its first birthday.

Military Strategy

In all guerrilla movements, indeed in all armies, combat experiences are frequently discussed in order to consolidate the victories, learn from the setbacks and strive to overcome the limitations. This exercise is so fundamental that it is the only way to fight the war effectively avoiding unnecessarily heavy losses. On the tactical level, junior officers discuss each and every major military operation before the commanding officer issues the necessary operation order which details out the missions and tasks for the units and personnel involved in the operation. This proven military practice has a tremendous morale-boosting effect on the young officers. They tend to fight better as they feel they were part and parcel of the decision to fight. On the strategic level, the High Command and senior filed commanders meet, at least once a year to work out the strategy of prosecuting the war all over the theatre of operations. The enemy with his garrisons in the South besieged still manages to hold an annual conference of the military area commanders at the Army General Headquarters in Khartoum to discuss the military strategy.

In the SPLA, the Chairman did not see it necessary to share with his colleagues in the High Command the task of formulating the military strategy for prosecuting the war. He took it upon himself to do the work alone. His orders in this respect since December 1986 are shown in the appendix and will be briefly discussed in what follows.

A. Axis Command

The directives and orders of December 31, 1986, were issued for the purpose that "the enemy offensive must be contained and repulsed and our own major offensive launched by the beginning of the rains." The Chairman and C-in-C went on:

> This military situation demands that all members of the SPLA/M High Command be physically present in the filed during the whole of the dry season to direct the operations.

According to the message, the overall objective was "to liberate the whole east Nile of Southern Sudan from Nimule to Renk by 31/12/1987 while intensifying guerrilla and semi-conventional warfare on the West Nile, Southern Kordofan and Southern Blue Nile." What military appreciation and appraisal the Chairman had done to make the realization of such a gargantuan mission possible was not explained.

This command policy introduced the concept of "Axis Command" for the first time. In most cases, it overlapped with the existing "Zonal Commands." It is axiomatic that wherever two military officers of the same organization shared territory, the most senior one assumes overall command of the forces. Therefore, there was no way the Zonal Commanders could not have come under the orders of the Axis Commanders in the territories they were together. The C-in-C, however, thought differently. Says he:

> The concept of Axis Command does not and should not contradict Zonal Command but rather is meant to reinforce it. The channel of command for Zonal Commanders still remains as before. But Axis Commanders submit their reports and requests directly to the C-in-C.

As it were to be expected, the C-in-C's assurances notwithstanding, problems of command in overlapping Axis and Zonal Commands cropped up almost immediately. For instance, there was confusion as to who would receive the logistics, is it the Axis or Zonal Commander? If the Axis Commander needs to deploy some forces of the zone, can the Zonal Commander object? Etc. In less than three months, the C-in-C had to issue another "command policy and directives" to explain the relationship between the Axis and Zonal commands. His message No. 043/3/87 dated 20/3/87 (see the appendix) opened thus:

> Ref my message of last December about the formation of Axis Commands, there are indications that the definition and aim of the Axis Command and its relation to zonal commands are not properly understood."

Problems continued. The concept was untenable. For instance in Axis Two, because of constant friction in command, the Zonal Commander had to be withdrawn and deployed as commander of Fangak and Ayod Independent Area Command. By the end of the year (the specified period), the overall objective of the command policy was not anywhere near achievement. By the end of 1987, only Pibor and Jekou had been liberated. Axis Two Commander, Cdr. Kerubino Kwanyin Bol, D/Chairman and D/C-in-C was languishing in jail. Axis Four Commander, Cdr. Salva Kiir, was fighting in Kurmuk instead. He did not take up command of his Axis. Axis Five Commander, Cdr. Arok Thon Arok, was still inside Ethiopia. The liberation of east Nile, not from Nimule to Renk but now bounded northward by Sobat river, had to wait until the first half of 1989.

B. Front Command

In the late 1987, the Chairman took over the command of Axis Four and started active operations on Kapoeta town. The town fell to the SPLA in January 1988. However, this victory was announced over Radio SPLA not as the work of Axis Four forces as was expected but was ascribed to forces of, the hitherto unknown, Bright Star Campaign (BSC). Radio SPLA broadcast of that afternoon carried an item of news that the official spokesman of the SPLA conveyed the congratulations of the Chairman and C-in-C to the BSC Cdr. on the magnificent victory scored by the BSC forces. It turned out later that the Chairman and C-in-C, the official spokesman, the BSC Cdr. and the author of the news item were one and the same man; Dr John Garang.

There was no official radio message to High Command members or SPLA units explaining the concept of BSC and how it related to the earlier concept of Axis Command.

On September 21, 1989, the Chairman and C-in-C issued another order, titled: "Organization Number 3", which instituted the concept of "Front". According to this order (message No. 185/9/89), the Axis formation was abolished and three Fronts created as follows:

1 First Front: under the command of the C-in-C, Cdr. John Garang, it was sub-divided into two parts (or "phases"):
   a) Phase one: comprising east of the Bahr el-Jebel and south of Sobat river and bordered by Ethiopia, Kenya and Uganda.

b) Phase two: comprising the part of Upper Nile Region north of the line made up by the Sobat and Bahr el-Jebel (in its northern bend) rivers.

2   Second Front: comprising the whole of Blue Nile province up to the 14th parallel. This was placed under the command of the Chief of Staff, Cdr. William Nyuon Bany.

3   Third Front: comprising the Lakes province, it was put under the command of the Deputy chief of staff, Cdr. Salva Kiir Mayardit.

Military operations in the three Fronts, respectively, were code-named: Bright Star Campaign (BSC), New Fung Campaign (NFC) and Kon Anok Campaign (KAC)[14].

In addition, the order stipulated that the administration of the GHQ and all the Central Training Centres shall fall under the C-in-C.

Significantly, the order did not define an overall objective for the concept of Front nor did it specify a time frame for achieving that objective. It just mentioned that the changes were made with effect from 21/9/1989 "for the coming phase of the war". What phase? Not a word.

C. BSC Expands

As mentioned already, the SPLA received a big setback in Southern Blue Nile in the first week of January 1990. The movement was literally driven out of the area. The Chief of Staff who commanded the area (Second Front) had just arrived Itang area in retreat when a new order reorganizing the command was issued by the Chairman on the 8th of January 1990.

All High Command members were ordered to be physically in the battlefield. The order (message No. 015/1/90) stated:

---

14 Kon Anok was an Aliab (Dinka) leader who fought the British forces in the Aliab country in the present Lakes State between October, 1919 and May 1920 scoring a major victory against the British troops near Ayilla between Mingkaman and Pab on December 8, 1919. Outgunned by his enemy and with almost all the cattle seized, Kon Anok surrendered on May 6, 1920, and the fighting between Aliab and the British came to an end..

In order to frustrate enemy plans, maintain our gains and capture
more territories, operations will be concentrated in BSC phase (I),
phase (II) and phase (III)...

These phases were defined in the order. Thus, the concept of "Front"
was implicitly abolished and all the areas that fell under NFC and
KAC were incorporated into the BSC, all under the command of the
C-in-C, Cdr. John Garang. Each phase was sub-divided into sectors.
Each sector was commanded by a High Command member and each
sector commander was also a Deputy to the BSC Cdr. Conspicuous by
his omission in this deployment was the Chief of Staff, Cdr. William
Nyuon Bany. He took this as a slap in the face and became apprehensive that the Chairman was planning to arrest him. Labouring
under the fear of the unknown, he seethed over this until at one stage
he burst out publicly. In a rally held in Itang, William poured scorn on
the Bor people whom he accused of being rumour mongers, presump-
tuous and doing much talk but less combat. He threatened that if
he were to leave the movement things would not be the same at all.
Visibly furious, he accused the Chairman, without mentioning him by
name, of stashing U.S. dollars in private accounts and warned those
who accuse him of corruption and amassing wealth to watch out as he
was not the only one in the field.

William's outburst was, of course, reported to the Chairman.
Knowing William's mentality, the Chairman's response was to appoint
William as commander of the Pibor area to mount a punitive campaign
against the Murle tribe for having shown lack of support for the SPLA.
All in the SPLA knew that in the process of subduing the Murle tribe,
Cdr. William Nyuon would amass as many thousand heads of cattle as
he wants. This would keep him quiet. As expected Cdr. William took
up the appointment with unbridled enthusiasm.

The main thrust of the 8th of January Orders was operations in
BSC Phase (II). The actual Operation Order for this phase was issued
in March 1990. In it (see the map) there was a new definition of
sectors and accordingly additional sector commanders were named.
BSC phase (II) was repeatedly reorganized ever since. On July 4,

1990 (message No. 025/7/90), sector 5 was frozen and sectors 4 and 6 separated; on December 1, 1990, sectors 4, 5 and 6 were again brought together under one command and so was the case with sectors 1, 2 and 3; and in just under two months later (message 078/1/91 dated 20/1/91) sectors 4, 5 and 6 were put under the command of Cdr. Salva Kiir Mayardit as D/Cdr of BSC phase II with the two High Command members (Manyiel and I) who commanded sectors previously becoming "assistant commanders" whatever the phrase meant in military terms. Again on April 2, 1991, all the six sectors of BSC phase (II) were put under Cdr. Salva Kiir as the Deputy BSC Cdr. Cdr. Riek Machar, Cdr. Gordon Kong and I became just his staff officers; respectively, as chief of Combat Operations, Chief of Civil - Military Operations and Chief of Servscom. This last order was to be in effect "until 31/5/91 or further orders."

D. Conclusion

From the foregoing, not only was the military strategy - if it could be termed as such - drawn up by one person but it was *ad hoc* in nature. The orders were almost always in reaction to "the enemy offensive". In Southern Sudan, enemy offensives are always in the dry season which period of the year is well known. Why then not plan in advance?

Another observation to make is the obvious under-deployment of High Command members. For instance, in the BSC Phase (II), apart from the C-in-C who was the BSC Cdr., there were five High Command members and one full Cdr. commanding just a Brigade-size force! Compare this with BSC phase (I), which was bigger in size and with more soldiers, that was commanded by only one High Command member, Cdr. Kuol Manyang Juuk, as Deputy BSC Cdr.

This under-deployment was costly too. Cdr. Martin Manyiel Ayuel was undergoing medial treatment in London when he was recalled to take part in the operations of BSC phase (II). It boggled the minds of many of us as to why the Chairman recalled him back when the treatment was not over. He was my deputy in the Maban operations and I personally knew he was still suffering. I took a decision in June 1990 and gave him permission for him to go to Itang to continue with the medical treatment. I could not have done more than that as permissions to go on medical treatment abroad was the sole prerogative of Dr John Garang. Cdr. Martin Manyiel Ayuel struggled with the disease and by the time he was in Nairobi it was too late. He passed away in a Nairobi Hospital on May 6, 1992. His strength of spirit never failed up to the last breath of his life when his frail hand scratched on the hospital wall near his death bed two letters: S.C. To all of us who knew him there was no doubt as to what he meant: the struggle continues.

Anybody with some military knowledge would immediately notice the oddity of the command structure in all the above deployments. Here is a C-in-C who runs the day-to-day administration of the army and, yet, still would want to be Axis Cdr., Front Cdr., BSC Cdr., etc., with the next layer in the hierarchy of the movement (High Command Members) as Deputy and "Assistant" Cdrs. of the Axes, Fronts, BSCs, etc. What assignments does such an arrangement leave for the other senior officers (Cdrs and A/Cdrs) to do? The whole arrangement defies any logic but the message the Chairman and C-in-C wanted to drive home was that nothing could be done except with his direct involvement. Certainly, this could not be true for the SPLM/A is among very few movements in the third world that attracted talents of all kinds: Military officers, police officers, prison warders, wild life officers, medial doctors, engineers, local government administrators, lawyers, economists, etc. All are there in big numbers. Therefore, the manpower, in quantity and quality, was abundant. What was lacking and still is are the organizational structures through which all these talents could be put to good use to serve the people's war of liberation. As it were, many of them stayed idle in refugees camps of Itang, Pinywudo and Dima. Naturally, disenchantment, disillusionment and frustration became widespread.

Finally, a reference was made in the C-in-C orders to the chain of command in relation to the zones. Some explanation is necessary in this regard. In March 1987, Cdr. James Wani Igga, Cdr. Yousif Kowa Mekki and I, who were about to move to take up our assignments as Zonal commanders, were briefed by the Chairman as to the chain of command we were to observe once in command of our zones. He told us that our messages on operations have to be sent to him and repeated to the Deputy Chief of Staff for Operations and Security, and the messages on Administration and Logistics to be sent to him and repeated to the Deputy Chief of Staff for Administration and Logistics. I personally asked the question as to why the same messages were not to be repeated to the Deputy C-in-C and the Chief of Staff. The Chairman's answer was that they will be getting their reports from the deputies of the Chief of Staff. It was a specious answer but was enough to protect our backs.

We all knew that there was no reporting system in the SPLA other than through the radio network. Why then the double reporting? Furthermore, if it were the chain of command which was to be strictly followed then the Zonal Commanders should have been reporting only to the deputies of the chief of staff and then each of them to report up the chain. We should not have been sending messages directly to the C-in-C. Once the C-in-C was included in our reporting system, there was no reason not to include the deputy C-in-C and the chief of staff. It was also inexplicable why the two deputies of the chief of staff should be getting partial reports. They should have been getting all reports on operations, administration, logistics, etc., to get an overall picture of what was going on in the zone concerned.

In any case, we complied with the order of the Chairman but it did not take long before we were taken to task by the deputy C-in-C and the chief of staff for having failed to observe the chain of command. In this challenge, the Chairman did not stand up to defend our position. We were left on our own.

The first warning to us came from the D/C-in-C, Lt. Col. Kerubino Kwanyin Bol. His message No. 088/7/87 dated 29/7/87 addressed to the chief of staff, his deputies and the Zonal Commanders read:

"It has come to my notice that some of you are corresponding directly with the C-in-C without informing me. This is unprocedural and incorrect to isolate me from the affairs of SPLM/SPLA. In my capacity as D/C-in-C, I order all of you to carefully observe the chain of command and norms of SPLA. Anybody who will act contrary to this order will definitely shoulder the consequences of this act."

Lt. Col. Kerubino's feeling of being isolated from the affairs of the SPLM/SPLA was definitely genuine as explained earlier. However, the Chairman's response was quite intriguing. In a long 7-point message (No. 001/8/87) he addressed all High Command members, Zonal commanders, Independent area commanders and rear bases commanders on 2/8/1987. The relevant parts were as follows:

1. Ref. D/C-in-C message 088/7/87 addressed to some of you without copy to me and others. There are many other similar messages addressed to some and not to others and all aiming to agitate groups or individuals on some local basis.

4. The truth is that D/C-in-C is very sick mentally and physically and some three or four non-combat officers have taken advantage of his condition and are the ones who draft the meaningless and illusionary agitational messages that you are receiving. These officers are: Major Atem Gualdit who just came from Sudan, Major Chol Biowei, 1st Lt. Ajak Boldit and 1st Lt. Korow, all of whom have never seen a battlefield nor moved an inch from Itang or Longkuei refugees camps. Despite all this they must be members of the High Command.

5. I want to assure all of you that there is no danger to the movement from these officers. D/C-in-C situation and erratic behaviour is a health problem and we wish him speedy recovery from both the mental breakdown and the appendix operation. D/C-in-C is, therefore, here given medical leave and you are to work with the C-in-C, chief of staff, D/chief of staff for operations and security and D/chief of staff for Administration and Logistics.

There was no evidence that the D/C-in-C was "very sick mentally" much less that he had a "mental breakdown". As to the physical sickness, having appendicitis could hardly pass as being "very sick" given the excellent hospital facilities in Asosa, where the D/C-in-C was, and Addis Ababa to carry out the relatively simple operation required to remove the appendix. The next thing heard about the D/C-in-C was that he was under detention incommunicado. Nobody bothered to ask the chairman about how fast his "recovery" was coming. People understood he was in an asylum Siberian style.

The D/C-in-C ended up in detention but the point he raised continued to linger on. It was now the turn of Cdr. William Nyuon, the new second in command, to draw attention that he was not being informed about what was going on in the SPLM/A. On December 12, 1987, William sent the following message to all units of the SPLA.

> From: Spear
> To: All Units
> Inf: Thunder
> 027/12/87

> Any operations must be sent to me with immediate effect from today onwards because it appears that some units fail to send to me messages and details of their operation. But I stay tuned only through Radio SPLA.

I expected, and I assume so must the other Zonal Commanders, the Chairman to explain to the chief of staff the chain of command he had earlier ordered us to observe. This was necessary so that if the Chief of Staff did not know about it he does not blame "some units" as came in his message. The Chairman did nothing of the sort. On the contrary, in his reply to William's message, he just ordered us to do as the chief of staff had ordered implying that it was our fault not to have done so before. The Chairman's reply dated 21/12/87, was short. It reads:

> From: Thunder
> To: All Units
> 129/12/87

> Ref. Spear's message 027/12/87. All messages concerning operations are to be addressed to THUNDER repeated to SPEAR and HAMMER.

Nothing is said about messages on administration and logistics; another time bomb.

For some reason, I received both messages on the same day: December 27, 1987. Four days later Cdr. William Nyuon revisited the subject. This time he was more specific on whom to blame. His message No. 042/12/87 dated 31/12/87 was as follows:

From: Spear
To: Alpha Beta
R: Merowe   R: Sennar
Inf: Hammer   Inf: Thunder
042/12/87

1. In order to achieve this war effectively, the military systems must be thoroughly followed.
2. Today, I am sorry to address you again since we are soldiers. I tried to address all units several times to stop such practices. But some of you failed to comply despite my message 027/12/87 which is clear to you all. That any operations conducted must be repeated to Cdr. Axis (3). There has always been no operations message from ALPHA BETA and MEROWE communicated to me.
3. ALPHA BETA and MEROWE are, therefore, advised that operations conducted should be communicated so that I understand full details. This is very necessary and coordinate.
4. In this connection, comrade, I presume that field report is much more encouraging indeed and should you in any case violate this, then what is that? So let us all hope for the best collaboration and hit hard. Good luck to all of us.

Thus, the chief of staff's complaint was directed against James Wani and me. Yousif Kowa could have been included where it not that by that time he was not in his zone. He had returned to Ethiopia after most of the soldiers of Volcano Bn he commanded in Southern Kordofan had deserted. As mentioned earlier, we were briefed together on the reporting system to follow. This did not include sending any messages to the chief of staff. On my part, in the four days between receiving William's first message and his sending of the second, I was in Dingjol area busy meeting the civil population in order to organize the civil administration. I do not remember having sent a message on operations or any other subject outside the zone in the four days. As such the impatience of the Chief of Staff was unjustified.

Cdr. James Wani Igga saw it imperative to explain the situation fully to the chief of staff. On January 4, 1988, he sent the following message.

From: Merowe
To: Spear
R: Hammer   R: Sennar   R: Alpha Beta
Inf: Thunder
005/1/88

Revolutionary greetings and best wishes for the new year. I am in receipt of your comradeship message 042/12/87. Comrade, I am really sorry to say that I have never at all received your message 027/12/87 which is the basis of your reproach on me. I should have otherwise essentially confirmed receipt. I am a soldier and as such I immediately acted according to superior orders. May I remind your comradeship humbly that I have been strongly innocently put to similar blame by DRAGON as per his former message 073/7/87 and mine 054/7/87.

The channel of communication to the best of my documentation and recollection is in full compliance of Cdr. C-in-C message 043/3/87. When the order of channel of command was reversed by THUNDER message 129/12/87, I immediately and accordingly began repeating my messages to your comradeship. Kindly refer to my messages 034/12/87, 035/12/87, 038/12/87, 039/12/87, 002/1/88 and 003/1/88 respectively which were subsequent to the new directives all repeated to you and shall be so henceforth.

I did not need to respond. Cdr. James Wani Igga humbly hit the nail on the head by placing the responsibility where it belongs: at the door of the C-in-C. Wani was referring to para (3) of the latter's message No. 043/3/87 (see the appendix) which re-explained the concept of Axis Command. The chain of command outlined therein is the gist of what the C-in-C briefed the three of us about in March 1987.

Strategy on Peace

The history of the South-North relations is a long catalogue of broken promises in which the South has been on the receiving end. The promise of "safeguards for the South" in the Juba conference of 1947, the "federation" resolution of the parliament in 1955 and the abrogation of the Addis Ababa Agreement of 1972, just to mention a few examples, are cases in point. Hence, the mutual mistrust between the North and South Sudan is deep-rooted. By 1983, and indeed up to today, there was no indication that the power brokers in Khartoum have undergone a change of heart. The radicalization of the Southern Youth and their resort to armed struggle stems from the bitter realization that Khartoum's arrogance in dismissing Southern legitimate demands could not be brought to an end as long as it had the monopoly of the means of state violence. This has always been ruthlessly employed to suppress and oppress the Southern Sudanese.

Like any other guerrilla warfare, the armed struggle waged by the SPLA was to rectify the wrongs meted out on the oppressed people in Sudan by the successive regimes in Khartoum in order to attain a political settlement which will ensure the establishment of a political arrangement in accord with the aspirations of the South and North Sudanese. The SPLA was either to defeat Khartoum's troops in orthodox battle or, through its military operations, enough pressure would be created to cause Khartoum to seek peace. Towards the end of 1984, at the height of Nimeri's unpopularity and increasing isolation, SPLA's leadership believed the SPLA could achieve an outright military victory over Khartoum's troops - at least in the South - and was, therefore, unprepared for a political settlement of the conflict. The events which led to the March/April Uprising that ousted Nimeri from power took the movement by surprise and its leaders were slow in adjusting to the concrete realities of the situation.

The previous chapters have shown how the Uprising brought to government Nimeiri's generals together with the NANS which staged the popular opposition to Nimeri's regime. The SPLA refused to negotiate with the former while considering itself an ally of the latter. But whatever differences the two groups had, they were agreed on one vital major item of policy: that the Sudanese army is the symbol of national unity and they will not allow it to be destroyed or defeated. In other words, whatever collaboration the NANS may have with the SPLA, it must rule out an outright SPLA victory in the battlefield. Few Northern Sudanese will publicly dare discuss the army excesses and atrocities in the South or even doubt the truthfulness of statements issued by the army on the war. This is an unwritten Charter uniting Northern Sudan. Dr John Garang had to learn this fact the hard way when Kurmuk was captured by the SPLA in 1987. The government whipped up a lot of bellicosity and war-like sentiments in the North and all were called upon to help defend the country from "aggression." Consequently, financial and material contributions were donated to the army in order to "liberate Kurmuk from the defilement of the rebels." Among those prominently displayed on the Sudanese media giving donations for this cleansing cause was Mohammed Ibrahim Nugud, the Secretary-General of the Sudanese Communist Party, flanked by his other two comrades who were members of the Constituent Assembly.

The Sudanese army has over the years grown into an institution of its own, a conservative one for that matter, impervious to the various changes of governments which took place in Khartoum since independence. The army always remained loyal to the government of the day. This is hardly surprising given the fact that its only record in combat was and still is fighting in the South (forget the jaunts to Egypt and Iraq); an issue on which Northerners hardly disagree. For instance, when the top leadership of the army which was overthrown by the present NIF military dictatorship claimed to be the "legitimate command" of the Sudanese Armed Forces and resolved to fight the regime, they refused to form an army of their own to fight the Sudanese army which remained loyal to its new C-in-C, Lt. General (PSC) Omar Hassan Ahmed al-Bashir.

Anybody who would want to score an outright military victory over the Sudanese Armed Forces must seriously scratch deeper into this special bond between the army and the political forces in Northern Sudan. The correct policy for the SPLA under the circumstances of Sudan must be to carry the gun in one hand and the olive branch in the other. The SPLA must fight as hard as it can to force the government to talk peace seriously. If and when it does, the SPLM should be ready and prepared to negotiate on the basis of a coherent peace programme which must not lose sight of the mistrust that has grown over the years. The aggrieved party must always know what went wrong for a solution to be found.

Since the war started in 1983, the first overt indication of the government's preparedness to talk peace came on March 3, 1985 when Nimeiri declared the formation of a peace committee under the chairmanship of Sirr El-Khatim El Khalifa. Reference has already been made to this committee in Chapter 2. There was no indication that the government was at all serious in seeking peace talks for there was no official contact made with the SPLM/A, directly or indirectly, on the matter. It appeared the formation of the committee was a propaganda stunt by Nimeiri to coincide with his expected trip to Washington late that month. The SPLM/A responded to Nimeiri's peace committee in a speech delivered over Radio SPLA by the Chairman and C-in-C on March 22, 1985. In this speech, the SPLA leader rejected any negotiations with Nimeiri and appealed instead to garrisons of the Sudanese army in the South to initiate talks directly with the SPLA and to ignore Nimeiri and his generals in Khartoum. There was no way the army in the South would have done as proposed by the SPLA leader. Despite his later claim that "the response from Sudan Army garrisons in the South has been positive and encouraging"[15], not a single enemy garrison took the call seriously, let alone engaging in talks of any kind with the SPLA.

---

15 Speech of the Chairman and C-in-C, SPLM/SPLA, March 22, 1985.

The overthrow of Nimeiri on April 6, 1985 and the new set-up that ensued demanded the movement to state its position vis-a-vis the developments in Khartoum. The reaction of the SPLM/A to these developments came in a statement by the Chairman and C-in-C broadcast over Radio SPLA on April 9, 1985. He ruled out any talks with "Swar al Dahab's Nimeiri's Regime of May-II" and presented a four-point programme of action[16]:

1 General Swar al Dahab must resign and hand over power to the people within seven days. Failing to do so, the SPLA will be obliged to continue the war in order to ensure that the people take over power.

2 The workers, professionals, trades and students unions to continue the strikes and demonstrations until the generals hand over power to the people.

3 The workers, professionals, trades and students unions to form agitational steering committees to continue the uprising and a General Steering Committee to take over power from the generals. The SPLA/SPLM is prepared to be a part of such a body in the process of taking over power.

4 The junior officers, NCOs and men in the Sudanese Army, police and prisons to disobey the orders of the generals and form their won steering committees in their units.

This call was tantamount to relaunching the Uprising without the steam that let it loose in the first place. In fact, the speech lists four major victories already achieved by the Uprising (throwing out Nimeiri, disbanding the state security organ, dissolution of the SSU and the release of all prisoners from Kober prison). Despite all these victories, could the assumption of power by the generals be enough motivation to take the masses on the streets again? A correct reading of the situation then suggested an emphatic 'No' for an answer. As was to be expected, none of the above four points materialized.

---

16 Speech of the Chairman and C-in-C, SPLM/SPLA, April 9, 1985.

When the 7-day ultimatum passed without the resignation of the generals, the Chairman and C-in-C of the SPLM/A had prepared a speech which was not broadcast until the 26th and 27th of May 1985[17] to coincide with the second anniversary of the battles in 1983 that led to the formation of the SPLA. Most of the speech concerned this occasion. It, however, dealt with the issue of war and peace in the country. While rejecting talks with the generals, the SPLA leader underlined that the SPLA/SPLM was "committed to an openminded dialogue on the fundamental problems of the Sudan." "Such a dialogue", he continued, "must be undertaken by all democratic and patriotic forces in the country so that a National Democratic Consensus is reached on the fundamental issues." Elaborating on the point, he went on:

> Such a national democratic consensus cannot be brought about by a bunch of generals, or interim political establishments; it can be brought about only through DIALOGUE among the national democratic and patriotic forces in the country, and the SPLA/SPLM is willing and ready to enter into such broad discussion that will study fundamental issues of the Sudan, such as the system of government, conditions for national unity, economic and social development, Sudan's foreign policy including its African and Arab commitments, and so forth.

On the question as to how to bring about a National Democratic Consensus, the Chairman answered:

> We believe that a national democratic consensus can be meaningfully brought about through struggle and the convergence in the process of struggle of all national democratic forces from all over the country."

He then proceeded to present a programme of National Democratic Revolution for the intensification of the struggle which, more or less, aimed at the isolation of the TMC and called for "round-2 of the

---

17 Speech of the Chairman and C-in-C, SPLM/SPLA, May 26th and 27th, 1985.

popular uprising." It was essentially a call to forge a political-military front against the government.

Therefore, the dialogue the Chairman had in mind was limited only to "the national democratic and patriotic forces in the country." This definition, of course, does not include the "real and potential enemies" of the SPLA/SPLM. The purpose of the dialogue is not to discuss peace but to work out how the popular movement in the streets of the cities and junior officers in the armed services could come together with the SPLA to intensify the struggle. It is this intensification of the struggle that will "bring about peace quickly." We have already shown in Chapter 3 that the perception of these forces about dialogue and peace as well as about the role of the generals was at variance, if not quite the opposite, of this view. Later on, the SPLM/A was to claim that its call for dialogue in this speech of the Chairman and a previous one in March 1985 was synonymous with calling for the National Constitutional conference. It is clear, however, the two concepts are miles apart both in their aims and who were to participate.

The next discourse on war and peace came with the Chairman's reply to the Prime Minister's letter. Some aspects of this letter have already been discussed in relation to the movement's commitment to democracy within it and in the country as a whole. In what follows, attention will be focused on the treatment of the issues of peace in the Chairman's reply letter. It must be acknowledged from the outset that there has been a considerable improvement in the movement's grasp of the reality in the country in this letter than was the case previously. The SPLA/SPLM was now ready to dialogue with all the political forces in the country in a National Constitutional Conference which will tackle Sudan's fundamental problems. But before this conference could convene, a number of pre-conditions must be fulfilled by the government of the day. The Chairman and C-in-C put it this way[18]:

> Since the Transitional Military Council has taken upon itself the responsibility for legislation in Khartoum, it must also take the respon-

---

18 Letter to the Prime Minister, Op. cit.

sibility of ensuring the necessary favourable conditions for national dialogue. Generally, the Government of the day in Khartoum must be seen by all to be genuinely interested in and "doing" not just talking peace. Specially, in the present situation in order for the SPLM/SPLA to come into national dialogue, the TMC, as the Government of the day in Khartoum, must first do the following:

1 Commit itself publicly to an agenda to discuss the "Problem of the Sudan", not the so-called "Problem of Southern Sudan." This concretely means convening a National Congress to discuss, first, the fundamental national issues (such as the system of Government in Khartoum, etc), and then the problem of Regional Governments (federations or regional autonomies), second, as reflections of the structure of power at the centre, in Khartoum.

2 Lift the state of emergency. It is incongruous and absurd for the TMC to declare a cease-fire, as it has done, and maintain the state of emergency at the same time.

3 Commit itself publicly to dissolve the TMC and the Council of Ministers, all to be replaced by a new Interim Government of National Unity, representing all the political forces, including the two warring armies (SPLA and Sudanese Army), and that as shall be agreed upon at the said National Congress. (The SPLM/SPLA was not a party to the formation of the TMC and the Council of Ministers. The two structures must, therefore, be dissolved and replaced by new structures agreed to by all involved.)

4 Cancel Nimeiri's Sharia Laws. It is pointless for the SPLM/SPLA to participate in a conference of national dialogue within the context of Sharia Laws. It is an objective indication of lack of seriousness to gloss things over by talking about exempting the South or any other region from (any) national laws: and it is meaningless to talk about "modifying" the Sharia Laws. Nobody will be amused by such phraseological niceties, and finally

5 Cancel two personal agreements made by Field Marshal Jaffar Nimeiri with Egypt, that is, the Defence Pact and the Economic

and Political Integration Treaty: and also cancel the other personal agreement made recently by Brigadier (PSC) Osman Abdhalla with Libya, also a defence arrangement. Without any prejudice to good-neighbourly relations with these two sister countries, such agreements, which commit the whole Sudanese people and which impinge on statehood (or sovereignty), can only be made by the whole Sudanese people in plebiscite, never by individuals.

The implementation of these pre-conditions (or pre-requisites, to sound palatable) continued to be the position of the SPLM/A in all the peace talks ever since. This was the case in the Koka Dam Conference and all its follow-up meetings; the Sudanese Peace Initiative meetings; the Ministerial Peace Committee meeting and the first two rounds of talks with the NIF Junta in Addis Ababa and Nairobi in 1989. The movement never produced a blueprint on its position on peace, i.e., on the movement's approach as to how the fundamental problems of Sudan could be resolved in order to bring the war to an end. In fact, the matter was never discussed on any level of the movement. The insistence of the Chairman on discussing only the pre-conditions leading to the convening of a peace conference rather than directly addressing the issues at the centre of the conflict; preferring to discuss these matters with the political parties rather than with the sitting government which was called upon to implement the pre-conditions; all these and other attitudes have left a negative impression on many observers leading them to cast doubt on the SPLA's readiness to give peace a chance.

If outsiders were in doubt about Dr John Garang's inclinations on a peaceful settlement to the conflict, those inside the SPLA knew exactly where he stood on the matter. He believes literally in that 'political power grows out of the barrel of a gun'. When addressing SPLA gatherings, he was in fond of telling them that "the war shall continue until all the objectives of the SPLA are achieved." Such a statement and similar ones are frequently broadcast over Radio SPLA. Some observers and political analysts dismiss such talk as rhetoric or just mere exhortation of troops. They are wrong. Consider, for example, his message No. 209/10/88 and 008/11/88 shown in the appendix. These messages were addressed not to the *hoi polloi* but to the members of the High Command. Therefore, the Chairman must have meant every word therein.

The first message was about the Prime Minister's attempts to meet the Chairman to discuss peace. Whatever wedge was being driven between the Umma party and the DUP, it was imperative to take the Prime Minister more seriously than the message had suggested. A basic correction is necessary in the 6 - point reply to President Museveni: Sayed Mohammed Osman El-Mirghani was not the Head of State; his brother was. I was personally disappointed to notice that the draft agreement between the SPLM/A and the DUP was just being sent to the High Command members (on 22/10/88) in the context of the propaganda war with the Prime Minister. It will be recalled that we had agreed with the Chairman in September (see Chapter 6) that the draft be sent to the High Command members to solicit their views on it before the second round of talks scheduled for October.

In the second message, the Chairman did not mince his words as to the purpose of the expected DUP/SPLM summit meeting. For him "Meeting DUP or anyone else is only political manoeuvring."

For Dr John Garang, a peace settlement is a compromise which can only mean capitulation or surrender. The Chairman had a special liking to one song among hundreds composed by the SPLA combatants. This particular song, of Bilpam battalion, was composed in 1984 in a mixture of Dinka and Arabic languages. The stanza that won the Chairman's admiration ran as follows: (unofficial translation):

John [Garang] grips the country,
And the Arabs say they want an agreement.
This John wouldn't accept.
How could he when the country is in ruins?
That thing of the past will not repeat itself.
We are a mighty force,
Bilpam is still in Bonga.
The day we go to Sudan,
All buildings shall be razed to the ground.
Bilpam Oyee!

Bilpam battalion has no mercy,
Even our fathers deserve to be shot.

The phrase "that thing of the past" is a reference to the Addis Ababa Agreement of 1972. Thus, the song makes it plain that since the SPLA is a mighty force, there can never be any peace settlement with the Sudan government in Khartoum. An African poet before composing a song about somebody, first collects enough information about the person, his background, his likes and dislikes, etc. In good African tradition, this composer of Bilpam battalion must have done his homework properly.

Made to Fit

The obvious question which poses itself is: why would Dr John Garang insist on running the movement alone contrary to any known and tested principle of guerrilla warfare where the fighters are all volunteers?

Informed gossip within the SPLA has it that Dr John Garang had a secret deal with President Mengistu Haile Mariam of Ethiopia. According to this theory, Mengistu's support for the SPLA was a *quid pro quo* for Sudan's support of the Ethiopian rebels and hence the deal was that the SPLA should continue fighting as long as the conflict in Ethiopia between the government and the rebels lasts. This is why, the theory goes on, Dr John Garang would not want anybody else take part in drawing up the strategy of the movement lest it may contradict his secret deal with Mengistu. This proposition lends credence to the "linkage theory" referred to in Chapter 6 but with a difference: it is being suggested by insiders.

There is no doubt in my mind that Dr John Garang has no programme for a peaceful settlement of the war in Sudan. I arrived at this conclusion from my personal experience as the chief negotiator of the movement for all the peace talks since 1988; be it the talks with the government or with Sudanese political parties and trade and professional unions. I was also an active participant in the Koka Dam Conference and in most of its follow-up meetings which were held in Addis Ababa to translate Koka Dam Declaration into action. This conclusion still remains valid up to today.

Therefore, one agrees with the suggestion that Dr John Garang would want the war to be fought *ad infinitum*. Fighting to him has sadly become an end in itself. The previous pages have sufficiently demonstrated this position. But whether this was part of a deal with Mengistu is more difficult to discern. Since 1986, I accompanied the Chairman to some of his meetings with President Mengistu Haile Mariam and I did not get any impression that the President was dictating terms towards a particular line of action. As a matter of fact, there were occasions when I felt that President Mengistu genuinely wanted the SPLA to expand outside Ethiopia such as his position on the Chairman's visit to Kenya discussed in Chapter 4.

A number of factors must have combined to let Dr John Garang behave the way he did. He became a prisoner of his own ambition. The means he used to become leader of the movement led him to feel insecure and uncertain of his position and in order to hold to it he became so protective to the extent of ignoring fundamental facts about the liberation struggle itself. It is like being on the back of a tiger. It will be remembered that in his struggle for the leadership of the SPLM/A, Dr John Garang manipulated the career army officers into an alliance against the "politicians". As a result, Kerubino, William and others supported him unreservedly against Mr Akwot Atem and Gai Tut. After the dust had settled with the politicians out of the way, the army officers wanted quick rewards. These were not coming as fast as they thought. More than the rest, Kerubino began to bully the Chairman reminding him often of the fact that he did not take part in the Bor battle of 1983 and that he joined the SPLA as "a colonel without a single soldier with him". Kerubino was later joined by Arok in questioning the military credentials of Dr John Garang pointing out that he never before commanded a combat unit of the army. Therefore, only quite a few were surprised that the two officers were among the first he detained without the due process of law.

The reaction of the Chairman to all the above challenges was a resolve to prove that he was the best military officer and the best politician ever. This meant conducting himself in a way which would make him appear to be the only hand behind every success. Hence, being the C-in-C was not enough, so, he made himself the BSC Cdr. and showed up everywhere there were major operations to capture a town. In this he moved with all the support weapons, enough ammos and all the necessary military hardware to ensure that the operations were successful at all costs. The number of casualties did not seem to bother him. All this to prove to the critics that he can after all command troops and capture towns. This was stretched to ridiculous proportions so much so that at one time in 1989, it appeared as if the SPLA was made up of two separate armies: the troops under the command of the BSC Cdr. (the Chairman himself) were well officered, well dressed, well armed and well equipped whereas the bulk of the army in Bahr el-Ghazal, Upper Nile and other areas were not only unclad and unshod but did not have ammos to fight the enemy. It became clear that there was no long term strategy for the fighting, it shifted with the targets and objectives determined by the C-in-C. Still when the BSC was sub-divided into phases in 1990, he continued to be the direct commander of each individual phase with senior High Command members as his deputy or assistant commanders. This was the case despite the fact that he did not set foot in any of these phases.

To ensure personal loyalty, the Chairman personally selects the recruits to undergo military training and no graduation can be done until he was there to personally issue out the rifles and the other military equipment. If he were abroad by the time the graduation was due nothing could be done and all will have to wait. These are but a few examples in the military field.

Politically, the sections of the Manifesto discussing the issue of leadership, were tailored to fit him personally. Section 23(b) of the Manifesto affirmed:

> Early determination of the correct leadership of the SPLA and SPLM so that the movement is not hi-jacked [sic] by counter revolutionaries.

What he meant by the "correct leadership" was none other than his person and "hi-jacking" the movement was synonymous with taking over the leadership from him. Guarding the movement against imagined hijackers became an obsession to Dr John Garang. In this, every experienced and educated Southerner who has joined or would want to join the movement was suspect. Section 24 of the Manifesto on "the real and potential enemies of the SPLA/SPLM" discusses in sub-section I(b) as to why "the Southern Sudanese Bourgeoisified and Bureaucratic elite" were an enemy to the SPLA/SPLA. It asserts:

> This elite falls into two main categories, those who were and those who were not associated with Anya-nya I. Their interest is the same, although they have internal difference as to who should be dominant politically in the South. Their real interest, like that of the Northern elite, is self-enrichment including the building of multi-storey buildings and amassment of other forms of wealth. Under the circumstances, either of these categories of the Southern elite will try to hi-jack the SPLA/SPLM by infiltrating its leadership and taking it over to their own advantage, or, failing to hi-jack the SPLA/SPLM they will try to organize their own political parties similar to those of 1960s with likely assistance from international reactionaries.

Thus, joining the movement was equated to infiltrating the SPLA/SPLM to hijack its leadership. Consequently, many intellectuals chose to keep out rather than undergo the harrowing experiences their colleagues have suffered.

Garang's preoccupation to remain leader at all cost made him to think that this could also be extended outside the SPLA to alliances made by the movement with other Sudanese political parties. Paragraph 23(K) of the first version of the Manifesto read:

> Contacting opposition groups in both North and South with the view of forming a United Front with these groups, provided the leadership of such a front remains under the SPLA/SPLM.

Thus, the "early determination of the correct leadership" was all permeating. In his trip to Tripoli in March 1984, the Chairman was confronted with a situation which put to test the above simplistic approach to alliances between different political groups. Col. Ghazafi wanted to forge a united front against Nimeiri comprising the SPLA and the Northern opposition groups including the DUP. The DUP could not buy a united front as prescribed by Dr John Garang. Hence, for Garang's delegation to proceed with the talks, the Manifesto had to be amended there and then. The words after the word "remains" were replaced by the expression: "armed and progressive." This was the expression which appeared in the later editions of the Manifesto. Even in this amended form, Dr John Garang read himself into leading the "united front" since the other groups were either unarmed or non-progressive.

The Chairman kept firm control over external political and diplomatic work. Given his distance in the field, the work in this important area tended to be on-and-off and lacked the necessary co-ordination and follow-up. Delegations on official visits abroad were ever changing and report to him alone rather than to the High Command. Also, although the leaders of the movement's delegations to peace talks have had some continuity, members of the delegations were not permanent and were selected mainly on the basis of "who was around in Addis" by that time. The establishment of OCER was a promising improvement. It was, however, as discussed in Chapter 6, not allowed to carry on with its mission.

It is a common saying in the SPLA that when Dr John Garang is in the field, the political and diplomatic work abroad stalls, and when he is abroad the war grinds to a halt. This is said by some with relish in tribute to the godsend gifted leader without whose industriousness the movement would certainly collapse!

Summary

This chapter gives an idea about the lack of organization within the SPLM/A and as a result of which there seems to be no coherence on all aspects of the struggle. That state of affairs was a legacy of the turbulent days in the birth of the movement.

Despite the attitudes that have developed over the years, some of us have always believed in the good sense of the Chairman and that it was still possible to persuade him to steer away from militarism and from the one man leadership to a collective one. One can say with absolute certainty, that Dr John Garang enjoyed the good will of the members of the SPLM/A in a way no other Southern politician ever enjoyed. None in the SPLA, as far as my knowledge goes, was after his position as Chairman and C-in-C. What everybody wanted, naturally, was the structuring of the movement so that they all can participate effectively in the prosecution of the war for which they have volunteered. This concern became a cause of suspicion from the Chairman and led him to lose trust in some genuine comrades who continued to advise him on the matter. As we all know, trust is a two-way street and hence the discontent among the intellectuals was a natural development from such an attitude. Since 1986, I never tired of reminding the Chairman, whenever an opportunity availed itself, of the utmost necessity and importance of activating the High Command which was the only leading organ of the movement. For me this was a matter of principle and it has nothing to do with the personality of anybody. My last attempt in this direction was a memo I presented in June 1990 titled "Towards Organizing the SPLM". It is reproduced verbatim as an appendix to this book. It does not purport to have ready answers to all the problems afflicting the movement. It was meant as just one contribution among many to stimulate healthy discussion of the affairs of the SPLM/A and chart a healthy course forward. To these points I do not for the moment, have much to add.

CHAPTER 10

The Comprehensive Peace Agreement

P EACE TALKS between the SPLM and the Government of Sudan
since the military takeover in Khartoum in June 1989, were
covered in Chapter 6 and in another book[19]. The period covered
was up to 1993. This chapter will focus on the peace talks that took
place thereafter which were known as the IGAD(D) Peace Process;
so named because they were mediated by the regional organization, IGAD(D). The process was successfully concluded with the
signing in Nairobi on 9 January 2005 of the Comprehensive Peace
Agreement (CPA).

The Beginnings

In a summit meeting of the Inter-Governmental Authority on
Drought and Development (IGADD) in September 1993, President
Omer Hassan Ahmed Al-Bashir requested the regional grouping to
help mediate the resolution of the conflict in Sudan. The request
was acceded to and the IGADD countries formed a four-country
committee headed by Kenya to mediate the Sudanese conflict. It was
named "the IGADD Sub-committee on Sudan". The other countries
in the committee were Eritrea, Ethiopia and Uganda; all were by then,
especially Ethiopia and Eritrea, friendly to GOS. The parties to the
conflict were by then three: the Government of Sudan (GOS), the
SPLM/A and the SPLM-United.

---

19 Akol, Lam, "SPLM/SPLA: The Nasir Declaration", i-Universe, Lincoln, Nebraska, 2003.

After a joint PTA/SADCC summit meeting in Kampala in November 1993, the committee of heads of state of the four countries met the leaders of the three parties to the conflict separately in Kampala. Each party presented its position on the resolution of the conflict and submitted to the committee all the necessary documents on the matter.

In January 1994, the Foreign Ministers of the IGADD committee met in Nairobi to chart out the course of the mediation. At that time the Foreign Minister of Kenya met the two leaders of the SPLM/A factions (Dr John Garang and Dr Riek Machar) with a view of reconciling them. The meeting came out with a joint statement on a unified position in the IGADD mediation. However, it fell short of a unified delegation or a united movement.

IGAD(D) in Action

The first formal round of talks under the IGADD mediation was held in March 1994 with all the parties mentioned earlier in attendance. Other rounds were held in May, July and September 1994. The last, held on the 6th of September, was a one-day conference which ended by the withdrawal of the GOS from the process.

It will be recalled that by the time the GOS withdrew from the IGADD process, the military balance on the ground was significantly in its favour. It had by then recaptured most of the garrisons previously held by the SPLA in Eastern Equatoria. The SPLA remained only with Nimule and the strip of land south of the 4th parallel. The GOS attention was then turned to 'peace from within'.

However, the IGADD mediators did develop on 20 July 1994, a framework for the negotiation process which became known as the Declaration of Principles (DOP)[20]. The two parties did accept it then. The DOP declared that "a military solution cannot bring lasting peace and stability to the country" and that "a peaceful and just political

---

20 IGADD Secretariat, "The IGADD Declaration of Principles", Nairobi, 20 July 1994..

solution must be the common objective of the parties to the conflict". It further stated that "the right of self-determination of the people of South Sudan to determine their future status through a referendum must be affirmed". The DOP stressed that "maintaining unity of the Sudan must be given priority by all the parties" and listed seven principles that need to be established to maintain that unity. Pointedly, the document concluded that in the absence of agreement on those principles, "the respective people will have the option to determine their future including independence, through a referendum".

In February 1994, the SPLM-United split into two factions; one led by Dr Riek Machar and the other by Dr Lam Akol. In September 1994, Dr Riek Machar's faction changed its name to South Sudan Independence Movement/Army (SSIM/A) which in April 1996 signed in Khartoum the 'Political Charter' with the GOS. The two sides agreed that the Charter would be transformed into a peace agreement within two months from its signing. This did not materialize.

By 1995, the hitherto friendly neighbours to Sudan, Ethiopia and Eritrea, had severed their diplomatic relations with the GOS. The first accused Sudan of masterminding the attempted assassination of the Egyptian President Hosni Mabarak in Addis Ababa that year. Contrary to all diplomatic norms, Eritrea, turned over the Sudanese embassy in Asmara to the opposition National Democratic Alliance (NDA) as the base for their opposition against the GOS. A striking shift of power occurred regionally when the three leaders of Uganda, Eritrea and Ethiopia coordinated their efforts against the Sudanese regime seeking its downfall with the direct support from the US administration. The GOS was accused by the USA and its neighbours of a conspiracy to disturb regional peace, topple regional governments and spread its version of Islamists ideology throughout the Horn of Africa. The US had in 1993 added Sudan to its list of states that sponsor terrorism.

In March 1996 in Nairobi, the Assembly of Heads of State and Government signed a Letter of Instrument to amend the IGADD agreement so as to establish a revitalized organization with a new name; Inter-Governmental Authority on Development (IGAD).

By early 1997, the military scale had shifted dramatically in SPLA's favour. The SPLA/NDA offensive of January 1997 in the East and Blue Nile brought these forces close to Damazine while the SPLA's March 1997 offensive in Eastern Equatoria brought the SPLA close to Juba. These offensives were with the covert support of the USA and the neighbouring countries, Ethiopia, Eritrea and Uganda.

In April 1997, the 'Sudan Peace Agreement', popularly known as the 'Khartoum Peace Agreement' was signed with pomp in Khartoum. The development was impelled by the military situation. The GOS was anxious to have the SSIM/A military wing, the South Sudan Defence Forces (SSDF), fight on its side in its war against the SPLA/NDA offensive. They in turn pressed for the now overdue transformation of the charter into a peace agreement.

The GOS returned to the IGAD mediation process in July 1997, almost three years since it had left it, and accepted once more the DOP as the framework for the negotiations. A number of rounds were held since then between the SPLM/A and the GOS in Nairobi and Addis Ababa up to August 1998. They were: the fifth, on 30 October 1997, the sixth, in May 1998, the seventh, on 4 August 1998 (in Addis Ababa). These rounds were characterized by being short, two to four days on average. Of relevance here is the fact that in the fifth round that commenced on 30 October 1997, the SPLM/A side tabled a confederation model as the arrangement to govern the Sudan during the interim period preceding the referendum on self-determination. It was based on two entities, the North and the South. The accompanying map showed the suggested borders of the two entities as the 13th parallel, which carved to the South areas outside Southern Sudan with its known borders of 1st January 1956. This position was rejected by the GOS side as being outside the framework of the DOP, especially that the suggested confederation assumed *a priori* the existence of two separate sovereign states.

During the same period a number of regional and international events took place that influenced the progress of peace talks. As the talks in Addis Ababa were winding up the American embassies in Nairobi and Dar-es-Salaam were bombed by terrorists with a lot of casualties.

The reaction of the US administration was to bomb using Cruise Missiles what it believed was a factory for manufacturing weapons in Khartoum North. It later turned out to be just a pharmaceutical facility. This aggression won Sudan some international sympathy as it was seen as the victim. The conflict between Ethiopia and Eritrea came to the open and the two countries fought a bitter war in 1998. As a result the relations between Sudan and each of them improved considerably. Also, the lifting of international embargo on Libya had the effect of opening the door for the Libyan leadership to exert efforts in conflict resolution in the region. In fact, Libya and the State of Qatar jointly mediated to improve the relations between Sudan and Eritrea. There was, also, positive progress in the relations between Sudan and Egypt which eliminated the previous tension between the two neighbours. On the visit of Dr John Garang to Cairo in October 1997, the Egyptian President made it clear to the SPLM/A and the NDA, that it will not compromise on the unity of Sudan and that it will play a role in the resolution of the Sudanese political crisis. The new position of Egypt and Ethiopia towards Sudan dealt a big blow to the international efforts to isolate Sudan using the Addis Ababa incident against President Mubarak. Furthermore, the war situation in the Democratic Republic of Congo pitted the allies of the SPLM/A against each other in their support of the different antagonists in that beleaguered country. Uganda, in particular, found itself embroiled politically and militarily by this situation. Hence, members of the alliance of neighbours the US administration had put together against Sudan were preoccupied with their own internal problems so much so that they no longer were able to devote attention to the mission of getting rid of the regime in Khartoum. Overall, this situation was favourable to the regime in Khartoum.

This is the backdrop to the eighth round of the IGAD peace talks that were held in the period 19-23 July 1999, more than a year since the last round took place. The end result of this round was the agreement of the parties to establish a permanent IGAD secretariat, formation of its committees and naming a Special Representative.

Change of Approach

The new administration in Washington led by President George W. Bush that assumed power in January 2001, reappraised US policy on Sudan. In relation to the peace process, President Bush appointed on 4 September 2001 (a week before the September 11 incident) Senator John C. Danforth as its envoy for peace in Sudan who then declared he was going to make a familiarization visit to the country. The September incident itself had a tremendous impact on peace in Sudan. Unexpectedly, the GOS declared its willingness to cooperate with the US government to combat terrorism and this pledge was put into action as streams of US security personnel visited Khartoum frequently and worked closely with the government on the issue. The policy changed from that of 'confrontation' to 'engagement' with the GOS.

Senator Danforth paid a visit to Sudan in January and again in March 2002 and produced a report which rejected the right of self-determination for the South, did not mention the word 'democracy' and slightingly described the Southern political forces as some 'political tribal factions', which, according to him, he was told they existed. The position of Senator Danforth was met with stiff opposition from the Southerners inside the country and abroad. In Khartoum, a number of Southern Sudan political parties issued a joint press statement in which they reaffirmed the right of self-determination as an inalienable right of the Southern Sudanese.

After that there was a shuttle diplomacy on the side of the IGAD secretariat and the IGAD partners, especially the USA, between the parties and in the region to reconvene the IGAD rounds of mediation. This was the origin of the 'Revamped IGAD process'. It was characterized by two important features: longer rounds (taking weeks instead of a few days previously) and more involvement of the partners than before.

The Breakthrough

All the previous rounds were stalled on the issue of 'State and Religion' which according to the DOP was central to the option of unity of the country.

The IGAD mediation under the new format commenced in June 2002 in Machakos, Kenya. It was under the auspices of the IGAD Secretariat in the presence of the IGAD partners (UK, USA, Italy and Norway) as mediators. The positions of the parties were still quite far apart on the issue of 'State and Religion' so much so that all observers thought this round like the previous ones was going to end up in deadlock. As the talks dragged on and on, the mediators decided to draft an agreement on the points discussed and present the draft to the parties, separately, on a take-it-or-leave-it basis. After consultations with their principals, the two parties accepted the draft which they signed on 20 July 2002 as the Machakos Protocol. This development took many observers by surprise. It was followed a week later by a meeting in Kampala between President Al-Bashir and Chairman John Garang, the first of its kind. It was a clear sign that the two parties were set on the course of peace.

The Machakos Protocol dealt with three basic issues: The system of rule, relationship between the state and religion, and the right of self-determination. It was widely supported by the Sudanese and it appeared the Sudan was at the threshold of attaining peace. Significantly, however, it was opposed by two important neighbours of Sudan, Egypt and Libya, although Libya later on changed its position in favour of what the Sudanese saw fit for themselves.

The Other Rounds of Talks

The Machakos Protocol gave a tremendous moral boost to the mediators and attention now turned to working out the details of the peace agreement. The two delegations returned to Machakos again to continue negotiations on the outstanding issues. The talks were, however, interrupted by military developments on the ground.

In September 2002, the SPLA attacked Torit which was held by the GOS forces and captured it. For quite some time the SPLA was opposed to agreeing on a ceasefire during the peace talks. The attack on Torit was part of SPLA's 'fight and talk' policy. The incident poisoned the cordial atmosphere created by the signing of the Machakos Protocol. The reaction of the GOS was swift. It withdrew from the talks and launched a big mobilization campaign for war and vowed not to return to the peace talks until Torit was recaptured. Heavy fighting ensued around Torit at the end of which the town was retaken by the GOS. In October 2002, as a result of a go-between by some personalities headed by Mr Abel Alier, the two sides signed a cessation of hostilities agreement and the talks resumed. This agreement held remarkably well up to the conclusion of the peace talks in 2005 and was a major factor in the progress made. Nonetheless, the developments following the fighting over Torit continued to deepen the lack of trust between the two sides.

In the rounds that followed (Karen, Nanyuki, Nakuru and Naivasha), the two sides were engaged in detailed discussions on   arrangements governing the interim period leading to the referendum; namely, the issues of power and wealth sharing, security arrangements and the Three Areas (Nuba Mountains, Blue Nile and Abyei). The level of the negotiating delegations was raised to be headed on the side of the GOS by the First Vice President of the Republic, Ali Osman Mohammed Taha, and on the side of the SPLM/A by its Chairman , Dr John Garang. Also, the mediators adopted a new approach to dealing with the negotiations through topical tracks, so that each round is devoted to one track at a time. The tracks were identified as five: power sharing, wealth sharing, security arrangements, the Three Areas, and the National Capital. This approach was taken together with the holistic approach to tackling the problem adopted earlier. Such a method would allow the parties trade-offs within each track or between them. Significant progress was made and differences were narrowed centring around only a couple of issues such as the Presidency, the national capital, the percentages of Southern Sudan participation in the national Government, the security arrangements and the Three Areas.

The Hiccough

The agreed procedure for the round of talks at Nakuru, Kenya, was for the Secretariat of IGAD mediation to present to the parties a draft framework on the resolution of the outstanding issues elaborationg the Machakos Protocol, the parties react to it and discussions to follow. Indeed, the Secretariat presented to the two parties a document entitled: *"Draft framework for the resolution of outstanding issues arising out of the elaboration of the Machakos Protocol"*. The two parties reacted to the document in writing and the session was closed officially by Lt. General (R) Lazarus Sumbeiywo on the 21st of July 2003 in order to give the parties time to study and respond to the draft framework presented by the IGAD Secretariat. It was made clear that the document was not on a take-it-or-leave-it basis but rather that it was open for discussion.

The reaction of the GOS to the document was dramatic. It rejected it outright as a nonstarter and embarked on a public mobilization campaign against the IGAD draft framework document. The acceptance of the SPLM/A of the document without amendment strengthened the GOS' fears and suspicion about the lack of neutrality of the IGAD Secretariat. The GOS position created an impasse in the peace talks.

Apart from the general statements, the GOS made specific objections to the provisions of the draft framework or the Nakuru document, as it became known. These include that the draft framework document:

1 is a back-pedalling from the unity option during the interim period that was affirmed by the Machakos Protocol, by providing for two armies, two central banks and two currencies; provisions which pave the way for secession;
2 had handed over the administration of the South to the SPLM/A alone, in total disregard to the participation of the other Southern political forces;
3 has tied the hands of the President of the Republic in decision-making by being required to get the consent of the Vice President on all decisions, which is tantamount to giving the latter the right of veto;

4   while denies the Central Government any effective role in running the South, gives the leader of the SPLM/A wide powers in running the North;

5   in raising the issue of the National Capital, deviates from the Machakos Protocol regarding the relationship between the state and religion. The provisions on the National Capital were, in the eyes of the Government, secularism itself;

6   is not fair on wealth sharing as it gives the South more than its share at the expense of the other regions of the Sudan.

These arguments found considerable support among the Northerners. However, the points raised are not an accurate representation neither of the provisions of the document nor the positions the GOS has taken previously. For instance:

1   the provision for the two armies during the interim period was contained in the Khartoum Peace Agreement (Articles 8(i) and 8(iii)) and embodied in the Constitution of the Republic of Sudan 1998;

2   paragraphs 25.1, 25.2 and 25.4 of the Nakuru document provide for one Central bank and one currency;

3   contrary to the claim that the South was handed over to the SPLM/A, paragraph 6.1 of the Nakuru document provides for inclusiveness of all political parties in the governments of the Northern and Southern states and the National government;

4   the consent of the Vice President is required only on three issues; namely, declaration of the state of emergency, summoning or proroguing parliament, and appointments to constitutional positions arising from the implementation of the Peace Agreement. All will agree that, in the context of the interim arrangements, these are matters that need the decisions of the two parties as equal partners in the implementation of the Peace Agreement;

5   The Vice President is only involved in the appointment of Governors. But, even this, is conditional on agreement between him and the President;

6   the GOS agreed to 75% share of oil for the South in the Khartoum Peace Agreement (Appendix 3) and therefore it is not reasonable to reject the 50% share contained in the Nakuru document.

The Nakuru document was silent on the elections during the interim period, a matter agreed upon by the two parties in the Memorandum of Understanding on November 18, 2002. Also, paragraph 31.2 of the Nakuru document ruled out the liberation movements that signed the Khartoum and the Fashoda Peace Agreements from participation in the interim security arrangements of the prospective peace agreement. These two issues should have been of concern to the GOS and hence form part of its public denunciation of the Nakuru document. The last issue in particular caused a lot of unease among the parties that signed those agreements with the GOS, especially that it was the GOS that represented them in the peace negotiations.

As will be seen later, all points objected to by the GOS in the Nakuru document, except for the National Capital and other minor details, were agreed upon in Naivasha under the various protocols.

The Protocols of the Peace Agreement[21]

It was pointed out earlier that following the signing of the Machakos Protocol, the parties got involved in long discussions on the details of governance during the interim period. Agreements on the matters discussed were in form of protocols. These protocols together with the Permanent Ceasefire and the Implementation Modalities constitute the peace agreement which became known as the "Comprehensive Peace Agreement" (CPA). We consider in what follows the main aspects of each protocol.

---

21   The Comprehensive Peace Agreement between The Government of the The Republic of The Sudan and The Sudan People's Liberation Movement/Sudan People's Liberation Army, Nairobi, 9 January 2005.

I. The Machakos Protocol

The protocol comprises of four components: agreed principles, the transition process, state and religion, and the structures of government.

On the agreed principles, it was acknowledged that the unity of the Sudan based on the free will of its people, democratic governance, accountability, equality, respect and justice is and shall be the priority of the Parties and that it is possible to redress the grievances of the people of South Sudan and to meet their aspirations within such a framework. It was further agreed that the people of South Sudan have the right to control and govern affairs in their region and participate equitably in the National government; and shall have the right to self-determination, *inter alia*, through a referendum to determine their future status. It promised to establish a democratic system of governance; find a comprehensive solution to the economic and social deterioration of Sudan; put in place a comprehensive ceasefire; and formulate a repatriation, resettlement, rehabilitation, reconstruction and development plan. It stressed that the Parties shall "design and implement the Peace Agreement so as to make the unity of the Sudan an attractive option especially for the people of South Sudan".

Regarding the transition process, it was agreed that the Parties shall collaborate in the task of governing the country, that the transition process will be made up of a pre-interim period of six months and an interim period of six years; and that at the end of the interim period the people of Southern Sudan shall, in an internationally monitored referendum, vote to either confirm the unity of Sudan by adopting the system of government established under the peace agreement or opt for secession. The Parties also agreed to establish, during the pre-interim period, an Assessment and Evaluation Commission (AEC) to monitor the implementation of the Peace Agreement. Its membership was to include, besides the Parties, the member states of the IGAD sub-committee on Sudan (Eritrea, Ethiopia, Kenya and Uganda), Observer states (Italy, Norway, UK and USA) and any other countries or regional or international bodies agreed upon by the Parties. Finally, the Parties agreed to "refrain from any form of unilateral revocation or abrogation of the Peace Agreement".

In relation to State and Religion, the Parties recognized that Sudan is a multi-cultural, multi-ethnic, multi-religious and multi-lingual country; that religion shall not be used as a divisive factor; that citizenship shall be the basis of enjoyment of all rights and duties; and that personal and family matters may be governed by the personal laws of those concerned.

On the structures of government, the Parties agreed to a framework of governance structured on the National Constitution as the supreme law of the land; that a National Constitutional Review Commission (NCRC) shall be established during the Pre-interim Period which shall draft the Legal and Constitutional Framework to govern the Interim Period and which incorporates the Peace Agreement; and that there shall be a National Government that shall exercise such functions and pass such laws as must necessarily be exercised by a sovereign state at national level.

Most importantly, the Parties agreed that national legislation affecting states outside Southern Sudan "shall have as its source of legislation Sharia and consensus of the people", and in regards to Southern Sudan "shall have as its source of legislation popular consensus, the values and the customs of the people of Sudan (including their traditions and religious beliefs, having regard to Sudan's diversity)".

The Security Arrangements Protocol

This protocol was signed in Naivasha on 25 September 2003. It covered five areas: status of the two armed forces, ceasefire, redeployment, Joint/Integrated Units (JIUs), command and control of the two forces, and the status of other armed groups in the country.

The Parties agreed that the Sudanese Armed Forces (SAF) and the SPLA shall remain separate during the Interim Period and both shall be considered and treated equally as Sudan's National Armed Forces. It was also agreed that there will be downsizing of the forces on both sides following the completion of the Comprehensive Ceasefire arrangements.

The JIUs, consisting of equal numbers from the SAF and the SPLA, shall constitute the nucleus of the army of Sudan should the result of the referendum confirm unity, otherwise they would be dissolved and the component parts integrated into their respective forces. Throughout the Interim Period, the size and deployment of the JIUs shall be: Southern Sudan, 24000; Nuba Mountains, 6000; Southern Blue Nile, 6000; Khartoum, 3000. In Eastern Sudan, the redeployment of the SPLA to the south of the South/North border of 1/1/1956 shall be completed within one year from the beginning of the Pre-Interim Period. The Parties further agreed to discuss the issue of establishing JIUs there.

On the redeployment, the Parties agreed that, except for the JIUs, the rest of the forces of SAF shall be redeployed north of the South/North border of 1/1/1956 within two and one half years. Similarly, the rest of the SPLA in the Nuba Mountains and Southern Blue Nile shall be redeployed south of the same border as soon as the JIUs are formed and deployed. All the redeployment shall be carried out under international monitoring and assistance. It was also agreed to implement with the assistance of the international community Downsizing, Demobilization and Reintegration (DDR) programmes for the benefit of the soldiers of both armies affected by the reduction, demobilization and downsizing of the forces.

Regarding the command and control of the two forces, it was agreed to establish a Joint Defence Board (JDB) under the Presidency comprising the Chiefs of Staff of the two forces, their deputies and other senior officers from both sides. The JDB shall co-ordinate between the SAF and the SPLA and command the JIUs. It was further agreed to develop a common military doctrine within the first year of the Interim Period. This doctrine was to be the basis of the training of the JIUs, the SPLA and SAF.

The protocol ruled that "no armed group allied to either party shall be allowed to operate outside the two forces". The Parties additionally agreed to address the status of the other armed groups in the country with the view of achieving comprehensive peace and stability in the country.

3. The Wealth Sharing Protocol

It was signed in Naivasha on 7 January 2004 after more than three weeks of negotiations. The protocol included guiding principles in respect of an equitable sharing of common wealth; ownership of land and natural resources; oil and non-oil revenues; fiscal and financial matters; government assets and liabilities; and reconstruction and development funds.

Some of the points agreed upon are of general applicability over the whole Sudan whereas others are related only to Southern Sudan and war-affected areas. The protocol opens with the statement that "the wealth of Sudan shall be shared equitably so as to enable each level of government to discharge its legal and constitutional responsibilities and duties". It also provides that Southern Sudan and other war-affected areas face serious needs to: be able to perform basic government functions, build civil administration, and rehabilitate and reconstruct/ construct the social and physical infrastructure in a post-conflict Sudan.

The Parties failed to agree on the ownership of land and subter-ranean natural resource, but agreed that the regulation of land tenure, usage and exercise of rights in land is to be a concurrent competency exercised at the appropriate levels of government. They further agreed to institute a process to progressively develop and amend the relevant laws to incorporate customary laws and practices, local heritage and inter-national trends and practices. To tackle such matters a National Land Commission and a Southern Sudan Land Commission were established, each with specified functions. The two commissions are to co-operate and co-ordinate their activities. In case of conflict between the findings of the two commissions, they are to reconcile their positions, otherwise the matter shall be referred to the Constitutional Court.

Regarding oil resources, the protocol spelt out principles guiding the management of the development of the petroleum sector. An independent National Petroleum Commission (NPC) was established to be constituted of equal numbers from the National Government and the Government of Southern Sudan (GOSS), in addition to not more than three representatives of oil producing State/Region as non-permanent members. The NPC was to formulate and oversee the implementation of policies related to the oil sector. The parties agreed to establish an Oil Revenue Stabilization Account (ORSA) from government net oil revenue derived from actual export sales above an agreed benchmark price. The basis of sharing the oil revenue was that at least 2% of oil revenue shall be allocated to the oil producing states in proportion to output produced in such state. After payment to the ORSA and the oil producing states, 50% of net oil revenue derived from oil producing wells in Southern Sudan shall be allocated to the GOSS as of the beginning of the Pre-Interim Period and the remaining 50% to the National Government and States in Northern Sudan. It was also agreed that a Future Generation Fund shall be established once national oil production reaches two million barrels per day.

In relation to non-oil revenue, the agreement listed the sources of taxes and other revenue for each of the National Government, GOSS and States governments. Additionally, the National Government shall allocate to GOSS 50% of the national non-oil revenue collected in Southern Sudan.

A Fiscal and Financial Allocation and Monitoring Commission (FFAMC) was agreed upon to "ensure transparency and fairness both in regard to the allocation of nationally collected funds to the States and the GOSS". It was to be comprised of experts nominated by the various States, the GOSS and the National Government.

On the monetary policy and banking, the Parties agreed to establish a Bank of Southern Sudan (BOSS) as a branch of the Central Bank of Sudan (CBOS). Two sets of banking instruments were to be used by the CBOS to regulate and supervise the implementation of a single monetary policy through: an Islamic financing window in Northern Sudan under a deputy governor of CBOS; and a conventional financing window in the BOSS headed by a deputy governor of CBOS.

The protocol also provided for the establishment of Reconstruction and Development Funds and the Multi-Donor Trust Funds each of them on the national and Southern Sudan levels.

It was moreover agreed that there shall be no legal impediments to interstate commerce or the flow of goods and services, capital or labour between the States.

4. The Power Sharing Protocol

Negotiations on this track took more than four months. On 26 May 2004, agreement on power sharing was concluded in Naivasha by the two parties and signed as the Power Sharing Protocol.

The protocol reaffirmed the principles agreed upon in the Machakos Protocol and defined four levels of government: national, Southern Sudan, the States and local government. Principles on the administration and inter-governmental linkages were listed as well as the human rights and fundamental freedoms. It was also agreed to "initiate a comprehensive process of national reconciliation and healing throughout the country as part of the peace building process". The parties further agreed to conduct a population census throughout the country before the end of the second year of the Interim Period and General Elections before the end of the third year.

The legislative authority shall be on the national, Southern Sudan and the States level. On the national level, there shall be a National Legislature comprising two chambers of Parliament: the National Assembly and the Council of States. The first is composed of members elected according to procedures set forth by an impartial and representative Electoral Commission. The second is to be composed of representatives from each State in the Sudan. Prior to the parliamentary elections, the seats of the National Assembly shall be allocated as follows: 52% for the National Congress Party (NCP); 28% for the SPLM; 14% for the other Northern political forces; and 6% for the other Southern political forces. The agreement provided that the National Constitution shall not be amended except by the approval of three-quarters of all members of each chamber, both chambers sitting separately. It was moreover agreed that amendments to the Interim National Constitution affecting the provisions of the Peace Agreement may be introduced only with the approval of both Parties signatory to the Agreement.

The protocol stated that the National Executive shall consist of the Presidency (The President and two Vice Presidents) and a Council of Ministers, and that there shall be a partnership and collegial decision-making process within the institution of the Presidency. The Council of Ministers was to be composed with the same representation ratios as the National Assembly. Until such time as the elections are held, the current incumbent President (or his successor) shall be the President and Commander-in-Chief of the Sudan Armed Forces (SAF), and the current SPLM Chairman (or his successor) shall be the First Vice President, President of the GOSS and the Commander-in- Chief of the SPLA. The President is to take decisions with the consent of the First Vice President in respect to four matters: declaration and termination of a state of emergency; declaration of war; appointments that the President is required to make according to the Peace Agreement; and summoning, adjourning or proroguing the National Legislature. There are provisions regarding the election of the President; appointments of the two Vice Presidents after the elections; measures to be taken in the event that the post of the President or that of the First Vice President falls vacant.

On the National Capital, it is provided that the law enforcement agencies shall be representative of the population of Sudan and guidelines are set for judges for the protection of non-Muslims. A special commission shall be set up by the Presidency for that purpose.

In relation to the civil service, the agreement listed principles that shall ensure balance, merit and justice in the civil service and ruled against discrimination on the basis of religion, ethnicity, region, gender or political beliefs. The need for training and creation of additional educational opportunities for war-affected people was stressed. A National Civil Service Commission was to be established with a task of formulating policies for training and recruitment into the civil service, and to ensure that not less than 20% of the middle and upper level positions in the National Civil Service (including the positions of Under Secretaries) are filled with qualified persons from the South within the first three years and achieving 25% in five years and the final target of 30% within six years. These figures are to be confirmed by the outcome of the population census.

Regarding the National Security, it was agreed that the National Security Service (NSS) shall be representative of the population and "reflect the partnership of the negotiating parties"; that the NSS shall be professional and its mandate shall be advisory and focused on information gathering and analysis; and that there shall be a National Security Council and security committees at the GOSS and State levels.

The protocol provided for the establishment of a number of independent commissions such as the National Electoral Commission, Human Rights Commission, etc.

The National Judiciary, according to the protocol, shall be independent of the legislature and the executive and shall exercise its powers through courts and other tribunals. It shall comprise: the Constitutional Court, National Supreme Court, National Courts of Appeal, and any other national courts or tribunals as deemed necessary to be established by law.

On the level of Southern Sudan, the Legislature is represented by the Southern Sudan Legislative Assembly which shall, prior to holding general elections, be comprised of 70% for the SPLM, 15% for the NCP and the remaining 15% for other Southern political forces. The same representation applies to the Council of Ministers of the GOSS. The Judiciary on the level of Southern Sudan shall comprise: Supreme Court of Southern Sudan, Courts of Appeal, and any other courts or tribunals as deemed necessary to be established in accordance with the Southern Sudan Constitution and law.

The protocol spelt out the institutions at the State level. Pending the holding of elections, the compositions of the State Legislature and Executive shall be comprised of: the NCP to hold 70% in the Northern States and the SPLM 70% in the Southern States; 10% in the Southern States to be filled by the NCP; and 10% in the Northern States to be filled by the SPLM; and 20% in the Northern and Southern States to be filled by representatives of the Northern and Southern political forces respectively. The State Constitutions shall provide for the establishment of such State courts by the State Judiciary as necessary.

The protocol concludes with five schedules of powers: National, GOSS, States, concurrent, and residual. There is also another "schedule" on the resolution of conflicts in respect of concurrent powers.

5. The Three Areas

Negotiations on the Three Areas were long and difficult. The main reason for the difficulty was that these areas are geographically part of northern Sudan on the basis of the South/North border of 1/1/1956 but a good number of the fighters in the SPLA hail from these areas and some of them occupy senior positions in the SPLM/A. Therefore, they had common cause with their Southern comrades-in-arms in the SPLM/A. Initially, the GOS delegation refused to negotiate on these areas on the grounds that the IGAD mediation was only about the South as came in the DOP. On the other hand, the SPLM/A delegation refused to negotiate on the other tracks if these areas are not part of the negotiations. The mediators exerted pressure on the GOS delegation urging them to accept negotiations on these areas. The compromise reached was to negotiate the conflict in these areas under Kenyan and not IGAD mediation. In other words, Lt. General (R) Sumbeiywo would, so to speak, put on the IGAD hat when negotiations were about the South and the Kenyan one when they are about the Three Areas. The two parties formed three committees, one for each area. After strenuous haggling, agreement was eventually reached on two areas and deadlock continued on Abyei. It was the intervention of the US envoy for peace in Sudan, Senator John C. Danforth, which saved the talks on this track. He tabled a proposal on Abyei before the two parties on a take-it-or-leave-it basis. Like they did in Machakos in 2002, the two parties accepted the proposal and signed it on 26 May 2004 together with the Protocol on the two states of Southern Kordofan and Blue Nile. Thus, what became known as the Abyei Protocol was merely this American proposal.

5.1. The Protocol on Southern Kordofan and Blue Nile States

The Parties agreed on power sharing, wealth sharing, SAF troops level and popular consultations in the two States.

The agreement included general principles such as the guarantee of human rights and fundamental freedoms, development and protection of the cultural heritage, and development of human resources and infra-structure. It provided for a State executive, legislature and judiciary.

Pending the elections, it was agreed that the executive and legis-lature in each of the two States be allocated to the two parties only: 55% to the NCP and 45% to the SPLM; that the governorship will rotate in the two States with each party holding the office of the Governor for half the pre-election period provided that no party holds it for both States at the same time. The same arrangement holds for the office of Deputy Governor.

The Parties agreed on the principle of "popular consultation" as a democratic mechanism for ascertaining the views of the people of the two States, through their respective elected legislatures, on the agreement and suggest possible rectification within the framework of the agreement.

The protocol also dealt with the share of each of the two states in the national wealth and established a State Land Commission.

The protocol ends with a number of schedules specifying exclusive competencies of the two States, concurrent powers, residual powers and sources of revenue.

5.2. The Protocol on Abyei Area

As mentioned earlier, the agreement on Abyei was the proposal made by the US envoy for peace in Sudan.

It defined the territory as "the area of the nine Ngok Dinka chiefdoms transferred to Kordofan in 1905" to be demarcated by an Abyei Boundary Commission, and defined the residents of Abyei as "the members of Ngok Dinka community and other Sudanese residing in the area". The Misseriya and other nomadic peoples were to "retain their traditional rights to graze cattle and move across the territory of Abyei".

At the end of the interim period and simultaneously with the referendum for Southern Sudan, the residents of Abyei are to cast a separate ballot to choose on either to retain its special administrative status in the north or be part of Bahr el Ghazal. A special referendum commission for that purpose shall be established by the Presidency.

Abyei is to have an administration falling under the institution of the Presidency. There shall be a local Executive Council composed of the Chief Administrator, his/her Deputy and not more than five heads of departments. There shall also be an Abyei Area Council comprised of not more than twenty members.

As a matter of urgency, the Presidency was to "start peace and reconciliation process for Abyei that shall work for harmony and peaceful coexistence in the area".

The agreement specified the sources of finance of the Abyei Area. In particular, the net oil revenue from the oil produced in Abyei Area is to be shared as follows: 50% to the National Government; 42% to the GOSS and 2% each for Bahr el Ghazal Region, Western Kordofan State, local Ngok Dinka and the local Misseriya people. It was further agreed to establish, under the Executive Council, an Abyei Resettlement, Construction and Development Fund.

On the redeployment of troops, the Parties agreed to deploy one joint battalion in the area.

6. Implementation Modalities

The last three protocols were signed on 26 May 2004. The Parties then turned their attention to the discussion on the implementation modalities. These were concluded on 31 December 2004. The modalities are timelines specifying the tasks of the Interim Period included in the protocols, the implementing authorities and the time frame for the implementation.

Of special significance here are the changes that were made to the protocols. The most outstanding change was in relation to the general elections. Article 1.8.3 of the power sharing protocol stipulates that "General Elections at all levels of government shall be completed by the end of the third year of the Interim Period". Point 9 of the "Implementation Modalities of the Machakos and Power Sharing Protocols" states that the general elections shall be held "not later than the end of the fourth year of the Interim Period", pushing the election date forward by one year. It is this last text that was incorporated into the Interim National Constitution.

The Parties also included what they termed "List of Corrections in the Protocols and Agreements", the most important in the list are:

1 Any reference to "State/Region" was to be replaced by the word "State" only. This came about as a result of the SPLM dropping its insistence on having three regions in the South (Bahr el Ghazal, Equatoria and Upper Nile) and agreeing to maintain the current ten States.

2 Western Kordofan State was abolished and its territory divided between Northern Kordofan State and the Nuba Mountains Area.

3 The debate on whether to name the State encompassing the Nuba Mountains "Southern Kordofan State" or "Nuba Mountains State" was settled in favour of the former.

4 The phrase "South Sudan" was to be replaced by "Southern Sudan" in all the protocols and agreements, so as to stress the unity of the country.

The implementation modalities included an appendix regarding an "understanding on Abyei Boundary Commission". It spelt out the composition of the Abyei Boundary Commission (ABC), the methodology of gathering information and the rendering of its report.

It is to be noted that in these implementation modalities no task was to be implemented by one of the two parties without the other; the implementation tasks are always to be implemented jointly by both of them.

The Signing Ceremony

On the 9th of January 2005 amid big regional and international presence the final peace agreement was signed in the Nyayo Stadium in Nairobi. The signing was witnessed by representatives of the IGAD countries, the African Union, the League of Arab States, the

Organization of the Islamic Conference, the European Union, the four IGAD Partners Forum countries (USA, UK, Italy and Norway), the United Nations Organization, the Royal Kingdom of the Netherlands and the Arab Republic of Egypt.

The occasion was also attended by a large number of Sudanese citizens especially Southerners, some came from Khartoum and others were in the region. They were extremely happy and jubilant with this singular achievement and delighted that at long last peace will prevail in the country.

Comments

The peace agreement took very long to negotiate. Under the Salvation Revolution Government, the peace talks began in August 1989. The IGAD(D) mediation alone lasted for eleven years. The agreement reached, the Comprehensive Peace Agreement, is very much detailed. That the CPA is bulky and took that long to conclude are a reflection of both the huge difference and lack of confidence that divided the two parties. As a matter of fact, the agreement provided for internal and external guarantees for its implementation. However, a smooth implementation of the agreement can only be assured if the two parties leave the past behind them to concentrate on building and nurturing confidence between them and among the Sudanese. They were conscious of this fact when they resolved to collaborate and be in partnership in the implementation of the CPA (see "the transition process" of the Machakos Protocol and sub-sections 2.3.4 and 2.7.2.2 of the Power Sharing Protocol). On the national level, it was thought urgent to initiate a comprehensive process of national reconciliation and healing as part of the peace building process (sub-section 1.7 of the Power Sharing Protocol). Such measures will set the Parties and the whole country on the path of peace and development.

The CPA is an agreement between the Government of the Republic of Sudan and the SPLM/SPLA. It is not between the NCP and the SPLM/SPLA as is erroneously made out by many. It is a North-South agreement with the SPLM negotiating for the South. The agreement is replete with the specification of the share of the South in all areas of power and wealth sharing. In fact, the SPLM painted itself as a Southern party when it agreed to the expression "other Southern political forces" used in the allocation of power sharing percentages (sub-sections 2.2.5, 2.5.5, 3.5.1, 3.6.4, 4.4.2, and 4.5.1). That is, the parties referred to are Southern political forces other than the SPLM. The same applies, *mutatis mutandis,* to the National Congress party as a Northern party.

The Machakos protocol was indeed the peace agreement. The other protocols were, so to speak, putting flesh into the skeleton constructed in Machakos. The most significant development in Machakos, without which an agreement would not have been possible, was that the two parties conceded on important pillars of their ideological persuasions. The NCP gave up on its hope to have the "Civilization Project" extend all over the Sudan as the South was exempted from the application of Sharia law; and the SPLM gave up on the hope to attain a secular Sudan as the application of Sharia was confirmed in the North. These were indeed irreversible concessions for it is almost impossible to change these arrangements constitutionally. A vote for unity in the 2011 referendum will be a vote to confirm these arrangements (sub-section 2.5 of the Machakos Protocol) and 75% majority is required in Parliament to amend the CPA. Even that requires a prior agreement of the two Parties (sub-section 2.2.7 of the Power sharing Protocol and Article 224(2) of the Interim National Constitution of the Republic of the Sudan 2005). In plain language, there is no way a secular united Sudan can be realized under the terms of the CPA unless the NCP is persuaded to adopt secularism. Similarly, the "Civilization Project" cannot apply for the whole country unless the SPLM is persuaded to accept Sharia law.

The war was caused and fuelled primarily by the lack of development. Therefore, the implementation of the CPA must focus on this central aspect. The role of the international community to stand by its obligations to provide the necessary funds for rehabilitation and development is, therefore, crucial.

It is true that it is the will of the Sudanese to make peace that made the agreement possible. Nevertheless, the role played by the international community to bring the agreement about cannot be underrated. They financed the peace talks, exerted the requisite pressure on the parties to negotiate in good faith ('the sticks and the carrots') and made pledges to finance the implementation process.

The contribution of the international community did not stop at that. Some influential countries, the IGAD(D) Partners Forum, are members of the Assessment and Evaluation Commission (AEC) and the United Nations Organization is charged with the monitoring of the security arrangements of the CPA. Its mission, the United Nations Mission in Sudan (UNMIS), is ten thousand men strong and is deployed in the South and the other war-affected areas, in addition to its headquarters in Khartoum.

The CPA was a magnificent achievement for the Sudanese people for it stopped bloodshed in the South and ushered in the country into an era of democratic transformation and socio-economic development. President Al-Bashir described the agreement as the beginning of the true independence of Sudan[22].

A lot have been said and written against the CPA. For instance, it is claimed that: it is bilateral and a deal and partnership between GOS and the SPLM; it ensured the monopoly of power by the two parties; it is asymmetrical federalism; and that it came about due to foreign pressure rather than as a result of an internal driving force.

It is necessary to consider such criticisms. From the outset, it must be stated that the overriding concern in the IGAD(D) peace talks was to bring the war to an end. It was not necessarily to look for the best system of rule in the country. Therefore, the talks were limited only to the warring parties. Initially, these were three and later on became two (the GOS and the SPLM/SPLA). And since it would not have been possible to end the war without addressing its root causes, doing so became the subject of all rounds of negotiations. The major demand of Southern Sudan was to get the right of self-determination and no peace

---

22 Speech of President Al-Bashir, Naivasha, 31 December 2004.

agreement would have been acceptable to them without agreement on this right. That the right of the people of Southern Sudan to self-determination became part of the peace agreement necessitated having a Government of Southern Sudan which together with the National Government shall supervise, oversee and lead the South to the exercise of that right. As such the GOSS became an additional level of government over and above the States in Southern Sudan. There is no similar level in the North. Hence, the asymmetrical federalism came about as a result of meeting the major demand of the people of Southern Sudan.

The partnership between the two parties to the agreement was essential to ensure its smooth implementation. The same consideration was behind the dominance of power by the NCP and the SPLM in the North and South, respectively (70% in power sharing). Dominance, yes, but not monopoly as other Northern and Southern political forces are represented in the North and South, respectively (20% in power sharing). These measures apply to the pre-election period only. It was decided to hold general elections during the Interim Period so that all the political parties can take part in the elections and the prospective government be formed on the basis of the popular score of each party in the elections. This is an important concession in the interest of democratic transformation.

As to foreign pressure, all will agree that the ramifications of the armed conflict have gone beyond Sudan's borders. In other words, the conflict was internationalized. It was not possible for the Sudanese to resolve the conflict on their own without a helping hand from other countries. The neighbours, through IGAD(D), undertook the direct mediation. In addition, as we have seen, other countries too played important roles in prodding the parties to reach a peaceful settlement of the conflict. However, the fact remains that whatever pressures are exerted from outside the country, no agreement was possible without the resolve of the Sudanese parties to make peace.

For some reason, the CPA did not include provisions for a general amnesty for both sides regarding crimes committed during the war. This makes it the first agreement to omit such an important aspect.

Finally, the CPA was to achieve two main objectives: to attain sustainable peace and bring about democratic transformation in the Sudan(s) whether Sudan remains united or Southern Sudan secedes. This is the litmus test to its success or failure.

Appendices

Radio Messages

1st   Relevant Code Names Used in the Radio Messages.
2nd   Command Policy and Directives.
3rd   General.

Appendix 1 (A)
Relevant Code Names Used In The Radio Messages

Note: These code names are no longer in use

S/No.	Code Name	Real Name	Other Code Names
1	Alpha Beta	Cdr. Lam Akol	Delta 3
2	Amara	Cdr. Daniel Awet Akot	
3	Arrow	Cdr. John Kulang Puol	
4	Badi	A/Cdr. Bona Bang Dhol	
5	Biar	A/Cdr. Peter Panom Thanypiny	
6	Delta-34	Cdr. Stephen Duol Chol	
7	Delta-39	Cdr. Vincent Kuany Latjor	Zulu-23
8	Dragon	Cdr. Kerubino Kuanyin Bol	
9	Fire	A/Cdr. Deng Alor Kuol	
10	Girraffe	Cdr. Arok Thon Arok	
11	Guat	1st Lt. Daniel Chwang Michar	
12	Hammer	Cdr. Salva Kiir Mayardit	
13	Ivory	Cdr. Gordon Kong Chol	Delta 1
14	Koom	A/Cdr. Daniel Deng Alony	
15	Kush	Cdr. Yousif Kowa Mekki	
16	Load	Cdr. Of Bilpam GHQ	
17	Matata	Cdr. Galerio Modi Hurnyang	
18	Mercury	Capt. William Bior Duot	
19	Merowe	Cdr. James Wani Igga	
20	Napata	Cdr. Kuol Manyang Juuk	Girraffe (2)
21	Nyok	A/Cdr. Oyai Deng Ajak	Piankhi, Delta 9
22	Sennar	Cdr. Riek Machar Teny	Delta 24
23	Soba	Cdr. Martin Manyiel Ayuel	Delta 26
24	Spear	Cdr. William Nyuon Bany	
25	Taseti	A/Cdr. Makuei Deng Majuc	Delta 18
26	Thunder	Cdr. John Garang	Delta 7
27	Wass	Capt. James Hoth Mai	
28	Wawat	A/Cdr. Taban Deng Gai	
29	Yarm	Capt. Moses Dhieu Kiir	
30	Yermuk	Cdr. Lual Diing Wol	

APPENDIX 1 (B)

Radio Messages On: Command Policy and Directives

S/No.	MESSAGE No.	MESSAGE DATE
1	Without No.	31/12/86
2	043/3/87	20/03/87
3	126/9/88	18/09/88
4	185/9/89	21/09/89
5	015/1/90	08/01/90
6	045/1/90	14/01/90
7	025/7/90	04/07/90
8	033/8/90	04/08/90
9	113/10/90	23/10/90
10	021/12/90	01/12/90
11	078/1/91	20/01/91
12	011/4/91	02/04/91
13	072/5/91	17/05/91

TOP SECRET
Date: 31/12/86
From: Thunder
To: Dragon
R: Spear   R: Hammer   R: Girraffe (1)   R: Arrow   R: Sennar   R: Amara
R: Maj/Dr Lam Akol   R: Maj/ James Wani   R: Maj/Yusuf Kua   R: Girraffe (2)
R: Soba   R: GHQ Cdr.

1. Attention: For the knowledge of those it is addressed to only.
2. The enemy is desperate and has launched and will continue to launch fierce and massive offensives during this dry season in their futile attempt to crush the SPLA and force a political settlement with or without the SPLA.   This is wishful thinking as the enemy plan cannot succeed.   However, we must take the challenge very seriously and avoid the same mistake of wishful thinking, that the enemy will fail while we do not take appropriate required action. The enemy offensive must be contained and repulsed and our own major offensive launched by the beginning of the rains.
3. This military situation demands that all members of SPLA/M High Command be physically present in the field during the whole of the dry season to direct the operations.
4. Whereas the alternate members command the zones, the five permanent members will command Axes, Fronts or Routes and these are here assigned as follows:

a) THUNDER commands and clears the Axis Pachalla-Pibor-Bor and establishes his forward HQs along the Nile between Shambe and Gemmeiza.
b) DRAGON commands and clears the Axis Dago-Maban-Melut and establishes his forward HQs along the Nile between Melut and Renk and is also the Zonal Commander of Southern Blue Nile.
c) SPEAR commands and clears the Axis Jekou-Nasir-Ulang and establishes his base along the Nile between Melut and the Sobat Mouth.

d) HAMMER commands and clears the Axis Raad-Boma-Kapoeta-Torit and establishes his forward base along the Nile between Gemmeiza and Nimule.

e) GIRRAFFE (1) commands and clears the Axis Akobo-Waat-Ayod and establishes his forward base along the Nile between Sobat Mouth and Shambe.

5. The above directives and orders are effective from 1/1/87 and the Axis commanders take up their duties and responsibilities from this date.

6. The overall objective is to liberate the whole east Nile of Southern Sudan from Nimule to Renk by 31/12/1987 while intensifying guerrilla and semi-conventional warfare on the west Nile, Southern Kordofan and Southern Blue Nile. Success of this plan will shift our logistical starting point right on the Nile by the end of 1987.

7. The concept of Axis command does not and should not contradict Zonal command but rather is meant to reinforce it. The channel of command for Zonal commanders still remains as before. But Axis commanders submit their reports and requests directly to the C-in-C.

8. Adjacent Axis commanders support each other as necessary by coordination or orders of the C-in-C and adjacent Zonal commanders support each other by coordination or orders of the normal chain of command.

9. Good luck and best wishes for the new year to all the Axis and Zonal Commanders. Victory is certain.

Reg. By/GC
31/12/86

TOP SECRET
Date: 20/3/87
Feom:Thunder
To: Dragon
R: Spear   R: Hammer   R: Girraffe (1)   R: All Zonal Cdrs:
R: Arrow   R: Sennar   R: Amara   R: Alpha Beta   R: James Wani   R: Yousif Kua
R: Girraffe (2)   R: Lt. Col Martin Manyiel   R: Badi   R: Matata   R: GHQs Bilpam
R: All Independent Areas Cdrs.   R: Lt. Col. Peter Panom   R: Lt. Col. Deng Alony
R: Lt. Col Peter Riir   R: Maj Alfred Akwoc   R: Capt. Kennedy Gayen
R: Capt. Oyai Deng Ajak   R: Capt. Moses Dhieu

043/3/87

Subject: Command Policy and Directives

Ref. my message of last December about the formation of Axis Commands, there are indications that the definition and aim of the Axis Command and its relation to Zonal Commands are not properly understood. The following points in this regard are implications to be noted and you are to work by them.

1. The Axis Commands are as follows:
   Axis One, Pachalla-Pibor-Bor with approximate river Nile boundries of Shambe and

Gemmeiza, Geographically, this includes the old districts of Pibor and Bor. It is commanded by the C-in-C, Col. Dr John Garang.

Axis Two, Dago-Maban-Renk with approximate river Nile boundaries of Renk and Kodok and consists of the old districts of Renk and Kurmuk. It is commanded by D/C-in-C, Lt. Col. Kerubino.

Axis Three, Jekou-Nasir-Malakal with approximate river boundaries of Kodok and Tonga and consists of the old districts of Nasir and Sobat. It is commanded by the Chief of Staff, Lt. Col. William Nyuon.

Axis Four, Narus-Kapoeta-Torit-Juba with approximate river Nile boundaries of Gemmeiza and Nimule. It consists of the old districts of Kapoeta and Torit and that small part of Juba district east of the Nile. It is commanded by the D/Chief of Staff for Operations and Security, Major Salva Kiir.

Axis Five, Akobo-Waat-Ayod-Fangak with the approximate river Nile boundaries of Tonga and Shambe. It consists of the old districts of Akobo and Fangak. It is commanded by the D/Chief of Staff for Administration and Logistics, Major Arok Thon.

2. The aim of the Axis Command is to reinforce the Zonal Commands along the axis and in order to capture all enemy garrisons east of the river Nile from Nimule to Renk and this to be accomplished within 1987, that is by 31/12/87.

3. The Axis Command does not replace the Zonal Command under the Axis Commands. Axis forces are different from Zonal forces and only reinforce them. In terms of channel of command Zonal Cdrs. Follow the normal already established chain of command. To this, matters regarding operations and security are referred to D/Chief of Staff for operations and security with information to C-in-C or D/C-in-C in the absence of the C-in-C and from there to the Chief of Staff and then to the C-in-C or D/C-in-C in the absence of the C-in-C. Similarly with matters regarding administration and logistics.

4. On the other hand, the Axis commanders are directly under the C-in-C in matters regarding their Axis Command and render their reports or messages directly to the C-in-C or D/C-in-C in the a bsence of the C-in-C.

5. The Zonal Commands and commanders are as follows:
- SOUTHERN BLUE NILE: Since DRAGON cannot be both Axis and Zonal Cdr., ARROW is here appointed Zonal Cdr. for Southern Blue Nile and moves there immediately.
- WESTERN UPPER NILE: SENNAR Cdr.
- BGAA: AMARA Cdr.
- NORTHERN UPPER NILE: Major Dr Lam Cdr. Until he arrives the zone, this zone now has four (4) independent area commands.
- CENTRAL and WESTERN EQUATORIA: Major James Wani Cdr.
- SOUTHERN KORDUFAN: Major Yusif Kua Cdr.
- CENTRAL SOUTHERN SUDAN: GIRRAFFE (2) Cdr.
- DIRECTORATE OF CHAIRMAN, C-in-C: Lt. Col Martin Manyiel Director.
- LAKES: BADI Cdr.
- EQUATORIA EAST OF THE NILE: MATATA Cdr.
- BILPAM SPLA/SPLM GHQs: Major Cagai Atem Cdr.

6. In addition to the Zonal Commands, there are Independent Area Commands that are like Zonal Commands in terms of channels of command and these are:

- RENK DISTRICT: Lt Col Deng Alony Cdr.
- SOUTH KODOK DISTRICT: Major Alfred Akwoc Cdr.
- NORTH KODOK: Capt Oyai Deng Ajak Cdr.
- SOBAT DISTRICT: Capt Moses Dhieu Kiir Cdr.

The above four (4) area commands fall under Major Dr Lam Akol as soon as he arrives the zone upon which they will cease to be independent area commands.
- AKOBO DISTRICT: Lt Col Peter Panom Cdr.
- FANGAK DISTRICT: Lt Col Peter Riir Cdr.
- NASIR DISTRICT: Capt James Oath Cdr.
The above three (3) Independent Area Commands will become central Upper Nile Zonal Command after NYAGAT bandits are wiped out in these districts. A Zonal Cdr will then be appointed.
- PIBOR DISTRICT: Capt Kennedy Gayien Cdr.
It is impractical for this district to be commanded from Eastern Equatoria as is previously or from Central Southern Sudan at the moment.

7. Only the C-in-C has authority to appoint, transfer or relieve Axis, Zonal, and Independent area commands while Axis, Zonal and Independent Area Commands respectively have authority to assign or transfer commanders within his command.

- FLASH -
Reg by/ GC
20/3/87

TOP SECRET
Date: 18/9/1988
From: Thunder
To: Napata
R: BADI   INFO: SPEAR   INFO: Hammer   INFO: Arrow   INFO: Alpha Beta
INFO: Merowe I   INFO: Kush   INFO: Amara   INFO: Soba   INFO: Ivory
INFO: GHQS Cdr.   INFO: Other Zonal Cdrs   INFO: Independent Areas
INFO: Fire   INFO: Radio SPLA (Not for announcement but to adjust your broadcasts).

126/9/88

1. The following structural and command changes are made in the Lakes Zonal Command.
2. With effect from 20/9/1988, Lakes Zonal Command comes under the INFIGAR theater of operations. This in effect means Lakes Zonal Command comes under command of NAPATA, the INFIGAR commander, from this date both in military operations and administration.
3. The former Central Upper Nile Zonal Command/Lakes Zonal Command is here reorganized into three (3) Independent Area Commands w.e.f. 20/9/1988:
   a) Tonj Independent Area Command
   b) Rumbek Independent Area Command
   c) Yirol Independent Area Command.

4. NAPATA, in consultation with and advice from BADI, to recommend the Independent Area Commanders and Civil administrators.
5. BADI is here w.e.f. 20/9/1988 appointed Deputy Commander of Campaign and joins the INFIGAR HQs of NAPATA immediately.
6. The above is for your execution, NAPATA and BADI to acknowledge receipt and compliance.

Op. Immediate

Dec/Kau Nak
20/9/1988

––––––––––

TOP SECRET
21/9/89
FM: THUNDER
TO: SPEAR
R: HAMMER   R: SENNAR   R: ALPHA BETA   R: MEROWE   R:KUSH
R: AMAR   R: NAPATA   R: SOBA   R:IVORY   R:CDR. LUAL DING
R: MATATA   R: MABAN CDR   R:GHQS/RECORDS   R: ROCK   R: PIANKHI
R: IRON   R: BONGA CDR   R: DIMA TRG CDR
R: A/CDR AYUEN ALIER   R:LULU

185/9/89

Organization number 3 (·) The following command reorganization, appointments and changes are made with effect from 21/9/89 for the coming phase of the war:

1. The axis formation is here abolished, since the objectives of 1st., 3rd., 4th., and 5th. Axis have been achieved (·) These objectives were to clear all enemy garrisons from the Ethiopian border to the River Nile (·) Only axis two, previous of DRAGON could not move from the border (·) The concept of axis is therefore no longer relevant (·) The concept of (front) is here instituted and three fronts are created as follows:

a) The first front phase one 1: This comprises the initial BSC area which is areas east of the Nile and south of the Sobat and bordered by Ethiopia, Kenya and Uganda (·) This remains under the C-in-C and deputy Cdr. Kuol Manyang Juuk .
b) The first front, phase 2: This comprises Northern Upper Nile, that is the OLD Kodok District and the rest of Upper Nile east of the Nile which consists of the Districts of Renk, Baliet (North of Sobat), Nasir (North of Sobat), Maiwut and Maban (·) This phase falls under the C-in-C and deputy Cdr. Gordon Kong Chol (·) Operations in this front both in phase 1 and phase 2 will continue to be code named bright star campaign (BSC).
c) The second front, this comprises the whole of Blue Nile Province both South and North up to the 14th parallel (·) The second front will be under command of COS Cdr. William Nyuon Bany, and deputy of Cdr. Galerio Modi Hurinyang (·) Military operations in this front will be code named the "NEW FUNG CAMPAIGN" (NFC).

d) The third font (·) This comprises the Lakes Province (·) The third front falls under command of the D/COS operations and security, Cdr. Salva Kiir Mayardit, and deputy of the most senior A/Cdr. in the front until a high command member appointed as deputy (·) Military operations in this front will be code named the "KON ANOK CAMPAIGN" (KAC).

e) The rest of the Zonal commands not affected by the above formation of front remains as before (·) However as campaign operations expand the C-in-C may issue directives incorporating zones into fronts or forming new fronts.

4. The GHQS Bilpam and alternate GHQ Boma and all central training centres such as Bonga and Dima, etc. will fall under the C-in-C (·) A/Cdr. Ayuen Alier Jongroor is here appointed Cdr. GHQS Bilpam to take over from A/Cdr. Cagai Atem Biar, who reports to C-in-C HQS after handing over to take a new assignment.

5. For execution (·) Above orders are with effect from today 21/9/98.

Copied by DY
Date: 24/9/89

TOP SECRET
Date 8/1/90
From Thunder
To: Spear   R: Hamme   R: Sennar   R: Alpha Beta   R: Merowe   R: Kush   R: Amara
R: Napata   R: Soba   R: Ivory   R: Yermuk   R: Matat   R: GHQs Cdr.
015/1/90

1. The Junta is determined to erode our gains and to impose their version of federation under Sharia. The months and days between now, January, and June are very decisive for both SPLA and the Junta and determines the future of the Sudan. Every day and every night counts we must therefore fight the Junta with all our reserve and to the maximum of our abilities.

2. All High Command members must physically be in war in this offensive time. The leaves of SENNAR, AMARA and SOBA are hereby cancelled and they report to the field immediately.

3. If we maintain our gains and even if we do not add to them, this would be victory for the SPLA and defeat for the Junta. Of course, if we add to our victories while maintaining our gains much the better. The core of our liberated areas is the area east of the Nile and South of Sobat river. These must be defended at all cost. The second priority are all of Yirol, Adok and Nasir. The latter to defend Itang as the enemy intends to proceed to capture Gambella after Nasir in order to disperse Itang and Panyidu refugees camps as they have done to Longkuei. Yirol is our gateway to BGAA. Adok and Leer are our gateway to WUN zonal command and S.K.

4. In order to frustrate enemy plans, maintain our gains and capture more territories, operations will be concentrated in BSC phase(I), phase (II) and phase (lll) as follows

A - BSC phase (I) Northern Sector comes under HAMMER as D/Cdr of BSC phase (I) Northern Sector. The mission here is to repulse and destroy any enemy convoys that attempt to move South of Sobat river and to capture Canal Mouth and Fm Zeraf garrisons as well as to be on standby to participate in the capture of Malakal.

2. Southern Sector comes under NAPATA as D/Cdr of BSC phase (I) Southern Sector. The mission here is to repulse any enemy convoys that attempt to move out of Juba and capture all enemy outposts of Juba on east bank, to close Juba airport and to be on standby to participate in the capture of Juba.

B - BSC phase (III) cornes directly under THUNDER with MEROWE as D/Cdr ofBSC phase (III) Southern Sector. The mission here is to capture all enemy garrisons on west bank of Equatoria and to be on standby to participate in the capture of Juba.

C - BSC phase (II) Northern Sector (Renk to Kodok on the Nile) under SENNAR asD/ Cdr of BSC phase (II) Northern Sector. The mission here is tocaptureallof Renk, Jelhak, Melut and Kodok and to be on standby to participate in the capture of Malakal as well as to repulse any enemy convoys coming from Kosti and to take guerrilla warfare to Kennana and beyond.

2. Eastern Sector (Maban to Ulu to Kurmuk) comes under ALPHA BETA as D/Cdr of BSC phase(II) Eastern Sector. The mission here is to capture all of Maban, Yabus, Ulu, Kurmuk and proceed to occupy the Ingessana Hills and to take guerrilla warfare to Damazine and to threaten the Roseires Darn.

3. Southern Sector (East of Malakal town to Adong to liberated districts of Nasir and Maiwut) comes under IVORY as D/Cdr of BSC phase (II) Southern Sector. The mission here is to repulse any enemy convoys moving into the sector from Malakal and to capture all enemy outposts of Malakal east of the Nile and to be on standby to participate in the capture of Malakal.

5. Other operations will be concentrated in NBGAA and Southern Kordofan. AMARA to take over command of NBGAA and Lakes w.e.f. today and concentrates the war on Wau Cok., Wau-Tonj road to be completely paralysed, Wau-Raja road to be closed, Aweil-Wau road to be completely paralysed and the rail road to South to be closed.

6. For execution.

Req by/ Wek Garang Nyang
24/8/90.

TOP SECRET
From: Thunder
To: Spear R: Hamrner R: Sennar R: Alpha Beta R: Merowe R: Kush R: Arnara
R: Napata R: Soba R: Ivory R: Yormuk R: Matata

045/1/90

1. Ref my 015/1/90 ordering all High Command members to participate physically in
confronting and repulsing the enemy dry season offensive.

2. Because of the above, the following appointments are made:

A - A/Cdr Elijah Malok Aleeng Deputy Head, Commission to Organize Production
and Services and acts in the absence of ALPHA BETA. He reports to ALPHA BETA
for handing over and briefing. FIRE to inform him to come immediately.

B - A/Cdr Deny Aloor Kuol Deputy Director Addis Office for Co-ordination and
External Relations and acts now in the absence of ALPHA BETA. He takes the Addis
Office.

3. Above are in effect until 30/6/1990 when the dry season offensive is over and after
which new relevant directives will be issued.

FLASH -
Dec / Lt Alison Adari
20/2/1990

TOP SECRET
Date : 4/7/90
From: DELTA 7
To: DELTA 3 R: DELTA 26 R: DELTA 18 INFO: DELTA 9

025/7/90
I. Ref your 060/6/90 dated 22/6/90 which I only received today 4/7/90.

2. Given the situation, we are to do the following:

A Sector 5 of DELTA 26 is untenable and is therefore frozen.

B- Sector 6 ceases to be an intersection command as the concept is also untenable. Sector
6 remains under DELTA 18 for both administrative and operational matters. Ulu is
near Maban and is to be included under Sector 6. The support weapons that were
assigned to Sector 5 go to Sector 6.

C- Sector 4 remains under DELTA 3 and you implement the recornmendation that came in your message. That is to use the available forces to reopen Longkuei to resettle the Uduk and to get food for the forces. Retain your HQs with the other forces around Yabus to continue pressure. DELTA 26 to organize Uduk soldiers at Itang and send them to DELTA 3 to help in the opening of Longkuei. Meanwhile on the deployment of Bonga recruits you will be sent forces after flow of food from Longkuei is secured. I have discussed Longkuei situation; that is its reopening with friends. They said neither Yes nor No. Instead of waiting you just go ahead and implement the plan so that they are faced with a refuge situation to solve. To avoid clash with their forces co-ordinate movement of our forces with General Zalege. Address him as JULIET and use the code DELTA BETA.

Op. Immediate
Dec/ Lt. John Peter
6/7/90.

TOP SECRET
Date: 4/8/90
From: Thunder
To: Spear
R: Hammer   R: Sennar   R: Alpha Beta   R: Merowe   R: Kush   R: Amara   R: Napata
R: Soba   R: Ivory   R: Yormuk   R: Matata   R: Cdr Stephen Duol Chol   R: Fire
R: S/G SRRA   R: S/G NEC   R: SRRA Liaison NBI   R: Mercury   R: Load   R: Rock
R: Root   R: Wawat   R: Steel   R: Taseti (B)   R: Stick   R: Kilo 43   R: Sickle   R: Wave

033/8/90
1. Subject : Assignment. By this order HAMMER takes over the Commission to Organize Production and Services (COPS) with immediate effect. FIRE to hand over the handing over notes that were left by ALPHA BETA for A/Cdr Elijah Malok who was appointed to act but did not report due to other assignments.

2. All COPS(SRRA, NGOs, etc.) messages are to follow the same channel of command as before, that is:

A -All messages from COPS units (SPRA, NEC) are to be addressed to Hammer with information to THUNDER and information to SPEAR.
B -HAMMER addresses COPS units with information to THUNDER and information to SPEAR.

3. For execution and information.

Op. Immediate
Reg by/ Malet Manoah Kot
5/8/90.

TOP SECRET
Date : 23/10/90
From: DELTA 7
To: DELTA 18(B)
INF: DELTA 24
INF: DELTA 3
113/10/90

1. In matters regarding military operations address your messages to Delta 7 with information to Delta 24, information to Delta 3 since they are Sectors adjacent to your sector and therefore have an interest in your military situation.

2. In matters regarding your sector administrative affairs address your messages only to Delta 7, unless any other party has reason to be informed.

Op. Immediate
Dec by/ Khristo Garang Akol
24/10/90

TOP SECRET
Date: 1/12/90
From: Thunder
To: Sennar
R:Alpha Beta   R: Ivory   R: DELTA 34   R: DELTA 18(B)   R: DELTA 11   R: Root
R: Wawat   R: Sickle   R:Load   R: Lulu-2
INF: Spear   INF: Hammer   NF: Merowe   INF: Kush   INF: Amara   INF: Napata
INF: Soba   INF: Yormuk.
021/12/90

1. Enemy is mobilizing A-2, popular Defence Forces and regular troops to make a major dry season offensive in Northern Upper Nile and Southern Blue Nile.

2. In order to deter, frustrate and repulse this enemy offensive, we must take extraordinary measures and all must play their respective roles effectively for overall success.

3. In light of the above, the following measures are taken and the following orders and directives issued with effect from today 1/12/90.

A command Restructuring and consolidation. In order to have unity and singleness of operational command Sector I of Delta I, Sector 2 of Delta 24 and Sector 3 of Delta 34 are here consolidated all under SENNAR for operational purposes for the next six (6) months up to 31/5/91, while they remain separate administratively.

B - Similarly, Sector 4 of Delta 3, Sector 5 of defunct Delta 26 and Sector 6 of Delta 18-B are here consolidated all under ALPHA BETA for operational purposes and since there is no other High Command member or full Cdr there, also for administrative purposes.

C All the reserve forces in Gambella area regroup in Pagak under Delta 11. These forces are
1. Two (2) TFs of INTISAR that were assigned to SICKLE,
2. One (1) TF of INTISAR that was targeted for SBN and deployed in SICKLE.
3. One (1) TF of INTISAR that was assigned to WAWAT.
4. Two (2) TFs of Uduk in WAWAT.

The old arms of these TFs which include AKMs, G-3, SKS and Muskovich will be collected and stored at Pagak when new AKMs and support weapons come from FIRE. The Uduk TFs will be issued with uniforms. The other TFS of INTISAR have uniforms.

D - ROOT with part of his staff and instructors move to Pagak to put the above force under refresher basic and unit training for the duration they may wait for equipment from FIRE, possibly up to two weeks. WAWAT to feed them. These will be deployed by 21/12/90 at the latest.

E- WAWAT to raise three(3) TFs or recruits, old soldiers and if necessary to complete with red army who would return to school after May 1991 and to put these under intensive training in Itang area. They will be armed with the old weapons of the TFs in para (C) above and charged with the security of Itang.

F- Similarly, SICKLE ditto as WAWAT above.

In the meantime WAWAT and SICKLE make local arrangements for maintenance of law and order in their areas in the absence of the present TFs with them and while they are training their security forces.

5. For execution.

- FLASH -

Cop by/ Lt Jobn Peter Wal
2/12/90.

TOP SECRET
Date : 20/1/91
From: Thunder
To: Spear
R: Hammer R: Sennar R: Alpha Beta R: Merowe R: Kush R: Amara R: Napata
R: Soba R: Ivory R: Yormuk R: Matata R: DELTA 34 R: Zulu 23 R: DELTA 11
R: GHQ/Records

078/1/91

1. Given the challenges of the dry season, the following reorganization and command changes are made with immediate effect today

A- NUN Sectors One(1), Two(2) and three(3) and SBN Sectors four(4), five(5) and six
(6) are here consolidated into one (1) command to be referred to as BSC phase Two(2)
and remain under the overall command of the C-in-C.

B- sectors four(4) , five(5) and six(6) fall under operational command of HAMMER
with ALPHA BETA and SOBA as Assistant commanders. In addition, HAMMER is
Deputy Cdr of phase Two(2).

C- Sectors One(1), Two(2) and Three(3) fall under operational command of SENNAR
with IVORY and DELTA 34 as Assistant Cdrs.

2. KUSH remains in command of Southern Kordofan and as adjacent command
coordinates with BSC phase Two(2) Cdr with respect to inter-related operations.

3. NAPATA takes over command of BSC phase One(1) Northern Sector from HAMMER
and as adjacent command to BSC phase Two(2) co-ordinates with BSC Phase Two(2)
Cdr. with respect to related operations.

4. ZULU 23 takes over command of all of the old Fangak district under NAPATA
with Fangak here made into a special Command. ZULU 23 is here given the special
assignment to bring under SPLA command all A-2 remnants, all armed Kujurs and
to mobilize these and SPLA forces in the area to expel the enemy forces in Fam Zeraf
before 31/3/91..

5. For execution
FLASH -
Dec by/Lt Alison Adari
21/1/91

TOP SECRET

Dae : 2/4/91.
From: Thunder
To: Hammer
R: Sennar R: Alpha Beta R: Ivory R: DELTA 34
INFO: Spear   INFO: Napata

011/4/91
1. A brigade size force consisting of Bn 105, Bn 165, Bn 190 and Bn 223 is assembled in
Renk under command of Brigadier (PSC) Fatahi Abdel Ghafur. They are waiting for
the steamers to bring some of their requirements. The steamers are moving to Malakal.
The formation is code-named FATAH AL-MUBAIN.
2. The mission of Fatah Al Mubain is to capture Nasir before the end of April. The enemy
has adequate information about the state of our forces and they appear confident.

3. Essentially, the enemy has only 60 days up to 30/5/91 within which they can do us significant damage. With respect to above, every day of the next 60 days therefore counts and especially the whole month of April. If we can frustrate their plans so that they are unable to take Nasir or to cross Canal during April, then they would run out of time.

4. To achieve above it is necessary not to divide up the 2,000 man force in Pagak but rather to have unity of command and means or concentration of forces including the pooling of all support weapons and to move quickly to engage the enemy in the Melut-Renk area so that the whole of April is exhausted fighting there far from Malakal and Nasir and so that even if eventually enemy makes it to Malakal being prevented from using a cross-country route to Nasir, they will have been exhausted and the month of May will already have been on them and advancing into the rain and thereby frustrating their plans for Nasir this year. Next year will be another matter.

5. Whereas the command got unified as BSC Phase(2) as came in my earlier directive, this is here reiterated again in view of the above threat and HAMMER as D/Cdr BSC Phase(2) takes direct operational command of all forces in BSC Phase(2), SENNAR is the Phase(2) Chief Combat Operations ALPHA BETA SERVSCOM and IVORY Civil-Military Operation.

6. Above until 31/5/91 or further orders.
- FLASH -
Dec by/ Lt John Peter Wal
3/4/91.

TOP SECRET
Date : 17/5/91
From: Thunder
To: Spear
R: Hammer   R:Sennar   R: Alpha Beta   R:Merowe   R: Kush   R: Amara   R: Napata
R:Soba   R:Ivory   R: Yormuk   R: Matata   R: S/G SRRA   R:S/G NEC
INFO: A/Cdr Elijah Malok.

072/5/91

1. Elijah Malok Aleeng is appointed w.e.f. 16/5/91 as Executive Director of COPS, Deputy to HAMMER for co-ordination of day to day running of COPS organizations.

2. COPS is a full time work and as HAMMER is engaged in military operations, deputy with delegated powers is necessary for efficient running of COPS.

- FLASH -
Dec by/ Lt John Peter

18/5/91.

APPENDIX 1 (C)

RADIO MESSAGES: GENERAL

S/No.	MESSAGE NO.	DATE	GENERAL SUBJECT
1	004/7/87	01/07/87	Assuming command of N.U.N. Zone
2	046/7/87	17/07/87	Major-General Gordon Kong of A-2
3	056/7/87	20/07/87	A/Cdr. Oyai Deng Ajak
4	122/1/88	11/01/88	Ditto
5	045/1/88	13/01/88	Ditto
6	172/1/88	15/01/88	Ditto
7	115/3/88	14/03/88	Arrest of Cdr. Arok Thon Arok
8	022/5/88	22/05/88	Recall to GHQ
9	209/10/88	22/10/88	Peace Talks with Sadiq and DUP
10	008/11/88	04/11/88	Peace Talks with the DUP
11	002/6/89	29/06/89	On the arrest of Cdr. John Kulang Puot
12	006/7/89	02/07/89	Coup d'etat in Khartoum
13	029/9/89	02/09/89	Chairman's foreign visit
14	188/9/89	21/09/89	Fighting in Itang and Pinywudo
15	238/3/90	31/03/90	Order to report to the C-in-C
16	001/6/90	01/06/90	Request for a PMHC meeting
17	018/6/90	22/06/90	Chairman's foreign visit
18	034/7/90	06/07/90	Chairman's response to 001/6/90
19	017/7/90	07/07/90	Reply to Chairman's 034/7/90
20	028/9/90	02/09/90	On Deployment of INTISAR
21	448/9/90	29/09/90	Singer Mohammed Wardi
22	255/12/90	31/12/90	Seminar in Cairo
23	002/1/91	01/01/91	Ditto
24	002/1/91	01/01/91	Ditto
25	056/1/91	18/01/91	Chairman's foreign visit
26	277/2/91	20/02/91	On drought animals
27	002/6/91	01/06/91	Chairman's foreign visit
28	003/6/91	01/06/91	Ditto
29	021/7/91	18/07/91	Ditto

TOP SECRET
Date : 1/7/87
From: Thunder
To: Koom
R: Koryom TF   R: Nyok   R: Yarm/Guat
Inf: Spear   Inf: Girraffe   Inf: All Units
004/7/87
1. Major Dr Lam Akol as of today, 1/7/87, takes over direct overall command of Northern Upper Nile Zone from the C-in-C.
2. Mazlum, Koryom TF, Fashoda, Abushok, Sobat, and all other SPLA military and paramilitary immediately come under direct command of Major Dr Lam Akol from this date and all their messages and reports directed to the (code) ALPHA BETA without repeating to THUNDER or any other member of High Command. It is Alpha Beta who in turn, as zonal Commander, will address the High commanders.

- FLASH -
Decoded by/Lt Joseph Petero
Date: 4/7/87.

TOP SECRET
Date : 17/7/87
From: Alpha Beta
To: Wass   R: Thunder   R: Spear   R: Hammer   R: Girraffe(1)
046/7/87
A I received a letter yesterday purported to be from Gordon Kong. Below is the text verbatim. Quote:
Anya-nya II Military High Command
Dolieb Hill Station
July 15, 1987
Comrade Col. Dr Lam Akol
Commander of SPLA units to Upper Nile

Comrade, The Anya-nya II military high command have issued the following statement as part of our peace process. The Anya-nya II military high command decree No. I stated that if you regard yourself as part of the peace process being negotiated between the SPLA and the Anya-nya II, we advice you to withdraw your all forces to the frontiers. If you are unable to apply this peace procedure, yours should be regard as deceive and baseless to our peace initiative.

(SGD)
Major General Gordon Kong Chol
Commander-in-Chief of Anya-nya II Armed Forces.

B - Unquote. I replied him as follows. Quote:
Northern Upper Nile Zonal Command
Date: 16/7/87

Major General Gordon Kong Chol
Commander-in-Chief of Anya-nya II Armed Forces
1. Your letter dated 15/7/87 is received. I have referred it to the Joint Peace Committee between the SPLA and Anya-nya (II).
While we await the reply of the Joint Peace Committee, I caution you that never again give orders to an SPLA officer. As an SPLA officer, I receive my orders only from the SPLM/ SPLA Political-Military High Command.
(SGD)
Major Dr Lam Akol Ajawin
Alternate Member of the SPLM/SPLA
Political-Military High Command and
Zonal Commander of Northern Upper Nile.

C COMMENT. Gordon Kong was in Malakal all this time. It was the day of our first battle with the enemy at Anakdiar, 12/7/87, that I gave permission to Anya-nya(II) that was coming from Nasir to pass safely to Dolieb Hill. That they did not fight us angered the enemy and Gordon Kong is under pressure to fight our forces here. Because he knows the consequences of his attack on us, he is resorting to the tactics of scaring us. Should we withdraw he would have hit two birds with one stone. This we should deny him. In the meantime he must be exposed to his Anya-nya(II) at JOKMIR and around NASIR. I advise that Capt. James Hoth makes copies of Kong's letter and gives a copy to D.K. Mathews.

Coded by/ Lt. John Peter Wal
17/7/87.

TOP SECRET
20/7/87
From: Alpha Beta
To: Thunder
056/7/87
Ref to our discussion on that you need Major Oyai Deng Ajak to be with you in August. I am forced by the situation I found here to put in a special request that his coming to you be delayed for at least six(6) more months. Of our old forces here, Fashoda Bn is the only one well organized and intact. Abushok is scattered in the villages and all the messages to you about the strength and operations are either not true or exaggerated. Most of the fighting was by Sobat Bn but most of its soldiers were disappointed by the leadership of Capt. Moses Dhieu and his malpractices of favouring Ngok to Atar Dinka and others. This created tribal and sectional feuds among the forces. The separation of Sobat frorn Abushok was highly popular but 1st Lt Daniel Chwang needs time to collect the soldiers from their villages and reorganize them. Mazlum is almost gone. The majority of Mazlum is from Dongjol. Lt Col Deng Alony's malpractices of favouring Abilang to Dongjol alienated the latter and he is now left with a very small force. The case of Koryom is a long story. The two(2) Majors (Alfred Akwoc and James Othow) are unable to unite and control the force. The new forces need time for good feeding and retraining to develop self-confidence.

In short, I need time to organize all the forces, old and new alike. Therefore, it is not opportune to change the command of Fashoda Bn at this juncture. The success of a force is admittedly a collective effort but in this the commander plays the pivotal role. Major Oyai Deng Ajak has gained respect among his force and the population through his clearmindedness, truthfulness, courage and commitment to our objectives. The wealth of experience he has gained in just over a year is amazing. I would, therefore, want him to continue commanding Fashoda Bn while I grapple with those formidable problems of reorganization of the army and establishing credible administration in the zone.

-FLASH -
Coded by/ Lt John Peter Wal
2 1/7/87

———————

TOP SECRET
Date: 11/1/88
From : Thunder
To: Alpha Beta
122/1/88
Let me know whether you are still needing A/Cdr Oyai Deng Ajak. Ref to our earlier messages about six(6) months ago.

- FLASH -
DEC. by/ Lt Joseph Machol Peter
13/1/88.

———————

TOP SECRET
Date: 13/1/88
From: Alpha Beta
To: Thunder
045/1/88
Ref your 122/1/88. A/Cdr Oyai Deng Ajak is now in the process of handing over Fashoda Bn to his Deputy, Capt Akwoc Mayong Jago. He will leave for your end any time within two(2) weeks. We are going to miss him in the zone but I am convinced of the need for him to join you.

Thanks a lot for your co-operation.

- FLASH -
Coded by/ Lt John Peter Wal
                    13/1/88.

———————

TOP SECRET
Date: 15/1/88
From: Thunder
To: Alpha Beta R: Napata
172/1/88
1. Ref your 045/1/88. I appreciated very much your decision to release A/Cdr Oyai Deng Ajak. I am confident that you will arrange for his escort to this end.
2. Let him come to Ayod and from there to Napata. Confirm his departure to me and inform Napata when he leaves.

FLASH -
Dec. by/ Lt Okwom Nyikang Adiang
18/1/88

TOP SECRET
Date: 14/3/88
From: Thunder
To: Spear
R: Hammer R: Arrow R: Sennar R:Alpha Beta R: Merowe R: Kush R:Amara
R: Napata R: Soba R:Ivory R: S.B.N Cdr. R: Badi R: Biar R: Matata
R: Load R: Fire R: Rock R:Boma Base Cdr R: Alpha-2 R: Nasir
IND. Area Cdr R: Itang Cdr R: Dima Cdr.

115/3/88

For your information,the arrest of Cdr Arok Thon Arok was effected on 8/3/88. Basically, Cdr Arok Thon Arok over the last year has been actively agitating for capitulation under some form of agreement with the enemy and has since then consequently refused to fight. In pursuit of this aim, Cdr Arok late last year held a series of unauthorized talks with enemy generals in London. In London, they reached agreement that Cdr Arok would take over the leadership of the SPLM/SPLA by any means including, as suggested by Cdr Arok himself, assassination of the Movement's leader. When Cdr Arok Thon Arok came back from London recently, he came to implement his London agreement with the enemy. He stationed himself in Itang, refused to go to his axis and actively went to work. He was pre-empted and arrested on 8/1/88 and without any bloodshed. Following is the full text of Order of Arrest and dismissal of Cdr Arok Thon Arok from the High Command:

THE ORDER OF ARREST OF CDR AROK THON AROK

1. Whereas the C-in-C specifically instructed Cdr Arok Thon Arok that his visit in London was a private one and that he was not to make any contacts with the Sudan Government, army, and/or political parties or foreign organizations but that should a situation arise, he must first get approval from the C-in-C before holding such meetings, and whereas Cdr Arok Thon Arok violated these orders within one (1) week of his arrival in London by holding many meetings among them with an enemy army delegation composed of the following

A - Major General Fadlalla Burma Nasir, Minister of State for Defence.
B - General Abdel-Azim Siddiq Mohammed, Chief of Staff.
C - Major General Salah Mustafa , Chief of Intelligence.
D - Brigadier Abdalla Ahmed Abdalla,   Military Attache, Sudan Embassy, London.

And whereas such meetings were made without the prior approval of the C-in-C as directed, this action constitutes flagrant disobedience and insubordinate behaviour, being offences under section (26) A and (24) H of the Movement's disciplinary laws 1984.

2. Whereas Cdr Arok Thon Arok has been reported by reliable sources to have made and continues to maintain contacts with the enemy and such contacts aimed at physical elimination of the Chairman and C-in-C, SPLM/A and/or defection of the said Cdr to the enemy and both courses of action aimed at agreement with and capitulation to the enemy, such actions constitute a crime under section (29) C of the Laws.

3. Whereas several reported that Cdr Arok Thon Arok has on many occasions and over some period unsuccessfully attempted to recruit them to wage counterrevolutionary activities against the SPLM/A, and whereas internal cells of the Movement have warned and expressed concern about these activities, such actions by Cdr Arok Thon Arok constitute an offence under section (29) D of the Laws.

4. Whereas on arrival from London, Cdr Arok Thon Arok has been given specific orders to report to his Axis immediately to participate in repulsing the enemy 1988 dry season offensive, Cdr Arok Thon Arok refused to obey the said orders from the C-in-C and instead presented several conditions that if not fulfilled he would not report to his Axis command. This action constitutes flagrant disobedience of lawful order from a superior under section (26)D as well as insubordinate behaviour under section (26)H.

5. In view of the above serious military and disciplinary offences committed by Cdr Arok Thon Arok as in paragraphs one(I), two(2), three(3) and Four(4) above, and after consultation with the other permanent members of the SPLM/A Political-Military High Command and after careful consideration and in exercise of my powers as Chairman and C-in-C, SPLA and in fulfilment of my sacred duty to protect the people's revolution from opportunism and counter revolution, I , Cdr. John Garang de Mabior, Chairman and C-in-C, SPLM/SPLA, here issue the following orders:

A - Cdr Arok Thon Arok is relieved of membership of the Political-Military High Command as of today, 8/3/88, as well as from his duties as D/C.O.S., Administration and Logistics and command of Axis Five(5) and from all other assignments in the SPLM/SPLA. Until the Chairman, C-in-C makes new appointments, the Chairman, C-in-C will perform or specifically delegate some or all the work and command of D/C.O.S., Administration and Logistics and Axis Five(5).

B - Having been relieved of all work and duties in the SPLM/SPLA, Cdr Arok Thon Arok is here today, 8/3/88, placed under arrest, confinement and investigation. Any SPLA officer so designated will guard him at a designated detention, legally charged for the offences in paragraphs one(l), two(2), three(3) and four(4) above.

(Issued and Signed)
Cdr John Garang de Mabior
Chairman and C-in-C, SPLM/SPLA.
Date: 8/3/1988.

End of the order. Axis, Zonal and Independent area commanders are to brief and enlighten those under them of above development and the reasons that necessitated this revolutionary action.

FLASH -
Decoded by/ Lt John Peter Wal

TOP SECRET
Date: 22/5/88
From: Thunder
To: Spear
R: Harnmer   R: Alpha Beta   R: Soba

022/5/88
1. Alpha Beta has an urgent assignment at HQs and must be at GHQs by 21/6/88 at the latest.

2. Soba is transferred to take over command of N.U.N. zonal command until Alpha Beta returns.

3. Soba is to leave immediately not later than 24/5/88 to meet Alpha Beta at ABWONG area where handing and taking over will take place.
4. For Execution.
      - FLASH -
Decoded by/ Lt John Peter Wal.

TOP SECRET
Date: 22/10/1988
From: Thunder
To: Spear
R: Hammer   R: Arrow   R: Sennar   R: Alpha Beta   R: Merowe   R: Kush   R: Amara
R:Napata   R: Soba   R: Ivory

209/10/88
1. In the last few days Sadiq and the international press have been announcing that I am meeting Sadiq on 25/10/1988 in Kampalla, and that this was arranged by President Museveni. When we denied this they turned it around and started to agitate that we did not want peace and in Khartoum Sadiq is maliciously telling everyone that it is Mengistu who refused.

2. The truth is that there was no such agreement. Sadiq made the suggestion to Museveni and Museveni seems to have assured him that this would be okay. Before Museveni could make the necessary contacts, Sadiq made the announcement thereby either forcing us to meet him or succeeding in straining relations between us and Museveni through embarrassment.

3 Among other motives, Sadiq made the announcement and desire to meet us for two main reasons, to solve two immediate problems

A - The meetings between us and the DUP are very painful to Sadiq. We have actually driven a wedge between Umma now on the one side and DUP on the other. By meeting us, Sadiq succeeds to remove the wedge and preserves the unholy trinity.

B There are Muslim members of the Assembly who do not want Sadiq/Turabi version of Sharia or Sharia in general. Sadiq wants to blackmail the SPLA and these secularists in Parliament by having handshake with me in Kampalla and then returning to Khartoum to challenge the secularists saying that look even that infidel rebel John Garang has accepted the alternative laws. We shall have actually voted for Sharia by proxy.

4. We will go ahead driving the wedge despite international media propaganda against us. I will go ahead to meet Mr EL Mirghani and hold joint or separate press conference. After that we will announce that we are meeting Sadiq. This will deny him the two objectives he wanted to achieve.

5. Find here the text of draft agreement reached by our side and DUP. This is the subject of our meeting with Mirghani and which we shall sign. If you have any comments let me know before I go to Addis. I will meet Mirghani with Hammer, Alpha Beta and Kush early next month.

6. Yesterday Museveni sent me one of his aides a captain. He, Museveni, has been put in an embarrassment by Sadiq, and the captain came to plead that I meet Sadiq. Sadiq has refused lower level preliminary meetings. We do not want to disappoint Museveni, at the same time we cannot be pressured into situations. The captain returned this morning with a 6-point reply. This is also here sent to you For your information and comment if any.

TEXT A   below is the full text of draft agreement with DUP.

DRAFT AGREEMENT BETWEEN THE DEMOCRATIC UNIONIST PARTY
(DUP)
AND THE SUDAN PEOPLE'S LIBERATION MOVEMENT/
SUDAN PEOPLE'S LIBERATION ARMY (SPLM/SPLA)

Inspired by the deep understanding of the suffering of the Sudanese masses who are yearning for genuine peace and stability;
Committed to the unity of the people and the territorial integrity of our country;
Rejecting the old policies that aim at escalating the war destruction and deprivation in all forms, such policies that will ultimately lead to disunity;

Resolute in the necessity of persistent efforts to consolidate and enrich the democratic practice within the beloved Sudan;

Convinced that genuine peace in Sudan cannot be attained in the context of the so-called "Southern Problem" but on the appreciation that the problem is national in nature and hence, its resolution is only possible through a serious, sincere and continuous dialogue between the Sudanese political forces on an equal basis in the proposed National Constitutional Conference, The SPLM/A and the DUP, after frank and sincere discussions and exchange of views at this critical stage in our country's history, here issue this statement to the Sudanese people

A Cognizant of the fact that the convening of the National Constitutional Conference is an urgent national necessity that demands of all the Sudanese political forces sincere and persistent efforts to bring about conductive atmosphere for the convening of the Conference, the two sides are totally convinced that the basic and necessary factors to bring about such an atmosphere are:

1. Although the firm stand of the SPLM/A remains the repeal of the September laws and to be replaced by the 1974 laws. It, nevertheless, and because of its keenness on the convening of the National Constitutional Conference has at this stage agreed with the DUP that in the period preceding the convening of the National Constitutional Conference, all the provisions involving the "Hodoud" and related articles that are contained in the September 1983 laws be frozen and that there shall be no legislation on any laws that contain such articles until the National Constitutional Conference is held and final agreement is reached on the alternative laws.

2. The abrogation of the military pacts concluded between Sudan and other countries and which impinge on Sudan's national sovereignty.

3. The lifting of the state of emergency.
4. Cease fire.

B - A preparatory committee shall be convened to agree on the time, place and procedures of holding the National Constitutional Conference.

C - The two sides have agreed on the necessity to hold the National Constitutional Conference not later than the end of 1988.

D - The two sides call upon all the Sudanese political forces to immediately join this sincere national effort so as to bring about peace and stability in the country.

Long Live the struggle of the Sudanese people.

TEXT B :Below is the 6-point reply to President Museveni

1. President Museveni's intermediation is welcome. The arguments for necessity of a meeting with the other side and of its urgency are appreciated and our positions are the same.
2. SPLA considers it expedient to have lower level meetings (whether at party or government basis) before the summit so that issues and agenda are thrashed out there.

3. SPLA held a first round talks with the DUP at delegation level last August and completed the second and last round on 17/10/1988. A basic draft agreement has been reached by the two sides.

4. Osman el-Mirghani, the head of the DUP and also the head of State in the present 3-party coalition government and Dr John Garang are scheduled to meet and sign this agreement within the next three weeks.

5. Because of the good offices of President Yoweri Museveni and in respect thereof, the SPLA drops the condition of low level delegation meetings and agrees to meet Mr Sadiq El-Mahdi at summit level if this will expedite the peace process.

6. After Dr John's meeting with Mr El-Mirghani and depending on the military situation, Dr John will be ready to meet Mr Sadiq El-Mahdi. In view of this and in order to avoid possible embarrassment and inconvenience, it is advisable not to put a definite time frame. But since we agree to the necessity and urgency of the meeting, it will be at the pearliest possible time. This will accordingly be conveyed to President Museveni.
- Op Immediate -
Dec/ Kau Nak
1/11/1988.

TOP SECRET
Date : 4/11/1988
From: Thunder
To: Spear R: Hammer R: Arrow R: Sennar R: Alpha Beta R: Merowe R: Kush
R: Arnara R: Napata R: Soba R: Ivory
008/11/88
1. 1 finally arrived Ethiopia this morning after 10 days journey from Torit/Katire area. The floods are still high. I was not able to receive your messages over this period because of the movement.

2. In Addis, I expect to meet the DUP leader if he does not pull out of the agreement. There is no reason why he should. Hammer, Alpha Beta and Kush will be with me in the meeting. On our side nothing is new. The struggle must continue. Meeting DUP or anyone else is only political manoeuvring. We ally or appear to ally with the weak to hit the strong and thereby weaken the total enemy situation. We have actually driven a wedge in the unholy trinity. If anyone of you has any ideas and suggestions that may help, send them before we meet El-Mirghani. The meeting should be within one week from today.

- FLASH -
Dec/ Kau Nak
5/11/1988.

TOP SECRET
Date 29/6/89
From: Alpha Beta
To: Thunder
R: Spear   R: Hammer
002/6/89
In a casual conversation I learned from SPEAR that ARROW is under detention for more than a month now. I did not have information before and it appears I am not the only Alternate Member of the PMHC who is not informed. I suppose the decision to detain ARROW was taken by the full members of the PMHC. It is just natural to inform the alternate members. This is what I think. Regards.

- FLASH -
Cod/Kau N.
29/6/1989

TOP SECRET
Date : 2/7/1989
From: Thunder
To: Spear
R: Hammer   R: Sennar   R: Alpha Beta   R: Morowe   R: Kush   R: Amara
R: Napata   R: Soba   R: Ivory   R: Cdr Lual Diing   R: Matata
006/7/89
1. Ref the coup in Khartoum. I have no other information other than what we are hearing on the radio. We did not have prior knowledge and the Movement was not involved in the coup.

2. The coup leaders or any government in Khartoum has no choice but to contact the SPLA. By their own announcement, they will be contacting the Movement soon. Our objectives remain the same and firm, and compromising them is out of question. The coup in Khartoum was expected and could have been done by any officer. Although we were not directly involved, it is the Movement's military and political activities that precipitated the coup. The coup is a symptom of the last kick of the dying old Sudan. We must, therefore, intensify the military and political struggle. Aluta Continua.

3. However, not to talk is unpolitical and untenable. The question is how to exploit the coup militarily and politically to make the situation worse for the new regime and thus to accelerate the birth of the new Sudan. On this I need your ideas and advices urgently and from time to time as events develop.

4. All forces are to be on full alert. A cease fire is out of the question Indications are that while the new regime is talking peace his real intention is vigorous prosecution of the war. We must preempt and demoralize them. SPLA Oye!

5. Send me your ideas and advices.

- FLASH -
Dec/ Kau Nak
2/7/1989.

———————

TOP SECRET
Date: 2/9/89
From: Thunder
To: Spear
R: Hammer   R: Sennar   R: Alpha Beta   R: Merowe   R: Kush   R: Amara
R: Napata   R: Soba   R: Ivory   R: Cdr Lual Diing   R: Matata
029/9/89

1. I have been away on foreign visits for the whole of August. I had been to Cuba, Nicaragua, Angola, Mali and Uganda. The visits were generally successful. I was able to get some armament and various types of ammos.

2. I arrived back from the last visit Uganda, yesterday 1/9/89. I will not go on any foreign visit for some time. I will remain in the rear areas to co-ordinate your operations and respond to your needs. The dry season is fast approaching and the enemy is expected to launch the ferocious attack on our positions so as to legitimize the rule.

3. We must pre-empt them to prevent their offensive from taking off. The coming dry season will be decisive on both sides. Our mission is to capture the whole of South Sudan by May 31, 1990. And to intensify guerrilla operations in Southern Blue Nile, White Nile and Kordofan provinces during that period so that we prepare conditions to capture them by the next dry/rainy season.

4. All commanders to be on alert and to prepare to execute the above mission. I will send you whatever else available to achieve your missions. Use whatever little you have or you get to maximum advantage to accomplish your mission. The international situation is very complex. We must be very economical in using whatever we get and must seek to capture from the enemy.

5. Because of my trip abroad, I have not been able to answer many of your messages. I will do this within 72 hours.

6. Above is for your information and where relevant for execution.

EMERGENCY -
Dec by/ Lt Deng Samuel Machar.
3/9/89.

———————

TOP SECRET
Date 21/9/89
From: Thunder
To: Spear
R: Hammer   R: Sennar   R: Alpha Beta   R: Merowe   R: Kush   R: Amara   R: Napata
R: Soba   R: Ivory   R: Cdr Lual Diing Wol   R: Matata   R: GHQ Records   R: Piankhi
R: A/Cdr Taban Deng Gai   R: Iron   R: Bonga Cdr   R: Sickle
188/9/89

I. There was indiscriminate fighting in both Panyidu on 11/9/89 and Itang on 15/9/89 between elements among the refugees and the friends militia. In Panyidu there was a clear case of provocation by the militia and the friends' counter revolutionaries. However, in Itang the situation was provoked by unruly elements among the refugees who had an eye on looting friends shops. The friends suffered many casualties and their houses and shops were thoroughly looted and set on fire. The looters themselves in Itang shot each other during the looting. There was complete break down of law and order.

2. Whatever the cause, our side was unable to exercise control and restraint. The Ethiopians must be highly complimented for their tolerance. All agree that no government will accept to host the refugees and fully support their Movement when these same refugees run wild to kill their citizens, loot their shops and set their villages on fire. No host can tolerate such guests, no matter what the situation must be as to give the other cheek. It must be us to go to all extents to tolerate, to accommodate, to befriend the local citizens and to avoid any clashes between us and the host citizens.

3. Disorder and lawlessness must immediately come to an end in all refugees camps. I am not pleading for this, I am taking the necessary measures to see that law and order are firmly established and that refugees camps in addition to taking proper care for the refugees also effectively contribute to the liberated areas.

4. Therefore, the following decisions and orders are issued:

A All refugees camps administration come under the C-in-C with effect from 21/9/89. Only the C-in-C will appoint or relieve refugees camps administrations.

B tang and Panyidu camps are put under martial law as of 21/9/89. A strict curfew will be in effect from 1800 hours to 0600 hours until law and order are established on a correct New Sudan basis.

C A/Cdr Oyai Deng Ajak is here given three(3) weeks assignment, 21/9/89 to 4/10/89, as martial law administrator for Itang and the surrounding areas to supervise the implementation of the necessary changes and orders that will be issued by the C-in-C. A/Cdr Gier Chuang Aluong is given a similar assignment for Panyidu. Their reports and co-ordination will be directly with the C-in-C.

D The administration of Itang, that is the administrator, commander and the rest of the co-ordinating committee is here relieved of their duties as of 0600 hours, Thursday 21/9/89, and replaced by the following committee:

1. A/Cdr Taban Deny Gai   - Chairman and Commander
2. Capt. Joseph Akol Giir   - Director, Finance committee
3. Capt. Simon Morris Didimo - Director, Production committee
4. Capt. Akol Diing Duot   - Director, Health Committee
5. Capt. Kuol Deng Abot   - Director, Security committee
6. Capt. Michael Manyuon Anyang - Director, Legal Affairs Committee
7. Capt. Timothy Tot Chol   - Director, Food and Materials Committee

8. 1st Lt Clement Katinya Nyelma   - Director, Social Services Committee
9. Comrade Dr Situna Abdullahi   - Director, Women Affairs Committee
10. Lt. Zakaria Mathen Riak   - Director, special Services Committee

E   A standing six(6)-man committee is here formed to advise the C-in-C at least once every six(6) months, or when there is need, on the running of the refugees camps and extent of implementation of C-in-C directives. These are:

1. Cdr Lual Diing Wol   - chairman
2. A/Cdr Isaac Tut Dhier   - member
3. A/Cdr Taban Deng Gai   - member
4. A/Cdr Pieng Deng Kuol   - member
5. Capt Mario Muor Muor   - member
6. Capt Michael Manyuon Anyang   - member.

F   Officers, NCOs and men that are relived from refugees camps administration are to report to Bonga with a departure order from the martial law administrator where they will be given assignment.

G   Officers, NCOs and men in Itang and Panyidu who have no assignments or units who are staying without proper documents are to report to Bonga with departure order from the martial law administrator.

Dec by/ DY
Date: 26/9/89.

———————

TOP SECRET
Date: 31/3/90
From: Thunder
To: Alpha Beta   R: Sennar   R: Soba   R: Fire
Inf : Spear   Inf: Hammer
238/3/90

1. All of you   Sennar, Alpha Beta and Soba, should be back by now. I understand that Sennar is in Nairobi and Soba should be back by now.
2. All three(3) of you report to my end within (72) hours by 1200 hours, 4/4/90, at the latest.
3. Alpha Beta to inform Sennar and Soba if they are not in Addis yet.
4. Fire remains responsible for Addis office.
5. For execution.

- FLASH -
Dec by/ Lt Alison Adari
31/3/90.

———————

TOP SECRET
Date: 1/6/90
From: Alpha Beta
To: Thunder
R: Spear   R: Hammer   R: Sennar R: Merowe   R: Kush   R: Amara
R: Napata   R: Soba   R: Ivory   R: Yermuk   R: Matata
001/6/90

1. Ref Thunder's 015/1/90 and 045/1/90 ordering all High Command members to be
   physically in the field to repulse the enemy's offensive in the dry season ending 30/6/90.
   I suggest that a meeting of the High Command be convened as soon as possible after
   30/6/96.

2. This is a matter of utmost urgency to discuss and take decisions on issues of strategy
   and policy in the conduct of our revolutionary war. As the Movement enters its eighth
   year, many political developments have taken place inside the Movement, in Sudan, in
   the region and internationally. These are bound to have an impact on us and this calls
   for our collective consideration.

3. We have two(2) Cdrs and a big number of A/Cdrs and they can take command of the
   forces while the meeting of the High Command is in progress

4. This is for your consideration.

- FLASH -
Coded by/ SGT Laat Mapour Awec
1/6/90

TOP SECRET
Date : 22/6/90
From: Thunder
To: Spear
R: Hammer   R: Sennar   R: Alpha Beta   R: Merowe   R: Kush   R: Amara   R: Napata
R: Soba R: Ivory   R: Yormuk   R: Matata   R: Cdr Stephen Duol   R: Delta 39
R: Taseti   R: Rock   R: Piankhi   R: Kilo 18   R: Load   R: Wawat   R: Root
R: Sickle   R: Steel   R: Tarhaka   R: Yam   R: Stick

018/6/90
1. I arrived back yesterday, 21/6/90, after (35) days away during which time I visited
   ten(10) countries and met their presidents. The visits were very successful as we are or
   will be getting some military assistance from seven (7) of these countries.

2. Because of my absence, many of your messages are probably unanswered. I replied
   some whenever I carne to a country where we have radio communication.

3. Above is for your information and also to allay fears of those under your command who might have been concerned about the recent developments in Europe and the Soviet Union. The truth is that since 1983, Eastern Europe, Soviet Union, USA, etc. of the big countries, none of these has ever given us any military assistance. The impact of the changes in the international situation on our military supplies is thus marginal and indirect. And to assure them there is no cause for alarm. In addition, what we get from Beshir, especially artillery and armour, adds to the above. The Sudan has many borders and whatever we get will enter.

4 Aluta Continua. El-Beshir's dry season offensive is over and in miserable failure. Let us tighten up and use every day of the dry season to go over the threshold to victory.
5. Thousands of congratulations for the military operations and victory is certain. Brief all under you that victory is imminent and for all to double up efforts.
Op. Immediate
Dec/ Khristo Garang
24/6/90.

TOP SECRET
Date: 6/7/90
From: Thunder
To: Alpha Beta
INFO: Spear   INFO : Hammer
034/7/90
Ref your 001/6/90. Whereas I agree with the recommendation, message is unprocedural. The repeated to all High command members is at best unnecessary.
Op. Immediate
Dec/ Khristo Garang
6/7/90

TOP SECRET
Date : 7/7/90
From: Alpha Beta
To: Thunder
INFO: Spear   INFO: Hammer
017/7/90
Ref your 034/7/90. I am glad that my suggestion for a meeting is accepted. As to the procedure, frankly, I am not aware of the procedures of the High Command as a political body. I was only relying on commonsense. I am deeply sorry if informing colleagues was unprocedural.
- FLASH -
Coded/Laat N. Awec
7/7/90.

TOP SECRET
Date: 2/9/90
From: Thunder
To: Sennar
R: Soba   INFO: Spear   R: Hammer   R: Alpha Beta   INFO: Fire
028/9/90

1. Ref your 145/8/90 and SOBA's 012/8/90. The points in both messages are appreciated.

2. Our problem in Sector (3) is not so much lack of manpower but difficulty of getting logistics there, ammos and food. As you recall last time I ordered four (4) Task Forces from Bentiu to report to Sector (2). You replied by suggesting that only Two (2) TFs will be necessary because of food problems. When those TFs arrived your end most of them deserted soon after. It would be a waste of manpower for us to send you the remaining two (2) TFs as they would either not go, desert on the way or desert after arrival. The problem of Sectors (4) and (5) is both manpower and logistics.

3. With INTISAR division, the composition is complex. The total was (6,000) about (50) percent, (7) TFs, of them were from Nuba Mountains. Deploying them to other areas would cause agitation among the Nuba and they may stop coming to the Movement. This would be very adverse. They would at any rate go and desert just as those from other areas do, especially from Sector (2) or (3) which is adjacent to their home, and this could be aggravated by hunger. We deployed the bulk of these forces to KUSH, up to Five (5) TFs of them; we deployed the remaining two (2) TFs in a direction that will hopefully eventually take them to Darfur. This second deployment can be told to them that they are going to bring the Darfur just as Volcano went to bring them. This leaves us eight (8) TFs of INTISAR.

4. Of the remaining eight (8) TFs, about (40) percent of these are from BGAA. Past experience also shows that because of their legitimate concern of Marahlein problem, more of these forces deserted home and it was evident that deploying them to Sector two (2), three (3) or four (4) at this time, they would start deserting even before reaching and on reaching, most of them would go and desert. The desertion would be aggravated by hunger, and the desertion would waste manpower.

5. The above, in addition to strategic considerations, lay behind the deployment we did to INTISAR. Of course, we gave serious consideration to Sectors (2), (3), (5) and (4), especially during the dry season, and this is included in the plan of deployment. Enemy penetration through Sectors (2), (3) and (4) renders us very vulnerable indeed. This will even be more so during this coming dry season with Omer now building up in Renk, Kosti and Maban and Chali areas. We reasoned that if we reinforce Delta 24, Delta 34 and Delta 3 now, these would go and be dissipated by desertion, especially under the present food conditions, and when El-Beshir's offensive comes we will have nothing to respond it with.

6. Consequently, the decision we took was to retain three (3) of the remaining eight (8) TFs in strategic reserve in Gambela area and the remaining five (5) TFs are moving to NAPATA area. This is the deployment of INTISAR. The three (3) TFs are tactically

deployed in Gambela area. By November, this strategic reserve will grow to six (6) TFs in the same area. So, we will not have problem of manpower as these six (6) TFs will combine with the old forces in Sectors (1), (2), (3) and (4) to provide sufficient force not only to contain Beshir but enable us to take the war to White Nile economic projects and to Ingessana.

7. Again our problem remains to be and will be transport. I discussed this problem thoroughly with EBONY in our last meeting some three (3) weeks ago. I requested a fund to buy draught transport animals (mules and donkeys). He approved Two hundred thousand(200,000) Birr for this purpose. The amount was received by FIRE last week and a committee under FIRE is now in the process of buying these animals. All will be deployed in sectors (2), (3), (4) and (5). These animals plus Equatoria (Yei, Maridi, etc.) should solve the transport problem of the dry season plus, of course, draught animals we can find in these areas and trucks we will get when we reach the projects.

8. Above is for your briefing and to put you in picture of general situation.
Op. Immediate
Dec by/Wek Garang Nyang
5/9/90.

TOP SECRET
Date : 29/9/90
From: Thunder
To: Spear
R: Hammer
INF: All Units
448/9/90
1. Singer Mohamed Wardi, a strong sympathizer of the Movement, arrived Ethiopia on 25/9/90 He had wanted to sing in the liberated areas but this is not feasible now.

2. He will sing in Addis Ababa and Dire Dawa in solidarity with the SPLM/A. He will donate half of the proceeds of his parties to SPLM/A's wounded heroes.

3. A committee composed of 1st Lt Chaw Mayol Juuk, 1st Lt Yasir Said Arman and Comrade Dr Wathig Kimeir is responsible for Wardi's parties.

4. Above is for your information and to underline the appeal and broad support the SPLM/A enjoys all over the Sudan as underlined by this famous Sudanese artist (Singer). SPLA Oye.
Op. Immediate
Dec by/ Khristo Garang
Akol Ater
30/9/90.

TOP SECRET
Date: 31/12/90
From: Thunder
To: Alpha Beta
R: Fire
INFO: Spear   INFO: Hammer   INFO: Sennar
255/12/90

1. There will be a seminar in Cairo on problems of the Horn of Africa from Jan. 7 to Jan. 10, 1991. It will be addressed by notables such as Herman Cohen, the U.S.A. Assistant Secretary of State for African Affairs. The Movement is invited to send one participant to present our position.

2. ALPHA BETA is here given the above assignment. The most senior A/Cdr commands in his absence and co-ordinates with SENNAR.

3. FIRE to process travel arrangements of ALPHA BETA so that he proceeds to Cairo on arrival and on time.

4. ALPHA BETA to start preparing the position paper while moving. FIRE to prepare and make references ready.

- FLASH -
V.U.
Dec by/ Khristo Garang
31/12/90

TOP SECRET
Date: 1/1/91
From: Alpha Beta
To: Thunder
INFO: Spear   INFO: Hammer   INFO: Sennar   INFO: Fire

002/1/91

A- Ref your 255/12/90. In view of the time element, it will not be practically possible for me to make it to the conference in time. I have no car with me and from where I am it takes not less than five (5) days good walk to Itang. I therefore, suggest that rather than miss the opportunity, somebody else can go to represent us.

B - This is for your information and directives.
- FLASH -
Coded by/Lt John Peter Wal
1/1/91.

TOP SECRET
Date : 1/1/91
From : Thunder
To: Alpha Beta
R: Piankhi   R: Fire   INFO: Spear   INFO: Hammer   INFO: Sennar
002/1/91
1. Ref your 002/1/91. I have already sent your name and FIRE will receive the ticket tomorrow in your name. It would be confusing to make the substitution.

2. PIANKHI is in Gambela. He has one of my HQ Toyotas with him. I will order him to send you this early tomorrow, 2/1/91. This means you can be in Gambela next tomorrow, 3/1/91, and proceed to Addis to arrive on 4/1/91 or 5/1/91. Your booking for Cairo is on 6/1/91.
- FLASH -
Dec: by/ Khristo Garang
1/1/91

TOP SECRET
Date: 18/1/91
From: Thunder
To: Spear
R: Hammer   R: Sennar   R: Alpha Beta   R: Merowe   R: Kush   R: Amara   R: Napata
R: Soba   R: Ivory   R: Yormuk   R: Matata
056/1/91
I. I arrived back today after three (3) weeks to Ethiopia, Kenya and Zaire on a begging mission for enemy dry season offensive.

2. Above is for your information.
- EMERGENCY -
Reg/ Lt Alison Adari
19/1/91.

TOP SECRET
Date: 20/2/91
From: Thunder
To: Hammer
INFO: Spear   INFO: Sennar   INFO: Alpha Beta   INFO: Wawat
277/2/91
1. As you must have found out in Cambela/Itang area, there is a lot of talk about alleged ill-advisability of buying draught animals(mules, donkeys, horses).

2. The money that was used to buy these animals was neither raised by any Zonal or Sector command nor was not collected in the refugees camp. This money was donated

by the friends' top man for this purpose. The animals are therefore an addition rather than a subtraction to what is deemed the best mode of transport.

3. It is alleged that there is no water, etc., for these animals when these vital items are available for other animals in the area such as the Gajak cattle, unless the grass and water escaped the area on arrival of C-in-C donkeys. Obviously, the donkeys, like support weapons, cannot capture garrisons. They must be managed to achieve the intended goal.

4. There are other areas where these animals can be effectively used such as between Tambura and Busere, where incidentally the enemy is using a fleet of donkeys for transport. If you found the local Cdrs persuaded that the donkeys are useless, then they cannot possibly manage them. In that case, you can send them to this end. If you can use them, of course, keep them as they were meant for your end. I have ordered Amara to get mules, donkeys, horses and camels for Yambio, Tambura, Busere, Raga transport. With a drum of diesel now (800) Birr in Addis in the black market and difficult to find, we really have little choice but to use vehicles when we can and use animals when we must. As is clear in Gambela even when there is money, there is no fuel to buy.

Op. Immediate.
Reg. by/ SGT Malet N. Kot
3/3/91.

――――――

TOP SECRET
Date: 1/6/91
From: Thunder
To: Spear
R: Hammer R: Sennar R: Alpha Beta R: Merowe R: Kush R: Amara R: Napata
R: Soba R: Ivory R: Yormuk R: Matata.
002/6/91

1. I arrived back to MERCURY country yesterday, 31/5/91, after fifteen (15) days during which I visited this country, Zambia (twice), Namibia, Nigeria (twice), Ghana (twice) and Zimbabwe (from where I just came).

2. I have been following the developments in Ethiopia over the media as all of you have been doing with great concern. I decided to extend the visits in view of these developments so that we secure in some of these countries the necessary ammos to defend and extend our gains. Despite the adverse situation in Ethiopia, I am glad to inform you that I was able to get (800) tons of ammos of various types from some of these countries. These include (15) million rounds of AKM (about 10,725 big boxes). The main problem is now air transport which I am working to solve. The total number of freight flights using a (727) Boeing is (20) trips at a cost of about (50,000) U.S. dollars. I have already secured money for (3) trips and hope to get today for another (6) trips. So we will be able to transport half of the ammos before June 15. 1 am still

working to transport the remaining half so that everything is at Napata's Rvs. before the end of June.

3. Above means that we will not have problem of ammos in the immediate future. Our people need not be worried, demoralized or panicked. We will turn the tables on Beshir despite the Ethiopian situation. All Cdrs are to keep up the morale of our forces and of our people. We will win. Victory shall sooner than later be ours, and the current celebrations in Khartoum by Omer's Junta will turn to sorrow and mourning.

4. All Cdrs are to start mobilizing as great a number of forces as possible, as we shall have no ammos problem, so that we give a final deadly blow to Omer El Beshir and as soon as possible. SPLA Oyee! Aluta Continua and Victory is certain.

- FLASH -
Reg by/Lt John Peter Wal
20/6/91.

TOP SECRET
Date: 1/6/91
From: Thunder
To: Spear
R: Hammer   R: Sennar   R: Alpha Beta   R: Merowe   R: Kush   R: Amara   R: Napata
R: Soba   R: Ivory   R: Yormuk   R: Matata
003/6/91
1. Ref my 002/1/91. The developments in Ethiopia are of course a very serious development. The situation demands our collective thoughts and decision making.

2. As soon as practical, I will call a meeting of the Political-Military High Command to review our situation in the light of the developments in Ethiopia.

3. In the meantime, HAMMER, ALPHA BETA and YORMUK are to do their best as they have been doing to manage the crisis of the refugees camps. SENNAR is to contain the enemy in Malakal as they will take advantage of the adverse situation in Ethiopia despite the rains. Similarly, MEROWE and NAPATA are to contain the enemy inside Juba so that none of our positions in BSC phase (1) and phase (3) is taken by the enemy. AMARA is to contain the enemy in Wau and assist ZULU 11 to contain the enemy not to advance beyond Bo.

4. With the situation remaining as it is and with logistics that we have secured, we will be able to teach Omer a big lesson before the dry season.

- FLASH -
Dec by/ Lt John Peter Wal
20/6/91

TOP SECRET
Date : 18/7/91
From: Thunder
To: Spear
R: Hammer   R: Sennar   R: Alpha Beta   R: Merowe   R: Kush   R: Amara   R: Napata
R:Soba   R: Ivory   R: Yormuk   R: Matata   INFO: All units.
021/7/91

I. I left Addis Ababa on 17/5/91 and went on diplomatic mission to southern and west Africa. On 12/6/91, I was joined by Cdr James Wani Igga, Cdr Daniel Awet, A/Cdr Deng Aloor and A/Cdr Richard K. Mulla. The five (5) of us plus a security officer continued with the diplomatic mission to west Africa, USA, UK, west Africa again and southern Africa again.

2. The delegation arrived back in Nairobi two (2) days ago on 16/7/91, on our way back home, and all are here informed that I have resumed normal radio contact and command as of 16/7/91.

3. As you all know many Movement events have occurred in the last two (2) months. The friendly Mengistu regime collapsed completely and a new EPDRF based government, currently hostile to the SPLA, took over in Addis Ababa. Their first act was to close down Radio SPLA and to expel our Addis office and to force the evacuation of all refugees and all SPLA presence in Ethiopia. This is why I stayed away for nearly two (2) months so as to seek solutions to the most serious problems created by the events in Ethiopia, such as the loss of Radio SPLA, ammos, etc.

4. At the same time Omer El Beshir's NIF military Junta tried very hard to take advantage of the situation to misinform, disinform and to try to achieve a decisive military victory. The junta misread the developments in Ethiopia as spelling the end of the SPLA and they were euphoric believing that the time for the killing to smash the SPLA had come. They started to bomb our people in Jekou, Nasir, Pachalla, Pibor, Torit, Maridi, Bor, Waat, etc. and launched two (2) major offensives in early June. One from Wau/Busere in an attempt to recapture Tambura before June 30th and from there consolidate and proceed to recapture Yambio and Maridi. This involved about (3,000) troops supported by heavy artillery, many tanks and over (100) trucks. The second offensive was launched at the same time from Juba to Yei, so as from there to proceed to recapture Morobo, Kaya and Lasu and open land route to/from Uganda and Zaire. The Chief of Staff, General Ishag advised against this, citing the rains, but he was overruled, dismissed and replaced by the more fundamentalist General Hassan.

5. The Junta could not be more wrong. I am happy to announce, brief and assure all SPLA officers, NCOs and men and all our people everywhere that the effect of the recent developments in Ethiopia will be minimal and minimised. Your Movement remains strong, will be further strengthened and will emerge, I assure you, even stronger than at any other time before. We must persist in the struggle, we must remain resolute, take courage, remain united and carry the struggle to the last mile, to its logical conclusion. Victory is certain and near.

6. The following points in the form of brief to you are to be noted and appreciated as SPLA's growing strength contrary to Beshir's propaganda and should allay the fears of some among our ranks that may think that the fall of Mengistu would weaken us.

A- Firstly, Omer El Beshir's two (2) offensives have failed miserably. The one from Wau has been halted, contained and is under destruction. After (48) days of heavy fighting from 01/6/91 to today, the enemy could advance only (33) miles. They are now in Basia. They have been unable to reach even Bo bridge, let alone Tambura. They have to date lost (184) KIA including one Major, two 1st Lts and four second Lts, and sustained (391) WIA including two Cols, one Major, one Capt, two 1st Lts and three 2nd Lts. Another (20) are reported MIA (missing). This is about (20) percent of their manpower put out of action. In addition, they have lost (19) trucks and three T-62 tanks destroyed, and our engineers have completely demolished the strategic Busere bridge behind them cutting them off from Wau. They have now run out of food and all types of ammos. Their problem is now not the recapture of Tambura and Maridi, but how to survive. Their GHQs has told them that food and ammos will be parachuted to them in Basia. This convoy is a mission to nowhere and it will certainly be destroyed. The C-in-C and the entire SPLA here warmly pass millions of our heartfelt congratulations to our gallant forces of BSC phase 3 and 4 who are fighting in the Busere-Bo sector and to the population of Tonj, Balanda, Tambura and Yambio for supporting them with food. SPLA Oyee! Victory is certain.

B -Similarly, Beshir's second offensive from Juba to Yei and which involved about (2,000) troops, tanks, heavy artillery and about (100) vehicles has been effectively contained. The enemy managed to reach Yei but after (35) days and after sustaining very heavy casualties on men and materials. The enemy lost (154) KIA and (268) WIA with (15) trucks and two T-62 tanks destroyed. More than (70) percent of the food they were taking to Yei got destroyed by our forces or by rains. Now the forces that were in Yei and the new arrivals are in deep crisis. They have no food and have run out of all types of ammos. They have only one tank operational and most of their vehicles are off road. The enemy GHQs ordered the old forces that were in Yei relieved to return to Juba while the new convoy take their place to defend Yei and go out to recapture Morobo and Kaya. Meanwhile our forces around Yei are shelling them daily with continuous raids, and both sets of enemy forces in Yei, the old and new, have notified Juba and GHQs that they all want to evacuate Yei for Juba. The C-in-C and the entire SPLA here pass millions of warm heartfelt congratulations to our gallant forces of BSC phase 3, sectors one and two, that fought the enemy convoy between Juba and Yei and that are now containing and hammering on the enemy inside Yei town. With Beshir's two rainy season offensives from Wau and Juba contained, victory is certain. SPLA Oyee! Omer and his scum will soon see what awaits them.

7. Apart from the above military victories, the other item any of you must be asking and of which you must be very concerned is the silence of Radio SPLA. I am happy to inform all of you that we have raised the necessary funds to purchase a powerful radio broadcasting station of our own that will cover the whole Sudan and beyond. Four (4) hours instead of two (2) hours radio RT transmission. The money for this is already in our hand and the delay is only in processing the purchase, transport of the equipment and installation. Given these technical factors, I cannot say exactly when we will start the actual broadcasting but most certainly much before the end of this year. As you can see,

when we start broadcasting soon, our situation with respect to Radio SPLA will be (100) percent our own and we will double the time of broadcasting. RADIO SPLA Oyee!

8. Lastly, I am happy to inform you that we have been able to acquire more ammos than at any other one time before. This includes (20) millions rounds of AKM ammos plus good quantities of shells: 60-mm, 82-mm, 120-mm, RPG-7, BM 122-mm, Howitzer, anti-tanks and anti-personnel mines. We have also raised the necessary funds to transport by air all these ammos to the field. As I write, (15) millions rounds of AKM has already reached and the rest is on the way. There should, therefore, be no excuse that we have no ammos because of the fall of Mengistu. Our ammos situation is actually better (much better). What we need now is more manpower and for the majority of SPLA forces to converge now on a decisive objective, and with more commitment, more dedication, so that we, like the guerrillas in Museveni's Uganda, Eritrea, Ethiopia, Somalia and Chad achieve a decisive military victory. All soldiers are to move according to orders from their Cdrs immediately beginning from today 18/7/91 to that objective! Victory is certain and near. SPLA Oyee!

9. All Cdrs at all levels to brief all under them of the contents and spirit of the above (as we have no Radio SPLA at present). Keep the morale and your necks high, we will win. Victory is certain. Greetings and regards. Millions of congratulations. SPLA Oyee! SPLA Oyee!

- FLASH -
Reg by/ Lt John Peter Wal
24/7/91

The National Democratic Alliance (NDA)

A Agreement of alliance between SPLM/SPLA and UMMA PARTY, January 29, 1990.

B Joint SPLM/SPLA - UMMA Party Communique, February 22, 1990.

C Position of the SPLM/SPLA on the charter of the National Democratic Alliance March 1990.

AGREEMEMT OF ALLIANCE BETWEEN SPLM/SPLA AND UMMA PARTY

Inspired by the suffering of the Sudanese people and present political, economic and exploding security crisis which our beloved country has lived in since 30th June, 1989, the SPLM/SPLA and the UMMA party succeeded to make political and military strategic alliance and agreed on the following programme of action:-

1. Basically the SPLM/SPLA agreed to the Charter and Programme of National Democratic Alliance (NDA) with the right of reservation that the details of the Charter and programme which were worked out in it's absence will be subject to necessary revision and rectification. Equally the two parties agreed to the importance of forming political bureau of NDA and to take upon themselves to convince the other signatories to the charter and Programme of NDA to come for a meeting on a date and venue to be agreed upon by SPLM/SPLA and the UMMA Party.

2. To topple the Muslim brothers Military Junta in Khartoum.

3. To bring about the democratic system in the Sudan.

4. To bring about peaceful settlement to the present conflict in Sudan, to convene national constitutional conference on the basis of Koka Dam and November 16th 1988 Peace Agreement and to rewrite the constitution of the Sudan.

5. To put forward Programme of Economic Reform.

6. To restructure the Sudanese army and all Security organs taking into account the following factors
   (a) to form balanced army from regional and ethnic point of view.

   (b) to incorporate into the new army those who are willing to join the army from the SPLM/SPLA and what is known now as tribal militias. This new army is to be established with the primary aim to defend the new democratic system.

7. The SPLM/SPLA in principle agreed to the suggestion of the UMMA Party of making short-cut to the present war by taking Power in Khartoum provided that the plan and the details of such a plan will be agreed upon before hand by all the parties involved.

8. The two parties agreed to bring to an end the hostilities between SPLM/SPLA and the tribal militias currently fighting along side with the government army. And that the UMMA Party will take responsibility to influence these tribal militias to join the alliance of UMMA Party and SPLM/SPLA and to join their ranks to fight their common enemy. To achieve this objective practically the agreement have to be reached in the field between the representatives of UMMA Party and SPLM/SPLA.

9. The two Parties agreed to follow the foreign Policy of non-alliance in the future, with special relationship with Libya, Ethiopia, Egypt, Uganda and other neighbours. In the light of the above principle, close and special relations will be gradually developed with

our brothers in Jamahiriya with ultimate aim of establishing unity between the two countries in the future on the basis of mutual respect and equality.

10.   The two parties are committed to maintain the relations and co-operation beyond the immediate tasks spelt out in the Programme.

The agreement was reached January 29th 1990 between SPLM/SPLA and UMMA Party delegations consisting of the following:

1. CDR James Wani Igga - Alternate member of SPLM/SPLA Political Military High Command and Leader of SPLM Delegation

2. CDR. Lual Diingwol - Alternate member of SPLM/ SPLA Political Military High Command and member of SPLM delegation.

3. CAPT. Mario Muor Muor - Member of SPLM/SPLA delegation and Secretary

4. Sayed Mubarak El Fadil El Mahdi – Representative of Umma Party Leadership.

Signed by:

(Cdr. James Wani Igga)   (Sayed Mubarak El Fadil El Mahdi)
Alternate Member of SPLM/   Member of Political Bureau and
SPLA Political-Military   Representative of Umma Party
High Command and Leader   Leadership
Of SPLM/SPLA Delegation

JOINT SPLM/SPLA - UMMA PARTY COMMUNIQUE

22/2/1990

After a careful study of the Charter and Programme of the National Democratic Alliance (NDA) signed on 31st. Oct. 1989 by the Confederation of the Trade Unions, Representatives of the regular forces and political parties, the SPLM/SPLA has agreed to the principles of the Charter with the reservation that it has the right to revise and/or amend the details of the Charter and programme which were worked out in its absence in a meeting of the signatories to the Charter.

Further to its endorsement of the Charter of the NDA; the SPLM/SPLA and Umma Party held a series of lengthy meetings after which both of them reached an agreement on the basic challenges and problems facing our beloved country. The essence of this agreement is the establishment of permanent peace, stability and national unity under a multi-party democratic system which will endeavour to realise the aspirations and goals of our toiling masses in political, economic and social fields. To achieve this objective, the two parties agreed to tirelessly work together with fellow brothers in the NDA to accelerate the removal of the military dictatorship of the Muslim Brothers in Khartoum, the holding of the Constitutional Conference and the establishment of the democratic government with the active participation of all the members of NDA.

The great history of the Sudan indicates that the dictatorship has failed our people more than enough; and it is time now for the real exercise of democracy. In the light of this understanding and based on the above agreement, the Umma Party and SPLM/SPLA call on the Sudanese Armed Forces to disassociate themselves from the NIF and its so-called Council of National Salvation and to stop them from using the Sudanese National Army to implement by force their malicious, evil and obsolete ideas which can only lead to the disintegration of the country. We urge our brothers in the armed forces that there is no justification for bloodshed and continuous war after the agreement of all the Sudanese popular forces and trade unions to bring to an end the war and establish a democratic system in the Sudan. It is only the NIF and its Military Council that stands against the unanimous agreement of the NDA for peace, stability and national unity. We, therefore, call on the armed forces to rebel against the Muslim Brothers military dictatorship and to side with the Sudanese masses represented in the NDA.

The Umma Party in compliance with the agreement calls on all tribal militias in Kordofan, Darfur and other parts of the country to immediately halt hostilities against the SPLA and turn their guns against the common enemy.

The SPLM/SPLA on its part hereby orders its Field Commanders to cease hostilities against and to cooperate with the above mentioned tribal militias to fight the common enemy. The SPLM/SPLA has also ordered its supporters in the army to do their part in the implementation of this agreement.

The two parties hereby call for a meeting of the General Assembly of NDA as soon as possible so as to work out the details of the Charter that will incorporate the views of the SPLM/SPLA and to discuss and agree on the necessary steps to be taken in order to put its provisions into effect.

In conclusion, we salute the struggle of the Sudanese people against the dictatorship of Muslim Brothers, we also salute all the political detainees.

Long live the unity of the Sudanese people.

Signed by:

(Sayed Mubarak El Fadil El Mahdi)
Member Of Political Bureau and
Representative of UMMA Party

(Cdr. Lual Diing Wol)
Alternate Member Of SPLM/
SPLA Political-Military High Command
and Representative of SPLM/SPLA

POSITION OF THE SPLM/SPLA ON THE CHARTER
OF THE NATIONAL DEMOCRATIC ALLIANCE.

Preamble

Since the exit of the colonial powers, our country has continued to experience a deep political crisis in the form of the civil war which has been raging for more than a quarter of a century and the chronic political instability which accompanied all the successive civil and military regimes. Therefore, it was hardly surprising that all the governments that came and went failed to resolve the basic problems facing our people and to open up prospects for development, for there can be no development without stability and there can be no stability without a comprehensive national consensus on the basic problems.

In spite of all the above, the period following the fall of the May regime has witnessed the emergence of a new dawn for a purposeful national action to build a stable New Sudan. Through the continuous efforts and hard work in which the SPLM/A was involved together with the various political and trade union forces before and after the April 1985 uprising, it was possible to reach agreement on several principles which guide the common national work on the way to peace. On the top of these principles is the adoption of dialogue rather than war, political, cultural and religious multiplicity rather than hegemony and democracy rather than one-man rule or tyranny be it civil or military.

The highest expressions of this comprehensive political consensus were the Koka Dam Agreement signed on March 26, 1986 and the Sudanese Peace Initiative signed on November 16, 1988. If this framework were allowed to reach its logical conclusion, Sudan would have realized stability and peace long time ago. However, the repeated manoeuvres to frustrate peace efforts, especially the conspiracies of the NIF, led to the continuation of war and destruction and consequently to the economic, political and administrative collapse. This group was consistent with itself and its obstruction of peace efforts because the attainment of a negotiated peaceful settlement based on political tolerance and respect of diversity is contrary to its fascist outlook in imposing its political thought under the guise of religion. It would also lead to its demise as a political force as it is incapable of operation within a multiparty democratic system. The coup d'etat which took place on June 30, 1989 was the last ring in that NIF conspiracy.

Therefore, it was not unexpected that the SPLM/A declared its position against that coup and its policies from the first month of its taking place. This stems from the SPLM/A's position as part and parcel of the national political forces opposed to military dictatorships.

In the same vein, the Movement welcomed the birth of the National Democratic Alliance (NDA) and declared its support of the basic principles contained in the Charter adopted by the NDA without reservation except in relation to high-lighting some of the principles, clarification of some details or reaffirmation of some methods of operation. In this the Movements position was based on the following facts;

Firstly: The experience of the SPLM/A in the struggle and its special nature. This demands reaffirmation of these principles so that the position of the Movement on the basic problems is unambiguous.

Secondly: The Movement appreciates the pressing conditions under which the Charter was formulated. Such conditions did not allow the political forces ample time to deal with some problems with the desired scrutiny and broad consultation.

Thirdly: The setbacks that accompanied popular uprisings especially in October 1964 and April 1985 for lack of clarity in some provisions of their Charters particularly when there was no joint vision on programmes of action or agreement on the mechanisms of carrying them out. Thus, the points the Movement strives to clarify represent an addition to and not subtraction from that Charter. In doing so, the Movement would like to affirm its strategic alliance with the forces of the NDA and throws into it its full moral and material weight and its political and military experience in the struggle. Therefore the Movement is keen from the outset to see that there are no loopholes which could be exploited by destructive elements, opportunists and the enemies of peace and stability, and also to close the door against all the wrong elements that have enjoyed hijacking the victories of our people after every popular Uprising.

On the basis of the above, the SPLM/A would like to present the following principles and facts about some issues raised in the Charter in the order they were raised therein. Apart from these, the Movement reiterates its full agreement with the other provisions of the Charter

The Programme of Daily Struggle
Firstly: Since the struggle for the attainment of peace is necessary under all conditions and more so under a dictatorship, the SPLM/SPLA believes that it is only logical that the first objective of the NDA should be the tireless search for peace and to fight all tendencies towards turning the present war in Sudan into a religious and racial one.

Secondly: The statement of the means of the struggle in the way it was done under para 5 rules out the armed struggle which represents an important dimension in the struggle of the Movement. Hence, the Movement affirms that the armed struggle is part and parcel of the popular struggle to overthrow the military dictatorship and to safeguard democracy.

System of Rule
Firstly: The SPLM/A agrees to the necessity of establishing an interim rule for a suitable period (five years) within which time the revolutionary authority could deal with the inherited problems that require effective revolutionary solutions so that the civil democratic rule that will follow is based on a solid and firm foundation. However, the Movement sees the need to distinguish between the duties assigned to this government on the basis of importance. The Movement also stresses the need to specify the duties of that authority in that period so that the programme avoids generalities that could be construed to mean the lack of seriousness such as the reference to stamping out illiteracy during the interim period.

The following should be at the top of the priorities at the interim period.

A- The Constitutional Conference - The Movement believes that there should be agreement to hold it within six months from the time the interim government was formed, and that the conference should complete its work within six months from its first sitting.

B . The Military Situation - In this respect, the Movement believes that it is necessary to agree from the very beginning on a flexible arrangement to deal with the reality of having two armies bearing in mind that the final solution to this problem will be achieved through the restructuring of power and its institutions including the armed forces and will be agreed upon in the Constitutional Conference.

Secondly: Whereas the Movement agrees to the suggested form of rule, it does not see any justification for the reference that one member of the Spreme Council be from the Southern region. Time has come to do away both in form and content, with the old moulds. The Movement also sees it necessary that the system of rotating Chairmanship of the Supreme Council be reintroduced. This is dictated by the sensitive nature of the interim period.

Thirdly: In spite of its recognition of the fact that there is need to establish Legislative and Executive Councils in the regions, the SPLM/A believes that the economic conditions of Sudan should be taken into account in forming these councils. It also considers the reference to governing the Southern Region on the basis of the Regional Self Government Act as out of place. This is not only because such a reference is guided by the old moulds that divide Sudan into South and North but because the Regional Self Government Act itself is a law governed by its provisions which include the provision that its institutions be freely elected rather than be appointed.

Fourthly: On the formation of the National Council, the Movement believes on the necessity of a prior agreement on the objective bases that determine which political party is entitled to take part. The SPLM/A also believes that there should be prior agreement on the representation of the two wings of the Movement (the political and the military) in that council.

Functions of the Interim Period

This chapter in the Charter deals with the principles, which will guide the work of the interim authority. It also contains broad outlines of the programme of that authority. On the basis of the Movement's analysis of the reality of the Sudanese society especially the countryside which has been neglected all through the previous regimes to the extent that it became a victim of famine in the mid-eighties, the SPLM/A believes that any solution to the chronic Sudanese crisis must first and foremost strive to stop the economic and environmental decay of the countryside and concentrate on policies which help in pulling out the countryside from its present state of collapse. It must be clear from the start that such policies will certainly have an impact on the ways of life in the most affluent areas. Therefore, it is imperative to put this into consideration when planning the national salvation programmes. This chapter also discusses issues concerned with safeguarding the government, purging the political work of malpractices, and the rectification of the performance of the state internally and externally. Hence, it is necessary to throw some light on these problems. They are:

Basic Freedoms:

Any provision on the basic rights must start with the right to life. This is a natural right which comes before any other right. The rights of the hungry in the countryside come before the freedom of association and expression, especially that the person who does not have something to eat is not in control of his fate. Nonetheless the Movement affirms its commitment to the defence of all the basic rights, their inclusion into the constitutional documents and protection in the laws. This is both internally and externally through the inclusion of these rights into the regional and international documents.

The Armed Forces:
In the SPLM/A's view, the national nature of the Armed Forces should not be limited to talking about keeping it out of partisan politics. The position of the Movement on this matter is that the Armed Forces must be restructured not only because it is the combative arm of the state that the Movement would like restructured but also to agree on a national formula on its composition and organization in order to defend the civil democratic authority against the adventures of some military officers.

Thus, the reference in the Charter to the Armed Forces in the context of discussing the national nature of mass media suggests an underrating of the issue of Armed Forces and the state. As mentioned before, this final formula on the position of the Armed Forces will be arrived at within the framework of the National Constitutional Conference. However, the interim government is called upon to introduce means that will tackle the military and security matters in the light of the presence of two armies carrying arms within the period that precedes agreement on the issue in the National Constitutional Conference.

Foreign Policy:
Whereas it supports all the principles mentioned under para 1(F), the Movement considers these principles need to be detailed in terms of priorities, especially that foreign policy is one of the areas that is prone to political manoeuvrings. Therefore, the Movement believes that the functions of foreign policy in terms of programmes during the interim period should be:
I   The use of diplomacy for the reconstruction and rehabilitation of Sudan.

2. To set a permanent framework to the relationship with Egypt, Libya, Ethiopia and the countries of the Nile Valley through agreements and principles that seek regional integration. This is because the neighbouring countries are the starting point in any regional integration especially with those countries where the historical ties, geographical facts and the immanent common interests demand to give those relations the highest priority.

3. Reactivation of the role of Sudan in the regional Arab and African organizations to play a more effective role especially on the issue of liberation and economic co-operation and to strive to concretize the programmes of this co-operation which Sudan's commitment to it in its internal policies and institutions has just been in form only. On the other hand, to strive to use the special position of Sudan within these two groupings that makes it more qualified than any other to support the organic unity between them in order to boost the Arab-African solidarity.

4. Reactivation of the role of Sudan in the international organizations and the non-aligned movement in light of the new changes in the world. In this it is still necessary to introduce new methods for diplomatic struggle between the third world countries in order to create a new world economic order as a substitute to the present system of

hegemony. and in order to step up co-operation between the countries of the South as an outside reflection of self-reliance.

5. So as not to have different interpretations to the provisions of para 2(B), the SPLM/A affirms that the agreements to which this provision applies are those mentioned after the Koka Dam Declaration, the Sudanese Peace Initiative and any other similar agreements that may be concluded in absence or without the agreement of the legislative organs which express the will of the nation.

Democracy:
To avoid misinterpretation, the Movement considers it necessary to tie up the provisions of para 2 (C) and (D) on the freedom of political and media activity and the contents of para 7 on the condemnation of corrupt practices under democratic regimes. One reason for the demise of democracy in Sudan is the irresponsibility and lack of concern displayed by some in the exercise of freedom, which emptied it from its contents. Democracy can only be protected by putting in place political and professional guidelines to govern the practice of partisan politics and the media and trade unions work. The following are among the guidelines envisaged:

A To determine the sources of financing of the political parties and to subject their budgets to general auditing.

B To adopt Charters for the media and trade unions work the violation of which could lead to disqualification of the violator from the professional practice.

C Agreement on special requirements which must obtain in any person interested to take part in the government during the interim period such as those mentioned at the conclusion of the Charter.

D To proscribe any organization which is based on religion, region or race.

The Movement considers also that the reference to the Elections Law and the representation of the Modern Forces as came under para 8 should be understood to mean reaffirmation of the principle of widening democratic participation in a way that will open opportunities for real representation of all the forces and groups which had remained politically marginalized. These include the workers, farmers, women and the professionals.

The Economy:
The Movement agrees with the general outlook of the economic reform programme as contained in the Charter. However, and on the basis of the above, it is necessary to reaffirm certain basic accepted principles. On the top of these is the principle of self-reliance, which should be the guiding principle in all our economic plans. Self-reliance has reflections on the policies of consumption, production and the priorities of energy and transport. All these must find expression in the body of the programme. Self-reliance as of necessity demands that due attention be paid to the rural production base which would reaffirm that top priority be given to the issue of arresting the collapse of the rural economy and the stoppage of the consequences of such collapse in towns and to lay the

foundation for programmes that will promote the rural manpower especially the women who represent a very important force in relation to labour and production.

Generally, the proposed economic programme is full of generalities and if adopted as it is for an interim period which is not more than five years would suggest, as pointed out earlier, lack of seriousness. Hence, the Movement believes that in this sensitive area, the interim government be charged with specific duties. As such there should be joint action before the interim period that will determine these duties and priorities. For example, the Movement points to the following:

A - The reconstruction of the areas directly affected by the war and the rehabilitation of the infrastructure, the agricultural and industrial projects and public services which collapsed as a result of neglect, erosion, lack of maintenance or the pressures of forced migration.

B- To relieve the difficult living conditions and meeting the basic requirements by adopting programmes that are based on self-reliance accompanied by controlling consumption and tightening expenditure starting from the state and its institutions.

C- On the problems of education and health, the interim authority will do well if it concentrates its efforts and succeeds in the rehabilitation of the present educational and curative health institutions coupled with soliciting external assistance to combat the endemic diseases especially those which started to spread again after having been brought under control.

The programme should also strive to reactivate preventive health programmes in the towns and countryside with special attention being paid to women and children.

D Comprehensive revision of the general expenditure in order to control it. This includes reviewing the status of public service and public institutions. This matter is not indicated in para 6 despite the fact that the interim government, given its broad base, is the most capable to undertake this revision. Therefore, the interim government should aim at reviewing the performance of the public service and institutions both qualitatively and quantitatively in order to improve performance, rehabilitation of manpower and directing its excess in government departments to productive employment. This fact also applies to the Armed Forces and other regular forces.

The Movement believes that the restructuring of these institutions must be made within a comprehensive evaluation of the real needs of Sudan in the areas of security and defence and the country's own ability to shoulder the responsibilities resulting from this.

E- Although it supports the necessity to severely punish those who have corrupted the banking system under the slogan of the Islamization of the economy, the SPLM/A does not consider that economic corruption was only limited to the above group as is referred to under paras 2(C) and 4(C). Hence, the Movement would like the formation of qualified committees in order to review all the activities and suspicious deals that were concluded under the previous regimes and especially in the fields of foreign trade, tax evasion, direct and indirect smuggling and speculation in real estate.

The Movement also considers that the reference made under para 4(C) on the dominant role of the Central Bank on the banking policies should only mean the domination of the Central Bank on the performance of the bank and not on the policies that direct the work of these banks. These policies will always remain one of the responsibilities of the executive authority.

CONCLUSION
The SPLM/A in presenting these clarifications on the Charter, is doing so from the stand point that it is a part of the National Democratic Alliance motivated by the miserable state our country is now in because of the war, wrong policies, and misrule. The Movement is determined that the people's victory cannot again be lost because of negligence and political manoeuvrings.

The American Initiative 1990

A   The Original Proposal.

B   Comments on the Proposal.

C   SPLM/SPLA's response to the proposal.

JOINT DECLARATION

(DRAFT)

AGREEMENT ON A FRAMEWORK FOR THE PEACEFUL SETTLEMENT OF SUDAN'S INTERNAL CONFLICT

A. BASIC PRINCIPLES FOR THE SETTLEMENT
1. Sudan will remain united in a single nation.
2. There will be a federal system of government.
3. The political system will be a democracy.
4. The present conflict will be demilitarised with a disengagement of forces under the supervision of international monitors.
5. Displaced Sudanese will be assisted with voluntary return to their homes.
6. Highest priority will be given to co-operation in the transport and delivery of relief supplies to the victims of drought, famine, and war.

THE PROCESS FOR A SETTLEMENT IN THREE PHASES

PHASE ONE:
- Will be completed within 30 days of the signing of the declaration.
- There will be an equitable disengagement of forces governed by the rule that the new disposition of troops can not result in a military disadvantage for either side.
- International monitors will arrive and be deployed.
- There will be an advance agreement on the modalities for forces disengagement which will be an <u>annex</u> to this declaration.
- A joint military commission will be established and will begin discussions on the implementation of disengagement of forces in accordance with the annexed modalities. These discussions will take place in_____.

PHASE TWO:
- Meeting of agreed representatives of relevant political forces will take place to plan a Constitutional Conference. This meeting will take place 45 days from the date of this declaration.

PHASE THREE:
A Constitutional Conference will begin 75 days from the date of this declaration.

Annex: Modalities for Disengagement of Forces in Sudan

- There is a cessation of hostilities and a separation of forces throughout Sudan. Particular steps will be taken to ensure separation of forces in Equatoria, Bahr-el-Ghazal, Kurdofan and Upper Nile provinces.

- All Government forces will be pulled back into defensive garrisons in the south.

- Government forces will be consolidated and "thinned out" so that not more than 20 thousand troops will remain with an appropriate command structure.

- SPLA forces will consolidate below the Bahr-el-Ghazal, Bahr-al-Arab, and Nahr Sobat line.

- Government military aircraft (except for transport planes in agreed air corridors for supply) will not fly below the Bahr-al-Arab line.

- Areas in Kurdofan province contested by SPLA forces will be "demilitarized".

- Areas of Blue Nile which are contested will also be "demilitarized".

- Any town held in part by both sides will be evacuated by both sides for a distance of 25 kms around.

- SPLA forces will pull back a minimum distance of 25 kms from Government controlled defensive garrisons. In areas where the existing defensive perimeter exceeds this, the SPLA will not advance.

- Forces of both sides can continue to be supplied non-lethal items: food, fuel, etc

- Each Government garrison will have an agreed "cordon sanitaire" supply route. The SPLA can designate an equal number of garrison towns to which controlled supply routes will be established.

- There will be a call for an appropriate African observer force.

- To facilitate effective observation and monitoring by the international group, which is in the interest of both parties, their respective forces should be assembled in larger units in identifiable and accessible places to the maximum extent possible.

- This force will monitor all resupply routes, areas designated demilitarized as well as place monitors at all headquarters battalion size and above. The monitors will also be stationed at any location they deem necessary to ensure the peace.

- In areas of known "bandit' activity either a Government or an SPLA force will be designated to police the area accompanied by observers.

- As soon as disengagement is complete civilian governors and senior administrators will be appointed in the three southern provinces, to take charge of existing civilian administration which will remain in place. Persons chosen to fill these positions will be acceptable to both sides.

- Talks on implementation of the above will begin immediately at the working level, followed in the near future by political level discussions about a federal system and the other basic issues in the Sudan civil conflict.

- A joint Military Commission will be established with a series of local subcommittees. It will begin discussions immediately on the details of implementation of this annex.

Comments On The Proposed

'AGREEMENT ON A FRAMEWORK FOR THE PEACEFUL SETTLEMENT OF SUDAN'S INTERNAL CONFLICT'

1. The proposal is made up of two components: The political and the military. The two are separated with the latter appearing as an annex.

2. The political component is made up of two parts and is the draft joint Declaration. The points are reasonable and it can be adopted as it stands.

3. The military component (i.e., the annex) raises a number of fundamental questions. In fact, it is an acceptance of a cease-fire in which the government is conceding nothing. On the contrary, the SPLA stands to lose as follows: -

a) Withdrawal from areas north of the line made up by Bahr-el-Ghazal, Bahr-el-Arab and Sobat rivers;
b) Withdrawal from Kordofan and Blue Nile Provinces;
c) Distancing itself to beyond 25 km radius from towns now under its siege.

4. on the political front the Annex secures to the Junta the holding of the Constitutional Conference without implementing any of the pre-requisites of the Koka Dam Declaration and the November peace Agreement. A great victory indeed.

5. The only government 'concession' to the SPLA is the implied consultation with it on the choice of civilian governors and senior administrators in the three Southern provinces as these 'will be acceptable to both sides'.

6. Recommendations:

We stick to the original proposal (Deng & Obasanjo). This can be achieved, within the present proposal, as follows:-

a) Endorsing the draft Joint Declaration, i.e., the political component; and
b) Proposing a new Annex (i.e., the military component) to go with it in place of the one suggested.

7. An amendment of the suggested annex is attached as a possible proposal from our side.

ANNEX: MODALITIES FOR CONSTRUCTIVE DISENGAGEMENT OF FORCES IN SUDAN.

1. There shall be an immediate cease-fire to facilitate the constructive disengagement of forces throughout Sudan.

2. All government forces will be disengaged to North of the 13th parallel.

3. Government military aircraft (except for transport planes in agreed air corridors for supply) will not fly below the 13th parallel.

4. There will be an appropriate African observer force to be agreed upon by the two sides.

5. This force will monitor all arrangements for the constructive disengagement of the forces as contained in this document. The monitors will be stationed at any location they deem necessary to ensure the peace.

6. In areas of known 'bandit' activity the respective government or SPLA force will be designated to police the area accompanied by observers.

7. The security of the national capital shall be the responsibility of the two armies.

8. Concurrent with the commencement of the disengagement, the SPLM/SPLA will appoint civilian governors and other administrators to take charge of civilian administration in the areas of its presence. Persons to fill the positions will be chosen by the SPLM/SPLA from amongst competent Sudanese who may or may not be members of the Movement and who may be inside or outside the country.

JOINT DECLARATION
(DRAFT)
AGREEMENT ON A FRAMEWORK FOR THE PEACEFUL
SETTLEMENT OF SUDAN'S CONFLICT

A. <u>BASIC PRINCIPLES FOR THE SETTLEMENT</u>

1. Sudan will remain united in a multi-national and multi-religious state. There shall be no discrimination among the citizens on the basis of race, religion, sex or area of origin.

2. There will be a federal system of government.

3. The political system will be a multi-party democracy.

4. The present conflict will be demilitarized with a constructive disengagement of forces under the supervision of international monitors.

5. Displaced Sudanese will be assisted with voluntary return to their homes.

6. Highest priority will be given to co-operation in the transport and delivery of relief supplies to the victims of drought, famine, and war.

B. <u>THE PROCESS FOR A SETTLENENT IN FOUR PHASES</u>:

PHASE ONE:

- Will be completed within 30 days of the signing of the declaration.

- There will be a constructive disengagement of forces in the spirit of Sudan's unity and territorial integrity.

- International monitors agreed upon by both sides will arrive and be deployed.

- There will be an advance agreement on the modalities for forces constructive disengagement which will be an Annex to this declaration.

- A joint Military Commission will be established and will begin discussions on the implementation of the constructive disengagement of forces in accordance with the modalities in the Annex. These discussions will take place in <u>a venue to be agreed</u> upon by both sides.

PHASE TWO:

- Meeting of agreed representatives of relevant political forces will take place to plan the National Constitutional Conference. This meeting will take place 45 days from the date of this declaration.

<u>PHASE THREE</u>:

- The National Constitutional Conference will begin 75 days from the date of this declaration.

<u>PHASE FOUR</u>:

- The formation of a broad-based government to implement the resolutions of the National Constitutional Conference and to hold free general elections.

<u>ANNEX</u>: MODALITIES FOR CONSTRUCTIVE DISENGAGEMENT OF FORCES IN SUDAN.

1. There shall be an immediate cease fire to facilitate the constructive disengagement of forces throughout Sudan.

2. All government forces will be disengaged to north of the 13th parallel.

3. Government military aircraft (except for transport planes in agreed air corridors for supply) will not fly below the 13th parallel.

4. There will be an appropriate African observer force to be agreed upon by the two sides.

5. This force will monitor all arrangements for the constructive disengagement of the forces as contained in this document. The monitors will be stationed at any location they deem necessary to ensure the peace.

6. In areas of known 'bandit' activity the respective government or SPLA force will be designated to police the area accompanied by observers.

7. The security of the national capital shall be the responsibility of the two armies.

8. Concurrent with the commencement of the disengagement, the SPLM/SPLA will appoint civilian governors and other administrators to take charge of civilian administration in the areas of its presence. Persons to fill the positions will be chosen by the SPLM/SPLA from amongst competent Sudanese who may or may not be members of the Movement and who may be inside or outside the country.

BSC Phase II and New Fung Campaign

A- OPERATION ORDER
B - COMMAND, STAFF AND ORGANIZATION

TOP SECRET

The Chairman
Ref. No. OPORDS
Date: March 21, 1990

Operation Order No: BSC/PHASE 2/NFC/01.
References: Sketches, Sudan Maps, Sand Models, Charts.
Time Zone: Sudan Local Time (SLT) is used throughout.

TASK ORGANIZATION: BSC PHASE II/NFC FORCES

(*) 6 TFs of Zajan:	(*)	2 TFs of NFC:
Zajan TF1		New Fung TF1
Zajan TF2		New Fung TF2
Zajan TF3	(*)	3 TFs of Commando:
Zajan TF4		Cmdo TF1
Zajan TF5		Cmdo TF2
Zajan TF6		Cmdo TF3
(*) 8 TFs of NUN:	(*)	3 TFs of Maban:
Abushok TF		Maban TF1
Sobat TF		Maban TF2
Fashoda TF		Gojam TF
Mazlum TF	(*)	4 TFs of Nasir Unity Campaign:
Bilpam/Koryom TF		NUC TF1
Khorfulus TF	NUC TF2	
Daniel Shogi TF	NUC TF3	

(*) Combat Support Command (COMSCOM):

Field Artillery:		AA/GPHMG and Missiles:	
BM-21 MRL	(2)	ZSU-37mm GPHMG	(1)
BM107mm MRL	(3)	ZSU-23mm GPHMG	(3)
105mm Howz	(1)	Cannon 20mm "	(1)
122mm Howz	(3)	14.5mm-4B "	(3)
76mm Gun	(2)	14.5mm-1B "	(6)
B-10 (82mm) ATL	(2)	12.7mm Doshka "	(4)
SPG-9 ATL	(7)	Strella M-2 Trigger	(3)
120mm Mortar	(8)	Strella M-2 Missiles	(18)
81mm Mortar	(21) – with Ivory.		
82mm Mortars	(15) – with Ivory.		

(*)   Sector Demarcation

The BSC Phase II/NFC theatre of operations will be divided into six sectors as follows:
1.   SECTOR I: Southern NUN, comprises Malakal and outstations, E/Bank.
2.   SECTOR II: Northern NUN, E/Bank, Melut to Gerger and beyond.

3. SECTOR III: Northern NUN, W/Bank, Tonga/Kodok Districts and beyond.
4. SECTOR IV: Southern SBN, from Yabus/Chali/Kurmuk/Qeissan and outskirts.
5. SECTOR V: Northern SBN: Ingessena Hills, Dendaru, Damazine, Projects.
6. SECTOR VI: Intersection of the five sectors: Maban and Ulu Garrisons.

2. <u>SITUATION:</u>

a. Brigadier Omer el Beshir took over power on 30/6/1990 with the avowed aim to achieve military victory over the SPLA, and to establish an Islamic Arab state and work for full Arab unity beginning with Sudan, Libya and Egypt. In pursuit of this aim, the Junta acquired lots of war material and launched a massive dry season military offensive beginning in October, 1989. The Junta vowed to wipe out the SPLA within two months, and when this was not possible they said they would certainly achieve this by the end of the dry season, that is, by the end of May, 1990, after which, they say, they would then negotiate from a position of strength to dictate terms from a position of strength.

b. The enemy had planned six major campaigns/missions to be executed and accomplished before 31/5/1990. These are:
(1) To clear the SPLA out of Southern Blue Nile.
(2) To clear the SPLA out from Western Equatoria.
(3) To drive the SPLA out from Southern Kordofan.
(4) To recapture all SPLA held garrisons East of the Nile and South of the Sobat River.
(5) To recapture Yirol and Shambe, and hence cut our logistics lines to Bahr el Ghazal, Bentiu and Southern Kordofan.
(6) To open up the River Nile route from Renk to Juba.

c. The enemy (till now) has failed to achieve any of the above, except the first mission. The enemy launched a surprise and massive broad-based attack against our forces of the 2nd Front, Southern Blue Nile (NFC), at the beginning of January, and quickly overran all our positions in Kurmuk area including rear positions inside Ethiopia at Katewarage, Agumbella, Qeissan and Training Centre as well as overunning the Refugee Camp at Longkwei, where they dispersed our Uduk refugees. The enemy subsequently captured and occupied Asosa, Beigi and Bambesi Garrisons of the Ethiopian army.

d. Exploiting their victory, the enemy pushed southwards from Kurmuk and recaptured Deim Mansur, Ora, Chali and Yabus and reinforced their Garrison at Maban. After this consolidation the enemy intends to clear out SPLA presence in the Maban area and to occupy Daga Post, and, possibly, to advance on Nasir and Jekou with an ultimate aim to overrun and disperse Itang and Panyidu Refugee camps as they did to Longkwei. In this event another force would come from Malakal to converge with the one from Maban.

e. Enemy logistics and reinforcements for SECTORS IV and VI come from Damazine by road through the Ingessina Hills. This route is open and devoid of any SPLA presence, and the enemy can move from Damazine to Kurmuk in matter of hours and proceed to Chali, Yabus or Maban the following day.

f. SPLA presence in the BSC Phase 2 area (SECTORS II and III) is very thin. This area has been devastated by enemy tribal militias, other bandits and natural disasters. As a result it has been difficult for the SPLA to maintain any effective presence in this area. The enemy logistics route Kosti/Renk/ Malakal has thus been quite open and safe for the enemy both by river and by land, on both East and West banks of the Nile.

g. The large enemy convoy, the so-called "Jundi al-waton al-Wahid" was able to reach Malakal early this year without a fight. A fleet of Nile barges (boats) also reached with little resistance. Last month a small convoy of 4 trucks, 1 APC and 192 men conducted what they called mopping up operations between Renk and Malakal burning villages of innocent civilians. Enemy morale and confidence is so high in the BSC Phase 2 area that they have declared NUN free of rebels, and they plan to start what they call development projects and resettlement of displaced southerners between Renk and Melut.

h. With the Renk/Malakal route secure, the next enemy objective from Malakal is to advance on Nasir and Jekou to capture them and to advance through the Canal Mouth southwards to try to recapture the areas of BSC Phase 1, East of the Nile and South of the Sobat.

i. On its side the SPLA must deny the enemy use of the Renk/Malakal road and, River contain the enemy inside Malakal so that they are unable to advance Eastwards to Nasir nor Southwards through the Canal Mouth, thus enabling BSC Phase 1 forces to capture Canal Mouth and Pam Zeraf. The SPLA must also deny the enemy use of the Damazine/Kurmuk road as well as to regain lost ground of the NFC in Southern Blue Nile.

j Generally, SPLA operations between Malakal/Renk, Kurmuk/Damazine and northwards to the Central Sudan agricultural projects are very sensitive. This is the soft belly of the enemy. Indeed the Gezira and the Roseires Dam are the backbone of the Sudanese economy. Effective SPLA military operations iin this area could precipitate immediate demise of the Junta as well as facilitate capture of the rest of War Zone One. Indeed, we have reached a phase in the war when it is very urgent that we take guerrilla warfare into the Gezira, the National capital Khartoum and elsewhere in the North.

3. MISSIONS:

The following 7 missions for BSC Phase 2/NFC forces have been identified for execution and accompli-shment over the next 100 days, ending 30/6/1990.

a. MISSION SPARK 1: Artillery bombardment of Malakal and deliberate raids into the town to pin down Malakal and capture its outstations, as well as eventually to capture Malakal itself.

b. MISSION SPARK 2: Capture of Jelhak and occupation and fortification of the Island south of it to effectively close the River route and to use this firm base as gateway to Renk and northwards into the agricultural projects of Central Sudan, as well as to capture Melut/Renk.

c. MISSION SPARK 3: Capture of Kodok, Kaka and Wadekona and blockage of enemy routes through Abujebeha and other routes into west Bank.

d. MISSION SPARK 4: Capture of Yabus, Chali, Kurmuk, Qeissan and their outskirts and to re-establish SPLA effective presence and administration in Southern Blue Nile and in Asosa Region, re-establish Longkwei Refugee camp and SPLA rear bases, including the training centre.

e. MISSION SPARK 5: Occupation of the Ingessina Hills to effectively close the Damazine/Kurmuk road and to conduct guerrilla warfare to Damazine/Roseires and northwards into the Gezira.

f. MISSION SPARK 6: Capture of Maban and Ulu to facilitate Missions SPARK 4 and SPARK 5 and to establish SPLA administration in that area.

g. MISSION SPARK 7: Recruitment of a total of at least 20,000 recruits by all the missions, and especially by SPARK 4, SPARK 5 and SPARK 2 that are each to recruit at least 5,000 recruits.

4. EXECUTION.
a) Concept of Operation: The mode of operation will be mixed, combining classical guerrilla and conventional warfare as and when appropriate, using to the maximum the principles of speed, surprise, flexibility and quick resolution, and allowing full initiative to sector and unit commanders. The missions are designed so that they are mutually supportive of each other. Guerrilla units will be infiltrated to harrass and disrupt the enemy rear, while the bulk of the forces capture his forward positions. Details of manoeuvre and fire support for a battle will be co-ordinated with the next higher HQs echelon.

b. Detailed Tasks:
(1) Mission SPARK 1 will be accomplished by 3 NUN TFs and 4 NUC TFs. COMSCOM elements, including one BM-21 and one coy of Combat Engineers, will be attached. Two TFs of COMMANDO will be on call.

(2) Mission SPARK 2 will be accomplished by 2 Zajan TFs and 5 NUN TFs. COMSCOM elements, including one BM-107mm and one coy of Combat Engineers, will be attached.

(3) Mission SPARK 3 will be accomplished by 2 NUC TFs and any other scattered forces that may be regrouped in the area. Priority of reinforcements to SPARK 3.

(4) Missions SPARK 4, SPARK 5 and SPARK 6 will be accomplished by 4 Zajan TFs, 2 NFC TFs and 3 Maban TFs. COMSCOM elements including one BM-21 and one copy of Combat Engineers, will be attached. Missions SPARK 4, SPARK 5 and SPARK 6 will initially be under combined (intersection) command until the fall of Maban and Ulu.

(5) Mission SPARK 5 will he accomplished by 2 TFs released from Para 4b(4) above after the fall of Maban and Ulu. This, of course, excludes guerrilla units that may be deployed here before the fall of Maban and Ulu.

(6) Mission SPARK 6 is as in Para 4b(4) above. Two Maban TFs will remain to secure Maban and Ulu, while the rest of the forces continue on to Missions SPARK 4 and SPARK 5, as detailed above.

(7) COMMANDO TFs remain in strategic reserve and will be deployed by the BSC Phase 2/NFC commander.

(8) COMSCOM and Combat Engineers are pooled and will be attached and detached by the Campaign commander according to mission or threat.

(9) Other Forces (scattered forces) not in the Task Organization will be regrouped by sector and unit commanders and sent to the rear for re-orientation, reorganization and redeployment by the Campaign HQs.

c. Co-ordinating Instructions:

(1) All radio sets Ru2/2K (where assigned) and Long range (TRC-340, Racal, RU/20A) will remain open for 24 hours throughout the operation during battle.

(2) No looting or banditry activity will be tolerated and commanders will take immediate disciplinary action.

(3) Sector and unit commanders must have own reserves when in battle.

(4) When the assigned mission is to capture an enemy position, there will be no withdrawal or relief from captured trenches (ground). Instead, the captured trenches (ground) will be extended and consolidated until the position is captured.

(5) Sector and unit commanders will have reserve ammos and within reach of the fighting units during any deliberate battle, so that the issue is brought to quick resolution.
(6) The object of battle is to make the other side non-combative. If an enemy soldier is unarmed disarmed or surrenders, he becomes essentially non-combative. Such POWs will be spared and immediately evacuated to the rear HQs at Nasir and Maiwut for processing.

(7) The integrity and dignity of the civil population (their lives, women, properties and honour) must be respected, and any actions to the contrary must be severely and immediately punished.

(8) Random shooting during or after a battle must be avoided. In BSC Phase 1 and Phase 2 and in other situations we have expended huge amounts of ammos after capture of a garrison to express happiness. Happiness will be expressed by other ways, such as singing, etc., and never by firing in the air. We badly need the ammos.

(9) Vehicles are pooled and assigned, attached or detached to missions by the Campaign HQs. We have very few vehicles and much less fuel. Trips unrelated or not significant to mission accomplishment must be avoided, and contrary behaviour will be severely punished.

(10) Each sector command will conduct limited local training within its sector to replenish own forces from weapons of martyrs, wounded heroes and other redundant arms in the sector.

5. ADMINISTRATION AND LOGISTICS (SERVSCOM).

a. Logistics resources will come from external sources and internal contributions. External contacts will be conducted only by the campaign HQs. Internal contributions will be raised by the sector and area CMA's under the overall planning and supervision of SERVSCOM.

b. The CMA's will be responsible for civil administration, political mobilization, services, development, recruitment, etc in their sectors and areas under the overall planning, direction and supervision by SERVSCOM. (See SERVSCOM Annexes).

c. Logistics transport will mainly be by the few trucks. Other means of transport will be investigated and secured. Those include canoes, fulukas, rafts and speed boats which should be secured now before the rains; and in northern areas more use will be made of animals such as camels, horses and donkeys.

d. Sectors and units will be assigned medical personnel. First aid medicines, as available, will be issued to the sectors and units. Serious cases will be transferred to the Campaign rear hospitals where the head of the medical services unit will process them. Sector or unit commanders are not allowed to make medical referals for any officer or soldier to Refugee camps or anywhere else without approval from the Campaign HQs medical department.

e. All levels of command must have registration hooks for all SPLA equipment. Ammos will be given special accountability. Constant checking of ammos issued and expended by each soldier will be done after each battle and during routine checking from time to time to eliminate random shooting and the very bad habit of selling ammos.

f. Sector and unit commanders must keep proper and update records of their personnel strengths, the KIA martyrs, WIA heroes, promotions, punishments, transfers, etc. and furnish the Campaign HQs and GHQ/Records with periodic reports as required. Sectors and independent units will send weekly parade to SERVSCOM/Admin Unit, as well as a monthly strength summary.

g. Local production will be vigorously promoted by the SERVSCOM production unit and the CMA's. There is plenty of fish in the rivers, lakes and swamps, and this can provide substantial protein supplement for our troops. The army must plant large fields for its own consumption to become self-sufficient in food requirements eventually.

6. COMMAND AND SIGNAL:

a. Signals (C.E.W.): All signal communication resources and work will be centralized directly under the BSC/NFC Cdr. The Signal (CEW) Operation Instructions (SOI) are in effect. (See the Signals Annex).

b. Command:
(1) Command and staff relationships are as in the chart in the Annex. (See Annex A: Command, Staff and Organization).
(2) The C-in-C commands all the BSC Phases (1,2 and 3) and the NFC.
(3) The SERVSCOM Chief and the Chief of Combat Operations are delegated command authority in their staff areas whenever the campaign commander, for some reason, becomes inaccessible and in emergencies.
(4) The most senior Sector CDR acts, if, for some reason, the campaign Commander is inaccessible.

7. ANNEXES:

a. Command, Staff and Organization Annex.	f. Medical Annex
b. SERVSCOM Annex.	g. COMSCOM Annex.
c. CMA Annex.	h. Signals Annex.
d. Logistics Annex.	i. Intelligence Annex.
e. Administration Annex.	j. Production Annex

8. DISTRIBUTION COPIES:

c. Campaign Cdr.	g. SERVSCOM Chief.
b. Sector 1 Cdr.	f. Chief of Operations.
d. Sector 2 Cdr.	k. COMSCOM Chief.
a. Sector 3 Cdr.	l. Extra, C-in-C Files.
h. Sector 4 Cdr.	i. Extra, C-in-C Files.
e. Sector 5 Cdr.	j. Extra, C-in-C Files.

9. AUTHENTICATION: (SIGNED)

BSC PHASE 2/NFC CDR. CDR. JOHN GARANG DE MABIOR
PLACE: MAIWUT, SUDAN.
DATE: 21/3/1990.

TOP SECRET
OPORD BSC/PHASE 2/NFC/01 ANNEXES
ANNEX A: COMMAND, STAFF AND ORGANIZATION

I- ORGANIZATION: As in the Chart, attached.

II- OVERALL CAMPAIGN COMMAND: The Chairman/C-in-C, CDR John Garang de Mabior.

III SECTOR COMMANDS:

1. Sector 1 Commander: Cdr. Gordon Kong Chol.
2. Sector 2 Commander: Cdr. Riek Machar Teny.
3. Sector 3 Commander: Cdr. Stephen Dhol Chol.
4. Sector 4 Commander: Cdr. Lam Akol Ajawin
5. Sector 5 Commander: Cdr. Martin Manyiel Ayuel.
6. Sector 6 Commander: A/Cdr. Makuei Deng Majuc (Independent Area Cdr.)

IV- PRINCIPAL STAFFS:

1. Combat Operations:
a. Chief of Combat Operations: A/Cdr. Oyai Deng Ajak.
b. Chief of Intelligence: A/Cdr. Isaac Tut Dhiar.
c. Operations officer: Capt. Nhial Deng Nhial.
d. Intelligence Officer: Capt. Elijah Atem Anyuon.
e. Movements Officer: Capt. Garang Akok Adut.

2. Service Support Command (SERVSCOM):
a. Chief of SERVSCOM: Cdr. Vincent Kuany.
b. Chief/Civil Military Administration (CMA): A/Cdr. Tot Wei.
c. Chief of Logistics: A/Cdr. Philip Ajak Deng.
d. Chief of Administration: Capt Kuereng Akoi Yaak.
e. Medical Officer: Caption Dau Aleer Abit.
f. Transport Officer: Capt. Garang Akok Adut.
g. Production Officer: Under the CMA.

V- SPECIAL COMMANDS:

1. Combat Engineers:
    a. Commander CE: A/Cdr. Tahir Bior Abdhala Ajak.
    b. D/Commander: Capt. Akuoc Jago.
2. Combat Electronics Warfare (CEW):
    a. Commander: A/Cdr. Gier Chuang Aluong.
    b. D/Commander:
3. Commando and HQs Security Forces:
    a. Commander: A/Cdr. James Oath Mai.
    b. D/Cdr. Capt. David Majok Mac.

4. Combat Service Command (COMSCOM):
   a. COMSCOM Cdr: Capt. Gatluak Gai Luoth.
   b. D/Cdr, AD and GPHMG: Capt. Ajak Deng Biar.
   c. D/Cdr, AT Weapons, Capt. Jurkuc Yaak Barac.
   d. D/Cdr, Field Artillery, Capt. David Makuol Ruot.

VI- SPECIAL STAFF:

1. Political Affairs and Secretaries:
   a. Capt. Edward Lino Abiei.
   b. Capt. Mohammed Said Bazara.
2. Aides de Camp and Personal Security:
   a. 1ˢᵗ Lt. Peter Atem Garang.
   b. 1ˢᵗ Lt. Madut Dut Yel.
   c. 1ˢᵗ Lt. Dut Cagai Biar.
3. Personal Physician:
   a. Capt. Dau Aleer Abit.

VII- TASK FORCE (UNIT) COMMANDS:

1. Zajan Task Forces:

a. Zajan TF1 Cdr.	Capt. George Kuac Wieu
" " D/Cdr.	Capt. Peter Yein Bedit.
b. Zajan TF2 Cdr.	Capt. John Duoth Nhial.
" " D/Cdr.	Henry Lam Juc.
c. Zajan TF3 Cdr.	Capt. Samuel Mayik Macar.
" " D/Cdr.	Capt. Garang Ngor Agany.
d. Zajan TF4 Cdr.	Capt. Daniel Ayual Makoi
" " D/Cdr.	Capt. Gatkuoth Hoth Yarhok.
e. Zajan TF5 Cdr.	Capt. Maker Thiong Mal.
" " Cdr.	Capt. Aleer Awan Ciengkuac.
f. Zajan TF6 Cdr.	Capt. Peter Duoth Kuany.
" " D/Cdr.	Capt. George Mut Nyang.

2. New Fung Campaign Task Forces:

a. NFC TF1 Cdr.	Capt. Nyang Chol Dhuor.
" " D/Cdr.	Capt. Isaac Mac Riak.
b. NFC TF2 Cdr.	Capt. Deng Lual Deng.
" " D/Cdr.	Capt. Isaac Makuac Chol.

3. Commando Task Forces:

a. Cmdo TF1 Cdr.	Capt.
" " D/Cdr.	1ˢᵗ Lt Nhial Jok Nhial.
b. Cmdo TF2 Cdr.	Capt.
" " D/Cdr.	1ˢᵗ Lt. Aloor Kuol Deng.
c. Cmdo TF3 Cdr.	Capt.
" " D/Cdr.	Garang Ater Koryom.

d. Cmdo HQ Coy Cdr.   2nd Lt. Abud Stephen Thionkol.
"   " D/Cdr   2nd Lt. Ajak Wuoi Alier.

4. Maban Independent Area Task Forces:
Maban TF1 Cdr.
"   " D/Cdr.
Maban TF2 Cdr.
"   " D/Cdr.
Gojam TF Cdr.
"   " D/Cdr.

5. Nasir Unit Campaign Task Forces:
a. NUC TF1 Commander   Capt.
"   " D/Cdr.   Capt.
b. NUC TF2 Cdr.   Capt.
"   " D/Cdr.   Capt.
c. NUC TF3 Cdr.   Capt.
"   " D/Cdr.   Capt.
d. NUC TF4 Cdr.   Capt.
"   " D/Cdr.   Capt.

6. Northern Upper Nile Task Forces:
a. Abushok TF Cdr.   Capt.
"   " D/Cdr.   Capt.
b. Sobat TF Cdr.   Capt.
"   " D/Cdr.   Capt.
c. Fashoda TF Cdr.   Capt.
"   " D/Cdr.   Capt.
d. Mazlum TF Cdr.   Capt.
"   " D/Cdr.   Capt.
e. Bilpam/Koryom TF Cdr.   Capt.
"   "D/Cdr.   Capt.
f. Khorfulus TF Cdr.   Capt
"   " D/Cdr.   Capt.
g. Daniel Shogi TF Cdr.   Capt.
"   " D/Cdr.   Capt.
h. Shamis TF Cdr.   Capt.
"   " D/Cdr.   Capt.

SIGNED

A/CDR OYAI DENG AJAK,
CHIEF OF COMBAT OPERATIONS
FOR/ CAMPAIGN COMMANDER

ANNEX A: COMMAND, STAFF AND ORGANIZATION
SECTOR DEMARCATION (APPROX.)

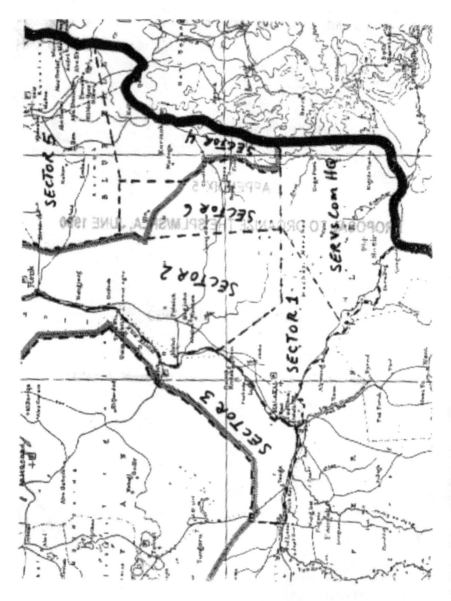

Annex A: Command Staff and Organisation. Sector Demarcation (approximate).

Proposal to Organize the SPLM/SPLA June 1990

TOWARDS ORGANIZING THE SPLM

Points to be discussed in the First Meeting of the Political-Military High Command of the SPLM/SPLA.

by

CDR/ LAM AKOL AJAWIN

(Alternate Member of the SPLM/SPLA Political-Military High Command)

June, 1990

TOWARDS ORGANIZING THE SPLM

Preface:
Seven full years have elapsed since the spark in Bor ignited the flame of our people's anger against oppression, misrule and dictatorship. The masses of our people joined the newly born Movement en masse. The objective and subjective conditions were ripe to turn such anger into a genuine social revolution of profound proportions under the leadership of the SPLM. Now, and as the Movement enters its eighth year many are not so sure. What went wrong?

The following pages are an attempt to answer this question. But before going through the pages it is essential to set the whole matter into its correct historical perspective as this is the only way to understand the twist of events and the ideas that developed.

It is a well known fact that the leadership of the Movement emerged after serious differences of opinion and squabbles among the contenders. However, and despite the bitterness of those days a structure of the SPLM was agreed upon based on a number of committees under the "Provisional Executive Committee" which in turn is headed by a Chairman. This was a great achievement and all those who took part in its formulation are to be commended for their political insight. The events that took place thereafter which led to the breakaway of the Chairman and some members is still a subject of great controversy and it is neither necessary nor helpful to delve into it here. Nonetheless, this rift proved to be very costly not only in human blood shed in the fratricidal fighting that followed but also in the organizational structure of the SPLM. Thereafter, the military committee, one of the committees of the Provisional Executive Committee, dominated the scene. The Movement took a sharp turn to militarism. It became the vogue those days to condemn the "politicians" and propagate that political work is quite unnecessary and that it is only the military might that will bring about victory. Soon after, the only two civilian members of the Provisional Executive Committee were arrested and their departure sealed the fate of any sembalance of collective leadership. The military committee subsequently changed its name to the "High Command". Whether this change of name had any practical significance is dealt with later on.

The present state of affairs is a legacy of those turbulent days in the birth of the Movement. The logjam can only be broken by steering away of militaristic tendencies and adopting a realistic approach to our problems, which are basically political in nature. The sine qua non for the victory of any revolution is a sound organization deep-rooted among the people. This is the course of history.

It is argued in what follows that there can be no alternative but to organize the SPLM and to widen the participation of its members in decision-making. This is the crux of the matter.

THE LEADERSHIP OF THE MOVEMENT:

The Movement has no political institutions of any kind. The "Political-military High Command", PMHC, has no rules governing it and has never held any formal meeting.

Some of its members have never seen each other.

It is axiomatic of any organisation to have regulations, rules, code of conduct, etc. Then the office bearers fill in the positions stipulated in these basic documents. This is not the case with the PMHC. It is hardly surprising, therefore, that it is never involved in decision-making and its members cannot claim to be better informed than the other members of the Movement.

Even as a military body, the PMHC never discusses matters of military strategy or tactics. The titles "Chief of Staff" and "Deputy Chief of Staff" are in reality without functions. You have to have general staff in the first place before you could have a Chief of Staff. Military experiences in the various theatres of operations are never shared or discussed by the leadership. In such a situation mistakes are bound to be repeated and great achievements in some Zones or areas worth emulating pass unnoticed by the other Zones and areas.

The above is on the organizational level. On the behavioural level, members of the PMHC are accused of being isolated from the people and insensitive to their problems, practising favouritism and nepotism, leading a life-style reminiscent of the old Sudan.

Few movements in history have attracted so many intellectuals, students and experienced people in the art of government as the SPLM/SPLA but these talents and skills have never been put to proper use to advance the people's struggle.

The direct result of this lack of participation is the present feeling of alienation among a wide cross section of the Movement's membership.

THE POLITICAL WORK:

This has two aspects, the political work among the forces and in liberated areas, and the political and diplomatic work inside and outside the Sudan. These will be discussed in turn.

(a) Political work among the forces and in liberated areas

Political training of our combatants leaves a lot to be desired. In our General Training Centres it is relegated to the lowest of priorities. As a result we end up with soldiers who learnt nothing new except to shoot. Hence, when in the field they are easily swayed away from the real cause of the struggle. The same could be said about the officers' training. Officers who are supposed to set the example to their soldiers do not size up to the expectation. As the struggle gets protracted it is the political will and commitment to identifiable political goals, both in practice and theory, that rekindle the flame and keep it burning, This is precisely what is lacking in the Movement now.

As a revolutionary movement we need to have political organs through which our people in liberated areas identify with us and exercise their power. This is the only way to develop our revolutionary cadres who will get steeled as the struggle progresses. No revolutionary movement can ever succeed without deep roots among the people. ZANU in Zimbabwe and SWAPO in Namibia, just to mention two examples, could not have won power at independence without the firm backing by their people.

(b) <u>Political and diplomatic work inside and outside the Sudan</u>

This is an area of utmost importance. The present efforts in this direction, however, have been on an ad hoc basis and lacked sustenance and follow-up. In consequence many opportunities and offers of help by some countries have not been made use of.

<u>THE ARMY:</u>
In spite of the military victories scored by the SPLA in the last two years or so. It remains a glaring fact that the fighting spirit of the average SPLA soldier has dropped significantly over the same period. This is a phenomenon worth close scrutiny. The best illustration of this situation is to be found in the liberated areas of Eastern Equatoria. There, several thousands of SPLA soldiers from the area are on the mountains and, indeed, most of the battles in Eastern Equatoria from 1988 onward were fought by soldiers from other areas. This attitude cannot be explained off as cowardice as some unwary minds contemptuously and arrogantly are in fond of spreading. Many of the tribes from which these soldiers come are renowned for their martial qualities under more difficult conditions.

The reasons have to be sought in the political sphere. It must be admitted that the Movement has failed to mobilize the people behind it especially in Equatoria which since the debate on the division of the South, remains an area that deserves special political attention. The enemy has persistently been playing up the Equatoria factor in a concerted propaganda over Radio Juba and other forums. And in the absence of a tangible rebuttal the repeated lie becomes the truth. The struggle to win the hearts of Equatorians is not so far in the SPLA's favour. This is not only worrying, it spells disaster.

A backward society like ours pays great attention to symbols and images. It is not what we say, however sincere it may be, that appeals to the people. It is what they see us doing. We need to move quickly and appoint competent Equatorians to all the civil and military assignments in Equatoria. Their practical presence among the people is more credible than volumes of written material and thousands of hours over Radio SPLA on how national and egalitarian the SPLM/SPLA is.

One final point on the issue of the army is the fact that we are running out of recruits. What is the implication of this on the maintenance of the present military gains and the future military situation?

<u>HUMAN RIGHTS:</u>
Right from the outset the Movement has pledged itself to fighting for equality, justice and respect of human rights. The record regarding this leaves a lot to be desired especially in relation to the dispensation of justice. Officers are sometimes arrested on the most frivolous and trivial reasons and are thrown into jail without charges to stay there for long periods. There are complaints that some officers have been tortured, and a good number lost their lives in the process, and others shared imprisonment with POWs. Another related problem is the issue of comrades detained for political reasons. Some of them have been under detention for more than five years and one of them died in prison. These cases and others need to be dispensed with immediately. A revolutionary movement has to be mindful of the fact that human honour and dignity should be held inviolable especially when dealing with comrades.

On another level, the arbitrary detentions and wanton torture without any legal protection has created a state of fear and suspicion among the rank and file of the Movement. In the Movement today very few will dare to express their opinions openly for the fear of being victimized. As a result gossip has become the order of the day. Gossip is not only the opiate of the idle, it is also a vent of suppressed opinion. Dissatisfaction bordering on discontent is now simmering. This reaction cannot and should not be shrugged away as the work of our enemies, who indeed will fan it up and exploit it, but needs to be probed very closely.

An immediate corrective action on the issue of human rights and the rule of law needs to be taken, otherwise, the possibility is real for our revolution to degenerate into a police state. A genuine revolution has nothing to lose and everything to gain in ensuring that justice is upheld.

<u>SUPPORT OUTSIDE THE LIBERATED AREAS:</u>
Since its birth the Movement espoused issues dear to the hearts of the disadvantaged Sudanese in general and the Southerners in particular. It was, therefore, expected that many conscious Southerners will join or at least symphasize with the Movement. Before passing a judgement on whether this was the case or not it is essential to note the following:

The former Anya-nya officers and men, except for a small fraction, stayed with the enemy and many of them were and are leading operations against the SPLA. Many had good opportunities to defect if they so wished but chose otherwise.

b- Very few of the southerners who were involved in active politics did join the Movement. Others have been outspoken against the Movement to the extent of co-operating with the Muslim Brothers.

c- Except for the first two or three years since the Movement started, the flow into the Movement of students, the intelligentsia and the peasants has come to an end. Even the unpopular fundamentalist policies of the present regime (Junta) could not be translated into numbers joining the Movement. This happens at a time when there are a lot of unemployed educated Southerners loitering in Khartoum.

d- The displaced Southerners around Khartoum alone are put by the most conservative estimates at 1.5 million. That they chose to walk hundreds of kilometres to the seat of the Government that perpetrated atrocities against them and their properties is by itself enough reason for concern. But it is mind boggling to discover that some of these displaced got recruited into the Government army and are fighting with extraordinary zeal against the SPLA.

e- Despite the strenuous and repeated propaganda efforts to win some sections of the enemy army to the side of the SPLA, it remains an indisputable fact that no defections from or dialogue with the enemy army did take place. The enemy army remained solid against the SPLA regardless of the political regime in Khartoum from Nirneiri to Omer El-Bashir inclusive.

f- The Movement failed to attract West European support, even humanitarian one, on a level comparable to that of the Anya-nya.

These points, and may be more, call for a serious study. We need to make a thorough soul-searching exercise to determine the real reasons behind this obvious failure to win constituencies whose grievances we articulate or who are sympathetic to our cause.

MEMBERSHIP OF THE MOVEMENT:

The Movement has reached a stage where it is neither necessary nor desirable for each and every member to be in the military. As a matter of fact, reality nowadays calls for the abandonment of military ranks in areas of civil activity such as the SRRA, NEC, etc. In these areas technical know-how and experience are the basic requirements for appointment, qualities hardly taken into consideration on commissioning or promotions. This is the only way to avoid a less competent senior officer heading a group of more experienced and better informed junior officers in areas of their specialization.

Such a policy will also help motivate others into action in areas where they can serve the Movement better. There is a widespread feeling within the Movement that whoever could not make it in the military field is good for nothing. This is erroneous and unrealistic. Human beings have different attitudes and aptitudes and there is no reason to expect the SPLA to be any different. The proponents of such thinking tend to forget the obvious fact that our armed struggle is not an end in itself but a means to achieve political objectives.

Comrades on civil assignments can be treated as a reserve force to be on call should the military situation demand general mobilization.

ORGANIZATION OF THE SPLM/SPLA

It cannot be overemphasized that it is a must to proceed immediately with the organization of the movement to ensure participation on the basis of collective leadership, accountability and individual responsibility.

Specialized committees have to be instituted to carry out specified duties. Their relationship to the High Command will also have to be spelt out very clearly.

The phrase "High Command" itself is inappropriate to designate a political body. Whatever qualifying words are attached, it remains, to connote the top brass of an army; any army. It is, therefore, proposed that it be replaced by the phrase "National Executive Committee", NEC. Hence the present "Political-military High Command" becomes the "National Executive Committee". Its membership, powers and functions to be specified in a document to be discussed by the present PMHC which after approval by it becomes law.

The following specialized committee of the SPLM/SPLA are proposed:
1. Political and Foreign Affairs
2. Administration and Justice
3. Finance and Economic Affairs
4. Services and Social Security
5. Agriculture and Wildlife Conservation
6. SPLA General staff.

Each of these specialized committees to be composed of suitably qualified members and to be headed by a member of the "National Executive Committee". Each committee may have sub-committees and commissions as its functions require. Again, membership, powers and duties of these committees will be regulated by law.

Simultaneous with the activation of the Movement's organs as above the political mobilisation in the liberated areas shall be stepped up and intensified to establish branches of the SPLM on various levels leading eventually to a General Congress. Many liberation movements, such as FRELIMO in Mozambique and many more, held party congresses a number of times while the struggle was still being waged. There is nothing novel here.

COMMAND ZONES

The organization of the SPLM necessitates the redefinition of the Command Zones to take into consideration two main points: a manageable size and zonal boundaries to conform as far as is practicable to the known administrative boundaries.

Fourteen zones are proposed: four in Bahr el-Ghazal Region, three in Equatoria Region and five in Upper Nile Region, and one each in Southern Blue Nile and Southern Kordofan.

The administrative councils comprising each of the twelve zones in southern Sudan are detailed in the Appendix.

THE PEACE PROCESS:

The present war will have to be settled eventually by political means. We are already involved in a peace process, which will have to reach its logical conclusion, i.e. a peaceful resolution to the present conflict. Like all such resolutions, compromises by all involved are unavoidable. The natural question that arises therefore is: at what stage of the war are we ready to compromise?

The answer to this question is a most fundamental and crucial in any war. It necessitates a continuous and accurate assessment of both the internal and external conditions and their effects on the conduct of the war at present and as projected into the future. The correct time can only be when the Movement has attained such a strength that can enable it by negotiations to achieve the basic objectives of the armed struggle through a settlement that allows the achievement of the rest of the objectives by peaceful means thereafter. If the balance of forces is projected to change in the enemy's favour, missing the right opportunity to compromise can be disastrous. This matter demands a careful appraisal by

the leadership of the Movement.
APPENDIX 1
Proposed Structure of the SPLM/SPLA Committees

1. POLITICAL AND FOREIGN AFFAIRS:

Political Orientation
- Information
- Radio
- Publications
- Documentation
- Culture
Religious Affairs
- Peace
- Foreign Relations and Offices abroad.

2. ADMINISTRATION AND JUSTICE:
- Administration in liberated areas
- Justice and Legal Affairs

3. FINANCE AND ECONOMIC AFFAIRS:
- Internal and Border Trade
- Transportation
- Mineral Resources
- Co-operatives
- Industry
- Economic Affairs.

4. SERVICES AND SOCIAL SECURITY:
- Health
- Education (General and Higher)
- Social Welfare
- Refugees Affairs
- Relief and Rehabilitation
- Construction

5. AGRICULTURE AND WILDLIFE CONSERVATION:
- Agronomy and Forestry
- Livestock and Fisheries
- Wildlife Conservation.

6. SPLA GENERAL STAFF:
- Operations
- Political work in the army
- Military Intelligence
- Training
- Administration
- Logistics

APPENDIX 2
Proposed Command Zones in Southern Sudan

BAHR EL-GHAZAL REGION:
1. Western:
Raga Rural Council
Wau Rural Council
Wau Town Council

2. Northern:
Aweil Town Council
Aweil Rural Council
Ariath Rural Council
Wanyjok Rural Council

3. Eastern:
Gogrial Rural Council
Twic Rural Council
Thiet Rural Council
Warrap Rural Council

4. Southeastern:
Rumbek Town Council
Rumbek Rural Council
Cueibet Rural Council
Yirol Rural Council
Awarial Rural Council

EQUATORIA REGION:
1. Eastern:
Kapoeta Rural Council
Chukudum Rural Council
Torit Rural Council
Ikotos Rural Council
Magwi Rural Council

2. Central:
Juba Town Council
Juba Rural Council
Terekeka Rural Council
Yei Rural Council
Kajokeji Rural Council

3. Western:
Maridi Rural Council
Mundri Rural Council
Ibba Rural Council
Yambio Rural Council
Yambio Town Council
Tambura Rural Council
Ezzo Rural Council

UPPER NILE REGION:
1. Southern:
Bor Rural Council
Kongor Rural Council
Pibor Rural Council
Pochala Rural Council

2. Central:
Akobo Rural Council
Waat Rural Council
Fangak Rural Council
Ayod Rural Council

3. Western:
Bentiu Rural Council
Leer Rural Council
Mayom Rural Council

4. Eastern:
Nasir Rural Council
Maiwut Rural Council
Maban Rural Council

5. Northern:
Malakal Town Council
Kodok Rural Council
Tonga Rural Council
Sobat Rural Council
Renk Rural Council
Melut Rural Council

APPENDIX 3
The Political-Military High Command

The Political-Military High Command (PMHC) is the only semblance of a political institution in the Movement. It is supposed to be the supreme policy-making body but the reality is very much different. That it has never held a single formal meeting is by now common knowledge among the rank and file of the Movement, yet major policy decisions are taken without the PMHC.

The following points illustrate how ineffectual the PMHC is.
A- Some major policy decisions taken without any meeting of the Political-Military High Command include the following:

1. Establishment of the SRRA, 1985.
2. The new structure of the officers' ranks,1987.
3. The agreement with the Anya-nya II, 1988.
4. Establishment of the National Economic Commission, 1988.
5. The agreement on the ICRC relief operations, 1988.
6. Establishment of the Political School in Isoke, 1988.
7. The agreement on Operation Lifeline Sudan, 1989.
8. The establishment of the Commission to Organize Production and Service (COPS), 1989.
9. Establishment of new colleges for Administration, Police, Prisons and Wildlife, 1989.
10. Policy Statements delivered over Radio SPLA are prepared and broadcast without the participation of the PMHC as a body. It is true that in some cases the opinion of the members is asked for to be sent by radio, but this cannot by any logic be a substitute for a meeting. Meetings do facilitate interactive exchange of views culminating in what can truly and genuinely be considered the position of the PMHC and hence of the Movement.

11. The decision to introduce a new currency into SPLA-liberated areas, 1990. Introduction of currency has far-reaching economic, social, and legal implications and repercussions that need to be carefully studied and evaluated before a firm decision is taken by the PMHC. The following questions need to be answered: who is the issuing authority of notes and coins? What is the amount of the covering reserve? What is the impact of issuing the currency on the combatants? , etc. It is not just a matter of design to be left to the artists. The work of the artist is to put into final form the decision of the PMHC on the currency and coinage.

B. It is sometimes argued that these vital decisions are taken without the PMHC because its members are far and busy in the field. Such an argument is faulty and unconvincing for the following reasons:

1. The function of the PMHC is to legislate, make policies and supervise the implementation of these policies. Hence, members of the PMHC should be available to be able to take part in the meetings of the PMHC where the necessary decisions are taken. This is their main function that comes above any other assignment.
2. The assignment of the members of the PMHC to be permanently in command of the zones has no justification. This assignment can be taken up with equal competence by

CDRs and A/CDRs. As a matter of fact, some of the zones and independent areas are at the moment commanded by A/CDRs. What is needed is to have high command members assigned as Supervisors of zones. The supervisor of the zone can spend up to 3-6 months, not necessarily consecutive, per year in his zone so that he is in full picture of what is going on there. The rest of his time is to be devoted to the work of PMHC.

3. Even if the necessity for the present assignment of high command members as zonal commanders were to be accepted, it should have been possible for the PMHC to be in session at least once a year during the rainy season. Such meetings of the PMHC could have taken the policy decisions required. The fact, however, is that no single such meeting was called for the last four years, at least.

C. Members of the high command know very little of what is going on in the Movement. For instance:
1. They are never informed about the training and, subsequently, the deployment of the recruits and officers. The criteria for commissioning officers are neither known to them nor documented.
2. They are not officially informed about the operations in the field. They have to get the news like everybody else on Radio SPLA.
3. They are not in picture of the political and diplomatic activities of the Movement externally.
4. High command members have never taken part in the formulation of any military strategy of the Movement. They are being deployed exactly like other SPLA officers. Since 1986, there has been a good number of such strategies: December 1986, March 1987, the "Bright Star Campaign", September 1989, January 1990, etc.
5. Promotions to the rank of A/CDR are made without consulting the high command members. They do not even know the criteria for such promotions.

D. High Command members are not informed of the Chairman's visits abroad before they occur and consequently they do not know who is in charge in his absence. After the visits no proper briefing about them is given to the PMHC. In the same vein, other delegations on missions abroad never report to the PMHC.

E. On appointment to the PMHC, candidates are neither consulted nor informed in advance of the announcement of their appointment. They hear of such appointment at the same time with the general public. As membership to the PMHC entails a political responsibility, the candidate for membership of the PMHC should be given the option to accept or decline the offer and this can only be ascertained by consultation. Above anything else, courtesy demands prior consultation.

Index